LANGUAGES
of
VISUALITY

Crossings

between

Edited by
BEATE ALLERT

Science, Art,

Politics, and

Literature

WAYNE STATE UNIVERSITY PRESS
DETROIT

Copyright © 1996 by Wayne State University Press,

Detroit, Michigan 48201. All rights are reserved.

No part of this book may be reproduced without formal permission.

Manufactured in the United States of America.

99 98 97 96   5 4 3 2 1

Library of Congress Cataloging-in-Publication Data

Languages of visuality : crossings between science, art, politics, and
   literature / edited by Beate Allert.
      p. cm. — (Kritik)
   Includes bibliographical references and index.
   Contents: Classical Greek origins of Western aesthetic theory /
John T. Kirby — Visible sounds and audible colors : the ocular
harpsichord of Louis-Bertrand Castel / Joachim Gessinger — Opera in
the light of technology / Friedrich A. Kittler — "Infinitely
repellant orbs" : visions of the self in the American Renaissance /
Richard Hardack — "Moral astronomy" : on a metaphor in Novalis and
its conceptual context / Karl Menges — The dialectic of
Romantic Enlightenment and the psychodynamics of the hypervisual in
Hölderlin's Hyperion / Harald Weilnböck — Aldo Palazzeschi and
Giorgio de Chirico : decentralized antitraditional aesthetics /
Anthony Julian Tamburri — Myth, invisibility, and politics in the
late work of Paul Klee / Kathryn E. Kramer — The eye's mind : Henry
James's The sacred fount and Vladimir Nabokov's The eye / Karen
Jacobs — "Teichoscopy" in the Wall novels of Peter Schneider and
Uri Orlev / Jeffrey Garrett — Visual citations : Walter Benjamin's
dialectic of text and image / Azade Seyhan — Writing and the nature
of the supernatural image, or Why ghosts float / Christopher
Collins.
    ISBN 0-8143-2540-8 (alk. paper). — ISBN 0-8143-2607-2 (pbk. : alk. paper)
    1. Aesthetics. 2. Image (Philosophy) 3. Vision. 4. Criticism.
5. Hermeneutics. I. Allert, Beate, 1954– . II. Series: Kritik
(Detroit, Mich.)
BH39.L295 1996
111'.85—dc20   95-45568

Cover and book design by Mary Krzewinski.

CONTENTS

Acknowledgments   *vii*

Contributors   *ix*

Introduction   *1*
BEATE ALLERT

I. VISUALITY AND RHETORIC: FROM THE GREEKS TO THE PRESENT

Classical Greek Origins of Western Aesthetic Theory   29
JOHN T. KIRBY

II. COLORS AND MUSIC: SCIENCE AND MEDIA TECHNOLOGY

Visible Sounds and Audible Colors: The Ocular Harpsichord of Louis-Bertrand Castel   49
JOACHIM GESSINGER

Opera in the Light of Technology   73
FRIEDRICH A. KITTLER
(translated by Anja E. Belz)

III. THE UNIVERSE AND THE SELF: MONADS, EYEBALLS, AND INDIVIDUALS

"Infinitely Repellent Orbs": Visions of the Self in the American Renaissance   89
RICHARD HARDACK

"Moral Astronomy": On a Metaphor in Novalis and Its Conceptual Context   111
KARL MENGES

v

▌CONTENTS

The Dialectic of Romantic Enlightenment and the Psychodynamics of the
Hypervisual in Hölderlin's Hyperion   132
HARALD WEILNBÖCK

IV. POETRY AND PAINTING: THE EMPTY CENTER, GAPS, AND HIEROGLYPHS

Aldo Palazzeschi and Giorgio de Chirico: Decentralized Antitraditional
Aesthetics   155
ANTHONY JULIAN TAMBURRI

Myth, Invisibility, and Politics in the Late Work of Paul Klee   174
KATHRYN E. KRAMER

V. POWER AND SEEING: CONTROL AND TRANSGRESSIONS

The Eye's Mind: Henry James's The Sacred Fount and Vladimir Nabokov's The
Eye   187
KAREN JACOBS

"Teichoscopy" in the Wall Novels of Peter Schneider and Uri Orlev   215
JEFFREY GARRETT

VI. THEORIES OF VISUALITY: CLOSER DEFINITIONS

Visual Citations: Walter Benjamin's Dialectic of Text and Image   229
AZADE SEYHAN

Writing and the Nature of the Supernatural Image, or Why Ghosts Float   242
CHRISTOPHER COLLINS

Index   263

vi

ACKNOWLEDGMENTS

The development of this book has been supported by a Faculty Incentive Grant from the School of Liberal Arts, Purdue University. I want to express my gratitude for this support, especially to Christiane Keck, Department Head of Foreign Languages and Literatures, and to the school of Liberal Arts. My warmest thanks to Deborah Starewich, who read the manuscript of this book with precision and care and made very valuable suggestions for improvement. Thanks to my dear friend Noemi Schwarz (University of Massachusetts) who helped me not only with last minute library searches but also with energizing talks, with her guitar music and paintings. Thanks to all the helpful librarians here at Purdue University and to Carla Nelson for her assistance. And I doubt I would have initiated this book without the productive imagination of Liliane Weissberg, Professor at the University of Pennsylvania and editor of the series *Kritik* for Wayne State University Press, whose work has always been an inspiration to me. She knew about my interest in the topic of this book and suggested that I contact scholars whom I knew working on related research in a variety of disciplines to propose this volume. I feel fortunate about the marvelous responses here, the interest of wonderful colleagues from various disciplines, and I treasure the contributions. They have opened exciting insights for me, some of which I hope to explore further in my next book, *Optics and Metaphor.* Thanks to Wayne State University Press, to Arthur Evans, Kathryn Wildfong, and the perceptive reader/copyeditor Jonathan Lawrence. Thanks above all to each one of the contributors, to all writers who have produced an interest in related questions, and to all interested readers. Thanks to everyone who helped to make this possible, including my parents, friends, and students.

CONTRIBUTORS

Beate Allert teaches German and Comparative Literature at Purdue University. She is the author of *Die Metapher und ihre Krise: Zur Dynamik der "Bilderschrift" Jean Pauls* (New York: Peter Lang, 1987) and has written on Lessing, Schiller, Novalis, and others. Her work links eighteenth-century literature with contemporary debates on verbal-visual dynamics. Questions on visuality that are being addressed in this collection of essays are further explored in the context of her work in progress, *Optics and Metaphor,* which will also take relevant aspects from feminist criticism and film studies into account.

Anja E. Belz, a translator living in London, is fluent in Bulgarian, Czechoslovakian, English, Dutch, German, and Russian. She holds an M.S.D. in Computing Science and is involved in the doctoral program at Imperial College, University of London, with a thesis on "Natural Language Processing."

Christopher Collins teaches in the English Department at New York University. Among his publications are *The Poetics of the Mind's Eye: Literature and the Psychology of Imagination* (Philadelphia: U of Philadelphia P, 1991), *Reading the Written Image: Verbal Play, Interpretation, and the Roots of Iconophobia* (University Park: Penn State UP, 1991), *The Uses of Observations: A Study of Correspondential Vision in the Writings of Emerson, Thoreau and Whitman* (The Hague: Mouton, 1971), and "Figure, Ground, and Open Field: Reader Response to Verbal Imagery" (*The Critic* 51.1 [Fall 1988]: 11–29). His research focuses on the intersection between poetic theory and cognitive psychology, and addresses, for instance, relations between literary and mental images, processes of visual perception, poiesis, imagination, and reading.

Jeffrey Garrett is humanities bibliographer at Northwestern University. Areas of scholarly interest include contemporary fiction for children, monastic library history, and the image of the library in postmodern fiction. Recent articles include "Missing Eco: On Reading *The Name of the Rose* as Library Criticism" (*Library Quarterly* 61 [October 1991]: 373–88) and "Bibliophiles with an Attitude: French Influences on Bavarian Library Secularization Policies, 1800–1810" (*Romance Languages Annual* 5 [1994]: 33–39).

Joachim Gessinger is chair of the German Department at the Universität Potsdam, Germany (Lehrstuhl für Geschichte der Sprache). He is author of *Auge und Ohr: Studien zur Erforschung der Sprache am Menschen 1700–1850* (Berlin: de Gruyter 1994) and *Sprache und Bürgertum: Zur Sozialgeschichte sprachlicher Verkehrsformen im Deutschland des 18 Jahrhunderts* (Stuttgart: Metzler, 1980). He has coedited *Schriftkultur und sprachlicher Wandel* (Osnabruck: OBST-Redaktion, 1993) and *Theorien vom Ursprung der Sprache* (Berlin: de Gruyter, 1989). He has written many articles on a variety of topics related to language development, communication theory, perception, and technology.

Richard Hardack recently received his Ph.D. in American Literature from the University of California at Berkeley. His recent publications include articles on double consciousness in Toni Morrison's *Jazz,* correspondence and intertextuality in Melville and Hawthorne, pantheism and race in Ishmael Reed's *Mumbo Jumbo,* transcendental American representations of the Pacific, and American slave and travel narratives. From 1994 to 1996, he is Visiting Professor at Haverford College, which he attended as an undergraduate. He is completing a book on pantheism, gender, and transcendental identity in American literature for Cambridge University Press.

Karen Jacobs is Assistant Professor of English at the University of Colorado, Boulder. She has recently completed a dissertation entitled "Engendering the Gaze: Modernist Fictions of the Viewing Subject" at the University of California at Berkeley. Her work has appeared in *Theory and Society* and *Qui Parle.*

Friedrich A. Kittler is Professor at the Humboldt University in Berlin, where he chairs the Institut für Ästhetik. He is also known via television and radio in Germany and has published *Computer als Medium* (München: Fink, 1994), *Discourse Networks 1800/1900* (Stanford: Stanford UP, 1990), *Dichtung als Sozialisationsspiel: Studien zu Goethe und Gottfried Keller* (Göttingen: Vandenhoeck & Ruprecht, 1978), *Der Taum und die Rede: eine Analyse der Kommunikationssituation Conrad Ferdinand Meyers* (Bern: Francke, 1977), and *Urszenen: Literaturwissenschaft als Diskursanalyse und Diskurskritik* (Frankfurt: Suhrkamp, 1977). He is an expert on Foucault, Lacan, poststructuralism, and the history of media technology.

John T. Kirby was chair of the Department of Classics at Purdue University for six years and is currently chairing the Comparative Literature program.

His scholarly interests range across classical and modern languages and literatures, from Homeric epic to French and Italian writers of the twentieth century. He is the author of *The Rhetoric of Cicero's* Pro Cluentio (Amsterdam: J. C. Gieben, 1990) and has written on Greek and Latin prose and poetry, including such topics as classical rhetoric and poetics, metrics, textual criticism, and on issues in current literary theory, particularly semiotics, narratology, and reader-response criticism.

Kathryn E. Kramer is Assistant Professor of Art and Design at Purdue University. She recently completed her dissertation, entitled "Mythopoetic Politics in the Late Work of Paul Klee." Her research interests include the visual culture of nineteenth- and twentieth-century Europe, the intersections of mythology and politics, and the institutional history of art.

Karl Menges is Professor of German at the University of California at Davis and cofounder of the International Herder Society. He is the editor of *Johann Gottfried Herder: Selected Early Works, 1764–1767* (University Park: Penn State UP, 1992), and the author of *Das private und das Politische: Bemerkungen zur Studentenliteratur, zu Handke, Celan und Grass* (Stuttgart: H.-D. Heinz, 1987), and *Kritische Studien zur Wertphilosophie Herman Brochs* (Tübingen: Niemeyer, 1970). His articles address many authors and topics, including Goethe, Schiller, Broch, Musil, Kraus, and H. Mann. His specialties are eighteenth- and twentieth-century literature, exile literature and literary theory.

Azade Seyhan chairs the German Department at Bryn Mawr College and is co-chairing the Bi-College Program in Comparative Literature of Bryn Mawr/Haverford College. Her most recent book is *Representation and Its Discontents: The Critical Legacy of German Romanticism* (Berkeley: U of California P, 1992). She has coedited a special issue of *New German Critique* on minorities in German culture and has written articles on such topics as poststructuralist debate, feminist literary theory, the politics of representation, and film studies. Special authors addressed are Nietzsche, W. Benjamin, and Heine.

Anthony Julian Tamburri, Professor of Italian and chair of Asian, Classical, Italian, and Semitic Languages and Literatures at Purdue University, has written *Of "Saltimbanchi" and "Incendiari": Aldo Palazzeschi and Avant-Gardism in Italy* (Madison, NJ: Fairleigh Dickinson UP, 1990), *To Hyphenate or Not to Hyphenate: The Italian/American Writer, or an "Other" American?* (Montreal: Guernica, 1991), and *Per una lettura retrospettiva: Prose giovanili di Aldo Palazzeschi* (Stony Brook: Gradiva, 1994). He is a contributing editor of the volume *From the Margin: Writings in Italian Americana* (West Lafayette: Purdue UP, 1991) and cofounding editor of the journal *Voices in Italian Americana,* a literary and cultural review. He is the cofounder of the Purdue

Conference on Romance Languages, Literatures, and Film and the *Romance Languages Annual*. Among his edited volumes and special issues, he most recently coedited a special issue of *Differentia* (spring/fall 1994) dedicated to Italian/American art and culture.

Harald Weilnböck, whose main theoretical focus is the application of post-Freudian psychoanalysis to literature and cultural studies, received his doctorate in German from the University of California at Los Angeles and has done postdoctoral work with the Critical Studies Program at the École des Hautes Études en Sciences Sociales, Paris. He has written on Heiner Müller, Irmtraud Morgner, Botho Strauß, Willem Hermans, and especially Hölderlin. Since 1994 he has held a position as lecturer at the Department of Literature and Pedagogy at the University of Eichstätt, Germany.

INTRODUCTION

BEATE ALLERT

Can the eye see itself, Yoomy? Taken out of its socket, will
it see at all? Its connection with the body imparts its virtue.[1]

It seems that the eye has had domination over all other senses from antiquity until now, and that various "regimes of vision" (Foucault) and simultaneously existing "scopic regimes" (Martin Jay) influence the ways we use
language, thus infiltrating our daily lives.[2] The history of seeing, however,
cannot be conceptualized as a straight line.[3] It requires a complex "metaphor-
ology" (Blumenberg) of visual language, research into the various uses of
visual metaphors, into the substructures of thinking where images are translated into words.[4] Furthermore, it involves many fields of study: it must be
truly interdisciplinary.[5] *Languages of Visuality* applies a variety of semiotic
and discourse analytical approaches, combining research from literature, visual and performing arts, media technology, physics, music, cognitive psychology, philosophy, and cultural studies. It draws from American, English,
French, German, Italian, and Russian literary sources. While it could therefore
be characterized as Eurocentric, it discovers within that tradition the noncen-
tric, the noncanonical, the marginal, and the suppressed. This book proposes
a pluralistic notion of "languages of visuality" and examines, as the title
suggests, crossings between science, art, politics, and literature. It explores
the textuality or sensuality of poetic images or of textual signs, which include
architecture, painting, dance, and other dynamic modes of expression. The
essays in this book are—perhaps in a Deleuzian sense—"multisensorial complexes," clusters that highlight "visuality" from different angles and disciplines. They are explorations of margins and zones where Jay's categories of
three scopic regimes in the Western tradition may not be sufficient, where we
discover slippages and moments of history that make us realize that the usual

1

categories are problematic and never capture everything. But how can we discover fine nuances and subtle shifts where the visual and textual interact if our vocabulary is outdated? What are the shifting relations between images and texts, between the visual and the verbal?[6] To what extent are texts visual and images textual? And how literally can we take the notion of "images" in our time when they can no longer be defined in terms of a text-based culture that used to characterize Western tradition since the invention of the printing press, but are increasingly defined by new simulation techniques and computerized vision?[7] These and other questions will be addressed in this study. It explores aesthetic, scientific, political, and, in some cases, gender-specific implications of the discourse of clarity, not only in its monopolizing and monocausal implications, which are often associated with Eurocentricity, but also in its antiocular, heterological aspects as they are now emerging.[8] *Languages of Visuality* raises even more questions, for example, about the translatability of the senses, the walls in people's minds, and the science of thresholds (Walter Benjamin's "Schwellenkunde").

In his 1994 book *Picture Theory: Essays on Verbal and Visual Representation,* W. J. T. Mitchell argues for what he calls a "pictorial turn" in postmodernity, a paradigm shift of major proportions, which he nevertheless traces back in Anglo-American philosophy to Charles Peirce's semiotics and to Nelson Goodman's *Languages of Art,* for both Peirce and Goodman explore conventions and codes that underlie nonlinguistic symbol systems and "do not begin with the assumption that language is paradigmatic for meaning" (12).[9] They indicate a shift away from the logocentric and toward forms of visuality that are not verbal. Related signals are found, Mitchell explains, in Europe with phenomenology's inquiry into imagination and "the visual, material forces of writing"; or, he adds, with the Frankfurt school's investigations of modernity, mass culture, and visual media; or with Foucault's insistence "on a history and theory of power/knowledge that exposes the rift between the seeable and the sayable, as the crucial fault-line in 'scopic regimes' of modernity" (12). This book will draw from such sources as well and contribute to a future map of scopic "fault-lines." It will address problems of visual/verbal relations, contiguities, crossings, and gaps.

In part I, "Visuality and Rhetoric: From the Greeks to the Present," John T. Kirby draws attention to intricate links between seeing and language, the visual and the textual. Kirby aims at an understanding of visual art and narrative theory in Western culture in his essay "Classical Greek Origins of Western Aesthetic Theory." Specifically, he makes connections between, first, the Greek models of mimesis and diegesis, while pointing out important differences between Plato and Aristotle; second, a recent theory by Noton and Stark on eye movements in ocular perception;[10] and third, Norman Bryson's theory of vision. Kirby shows the relevance of Greek rhetoric for contemporary aesthetic theory and especially for the notion of "reading" such nonverbal "texts" as musical scores, paintings, sculptures, films, and performances of drama and dance. He shows the root of this discourse in the actual process of textualization of the visual, not only as implied in scientific studies on "scan-path" and "saccades," referring to the movements of the eyes in the process of visual perception, but already in the classical models of mimesis and diegesis as offered by Plato and Aristotle. Kirby provides a sophisticated reading of their uses of the terms *mimesis* and *diegesis* and demonstrates that Greek rhetoric is of vital importance to the understanding of aesthetic theory and art today. In his theory of the textualization of the visual he refers to Norman Bryson, who made the distinction between discursive and figural aspects of an image, thus drawing attention to interesting image/text relations. The discursive aspects of an image emphasize the influence of the word over the image, texts that precede it (as in the case of the window in the Canterbury cathedral), or the domination of its meaning by inscriptions. The figural aspects of an image belong to the visual experience independent of language, its "being-as-image." Kirby goes one step further than Bryson by arguing that all images have a discursive aspect and that—at least cognitively—we textualize them to communicate our cognition to another person. He makes clear that no images can be understood without some process of textualizing. This is where he asks interesting questions about multiple ways to textualize images and where the reader may have to perform some mental diegesis as well. He shows that the visual and the textual are inseparably intertwined and that this connection has already been established with Greek rhetoric. It must be noted that the models Kirby provides in this context are not dualistic but rather triangular.

Part II, "Colors and Music: Science and Media Technology," is in certain respects not about the link between image and word, the visual and the textual, but about a gap between them. It draws attention to various art forms and disciplines, to discourse analysis, and shows that meanings change whenever other media are used. It also emphasizes the performance of the sensorium in processes of perception, or, in the words used in the eighteenth century, the associations of sensations ("Seelenassoziation"), the ways they are processed and communicated. Joachim Gessinger's essay "Visible Sounds and Audible Colors: The Ocular Harpsichord of Louis-Bertrand Castel" addresses the question of the translatability of the senses as explored in the context of the invention of Castel's ocular harpsichord, which had to test how colors can be presented as music—how to make the visible acoustic. Gessinger examines the various roles Castel's invention of the "clavecin oculaire" played in the epistemological and philosophical discussions in the eighteenth century, including arguments by Diderot, Newton, Locke, Berkeley, Condillac, Herder, Telemann, Montesquieu, Voltaire, Burke, Mendels-

3

sohn, and Rousseau.[11] Castel's "discourse of colours" opened a new dimension in art, aesthetics, and the theory of signs, semiotics. It contributed to a shift from concerns in physics, mathematics, and epistemology to aesthetics, language, and a psychology of art. Castel's dissent from Newton implies a turn from calculation to examination of the material of painting, the coloring matter, the musical instrument, and the principles of composing. He replaced the prismatic reduction of colors, the camera obscura, with the "natural production of colors." His instrument was not intended as a tool for discourse analysis, for which Gessinger uses it effectively here, but to test a previously unchallenged tripartite harmony: the analogies between the physical nature of sound and light, between their perceived forms as tone and color, and between the different kinds of artistic performance—music and painting. This experiment involves aspects of physics, perception, and cognition and raises fascinating questions in multiple disciplines.

Friedrich A. Kittler's "Opera in the Light of Technology" shows the impact of science and media technology on art, the role of the invention of electric light for the history of the opera, and the emancipation of music from previously established codes.[12] He probes the boundaries of the visual and the acoustic and highlights scientific discoveries in this context. He documents that the gap between art and nature was, to a large extent, a result of limited media technologies and terminologies. When in 1876 Wagner had gaslight installed in the opera house in Bayreuth, and when in 1881 electric light was used in the London Savoy Theater for the first time, a major change occurred: performances were no longer limited to the burning time of candles, and a new world of perception and signification (with Benjamin a new "Merkwelt") was created. When in 1739 Euler's "Essay on New Music Theory" replaced the concept of interval with that of frequency, sound was no longer measured in terms of the length of strings in space but in terms of oscillations in time. Fourier's spectral analysis did for sounds what Newton had done for the visual: a new computability exceeded previously established limits of perception, which had been defined in a way by nothing but cultural codes. When the sounds of nature, such as murmuring, buzzing, and swishing, were introduced into music, the role of art changed. Senses that had been repressed became recognized and communicated or textualized beyond previously available measures of calculation. Debussy preferred Wagner to Beethoven because Wagner was interested in the entire range of sounds and tried for himself to get mimesis back into art, to let nature speak. While musical intervals and the alphabet were "dissolved" by mathematics and differential calculus, notions of art, image, and text were also radically in flux. A new dimension to such a development was achieved by gramophone, film, and television.[13] Kittler's essay crosses borders in various directions; it opens insights to cryptograms and anagrams, to Nietzsche, Babbage, and others, and ignites sparks for further research and discussion. Kittler explores fractures among visual and textual representation, technologically defined languages of visual and acoustic signification, shifting relations between nature and art. His essay raises new questions about worlds of perception as they differ, but communicate, across the disciplines.

The three essays in part III, which is entitled ''The Universe and the Self: Monads, Eyeballs, and Individuals,'' all link the discourse of the eye and seeing as it can be found in American and European literature, with psychological, sociological, anthropological, political, and gender-specific questions. In '' 'Infinitely Repellent Orbs': Visions of the Self in the American Renaissance,'' Richard Hardack argues that the language of visual self-representation determines the nature of identity. He points out that the tropes of eyes and orbs in the language of American Renaissance transcendentalists, which are influenced initially by the Leibnizian theory of the monads and Goethe's classical social pantheism, are significant self-representations of the American male individual at that time.[14] In Emerson's taxonomy, particularity is negated in favor of universality, and the transparent eyeball is the central visual, linguistic, scientific, and representational motif. This constellation is mobile, even in Emerson's cosmos, and becomes fragile in the reception of Melville: the I disappears as an eye and becomes nothing, merges with nature and becomes diffusely All, sees everything. Interestingly, however, Hardack points out that even in the work of one writer (Emerson) we may find two competing versions (conceptions of the self as well as types of ''visual language'') simultaneously: one of the sublime and universal order with the self merged into the eye of the All, and the other of those orbs colliding with, absorbing, and repelling each other. Melville poignantly dramatizes such conflicting models, which he found in Emerson's work, makes a parody, and shows in his fiction what happens to someone who holds both positions at once: Pierre's eyes pop out, they roll away from ''their orbit.'' What may be interpreted as dismemberment for some readers may indicate the rise of democracy for others. Hardack's discussion and other interesting remarks invite further research and discussion, particularly into the areas of gender studies and feminist criticism.

In '' 'Moral Astronomy': On a Metaphor in Novalis and Its Conceptual Context,'' Karl Menges also examines a transition or slippage between scopic regimes. Menges shows that Novalis's literary and theoretical work illustrates the paradigm shift that Foucault has described as ''from the classical to the modern 'episteme' '' by focusing on its ''literal, that is, precisely its visual implications.'' Menges points out that Novalis's essay ''Die Christenheit oder Europa'' offers a highly differentiated account of Western civilization and a critique of the Enlightenment. In contrast to preclassical thought, Enlightenment rationality dismissed all semiotic correspondences in favor of ''a new order of things,'' a different episteme of regulatory systems and grammatical taxonomies, promoting exclusively analytical reasoning over analogical associations. Whereas the previous "Thomistic theorem" suggested an approximation between inner and outer worlds, it is specifically the Cartesian model that exploits the ocular image of the mind's eye in terms of a complete dualism, surveying and controlling whatever occurs in the world outside.

Novalis rejects such a "new age of judgment" associated with Cartesian vision and the form of linguistic representation that takes control of reality with an all-consuming, appropriating force. Menges further explains in this context that Enlightenment logic had displaced the traditional ternary concept of signification (sign, signifier, signified) in favor of a strictly binary organization. Foucault posits in this context a "duplicated representation" whose syntax not only reflects an exterior reality but, in a quasi-transcendental dimension, reflects its own logical predisposition. He mentions Hölderlin and Mallarmé but not Novalis, whom Menges adds for excellent reasons here. Such inscription of logic into grammar affects signification to the extent that irrational or magical events are excluded whenever they are literally beyond comprehension. This is what Novalis and the romantics' model of representation turned against. While abandoning the notion of transparency, they hope for a new linguistic unity not unlike that of the pre-Enlightenment totality of resemblances. But whereas the Renaissance text was ultimately controlled and limited by the primal text of the world, language of modern literature remains ungrounded. Novalis's Klingsohr tale is an example here. What the scribe writes gets erased in the water test, his ugliness stands for the condition of denaturation, his fixation on numbers for the limits of rationalistic literacy or the "dryness of a book culture that has lost its natural moorings in a semiosis of representational power and calculability." Menges shows how Novalis's writings are intertextual, transitory, and therefore escape intentionality, as his "Monolog" best articulates. Where language is "ein Wortspiel," fundamentally playful, words no longer carry preexisting meanings. Language is redefined as the autonomous, self-referential play of differences.[15] Intentional speech and representational writing correspond to the gaze. Novalis develops a reorientation of vision that should not be binary as in the closed circuitry of logic and grammatical representation, a free play recognizing infinity of all differential manifestations, and against all one-dimensional fixation. Novalis states, with an almost Wittgensteinian radicality, that the borders of feeling and intuition are also the borders of philosophy. Feeling is beyond articulation, precedes teleological reflection, is mute.[16] It cannot feel itself, only reflect on itself. Looking at feeling in a reflective way leaves us with a loss of feeling, and vice versa. Novalis expresses this idea of an "ordo-inversus" principle and develops a new way of seeing that he associates with "intellectual intuition," "reflected consciousness," a "second inversion." Such vision mirrors the inverted image and does not fall victim to the inversion that afflicts simple consciousness. His alternative visual paradigm, Menges explains, is expressed in a variety of metaphors, including that of a "poetic theory of telescope" where perception is not only tied to linear technological innovations but linked to imagination and intuition. Such synthesizing vision connects philosophy with poetry, science with art. It is no longer captured by the analytical, appropriating gaze. True enlightenment is therefore—for Novalis and Menges—broken reflexivity, reflected reflection, intellectual intuition. It is not reflection in the finite but, through an extended double mirror effect, a "moral astronomy." This term, which alludes to Herder, Hemsterhuis, and Shaftesbury, characterizes thoughts as reflections of sensations and links philosophical assertions with human interactions. It also links language with bodily sensations, but not in any simplistic way.[17]

The final essay in part III, Harald Weinböck's "The Dialectic of Romantic En*light*enment and the Psychodynamics of the Hypervisual in Hölderlin's *Hyperion*," explores the darker sides of romantic vision: the hypervisual, its extremes. It highlights the borders of romantic vision, not where it seems to fade in the margins but where its textuality is so thick that blackness occurs. It examines a language of visuality where imagination dominates seeing and becomes dangerously psychosomatic.

The essay is theoretically situated in a post-Freudian context of sociological psychoanalysis, including theories by Kohut, Winnicott, Reich, and Klein. It also applies studies by Horkheimer and Adorno, Habermas, Jameson, Virilio, and others, and mentions some recent research on seeing, sense perception, vision, and cinema. While combining these various theoretical approaches, Weinböck offers a close and provocative new reading of key passages from Hölderlin's *Empedokles* and *Hyperion*. Although one may not agree with Weinböck's statement that "Hölderlin's romantic emphasis on visual language represents the (identical) binary opposite of the Enlightenment's obsession with clarifying vision," one must admit that the Hölderlin passages he highlights in the context of this essay do, in fact, draw attention to obsessive and extreme qualities of the visual and link the romantic language of visuality with narcissism and alienation. It would be misleading to connect these motifs with the author or with Hölderlin as a person. It must be emphasized, and there is no doubt to that effect in Weinböck's interpretation, that the issue is how Hölderlin's texts reveal, via constellations and dynamics of their use of visual language, substructures of perception, cognition, and communication that do exist in the conscious or unconscious "regime of vision" (Foucault) already at Hölderlin's time, during the French Revolution. The early romantics, Novalis and Hölderlin, proposed a kind of vision that differs from the gaze, which questions it, and which goes beyond opposition and intensification of Enlightenment's visuality. It may have been not only desire but also fear that motivated the intended "astronomical" look. Weinböck's essay is complementary to Menges's. Weilnböck is obviously not interested in the balanced or ideal notion of the romantics' visuality, but rather in its most extreme manifestations in literature. In the case of Hölderlin, it has indeed become highly self-reflexive and therefore provides a kind of X-ray vision, a delayering or scaling of its own textuality of the visual. This reveals shocking insights for psychosomatics and cultural criticism.

In analogy to Caspar David Friedrich's paintings of the *Rückenfiguren,* Weilnböck thematizes the position of the contemplative onlooker, the painter's eye in the picture.[18] Hölderlin's intense visual troping and his grammatically paratactical style seem to anticipate "impressionistic styles of painting and writing" and an "almost cinematographic mode of image sequencing." Hölderlin's abundant use of metaphor and metonymy indicates "a profound change of the individual's psychosomatic organization." The Enlightenment's "clear vision" of quasi-transparency and romanticism's synaesthetic countervision of multiple reflection display vicious undercurrents. Extremes get exposed in Hölderlin's literature where "vision and visual language collapse or turn compulsive, indulging in a symbiotic gaze of fusion and total narcissistic identification with the viewed object." Weilnböck applies Kohut's term "mirror transference" in his reading of Hölderlin. He shows how the aesthetic gaze tends to fuse and melt everything, and examines underlying power structures of possession and appropriation.

A fusion with a romanticized and intensely eroticized landscape can be found in *Hyperion,* where the hero is longing for a symbiotic connection with the cave. Hyperion has fantasies about withdrawing with Diotima into the depth of the mountain and looking into the mirror image of the water on the ground. The motif of narcissism is obvious. Weilnböck finds that the intensified sense of vision does not coincide with increased sharpness or richness of perception and that the tremendous dynamic of visuality has its roots more in social alienation than in creative liberation. He diagnoses "intensely projective visuality" in Hölderlin's work and experiments with almost overloaded borders of representation where seeing has been entirely replaced by projection. The totalizing, if not totalitarian, role of imagination anticipates control mechanisms that are politically very suspect, but also anticipates precinematic forms of perception. Two extreme types of languages of visuality, as well as two forms of psychosomatic alienation, are shown in Hölderlin's work: in *Empedokles* the hero suicidally and masochistically leaps into the volcano, thus trying to fuse with totality; in *Hyperion* the hero turns around, looking down on civilization, and then becomes a sadistic volcano himself. He attends to warfare in the end. In both cases, notions of self and individuality collapse, communication and intimacy are impossible, and women are entirely removed from the plot.[19]

Weilnböck states that Hölderlin's reception was delayed and that when he was finally discovered—by Heidegger, Benjamin, Adorno, and others—as one of the most advanced writers of modernity he was still never fully recognized in terms of the visual. Weilnböck does for Hölderlin what Menges does with respect to Foucault for Novalis: he introduces the importance of his visual language into literary criticism and cultural studies.

Part IV, "Poetry and Painting: The Empty Center, Gaps, and Hieroglyphs," begins with Anthony Julian Tamburri's essay "Aldo Palazzeschi and Giorgio de Chirico: Decentralized Antitraditional Aesthetics." Tamburri explores epistemological analogies and perhaps ideological commonality between Palazzeschi's poetry and de Chirico's paintings. He finds that both artists resist, "in a (proto)postmodern way," notions of hierarchy, universality, and absoluteness, and he links them with notions of a postmodern discourse, including such terms as "stability/subversion, hierarchy/anarchy, determinacy/indeterminacy, genital/polymorphous." Palazzeschi and de Chirico both reject the hegemony of seeing and signification, the usual expectations of their culture, the norms of the canon. They develop, as Tamburri convincingly demonstrates, a "decentralized antitraditional aesthetics." He also distinguishes them from the majority of their rebellious contemporaries. Tamburri uses Bakhtin's notion of decentralizing the "verbal-ideological world," modifies these categories slightly ("the signifier-ideological world . . . be it verbal or visual"), and also integrates ideas from Iser's reader-response theory, as well as theoretical considerations from Calvino, Eco, and Lyotard, one of whose sentences may remind us that it is not these artists' "business . . . to supply reality but to invent allusions to the conceivable which cannot be presented" (81).

Tamburri's essay examines interfaces among the disciplines of art and contributes to a study on intertextuality—or "multivisuality," I might add—thus opening a new methodological dimension and offering a terminologically advanced instrumentarium. The painter and poet, whose works under consideration here were created about at the same time (early twentieth century), are not making explicit references to one another. The kind of intertextuality Tamburri explores is not given by any previous statement or text but created by him, the reader/observer, who actively participates in the construction of meaning. Tamburri argues that language cannot be but ideologically invested, that it can therefore be oppressive and restrictive. He shows that it is indeed possible to escape the scopic regime of a given culture without falling into the dualistic trap of the major counterdiscourse. His interpretation offers fine examples of two avant-garde artists whose work contributes to a pluralistic notion of artistic invention and interpretation. It presents the idea of "the individual—author *and* reader—who has (re-)created and developed a different repertoire of signs." Such a repertoire exists in the poems by Palazzeschi. Their techniques are suspension of time, monotony, descriptions devoid of emotion, suspension of reference, mollified actions and colors, opacity, and lack of communication. These poems leave the reader with the effect of inscrutability, with a void. They could be considered examples of "non-sense verse." While etymologically speaking the term *image* was once linked with the idea of imitating reality, such "images" lack representation and reference to any previous knowledge.

Similarly, de Chirico's paintings can be characterized as uncentralized and seem to reveal a narrative irresponsibility. Iserian blanks can be concretized in the text of these paintings: there is a void in the middle of the canvas. This has an immobilizing effect on the observer: the blanks lead to confusion and puzzlement; they force the reader to stop, think, and reflect. Thus they challenge the reader/observer to use this blank for his or her own constructions of meanings.[20] The blanks are the messages themselves—the missing statue, for example, the enigmatic central image, empty space. Tamburri notices that the light in de Chirico's paintings seems to come from the left, but he concludes that Palazzeschi and de Chirico "deprivilege narrative and coherent textuality in favor of liberating the signifier from an extrinsic signifying force." His interpretation adds new image/text relations to our debate and suggests new answers to the problem of mimesis. By drawing attention from the empty space on the canvas to the observer and reader, he deauthorizes the text and shifts the construction of meanings to us, while offering new theoretical considerations about the process of interpretation and the dynamics of unlimited semiosis.

Kathryn E. Kramer's essay "Myth, Invisibility, and Politics in the Late Work of Paul Klee" demonstrates how metaphorical strategies of verbal and visual language may be viewed as techniques to circumvent or immobilize fascist power. Such an attempt seems to have been the case for Paul Klee, for whom it led to the discovery of ancient chthonic myths and to *chiffres* in his paintings, which replace the "images" of the earlier Bauhaus period. The fascist notion of "degenerate art" reflects iconophobia and provokes antivisual troping, counterdetective moves, and subversive signs of resistance.

Klee's work from the last three years of his life (1937–40) seems to transform and recombine earlier image complexes into glyphic signs that are not quite figures and not quite written characters. Their distorted linear formations seem to hover between the pictographic and the ideographic. Kramer refers to some primal state of writing where signifier and signified are almost equal and uses Lyotard's concept of a figure-matrix, where internal phantasms are generated and where a force transgresses the visual field as invisibility. It is a place where discourse, image, and forms coexist without friction before they are put into oppositions by their expression. She explains that as a native Swiss (though a German citizen), it must have been quite troubling for Klee to find some of his paintings placed on the "dada wall" (most rejected, from the fascist perspective) in the Degenerate Art exhibition. Klee was, as Kramer puts it, "never really a political animal" and preferred the role of a rather remote, contemplative artist. But any political image was dangerous for him, as it could also jeopardize his chance to obtain Swiss citizenship. In addition, Klee had numerous reasons to avoid any overt political action under Germany's censorship at that time. Kramer argues that the new mode of expression in the late work of Klee, characterized by Werckmeister in terms of "crypto-mythic figuration," must be understood as an antifascist strategy, as a kind of politicization, even in what seems to be the most unpolitical.

Kramer offers a fascinating reading of Klee's "private alphabet," the "secret language" of his late work, precisely by resisting any available code or previously formulated language of visuality. She claims that the indecipherability of the secret hieroglyphs is in Klee's case intentional. The signs are not blocks of the narrative; they avoid textualization in that sense and are evocative of an archaic "translinguistic state that exists between an original phenomenon and the language that evolves to refer to that phenomenon." Kramer is not so much interested in the themes from classical mythology in Klee's late work as she is in how they operate in his specific art works. She resists the danger of imposing the methodology of literary criticism on visual art or imperializing images by texts, an acute problem with a long history, which has recently been challenged by Barbara Stafford.[21]

Kramer combines multiple aspects in her considerations. She is interested in the dynamics between various visual languages and raises the following questions: How does Klee's "hybridization" of the mimetic/nonmimetic reflect the apocalyptic tenor of Europe at the threshold of World War II? How do the operations of Klee's fractured signs relate to classical Greek literature, especially tragedy? With respect to Klee's "primitive signs," she detects a border between primal chaos and the origination of myth where they seem to act as frontiers, to signal a zone of residue of meaning in which there is a retreat from visual form. Kramer compares Klee in such terms with other intellectuals in exile who had the need to express and assert themselves without transgressing the confines of their habitually nonactivist, nonpolitical culture.

In addition, Kramer's essay offers new insights into the disagreement between Bataille and Breton and places Klee on the side with Bataille. They share a love for the archaic myth, for the lower forces of the senses, and a critique of ocularcentricity. In this respect Klee also contributes to what Martin Jay has recently described as "antiocular discourse." Bataille's revolution could not take place by Hegelian means, which would replace one order with another. Kramer is convincing in her assessment that it was a shared notion between Bataille and Klee that "the acephalic enterprise was devoted to perpetual revolution, to continual destruction, to an extreme *heterogeneity* in the face of fascism's extreme *homogeneity.*''

Part IV could be summarized in terms of *possibilities* of border crossings away from traditional scopic regimes and toward liberation of the ''individual'' (a term that has undergone a radical transformation, has become pluralistic and newly defined in postmodern notions of multiple subjectivity and intersubjectivity). Tamburri and Kramer challenge traditional assumptions of authorship or any given meaning, whether they are visually or textually encoded. Part V, ''Power and Seeing: Control and Transgressions,'' examines the *limits* of certain border crossings and liberations and shows how scopic regimes and forms of supervision pervade when we may least expect them. At the same time, it encourages us again to think of counterstrategies and ways to circumvent the predictable.

To begin part V, Karen Jacobs's essay ''The Eye's Mind: Henry James's *The Sacred Fount* and Vladimir Nabokov's *The Eye*'' explores how far ''tactics of supervision'' reach while traditions are being eroded. In contrast to Tamburri's interest in the empty center in poems and painting, Jacobs deals with the realist narrator in detective fiction. She turns to a subgenre of realism, detective fiction, where narrative omniscience and authorial ''objectivity'' become very problematic. An apparent sign may no more lead to ''truth'' than will any given blank. She begins her own investigation by making an analogy between the Marxist (Jameson) and Cartesian models of seeing, an idea that may prompt further discussion. Then she investigates signs of the Cartesian model in modern fiction, where, at the same time, it becomes challenged and overturned. In a third step, she offers important distinctions and theoretical considerations while including approaches from Freud, Lacan, Žižek, and others.

Jacobs argues that Jameson's division of realism into aesthetic and epistemological models of form and content in *Signatures of the Visible* entails some components of Cartesian spectatorship, a model of seeing that ''repeatedly has been described as hegemonic in Western thought up until this century.'' The Cartesian spectator's transcendent, universal view can be seen in Paul Ricoeur's definition as ''a vision of the world in which the whole of objectivity is spread out like a spectacle on which the *cogito* casts its sovereign gaze'' (236); or in Richard Rorty's ''mirror of nature'' with the detached objectivity of science; or in Martin Jay's critical assessment as ''ahistorical, disinterested, disembodied subject entirely outside of the world it claims to know only from afar'' (''Scopic Regimes'' 10). All these versions seem to correspond with the narrator in realist fiction, who, as Jacobs puts it, ''invisibly presides over the fictive world it represents as transparently available to it.'' Jacobs's thesis is that the Cartesian spectator and the omniscient-realist narrator are both historically overlapping and theoretically contingent and that the realist narrator can be interpreted as "the virtual embodiment of the assumptions of Cartesian spectatorship." Borrowing from Foucault and Selzer, she makes use of the expressions "panoptic eye of surveillance" and "society of surveillance."

This is where the subgenre of detective fiction becomes a tool for the study of control mechanisms and codes of visual language; it also shows how Cartesian spectatorship becomes more and more eroded. Instead of the neutral, detached gaze, we find "subjectivized forms" of vision and the breakdown of the traditional equation between sign and meaning. The finding of truth in detective fiction is associated with the finding of criminal acts, and it is not likely to be the neutral, disinterested observer who finds evidence for the crime from a distance, but rather the personally engaged observer who looks for details, knows differences and similarities between facts and traps, and arrives at answers often only by using tricks, intuition, speculation, and a microscope. This may be an especially interesting comment if we read it intertextually, as suggested in Menges's essay on Novalis's notion of "moral astronomy." Jacobs examines the strategies of detective fiction that challenge the assumptions of the realist tradition and notices a change from transparency to opacity. The unmediated view of objects through the eyes of the omniscient narrator is disturbed for the reader, and meanings are suspended. She argues that narrative techniques of detective fiction replace the Cartesian spectator with varying forms of subjectivization. She finds the "obsessive, voyeuristic gaze" in Henry James's *The Sacred Fount* a "vehicle for an extended critique of the possibility of the detached, disinterested, omniscient version of the Cartesian spectator and the supervisory force with which it is associated." The notion of objectivity becomes anatomized—dissolved, for example, when the fictional characters look at an "object" that has internally become ambiguous: the painting *The Man with the Mask.* It offers a surplus of conflicting, if not mutually exclusive meanings, but not the expected evidence. Nabokov's *The Eye* similarly anatomizes the notion of subjectivity when Smurov, for example, does not have a "self" apart from the images others make of him. The politics of the gaze is under scrutiny in both texts. The distinction between subjective and objective is undermined, and perceptual indeterminacy and the mechanisms by which the narrator tries to exercise control are pathologized and turn—from another perspective than in Weilnböck's critique of the gaze in Hölderlin—narcissistic and potentially violent. The discrepancy between seeing and knowing, between a genre and a subgenre, mobilizes the invention of what I call miniature "scopic deregulators" as particularized, marginalized languages of visuality, codes of resistance and undercurrents that could not be captured or channeled by any totalizing regime of sight, whether Cartesian, realist, or of any "panoptic" persuasion.

The term *panopticon,* which is especially important in Jeffrey Garrett's essay " 'Teichoscopy' in the Wall Novels of Peter Schneider and Uri Orlev," was first introduced into the discourse, to which Foucault has also contributed, by the English philosopher Jeremy Bentham via letters from Russia to England, published in 1791. The term describes a "rotunda-shaped building offering an unobstructed view from a central tower into hundreds of rooms or cells arranged radially around it." Garrett analyzes the uses of the panopticon and other wall technologies, control mechanisms, and devices for visual and political control, including the poetic strategy of *teichoscopia* (wall-viewing) in the context of two recent novels. In both novels, walls are linked with optical instruments, not only with obstruction of sight but also with openings and optical devices such as windows and lenses. They can be used with opposite functions, dependent on inside or outside perspectives. Schneider's novel *Der Mauerspringer* (1982) presents the Berlin Wall as a primarily psychological barrier with a very different effect for East and West. Its effects include, for example, the use of television on both sides: things look distorted from either direction. Garrett argues that Schneider develops, in his novel, strategies to counteract such optical fragmentation and asks how the distorted views might be creatively corrected. Reversed mirrors and other strategies are used. The narrator himself seems to act as a *Grenzgänger*, oscillating between opposite views, but there is also a "wall-jumper" whose *Wallsprünge* are not only pathological signs but attempts to neutralize the sensory deprivations caused by the wall. Garrett refers to Goethe's *Colour Theory* and the effect of afterimages, actualizes Schneider's notion of walls in people's heads, and asks how to get rid of those walls in Germany today. Garrett offers another type of visual criticism related to Bentham's model of the panopticon in the context of Orlev's *Haii Berehov Hatziporim* (1981), where one theme is fascist surveillance. At the end of the novel Garrett detects the phantastic image of a reversal of optical/political surveillance. Its mechanisms become immobilized when, in an almost paradoxical move, Alex, the Jewish boy who was captured in the panoptic walls of a ghetto, discovers countermirror effects, finds a moment to become invisible in the pupil of the "panoptic eye" of surveillance itself, and succeeds in escaping. Such a countervisual strategy is nonmimetic and its image is irreversible, but it makes us think of moments to challenge the regime of any repressive power. Garrett suggests teichoscopy in more than one way.

   Part VI, entitled "Theories of Visuality: Closer Definitions," draws some of the presented arguments together and opens new vistas for further investigation. It contains two essays that again challenge notions of equation, factual knowledge, authority, representation, and continuity. They offer new approaches and more precise terminologies for the development of interdisciplinary studies. Whereas the essay by Azade Seyhan on Walter Benjamin's "Schwellenkunde" (science of thresholds) makes us think of momentary contiguities, transitions, and translations, Christopher Collins makes us realize the radical break between oral- and text-based cultures, between "outer" and "inner" imaging, while drawing attention not only to different types of "images" but also to diverse processes of image cognition, imagination, and textualization.

In "Visual Citations: Walter Benjamin's Dialectic of Text and Image," Azade Seyhan offers a third element to the image/text debate: the concept of allegory, which she finds just as important. The term *allegory* captures an image of unrest, the simultaneity of erasures and constructions, oscillations between absence and presence, coextensive elements between the image and the script. Seyhan draws attention to Benjamin's "Zentralpark," a "text" or intertext of multiple fragments, where he offers a reading of Baudelaire and, almost via subtext, indirectly, at the margin, his theory of allegory. Seyhan makes us understand why Benjamin liked this term: "Like the works of art that always point beyond their time and place, allegory is a transformative and open-ended figural force. As a mediating term between image and text and between destruction and preservation, it transforms and translates the memory it touches." While Benjamin sees images as texts to be deciphered, and while he reads texts as visual phenomena, he finds both terms and any such one-sided process of translation restrictive. He asks how such "translations," which apply to every act of citation, could possibly energize the repertoire of each of the two separate "languages," the visual and the verbal, and, at the same time, surpass both categories.

His "science of thresholds" contributes to multiple translations and to the interdisciplinary study of languages of visuality. While Benjamin's "translator" attempts to rescue hidden memories from the unconscious, his interest is not limited to reflection. He aims at a revolutionary interpretation of the past for the present: a border crossing. This is associated with the idea that history has never been realized fully, that its images help us trace what has been forgotten, marginalized, and suppressed. The translator's task is to illuminate, to break the frame of history's formulas, to disturb momentarily the continuum of time, and to shatter the surface. While these seem to be techniques that have also been "translated," at least considering some of these aspects in the production of and reception of film, Seyhan notices that Benjamin's techniques can create disturbing new mirror effects and opens the heterogenous as the dynamics in *Passagen-Werk*.

What Benjamin develops in the context of an aesthetic theory is no longer limited to the realm of art and aesthetics. The "translations" of texts into images and of images into texts are always political acts and contribute to cultural change. Seyhan emphasizes that this involves all disciplines of study and every aspect of human life. Now that the aesthetic domain is no longer marginalized by the discourse of science and philosophy, it includes all manifestations of collective memory, everything "from comic strips to hard-rock lyrics to videos and highway billboards," and now that boundaries of the canonical no longer prevail, it may be—as Barbara Stafford has recently argued—the task of the "imagists" to speak up.

With Benjamin's allegory we have gone one step further into the many zones of passage between images and texts, counterimages and subtexts, margins and covers, and so on. But there are more than "phantasmagoric zones between dreams and awakenings" to explore; there are also—along the same lines on different plateaus—the "electrical images" and the "techniques of cutting," as outlined, for example, in a recent study by Richard Dienst with reference to Godard and Deleuze, as the "interstice between images, as the upsurge of a power of difference in the ruins of the old logic of sense" (157).[22]

With Christopher Collins's study "Writing and the Nature of the Supernatural Image, or Why Ghosts Float" we are now faced with the gaps between "outer" and "inner" imaging. Hovering ghosts can be better understood if we consider the differences between media and corresponding processes of imagination. Collins connects "outer imaging" with traditional mimesis and diegesis, drama, or recited narration, "inner imaging" with anamnesis (reproductive imagination) and phantasia (productive imagination). There are distinctions between the images of dreams, reveries, hallucinations, and literate, chirographic, and typographic imaging, but they share important features that separate them from mimesis and diegesis. Since they are private actions with the only possible visual interference being the words that appear on a page, they allow the production of imaginal, free-floating signifieds, which were not available before standardized print and movable type. Collins characterizes this advance in phantasia in the context of the development from outer to inner imaging, from oral to written communication. Changing representations of the supernatural are the result of changing figure-ground relations. While ghosts were once fully grounded as the figures in the performance of a Greek drama, they are now associated with "absent grounds," "ganzfeld simulations," or "transparent writing." Collins offers fascinating distinctions and aspects from cognitive psychology while using examples from Shakespeare, Hölderlin, Rilke, and others. He motivates our attempt to come to terms with the fractures, shifts, and slippages from one scopic regime to another in terms of the different media involved. Collins develops an entire "typology of ghostly gestalts" and asks what roles visual representations of the supernatural play in the contexts of shifting cultures, from orality to textuality, from written page to film, and so on. His study addresses different processes of imagination, and it raises, among a myriad of others, the following questions: What kinds of translations, transformations, and crossings will follow in our postmodern age, where new simulation techniques and computerized vision further replace the written text? Do the gaps between figures and ground get bigger or smaller? Or do they eventually get erased? Do they provoke new forms of productive imagination, or will they have counterliterate and counterimaginary side effects?

Notes

1. Herman Melville, *Mardi* (New York: Signet, 1964), 402.
2. Martin Jay, with whom the term *scopic regime* is associated, indicates in ''Scopic Regimes of Modernity'' (3) that he borrowed it from Christian Metz. What I like about Jay's use of the term is that he conceptualizes seeing in pluralistic terms and does away with any linear notion of worldviews. He heuristically suggests three scopic regimes: The first is Cartesian perspectivalism, which became the basis for modern epistemology. The second is Baconian empiricism of the detached, ''scientific'' view, as it plays a role, e.g., also in Svetlana Alpers, where the eye is cast on the detailed, articulated surface of the world where more is described than explained. Jay associates this model not only with the valorization of material surfaces in Dutch art but also with ''the fetishism of commodities no less characteristic of a market economy'' (15). The third is called ''baroque''; it expresses the bizarre and peculiar, the irregular, and seems to be the most significant alternative to the hegemonic style of Cartesian perspectivalism. It marks a surplus of images, opacity, and unreadability and has been of special interest to Christine Buci-Glucksmann. It rejects monocular geometricalization, the illusion of a homogeneous world seen from a distance from a God's-eye view, and it notices contradictions between surface and depth, a nonhierarchical multiplicity of visual spaces. Jay acknowledges the plurality of scopic regimes and finds that they can interact, compete, and sometimes overlap. I would be curious to find slippages, translations, and gaps between these models, which are nothing less than simplifying constructions in the attempt to comprehend the entire cosmos of ''languages of visuality.'' The problem will be in deciding what framing devices to use, or how to ''cut'' the film of shifting images and constellations so that we can discuss or express them. For further explorations on Jay's baroque scopic regime see also Rodophe Gasché.
3. Compare, e.g., studies on the history of optics—on seeing, eye, images, film, media technology—and related philosophical, literary, and theoretical discourses: Gerard Simon, Liliane Weissberg, Frederick Burwick, Katharina Weisrock, Thomas Zacharias, Vivian Sobchack, and Arthur Zajonc. Or, even if we want to compare studies that address the mirror motif, there is a wide spectrum between Richard Rorty, Hart Nibbrig, Kaja Silverman, and Umberto Eco. These few examples show how interwoven these discourses are, while each of these studies has its own intricate and specific research spectrum. All linkages and analogies, if they are made to show semblances and not differences, always seem to leave us, even if done for legitimate scholarly purposes, with a sense of neglect and unease.
4. See Blumenberg (especially the introduction and 84–105). An English translation of Blumenberg's pathbreaking essay ''Licht als Metapher der Wahrheit: im Vor-

feld der philosophischen Begriffsbildung'' has recently been published in Levin 30–62. It is translated by Joel Anderson and titled "Light as Metaphor for Truth: At the Preliminary Stage of Philosophical Concept Formation." For excellent comments see Haverkamp, *Die Theorie der Metapher* 285–315 and "The Memory of Pictures." Haverkamp challenges with respect to Barthes and Augustine any simplistic notion of "translation" from image to text. He argues on the basis of Blumenberg's concept of "absolute metaphor" and Derrida's "white mythology" that the photographic image does not represent anything that ever existed outside or before that photograph. He applies Barthes's notion of "the death of the author," which has usually only been related to the textual, to the visual.

5. Interdisciplinary studies that I find exemplary are offered by Amrine, Bal, and Baumgart et al. One breakthrough in this direction was already offered by Hofstadter.

6. On differences between oral and written cultures and on shifting verbal/visual relations see Assmann, Assmann, and Hardmeier; Dümchen and Nerlich; Eco; Flusser; and Kittler.

7. Baudrillard writes, "To dissimulate is to feign not to have what one has. To simulate is to have what one hasn't. One implies a presence, the other an absence. But the matter is more complicated, since to simulate is not simply to feign: 'Someone who feigns an illness can simply go to bed and make believe he is ill. Someone who simulates an illness produces in himself some of the symptoms' (Littre). Thus, feigning or dissimulating leaves the reality principle intact: the difference is always clear, it is not masked; whereas simulation threatens the difference between 'true' and 'false,' between 'real' and 'imaginary.' Since the simulator produces 'true' symptoms, is he ill or not? He cannot be treated objectively either as ill, or as not-ill" (5). This is an excellent example of how the dissolution of binaries can be conceptualized. What I find troublesome and questionable is how Baudrillard draws his conclusion, which seems almost simplistic, nostalgic, or fatalistic: "The cool universe of digitality has absorbed the world of metaphor and metonymy. The principle of simulation wins out over the reality principle just as over the principle of pleasure" (152). Wouldn't it make more sense to claim more than one "reality principle" and more than one "pleasure principle," or question both as they have been defined by the dominant (male) Western culture?

8. In *Heterologies: Discourse of the Other,* Michel de Certeau compares and correlates two discourses whose taxonomy of "time" and notion of "space of memory" work quite differently: historiography postulates a continuity, is based on a clean break between past and present, and is the product of knowledge and power linking these two domains; psychoanalysis recognizes the past in the present and treats the relation as equivocal, not as a succession. Forgetting and remembering are, according to Freud and others, not simply arbitrary and passive; they have their own logic. De Certeau's undertaking could be compared to our own interdisciplinary interest. Bringing various discourses together, he does not aim at their fusion but at the spaces between, the forgotten and eliminated.

9. Perhaps one should respond to Mitchell that Goodman remains "linguicentric."

Other, related uses of the word *language,* in the plural, and not limited to the verbal—in fact, often rather used in opposition to verbal languages—are, e.g., indicated in the notions of "the languages of psyche" by G. S. Rousseau and "semiotics of visual language" in the three-dimensional sense of Saint-Martin, who uses the term referring to architecture, nonverbal signs, and movements in space, and who develops, in addition, the notion of a "grammar of sculpture." Such "languages" address topological regions beyond previous textualization.

10. Also on Noton and Stark's saccades, on scanning in the process of seeing, and on gestures of demonstration, compare Kirby with Gandelman, who offers, e.g., the reprint of a scanning diagram of an eye looking at Paul Klee's *Figuring Old Man,* as used by Noton and Stark to illustrate their theory (9). This intertextually links Kirby's essay further with the essay by Kathryn Kramer in this book. Gandelman uses the directions of the scanning path with two types of seeing, which correspond to two types of thinking: the "linear-pictorial" or the "optical-haptical" (9). He correlates these with Jakobson's well-known dichotomy between metaphor and metonymy as two main types of verbal association. The double scanning, the "touching" and the "jumping," is, according to Gandelman, a translation into the pictorial modality of the language. He summarizes his thesis: "One axis is that of metaphoric, optic scanning which proceeds through semantic jumps from one corner of the picture or text to another. The other axis is that of haptic or contact vision, which bores through texture and color and fixes on nonsemantic elements in picture or text. Such a deconstruction of picture or text into a twofold structure gives the fullest legitimacy to the linguistic or semiotic approach used by contemporary researchers in their analyses" (12). Perhaps we should realize that most recent semiotics have gone much beyond Jakobson's semiology and beyond Saussure's dualistic concept and come to terms with the most recent studies, as offered by Floyd Merrell and, in this book, John Kirby.

11. A contribution on Herder's critique of ocularcentricity has been provided by Hans Adler in *Die Prägnanz des Dunklen.* Peter Sprengel connects Herder, Jacobi, and Jean Paul as opponents to dominant Weimar classicism. In contradiction to Goethe (and his notion of symbol), Jean Paul prefers allegory and metaphor over other forms of writing. This is where Walter Benjamin explicitly connects with Jean Paul, whose motto is "fictio supra naturam"—the less "mimetic," the better. His question is how to break out of frames that are imposed by representational language. I have commented on his specific "Bilderschrift" and its dynamics in *Die Metapher und ihre Krise.*

12. The so-called "Shepard tones," named after the psychologist Roger Shepard, are another excellent example. Shepard discovered the principle of the hexagonal modulation scheme of Bach's endlessly rising fugue forms in "The Musical Offering," which could be "read" or textualized in terms of irony: The royal theme or the idea of rising, along and with the notion of hierarchy altogether, is undercut by the internal logic of the music. Hofstadter has already pointed out (717–19) how the shifting weights of the tones contribute to a kind of border crossing with puzzling and thought-provoking effects that challenge the habitual notion of the octave. And there is also the limited scope of the piano in comparison with today's

19

computerized music, where more under- and overtones can be perceived, which has counter-hierarchic effects.

13. See also Kittler's *Discourse Networks 1800–1900.*

14. Hardack's critique of the male notion of an "infinitely repellent orb" is an excellent contribution to gender studies. Melville's detachable eye of the transcendent postindividual reflects an adaption and a parody of Emersonian pantheistic ideas. And, one may add: what is the Gaea, the giant monster, if not the return of the repressed, the neglected and excluded female, a voice lacking in both authors' work? And isn't the detached eye, which has lost its function due to lacking connections with other parts of the body, a "poetic" warning of female repression, which has, of course, political implications and consequences? This shows how images and metaphors can reveal substructures of thinking, including messages from the unconscious, which transgress limits of intentionality. Feminist studies on seeing and the gaze are most often contributions of film studies but are also relevant in this context: Wendy Lesser, Teresa de Lauretis, Laura Mulvey, Susan Rubin Suleiman, Mary Ann Doane, and others.

15. This is where Novalis can be linked with Derrida's notion of difference.

16. There are related kinds of muteness, silence, in Novalis and Wittgenstein. Also, Wittgenstein's *Blue Book* could well be an allusion to Novalis's "blue flower" in *Heinrich von Ofterdingen,* which changes meaning and is ultimately unattainable. Wittgenstein begins his *Blue Book* by asking what explanations are. This question about the explanation of the explanation (and so on) becomes ridiculously entangled and complex and draws attention to the modalities of language, to what Wittgenstein has coined "philosophical grammar." Jean Paul uses the term "blue milk" in the sense of ink, possibly also referring to Novalis and with related connotation. For exciting research on Novalis see also Kuzniar, Mahoney, and Calhoon.

17. Cf. on this topic also Weissberg and Trabant.

18. In *The Science of Art* Martin Kemp points out that the paintings of Caspar David Friedrich were influenced by Goethe and scientific theory, but that Friedrich "inconsistently employed coloured shadows and exploited some degree of optical mixing, but the balance in his art was tipped decisively away from scientific theory" (299). Maybe it is precisely this inconsistency that makes him modern, and this connects him even more with science than any predictable application of one or the other formula. On a different account of "science," see, e.g., Merrell, *Semiosis in a Postmodern Age* (1995) and *Unthinking Thinking* (1991).

19. The same is also true for Novalis in *Heinrich von Ofterdingen.* This comment has already been made by Kittler and Kuzniar, who both make references to Lacan but with interesting differences in their conclusions. While Kuzniar (like Kittler) notices the disappearance of women in the plot of the novel, she draws attention to female voices in the text nevertheless. They appear unattached to any notion of subject or object. Kuzniar associates these female voices in the writing of this male author, Novalis, with Julia Kristeva's *écriture feminine,* draws from Jacques Lacan, Judith Butler, and others, and states the return of the repressed. I definitely agree with her.

20

20. Compare Tamburri's intriguing use of Iser's reception theory with other "readings" of visual art based on reception theory—e.g., Kemp, especially 253–78.
21. See Stafford on this problem, especially in her introduction to *Body Criticism* (1–45). While she argues that visual artists, art critics—"imagists," as she summarizes them (herself included)—have been dominated and suppressed by the "text-based disciplines" (6) in the hierarchy of institutionalized knowledge, she draws attention to an increased importance of the visual in the twenty-first century, to medical imaging technologies (CT, PET, and MRI scanners), electronic imagery, and the "inescapable universalization of vision." These developments are replacing the previously text-based culture and require multiple languages of visuality (if we want to come to terms with them). These changes have been summarized by Mitchell under the rubric "pictorial turn." Stafford calls for the imagists' liberation and writes: "My overarching conviction is that we bring, and must continue to bring, something special and distinctive to the humanities and the sciences. . . . We must respond to the dire need our civilization has for the intelligent thought concerning nondiscursive expression. Here lies an opportunity for hope and an incentive for performance" (6–7).
22. Richard Dienst has a brilliant chapter on Deleuze in *Still Life in Real Time* 144–69.

References

Adler, Hans. *Die Prägnanz des Dunklen: Gnoseologie-Ästhetik- Geschichtsphilosophie bei Johann Gottfried Herder.* Hamburg: Felix Meiner, 1990.

Allert, Beate. *Die Metapher und ihre Krise: Zur Dynamik der "Bilderschrift" Jean Pauls.* New York: Peter Lang, 1987.

Alpers, Svetlana. *The Art of Describing: Dutch Art in the Seventeenth Century.* Chicago: U of Chicago P, 1983.

Amrine, Frederick, ed. *Literature and Science as Modes of Expression.* Dordrecht: Kluwer, 1989.

Amrine, Frederick, F. J. Zucker, and H. Wheeler, eds. *Goethe and the Sciences: A Reappraisal.* Dordrecht: D. Reidel, 1987.

Assmann, Aleida, Jan Assmann, and Christof Hardmeier, eds. *Schrift und Gedächtnis: Archeologie der literarischen Kommunikation I.* 1983. München: Carl Hanser, 1993.

Bal, Mieke. *Reading Rembrandt: Beyond the Word-Image Opposition.* Cambridge: MIT P, 1991.

Barthes, Roland. *Camera Lucida: Reflections on Photography.* Trans. Richard Howard. New York: Hill & Wang, 1981.

———. *Image-Music-Text.* Trans. Stephen Heath. New York: Noonday, 1977.

Baudrillard, Jean. *Simulations.* Trans. Paul Foss, Paul Patton, and Philip Beitchman. New York: Semiotext(e), 1983.

Baumgart, Silvia, et al., eds. *Denkräume zwischen Kunst und Wissenschaft.* Fifth International Congress of Female Art Historians. Berlin: Dietrich Reimer, 1993.

Bender, John, and David E. Wellbery, eds. *The Ends of Rhetoric: History, Theory, Practice.* Stanford: Stanford UP, 1990.

21

Blumenberg, Hans. *Paradigmen zu einer Metaphorologie.* Archiv für Begriffsgeschichte 6. Bonn: Bouvier, 1960.

Bohn, Volker, ed. *Bildlichkeit: Internationale Beiträge zur Poetik.* Frankfurt: Suhrkamp, 1990.

Bryson, Norman, Michel Ann Holly, and Keith Moxey, eds. *Visual Theory: Painting and Interpretation.* New York: HarperCollins, 1991.

Buci-Glucksmann, Christine. *La Folie du voir: De L'esthetique baroque.* Paris: Galilee, 1986.

Burwick, Frederick. *The Damnation of Newton: Goethe's Colour Theory and Romantic Perception.* Berlin: Walter de Gruyter, 1986.

———. *The Haunted Eye: Perception and the Grotesque in English and German Romanticism.* Heidelberg: Carl Winter Universitätsverlag, 1987.

Calhoon, Kenneth S. *Fatherland: Novalis, Freud, and the Discipline of Romance.* Detroit: Wayne State UP, 1992.

Caws, Mary Ann. *The Eye in the Text: Essays on Perception, Mannerist to Modern.* Princeton, NJ: Princeton UP, 1981.

Christ, Jan. *Glas.* Klagenfurt: Ritter, 1990.

———. *Rauchschrift.* Klagenfurt: Ritter, 1991.

De Certeau. *Heterologies: Discourse on the Other.* Trans. Brian Massumi. 1986. Minneapolis: U of Minnesota P, 1989.

De Lauretis, Teresa. *Alice Doesn't: Feminism, Semiotics, Cinema.* Bloomington: Indiana UP, 1984.

———. *Technologies of Gender: Essays on Theory, Film, and Fiction.* Bloomington: Indiana UP, 1987.

Deleuze, Gilles. *Critique et Clinique.* Paris: Les Editions de Minuit, 1993.

———. *Le Pli: Leibniz et le Baroque.* Paris: Les Editions de Minuit, 1988.

Derrida, Jacques. *Glas.* Trans. John P. Leavey Jr. and Richard Rand. Lincoln: U of Nebraska P, 1986.

———. "White Mythology: Metaphor in the Text of Philosophy." *Margins of Philosophy.* Trans. with additional notes by Alan Bass. Chicago: U of Chicago P, 1982. 209–71.

Dienst, Richard. *Still Life in Real Time: Theory after Television.* Durham: Duke UP, 1994.

Doane, Mary Ann. "Technology's Body: Cinematic Vision in Modernity." *Differences: A Journal of Feminist Cultural Studies* 5 (1993): 1–23.

Dümchen, Sybil, and Michael Nerlich, eds. *Text-Image, Bild-Text.* Berlin: Technische Universität Berlin, 1990.

Eco, Umberto. *Yber Spiegel und andere Phänomene.* Trans. from Italian to German by Burkhardt Kroeber. München: Carl Hanser, 1988.

Fink, Karl J. *Goethe's History of Science.* Cambridge: Cambridge UP, 1991.

Flusser, Vilem. *Lob der Oberflächlichkeit: Für eine Phänomenologie der Medien.* Bensheim: Bollmann Verlag GmbH, 1993.

Foster, Hal, ed. *Vision and Visuality.* Seattle: Bay, 1988.

Gandelman, Claude. *Reading Pictures, Viewing Texts.* Bloomington: Indiana UP, 1992.

Gasché, Rodophe. *The Tain of the Mirror: Derrida and the Philosophy of Reflection.* Cambridge: Harvard UP, 1986.

Goffman, Ervin. *Frame Analysis: An Essay on the Organization of Experience.* 1968. Boston: Northeastern UP, 1986.

Gordon, Ian E. *Theories of Visual Perception.* Chichester: U of Exeter P, 1989.

Haverkamp, Anselm. "The Memory of Pictures: Roland Barthes and Augustine on Photography." *Comparative Literature* 45.3 (1993): 258–79.

————, ed. *Die Theorie des Metapher.* Darmstadt: Wissenschaftliche Buchgesellschaft, 1983.

Haverkamp, Anselm, and Renate Lachmann, eds. *Gedächtniskunst. Raum-Bild-Schrift: Studien zur Mnemotechnik.* Frankfurt: Suhrkamp, 1991.

Hoesterey, Ingeborg, ed. *Zeitgeist in Babel: The Postmodernist Controversy.* Bloomington: Indiana UP, 1993.

Hoesterey, Ingeborg, and Ulrich Weisstein, eds. *Intertextuality: German Literature and Visual Art from the Renaissance to the Twentieth Century.* Columbia, SC: Camden, 1993.

Hofstadter, Douglas R. *Gödel, Escher, Bach: An Eternal Golden Braid. A Metaphorical Fugue on Minds and Machines in the Spirit of Lewis Carroll.* New York: Vintage, 1979.

Höpfner, Felix. *Wissenschaft wider die Zeit: Goethes Farbenlehre aus rezeptionsgeschichtlicher Sicht. Mit einer Bibliographie zur Farbenlehre.* Heidelberg: Carl Winter Universitätsverlag, 1990.

Jakobson, Roman. *Fundamentals of Language.* The Hague: Mouton, 1971.

Jay, Martin. "The Disenchantment of the Eye: Surrealism and the Crisis of Ocularcentrism." *Visual Anthropology Review* 7.1 (1991): 12–37.

————. *Downcast Eyes: The Denigration of Vision in Twentieth-Century French Thought.* Berkeley: U of California P, 1993.

————. "Scopic Regimes of Modernity." *Vision and Visuality.* Ed. Hal Foster. Seattle: Bay, 1988. 3–23.

Kemp, Martin. *The Science of Art: Optical Themes in Western Art from Brunelleschi to Seurat.* New Haven: Yale UP, 1990.

Kemp, Wolfgang, ed. *Der Betrachter ist im Bild: Kunstwissenschaft und Rezeptionsästhetik.* Köln: DuMont, 1985.

Kittler, Friedrich. *Discourse Networks, 1800–1900.* Stanford: Stanford UP, 1990.

Kristeva, Julia. *Black Sun: Depression and Melancholia.* Trans. Leon Roudiez. New York: Columbia UP, 1989.

Kuzniar, Alice. "Hearing Woman's Voices in 'Heinrich von Ofterdingen.'" *PMLA* 107 (1992): 1196–1207.

Lacoue-LaBarthe, Phillipe. *Typography: Mimesis, Philosophy, Politics.* Ed. Christopher Fynsk. Cambridge: Harvard UP, 1989.

Lesser, Wendy. *His Other Half: Men Looking at Women through Art.* Cambridge: Harvard UP, 1991.

Levin, David Michael, ed. *Modernity and the Hegemony of Vision.* Berkeley: U of California P, 1993.

Lyotard, Jean-François. *The Postmodern Condition: A Report on Knowledge.* Trans. Geoff Bennington and Brian Massumi. Minneapolis: U of Minnesota P, 1984.

Mahoney, Dennis F. *The Critical Fortunes of a Romantic Novel: Novalis's* Heinrich von Ofterdingen. Studies in German Literature, Linguistics, and Culture. Columbia, SC: Camden House, 1994.

———. "Human History as Natural History in the 'Novices of Sais' and 'Heinrich von Ofterdingen.' " *Historical Reflections* 18.3 (1992): 111–24.

———. "The Myth of Death and Resurrection in 'Heinrich von Ofterdingen.' " *South Atlantic Review* 48 (1983): 52–66.

———. *Die Poetisierung der Natur bei Novalis.* Bonn: Bouvier Verlag Herbert Grundmann, 1980.

Matthaei, Rupprecht, ed. *Goethes Farbenlehre.* 1987. Ravensburg: Otto Maier, 1988.

Merleau-Ponty, Maurice. *Das Auge und der Geist: Philosophische Essays.* Trans. Hans Werner Arndt. Hamburg: Max Meiner, 1984.

———. *Phenomenology of Perception.* Trans. from the French by Colin Smith. 1989. London: Routledge, 1992.

———. *The Visible and the Invisible.* Ed. Claude Lefort. Trans. Alfonso Lingis. Evanston: Northwestern UP, 1968.

Merrell, Floyd. *Deconstruction Reframed.* West Lafayette, IN: Purdue UP, 1984.

———. "Who Purloined Ariadne's Thread?" *Semiotica* 95.1–2 (1993): 107–39.

———. *Unthinking Thinking: Jorge Luis Borges, Mathematics, and the New Physics.* West Lafayette, IN: Purdue UP, 1991.

Mitchell, W. J. T. *Iconology: Image, Text, Ideology.* Chicago: U of Chicago P, 1989.

———. *Picture Theory: Essays on Verbal and Visual Representation.* Chicago: U of Chicago P, 1994.

Moxey, Keith. *The Practice of Theory: Poststructuralism, Cultural Politics, and Art History.* Ithaca: Cornell UP, 1994.

Mulvey, Laura. *Visual and Other Pleasures.* Bloomington: Indiana UP, 1989.

Nibbrig, Hart. *Spiegelschrift: Spekulationen über Malerei und Literatur.* Frankfurt: Suhrkamp, 1987.

Peterfreund, Stuart. "Scientific Models in Optics: From Metaphor to Metonymy and Back." *Journal of the History of Ideas* 55.1 (1994): 59–73.

Ricoeur, Paul. "The Question of the Subject: The Challenge of Semiology." *The Conflict of Interpretations.* Trans. Don Ihde. Evanston: Northwestern UP, 1974.

Ritter-Santini, Lea, ed. *Mit den Augen geschrieben: Von gedichteten und erzählten Bildern.* München: Hanser, 1991.

Rousseau, G. S., ed. *The Languages of Psyche: Mind and Body in Enlightenment Thought.* Berkeley: U of California P, 1990.

Rubin Suleiman, Susan. *Subversive Intent: Gender, Politics, and the Avant-garde.* Cambridge: Harvard UP, 1990.

Saint-Martin, Fernande. "From Visible to Visual Language: Artificial Intelligence and Visual Semiology." *Semiotica* 77.1–3 (1989): 303–16.

———. *Semiotics of Visual Language.* Bloomington: Indiana UP, 1990.

Silverman, Kaja. *The Acoustic Mirror: The Female Voice in Psychoanalysis and Cinema.* Bloomington: Indiana UP, 1988.

Simon, Gerard. *Der Blick, das Sein und die Erscheinung in der antiken Optik, mit einem Anhang: Die Wissenschaft vom Sehen und die Darstellung des Sichtbaren.* Trans. from French to German by Henz Jatho. München: Fink, 1992.

Sobchack, Vivian. *The Address of the Eye: A Phenomenology of Film Experience.* Princeton, NJ: Princeton UP, 1992.

Sprengel, Peter. "Antiklassische Opposition: Herder—Jacobi—Jean Paul." *Europäische Romantik I.* Ed. Karl Robert Mandelkow. Wiesbaden: Akademische Verlagsgesellschaft Athenaion, 1982. 249–70.

Stafford, Barbara. *Body Criticism: Imaging the Unseen in Enlightenment Art and Medicine.* Cambridge: MIT P, 1991.

Steiner, Wendy. *Image and Code.* Ann Arbor: U of Michigan P, 1981.

Trabant, Jürgen. *Apeliotes oder der Sinn der Sprache: Wilhelm von Humboldts Sprach-Bild.* München: Wilhelm Fink, 1986.

Utz, Peter. *Das Auge und das Ohr im Text: Literarische Sinneswahrnehmung in der Goethezeit.* München: Wilhelm Fink, 1990.

Weisrock, Katharina. *Götter und Zauberblick: Auge, Blick und Wahrnehmung in Aufklärung und Romantik.* Opladen: Westdeutscher Verlag, 1990.

Weissberg, Liliane. *Geistersprache: Philosophischer und literarischer Diskurs im späten achtzehnten Jahrhundert.* Würzburg: Königshausen & Neumann, 1990.

Wittgenstein, Ludwig. *Das Blaue Buch: Eine Philosophische Betrachtung.* 1958. Frankfurt: Suhrkamp, 1984.

———. *Philosophische Grammatik.* 1969. Frankfurt: Suhrkamp, 1973.

Zacharias, Thomas. *Blick der Moderne:Einführung in die Kunst.* München: Schnell & Steiner, 1984.

Zajonc, Arthur. *Catching the Light: The Entwined History of Light and Mind.* New York: Bantam, 1993.

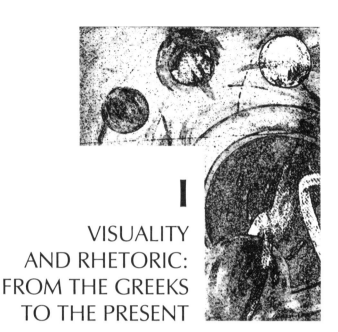

I
VISUALITY
AND RHETORIC:
FROM THE GREEKS
TO THE PRESENT

Classical Greek Origins of Western Aesthetic Theory

JOHN T. KIRBY

Theorists of art have since time immemorial found the comparison of the visual and verbal arts an irresistible one. The Greek poet Simonides is reported to have said that a picture is silent poetry, poetry a speaking picture;[1] Horace makes a famous comparison in the passage beginning *ut pictura poesis.*[2] The notion continues to entrance us today, the more so as we train ourselves to think of "reading" such nonverbal texts as musical scores, films, performances of drama or dance, and static works of visual art such as paintings, drawings, or sculptures. In view of this, it is perhaps worthwhile to investigate the roots of this discourse (in Western thought at least) and to see what further inferences may be drawn about the textualization of the visual.

It is no exaggeration to say that Plato and Aristotle pioneered the study of narrative in Western culture. In developing theories of texts, of creativity, and of the psychosocial roles of art, they found it necessary to develop a working vocabulary. I propose in this essay to consider certain terms that recur in their writings on literature in order to provide an understanding of how these have affected modern narrative theory. On a broader scale, I will suggest that the classical models may, in fact, afford us an even more far-reaching tool for understanding the nature of art in general, including, as we shall see, the visual arts: what I shall call a comprehensive typology of aesthetics. (Such a typology will, of course, be too vast to delineate *in extenso* here, but some directions can at least be adumbrated.) We shall, I submit, discover that Aristotle turns Plato's schema (literally) upside down, and that Aristotle's reinscription of the fundamental issues may open up broad, unforeseen vistas. The relationship of diegesis to mimesis has weighty implications not only for the verbal text but for other art forms as well.

Plato

Socrates, beginning at *Republic* 392e, sets out a schema of what he calls *diêgêsis,* "narrative," which may or may not include *mimêsis,* "imitation."[3] In constructing this schema, he engages in the process of *diairesis,* that is, the "division" of a thing into its constituent parts, in order to understand its nature.[4] In this case, the division is determined by the presence or absence of direct quotation. Diegesis entailing mimesis (1) may be further subdivided into (1a) diegesis consisting entirely of mimesis, such as tragedy and comedy, and (1b) diegesis that includes some mimesis, such as epic. (2) Pure diegesis, without any mimesis, is found in poetic genres such as the dithyramb (see fig. 1).

Once this spectrum is delineated, the question is posed: Should we allow *any* mimesis in our poets' diegesis (394d 1–4)? That is, the whole issue has been raised for its relevance to the moral parameters of the ideal state under discussion. Socrates places certain restrictions on mimesis (395b–396a) and, later in the *Republic,* elaborates further his reservations about the concept of imitation (601c ff.).[5] The problem is intimately connected with the doctrine of the Forms. For Plato's Socrates, what is real and true does not change; consequently, the mutable, sensible world around us is not "real" in this sense. It is a reflection or representation—one might say an "imitation"—of what is real (597a).[6] But the mimetic artist—whether poet, painter, or musician—represents not the Forms but merely the sensibles (597d–e). Thus mimesis is at third remove from reality.[7]

Concomitant with all this is the assumption that there exists a hierarchy of perception, with sensory operations ranking well below reason (*nous*). And the latter is held to be closely connected with the Good (*tagathon*): in expounding the analogy of the Sun, Socrates maintains that the relation of the Good to reason is the same as that of the Sun to vision (508b–e). The analogy

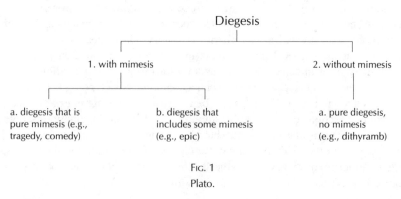

Fig. 1

Plato.

of the Divided Line (509–11) clearly valorizes the operation of reason over any kind of sensory perception; moreover, it seems that the idea of the Good belongs at the very top of the hierarchy, even above the other Forms.

The groundwork is laid in this fashion. Socrates proceeds to say that the perpetration of mimesis is the creation of illusion and, consequently, the distortion of reality (602c–d). The effect of this illusion and distortion, he says, is to hobble the *logistikon* of the soul—our capacity to measure, number, and weigh that which is real and undistorted (602d). Therefore, the mimetic artist arouses, nurtures, and strengthens the tendency of the soul toward slavery to the emotions, a danger to which even the best of us are susceptible (605b–607a).

It is understandable that an epistemology such as that underlying the *Republic* would cast suspicion on anything that might threaten the smooth and efficient operation of the *logistikon*. Since accurate understanding is a principal goal of philosophy, and since mimesis is held to hamper accurate understanding, it could hardly be seen as anything other than a stumbling block to the philosophic life; and Plato's Socrates is not one to allow any confused notion of pleasure or beauty to usurp the primacy of the Good.[8]

Plato's unremitting attitude toward mimesis seems somewhat modified (and mollified) in his later work. In the *Laws,* for example, all *mousikê* is said to be *eikastikê* and *mimêtikê*—productive of likenesses and representations (668b)—and while the springboard of the discussion is choral singing (*hê tôn khorôn* [scil. *mousa*], 666d), the context broadens to include the visual arts (*kata tên opsin . . . apeikasai,* 668d) and eventually every kind of mimesis (*peri hekastên eikona, kai en graphikêi kai en mousikêi kai pantêi,* 669a; verbal texts are explicitly considered in this passage as well, *rhêmasi te kai melesi kai tois rhuthmois,* 669b). On the basis of what we have seen in the *Republic,* we might expect Plato to condemn all such activities out of hand. But instead, in full recognition of this universally mimetic character of *mousikê,* he offers some criteria for evaluating the nature and quality of these artistic productions—confirming, in the process, their (potential) moral and social value.[9] Here poetry "cannot, so to speak, be trusted on its own, but as the ward of a philosophic guardian can put its talent to good use" (Ferrari 108).[10]

Even in the *Laws,* it should be noted, the cherished values of the *Republic,* such as truth and goodness, are maintained. There is also a deep appreciation of, indeed an insistence on, the "rightness" (*orthotês*) of a representation; this is said to depend, not on pleasure (*hêdonê,* 667d), but on "equality of quantity and quality" between original and likeness (*isotês . . . tou te tosoutou kai tou toioutou,* 667d; cf. 668b, *mimêseôs gar ên, hôs phamen, orthotês, ei to mimêthen hoson te kai hoion ên apoteloito*). The judgment of such quantitative and qualitative *isotês,* and hence of *orthotês,* is, of course, the purview par excellence of the *logistikon.* So the concern for the potential dangers of distortion and blurred understanding is still very much alive in what is perhaps Plato's last dialogue.

Aristotle

Aristotle's *Poetics* forms a part of his anti-Platonic program.[11] His solution to the problem could hardly be bolder: rather than worry at all about the "reality" of imitation, he begins with a defense of *poiêtikê* on the grounds that it is a natural result of the mimetic urge, and then asserts point-blank that mimesis itself is natural (and peculiar) to humans (1448b). That is, he shifts out of the original realm of inquiry entirely. Furthermore, in what is perhaps the boldest stroke of all, he *reverses* the genus/differentiae distinction originally posited by Plato in book 3 of the *Republic*.[12] There, as we saw, diegesis was the genus, and the presence and absence of mimesis were its differentiae. In the *Poetics,* mimesis becomes the genus, the topic of *diairesis.* Nor is this all Aristotle does to controvert the Platonic *diairesis:* he supplies entirely new differentiae, namely, the medium, object, and mode of imitation. It is not until he comes to the last of these three (1448a) that he picks up Plato's distinctions as a further subdivision of the mode of imitation (see fig. 2).

As if this were not enough, Aristotle takes the third (and presumably the most heinous) of Plato's genres—pure mimesis, or drama—and makes it the topic of a minute sixfold *diairesis.* His analysis of the six *merê* (parts) of tragedy constitutes the central portion of our extant torso of the *Poetics.*

Aristotle's system is not only visibly more sophisticated than that propounded in the *Republic;* it unfolds as a solution to problems raised by Platonic metaphysics and ethics. Plato is interested in detecting (and eradicating) every trace of mimesis in the narrative. Aristotle, on the other hand, boldly contends that mimesis is a topic good and worthy of study, and pursues a *diairesis* of it in order to understand its essential nature. For it is not merely natural human behavior; through it we are susceptible of learning (1448b)— another typically human activity,[13] and one supremely worthy of the philosopher. So Plato's premise that mimesis obstructs knowledge is disallowed. In this way, the mimesis/diegesis relation is used precisely to legitimize the discipline[14] in the face of Platonic objections.

A Comprehensive Typology of Aesthetics

Though he mentions other arts, Plato's primary concern with mimesis is *qua* aspect of literary diegesis. Aristotle's reversal of the diegesis/mimesis hierarchy is behavior no less polemical than that of Plato, and indeed is a counterpolemic to the Platonic position. But the shift to mimesis has far-reaching consequences: by beginning with neither the act of narration nor the resulting narrative, Aristotle opens the realm of genres and even of media. Whereas

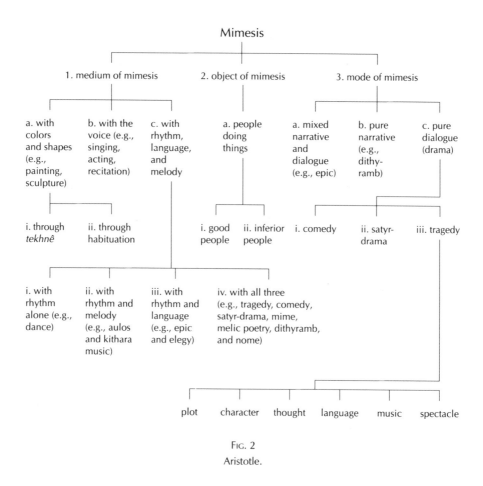

Fig. 2
Aristotle.

Plato's system sets verbal texts as the *definiendum*, the *Poetics* makes it clear that verbal texts are only one kind of star in the mimetic constellation.[15]

Aristotle's schema is designed to take into account not just narrative, but potentially all *poiêtikê tekhnê*. Our text of the *Poetics* concentrates on just one portion of his *diairesis*, namely, the six *merê* of tragedy; hence its specifically literary orientation. With world enough and time, however, it could be expanded to embrace in comparable detail all the fine arts of Aristotle's culture (and virtually all of ours; see my Postscript). In other words, it approaches the status of a comprehensive typology of aesthetics. To do so, it was essential that Aristotle shift from diegesis to mimesis as the genus under scrutiny. This shift, then, has the practical virtue of expanding the realm of inquiry; at the same time, it has the theoretical strength of allowing for the fact that all sign-based communication and interpretation is mimetic. Every work of art, regardless of the medium employed, *represents* something, if no more than a thought or conception of the artist; and every viewer or audience of an art object or event receives an internal *impression* of it.[16] This impression is, I contend, also mimetic.[17]

But I do not think that we can therefore jettison diegesis as a crucial element of our appreciation of art. Indeed, while we are sometimes able to dispense with the concept of diegesis in analyzing the *production* of mimesis, we must nonetheless adopt what may be called modes of diegesis in order to *appropriate* mimesis mentally, in terms both of intake and of contemplation. I would like to consider the issue on these two levels,[18] focusing attention particularly on vision and the visual arts.

First, as to intake, which is a physiological process: the research of Noton and Stark in ocular perception demonstrates the role played in human vision by "saccades," rapid movements of the eyes connecting a series of fixations on isolable points in the visual field.[19] What is more, this leads to the internal representation of the image in the viewer's memory; and when the viewer sees the image again, he or she recognizes it, not only by the peculiarities of the isolated points he or she fixes on, but by scanning it, point by point, *along the same series of saccades followed originally.* Noton and Stark call this the "scanpath" ("Eye Movements and Visual Perception" 38).

An analogy may be drawn between this and what Aristotle calls the *sunthesis pragmatôn,* the "putting-together of events" (*Poetics* 1450a; a synonym of *muthos,* or "plot"). Each feature of a visual image might be considered in some sense a *pragma* or event in the image, and there is a progression from feature to feature. We invest the image with an internal logic so as to order the series of movements; the repetition of this series of movements constitutes an act of visual recognition. In other words, there is a kind of diegesis to our process of seeing.[20] And it seems that this process will obtain for any mimetic experience involving sight. In the case of auditory intake (as with musical performances) a similar diegesis must also occur, whether the musical "language" is readily recognizable or not.

On a second, larger level as well—that of contemplating and understanding what we have taken in—I think it must be said that we can appropriate mimesis only via diegesis. *Muthos* can only be spun out, and apprehended, in time.[21] This is not to say that an iconic representation (such as a painting) cannot embody a *muthos*—on the contrary!—nor that we are incapable of appropriating the iconic (to some extent) in an instant, at least on the intake level. But to "unpack" the *muthos* embodied in such a representation, even silently—much more so orally or in writing—does indeed consume time.

Take, for example, Seurat's *Un dimanche après-midi à l'île de la Grande Jatte* (see fig. 3). At a glance we know that this is a group of what Aristotle would call *prattontes*—people doing things (*Poetics* 1448a).[22] We know that

they are in some sort of integrated social setting, because there are men, women, children, even pets. We know from their clothing that they come from a certain portion of the socioeconomic spectrum, and from their attitudes that they are at leisure, not (for example) at war. All this comes, perhaps subliminally in part, from no more than a look at the painting.[23] Certain other things are as immediately apparent, though these begin to lead us toward another issue of time: the costumes give some indication of the historical period and (along with the flora) of the season of the year.[24] These questions of period and season offer us a point of reference for the *praxis,* the activity pictured. Moving to a more expansive consideration of the painting, we may ask questions of a different nature: Where have these people come from? How did they get there? Whom do they hope or fear to see at this park? What are their joys and woes? Now each one of these questions, and many more such, might elicit a *muthos.* But to answer them, to weave the answers together into a *sunthesis pragmatôn,* and to represent or report that *sunthesis,* would all take time.

This is somehow profoundly connected with the way our minds digest or process information. Norman Bryson remarks on the discursive and figural aspects of an image:

By the "discursive" aspect of an image, I mean those features which show the influence over the image of language—in the case of the window at Canterbury [scil. the East Window at Christchurch Cathedral], the biblical texts which precede it and on which it depends, the inscriptions it contains within itself to tell us how to perceive the different panels, and also the new overall meaning generated by its internal juxtapositions. By the "figural" aspect of an image, I mean those features which belong to the image as a visual experience independent of language—its "being-as-image." (6)

I would like to borrow this terminology and to contend that *all* images have a discursive aspect, at least insofar as we attempt to consider them cognitively or (especially) to communicate our cognition to another person. And to consider an image cognitively, to engage in discourse about it—be it a stained-glass Crucifixus or a Vasarely "composition"—is to textualize it.

I reiterate: to textualize takes time. We may textualize in myriad ways. Do we try to imagine the original *promeneurs* at the Grande Jatte that Sunday afternoon? Consider the woman with the parasol and the pet monkey. Is that her husband next to her, or her brother, or is this some Flaubertian assignation? Are they calmly observing the boats on the Seine, or are they tense with conflict, maintaining a brittle composure? On another level, was the model for this woman a friend Seurat had asked to pose especially for him, or a mere stranger, like the grotesques that da Vinci would pass in the street and then sketch from memory at home?[25] Or, to begin afresh, who is to say that the whole painting is not an iconic *mise-en-abyme*, the representation of a group of actors who are dressed to replicate the Paris of the 1880s? After all, the lighting changes drastically as we progress into the deeper registers of the painting. Who is to say that the seven people in the foreground, and their animals, are not standing in front of a backdrop painted to look like the park at the Grande Jatte? And so on, and on. We can textualize the image endlessly, can make innumerable discursive evaluations of it, but each time we do so we incarnate this in narrative. Not only does the spinning of narrative take time: the very *fabula* takes some time as well, however much or little.[26] We may organize it in any number of chronologies, depending on whether we wish to emphasize that the woman with the monkey has just walked into the field of vision, or that the rowers are passing by as we watch, or that the dog is about to run off with the seated woman's fan. And we may wish to triangulate ourselves with the mimesis and its creator in a nexus of chronological relations that depend on how closely our own narrative coincides with Seurat's. We may order these, for example, (1) the occurrence of the event, (2) its capture on the canvas, (3) our viewing of it; or (1) the conception of the image by the painter, (2) our apprehension of it, (3) the materialization (at some future time) of the narrative we fabricate; or we may imagine ourselves synchronic with the characters as well as with the creation of the mimesis. For the light is behind us, to the left, but if we are under the tree with these people we will cast no shadow before us.[27]

So we come full circle, in a way, when we admit to the discursive aspect of an image, for we thereby unite the activity of the artist—which, with Aristotle, we identify as quintessentially mimesis—with that of the viewer/audience—which inevitably involves diegesis as well. The viewer/audience performs a mental diegesis in apprehending the work of art, whatever sensory means are used to apprehend it: one has a series of (re)actions whereby one takes in information about the painting or song or drama; and one situates the memory of these reactions in the brain, and reexamines them, as a series. One also performs diegesis in comprehending the work of art, for in assessing aesthetically the data we have taken in, we tend to look for unifying schemata, whether (with Aristotle) in terms of causality or in some other system. Human consciousness as a whole sometimes functions as such a system; that is, apart from the issue of causality, the consciousness of the viewer/audience may itself be the linchpin, the unifying point at which otherwise disparate and atomized elements of a work of art converge.

And articulated diegesis, in human communication, inevitably involves some kind of sign-system—most typically, words. This is surely why Plato is most exercised over the activity of the writer in his ideal state, and why, of all the differentiae of mimesis, Aristotle focuses particularly on the literary. As mortals we are caught up in the flow of time. Insofar as we attempt to articulate our (inevitably temporal) apprehension of mimesis, it seems that diegesis has the last word after all.

Postscript: Modern Art Forms

Even in the case of a medium such as cinema, the Aristotelian system can be adapted to make accommodation: a narrator's voice-over in film, simultaneous with the action of the characters, might in its own way be considered a mixture of diegesis and mimesis. A more initially complex issue is that of abstract art, for Aristotle's approach at first seems unremittingly representationalist. But there seems little question to me that an abstract composition could fairly be said to be the representation or mimesis of a concept in the mind of the artist. I would expect the issue of organic compositional unity to be more essential to Aristotle than whether the work represents an object in the real universe.

But Aristotle's teleological approach to all things placed a premium on causality—on doing something by design (*tekhnêi*) and not by chance (*tukhêi*) or haphazardly (*eikêi*). For the modern theoretician interested in adopting the

Aristotelian schema, then, perhaps the thorniest question is how to account for aleatory art. The very term would probably have seemed oxymoronic to the average Greek of Aristotle's time, as they were accustomed to thinking antithetically in terms of *tukhê/tekhnê* and *kosmos/khaos*. To circumvent this cultural specificity of Greek art theory, it would be necessary to retreat within the *diairesis* and introduce a new differentia, as is seen in figure 4. At this point, figure 2 could be inserted under "mimesis." Or is aleatory art to be taken as "mimetic" of the randomness and "Mutabilitie" of the universe? If so, the *diairesis*—once again of Aristotle's original genus "mimesis"—might be as shown in figure 5, with the medium, object, and mode of mimesis (from fig. 2) inserted under "by design." Or, more radically, one might abandon the Platonic/Aristotelian tradition of *diairesis* entirely and make the schema shown in figure 6, thereby recognizing, at a single stroke, both that the artist's intention of including chance constitutes in itself a kind of *tekhnê,* and that where chance is concerned (including the "real" universe) there can be no full determinacy. In this schema, it turns out, mimesis and the aleatory mirror each other (however imperfectly or unfaithfully) through the mediation of "chance" and "design."

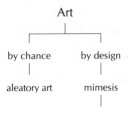

Fɪɢ. 4

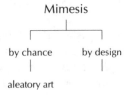

Fɪɢ. 5

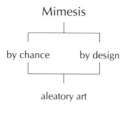

FIG. 6

Notes

1. Cited in Plutarch's *Moralia* (e.g., 17f, 58b) and, in Latin, in the *Rhetorica ad Herennium* (4.39).
2. *Ars poetica* 361–65; a much-appropriated and insufficiently understood portion of the text.
3. We have largely to thank Gérard Genette for the recent popularity of the terms *mimesis* and *diegesis* in discussions of literary theory ("Boundaries of Narrative" 1–2; cf. *Narrative Discourse* 162–70). Relying solely on his précis of the classical models, however, one might come away with a somewhat distorted conception of their import (and of their symbiotic relationship) in the original texts. I have discussed this in some detail in my "Mimesis and Diegesis."

    Diêgêsis is related to the verb *diêgeomai,* to "describe" or "narrate"; *mimêsis* is related to the verb *mimeomai,* to "imitate," "represent," "portray," which in turn seems to be denominal from *mimos,* an "imitator" or "mimic" (particularly in drama). Whether mimesis in Aristotle's sense can mean "imitation" or "representation" or (as I think) both, is disputed; see Dupont-Roc and Lallot 20–22 and Janko xiv–xv.

    On mimesis generally see (among many others) McKeon; Webster; Verdenius; Koller; Else, " 'Imitation' in the Fifth Century"; Sörbom; Golden, "Mimesis and Katharsis" and "Plato's Concept of Mimesis"; Nehamas, "Plato on Imitation and Poetry"; Ricoeur 52–87; Eden 64–75; and Halliwell, *Aristotle's Poetics,* especially 109–37, and "Aristotelian Mimesis Reevaluated."

4. *Diairesis* is touched on in the *Republic* (454a) and discussed in several other dialogues, including the *Phaedrus* (266a–b, 270d, 277b–c), the *Sophist* (e.g., 235b–d, 253d–e, 267d), the *Statesman* (e.g., 258c, 287c), and the *Philebus* (15–16). Whether it is intended to provide a definition or to elaborate an already-posited definition is debated: see, e.g., Adam 2:142, 174; Shorey, "Origin of the Syllogism" 4 and "Origin of the Syllogism Again"; Robinson 52; Hackforth 5; Cherniss 1–82; and Kirby, *Rhetoric* 92–93. For more on Platonic diairesis and dialectic, see, e.g., Stenzel; Cornford, "Mathematics and Dialectic" and *Plato's Theory of Knowledge;* Lloyd; Sayre; and Gómez-Lobo.
5. It is sometimes alleged that the mimesis discussed in *Republic* book 3 is entirely foreign to that discussed in book 10. In fact, despite differences of focus, they are

39

intimately related, as is demonstrated in Rosenstock 235–40 and 244–45 n. 9; Nehamas, "Plato and the Mass Media" 214–15; Halliwell, *Plato* 5–6 and 24 n. 7 and "Aristotelian Mimesis Reevaluated" 488–89; Ferrari 114–25; and especially the careful study in Belfiore. Notes 1–8 of the latter essay collect and categorize an extensive bibliography of the opposing view, in preparation for a detailed refutation thereof.

6. The doctrine is accepted as a given in the discussion at 595ff., having been worked out in some detail at the end of *Republic* book 6 (509–11, where the concept of the Divided Line is expounded).

7. *Republic* 597e. Plato is of course counting in the ancient manner. We would say "at second remove."

8. On the place of pleasure and beauty in Plato's aesthetic system, see particularly Maguire.

9. See *Laws* 667–71. It is important not to lose sight of the fact that there was already some cautious consideration, in *Republic* book 3, of the viability of the mimesis of good characters, both in the behavior of the guardians (395c) and in literary texts (397d). But book 10 is quite stern in its exclusion of mimetic poetry (595).

10. This change of attitude is, I think, to be associated with Plato's "new concern with the physical world, after the *Republic* . . . it is not until the *Theaetetus* and later dialogues that he clearly abandons the old view that sensation and the objects of sense-experience are mere 'rubbish' " (Hackforth 9).

   So Plato eventually extends the designation of "mimesis" to *all* artistic endeavor, and also softens in his assessment of its place in human life. Given the late date of the *Laws,* it is conceivable that these two significant changes could have taken place after the formulation of Aristotle's position as sketched out in *Poetics* 4. When Aristotle actually committed that position to writing is another (very thorny) issue; on the dating of the text of the *Poetics* see, e.g., Halliwell, *Aristotle's Poetics* appendix 1. And whether Plato's shift is as a result of any discussion with Aristotle is not a question I care to address here.

11. Despite the denial of, e.g., Gudeman (21–28), this is clear from every line of the treatise. The topic is well treated by Else in *Aristotle's Poetics* and *Plato and Aristotle on Poetry.* There is a very convenient collection of Platonic *loci* in Halliwell, *Aristotle's Poetics* 121, n. 23 and appendix 2.

12. Noticed too by Halliwell, *Aristotle's Poetics* 128, n. 34.

13. Cf. *Metaphysics* 980a: "All people desire by nature to know. An indication of this is our delight in the senses; for even apart from their usefulness, they are loved for their own sake, especially the sense of sight. . . . The reason for this is that, of the senses, sight most of all makes us know, and makes many differences [*diaphoras*] clear." This text is remarkable for us because of (1) its focus on the desire for *knowledge,* that most Platonic of goals; (2) its emphasis on *sight* (which is perhaps significant in connection with the phenomenon of performed drama); and (3) its mention of the interest in *diaphora*—a pursuit most highly developed in the philosophic procedure of *diairesis.*

14. That it is in fact a discipline—a *tekhnê*—is also an aspect of Aristotle's defense

against the accusation made at *Republic* 602b. Plato had similarly accused rhetoric of being not a real *tekhnê* but merely a knack that one picked up by practice (*Gorgias* 500e–501a). Aristotle shows, in the *Rhetoric* as in the *Poetics,* that the topic of discussion is indeed a discipline with demonstrable principles.

15. In fact, Plato himself makes an explicit analogy between the poet and the painter (*Republic* 598, 605), but only to condemn both equally as threats to society and to assert that both arts are equally skewed.

16. Cf. Bal, ''Rhetoric of Subjectivity'': ''It is an easy and satisfying solution to interpret the concept in terms of Peircean semiotics. Mimesis is then regarded as the representation of an *interpretant''* (339). My assertion that *all* sign-based communication is mimetic may at first seem to out-mimeticize Aristotle, but I have in mind his famous semiotic formulation at *On Interpretation* 16a. Bal (340) is, however, correct to point out that Aristotle says Empedocles is not a *poiêtês* but a *phusiologos* (*Poetics* 1447b 17–20), that is to say, not that his language does not *represent* his thought—which it does—but that he is not about the business of making *muthoi* in his texts. For more on mimesis as a mode of signification see Halliwell, ''Aristotelian Mimesis Reevaluated.''

17. I realize that these assertions deny the possibility of a fully autonomous ''heterocosm'' (as the term is used by Abrams 35 et passim). On heterocosm and mimesis see McHale 27–29.

18. This is not to say that other levels might not be considered. Bloom, e.g., discerns a complex taxonomy of educational objectives in the cognitive domain, including knowledge, comprehension, application, analysis, synthesis, and evaluation. All of these will perhaps be deployed in one way or another in an aesthetic experience. But I have chosen to discuss intake and contemplation because both of these are, as I have said, modes of diegesis.

19. See Noton and Stark, ''Eye Movements and Visual Perception,'' ''Scanpaths in Eye Movements,'' and ''Scanpaths in Saccadic Eye Movements.'' Eye movement is classified under two basic headings (Hallett 16): smooth and abrupt. Smooth eye movement may be either conjugate or disjunctive, i.e., similarly or oppositely directed in the two eyes; smooth conjugate movement may be further subdivided into smooth pursuit, optokinetic slow phase, and vestibular slow phase, while smooth disjunctive movement allows for vergence. Saccades are classified as abrupt conjugate movement; they are of 20–150 milliseconds in duration, and of longer duration when larger. For more on perception and pictorial representation see Nodine and Fisher.

20. The exception to this seems to be that certain objects, by their familiarity, earn a holistic internal representation and do not require serial recognition (Noton and Stark, ''Eye Movements and Visual Perception'' 36). As an accompaniment to their observations on the scanpath, Noton and Stark originally postulated a ''feature ring'' as ''a sequence of sensory and motor memory traces, alternately recording a feature of the object and the eye movement required to reach the next feature. The feature ring establishes a fixed ordering of features and eye movements, corresponding to a scan path on the object . . . during recognition the internal representation is matched serially with the object, feature by feature''

41

(38–39). This theory later underwent some revision when it was determined that a viewer's cognitive models can actually direct scanpaths; i.e., "eye movements change considerably with different cognitive states" (Stark and Ellis 214). Stark (but not Ellis) goes so far as to draw an analogy between such cognitive models and, of all things, the Platonic Forms, suggesting that (1) these models exist in us at birth and (2) the scanpath is evidence of how they are brought out in "an hierarchical set of pattern recognition checking phases" (216–18). In this respect he shows his affinity with Gestalt psychology. For a useful outline of various theories of perception, see chapter 2 of Rock.

21. Ricoeur points out that epic and drama, despite the absence of a narrator in the latter, can nonetheless be united under the term "narrative," because he characterizes narrative not by its "mode"—the author's attitude—but by its "object," the *muthos* (36). (He does, however, distinguish diegesis as "narrative in the narrow sense.") True to the title of his work, Ricoeur (in chapter 1) connects the Aristotelian *muthos* with Augustine's concept of the experience of time as *distentio animi* (*Confessions* 11.14).

I find it noteworthy that Jakobson deems time "the vital question of our period" (15). Certainly one thinks of the work of Heidegger and Einstein in this regard. Aristotle made great advances in the philosophical consideration of time as a measure of *change;* see Lear chapter 3, especially 74–97.

22. This is my contention in spite of the fact that most of the figures in the painting appear to be doing nothing in particular. Indeed, I chose to discuss this work because of its extremely static quality: on a spectrum of movement or activity in painting, it would surely find a place very near the low end. (The high end would be occupied by such works as, say, Poussin's versions of *L'enlèvement des Sabines;* David's *Les Sabines* I would place somewhere in the middle of the spectrum, since it depicts a moment of pause or hiatus in a situation of frenzied activity.) At any rate, the Seurat piece provides us with an interesting test case because, despite its apparent repose, we find ourselves induced—both physiologically and sociologically—to "narrate" the painting to ourselves in various ways, as I shall demonstrate.

Much to my amusement, after deciding to concentrate on the *Grande Jatte,* I discovered that my contention had already been illustrated: the painting has been elaborately "narrated," in fact dramatized, in Stephen Sondheim's musical comedy *Sunday in the Park with George.*

23. I have said "subliminally." I would like to allow for the possibility that there is what amounts to a simultaneous diegesis on the subconscious level, which we are as yet incapable of diagnosing. If this is the case, such "subliminal" perceptions may not be as immediate or as monolithic as one might think.

24. It has also been ascertained that the angle of sunlight in the painting would match that at the actual Grande Jatte at 4 P.M. (Minervino 103). This is of interest to the extent that one attempts to connect the picture with phenomenal reality—to the extent that the painting is seen as the "portrait" of a geographic locale on the outskirts of Paris.

25. In fact we know that in addition to preliminary paintings of the whole tableau,

Seurat did at least one *crayon conté* study specifically of this figure; and that he painted much of the final version at night, by gaslight, in his studio. It is important to remember that the artist engages in textualization of his or her images fully as much as the spectator does.

26. Aristotle himself is aware of this (*Poetics* 1449b 24–25, 1450b 34–1451a 15, 1459b 18–31). For more on *fabula* see Chatman 19–20; Bal, *Narratology* 5; and Brooks 12–14.

27. All of this dovetails very well with Genette's schema of tense; more than half of the *Discours du récit* is focused on issues of what he calls "order," "duration," and "frequency," each of which deals with a different facet of narrative temporality.

References

*Page references in the Notes are to the latest edition cited, and to the English edition where one is listed.

Abrams, M. H. *The Mirror and the Lamp: Romantic Theory and the Critical Tradition.* New York: Oxford UP, 1953.

Adam, James M. *The Republic of Plato.* 1902. 2 vols. 2nd ed. Cambridge: Cambridge UP, 1963 (revised by D. A. Rees).

Bal, Mieke. *Narratology: Introduction to the Theory of Narrative.* Toronto: U of Toronto P, 1985 (a translation of *De theorie van vertellen en verhalen*).

———. "Notes on Narrative Embedding." *Poetics Today* 2.2 (1981): 41–59.

———. "The Rhetoric of Subjectivity." *Poetics Today* 5.2 (1984): 337–76.

Belfiore, Elizabeth. "A Theory of Imitation in Plato's Republic." *Transactions of the American Philological Association* 114 (1984): 121–46.

Bloom, B. S. *Taxonomy of Educational Objectives: The Classification of Educational Goals. Handbook I: Cognitive Domain.* New York: David McKay, 1956.

Brooks, Peter. *Reading for the Plot: Design and Intention in Narrative.* New York: Random, 1984.

Bryson, Norman. *Word and Image: French Painting of the Ancien Régime.* Cambridge: Cambridge UP, 1981.

Chatman, Seymour. *Story and Discourse: Narrative Structure in Fiction and Film.* Ithaca: Cornell UP, 1978.

Cherniss, H. *Aristotle's Criticism of Plato and the Academy.* Baltimore: Johns Hopkins UP, 1944. New York: Russell & Russell, 1962.

Cornford, F. M. "Mathematics and Dialectic in the *Republic* VI–VII." *Mind* ns 41 (1932): 37–52, 173–90.

———. *Plato's Theory of Knowledge.* London: Routledge & Kegan Paul, 1935.

Dupont-Roc, Roselyn, and J. Lallot. *Aristote: La Poétique. Le texte grec avec une traduction et des notes de lecture.* Paris: Editions du Seuil, 1980.

Eden, Kathy. *Poetic and Legal Fiction in the Aristotelian Tradition.* Princeton: Princeton UP, 1986.

Else, Gerald F. *Aristotle's Poetics: The Argument.* Cambridge: Harvard UP, 1957.

———. " 'Imitation' in the Fifth Century." *Classical Philology* 53 (1958): 73–90, 245.

——. *Plato and Aristotle on Poetry*. Chapel Hill: U of North Carolina P, 1986 (published posthumously).

Ferrari, G. R. F. "Plato on Poetry." *The Cambridge History of Literary Criticism*. Ed. G. A. Kennedy. Vol. 1: *Classical Criticism*. Cambridge: Cambridge UP, 1989. 92–148.

Genette, Gérard. "Boundaries of Narrative." *New Literary History* 8 (1976): 1–13 (originally published as "Frontières du récit" in *Figures II*. Paris: Seuil, 1969).

——. *Narrative Discourse: An Essay in Method*. Ithaca: Cornell UP, 1980 (published as *Discours du récit* in *Figures III*. Paris: Seuil, 1972).

——. *Narrative Discourse Revisited*. Ithaca: Cornell UP, 1988 (a translation of *Nouveau discours du récit*. Paris: Seuil, 1983).

Golden, L. "Mimesis and Katharsis." *Classical Philology* 64 (1969): 145–53.

——. "Plato's Concept of Mimesis." *British Journal of Aesthetics* 15 (1975): 118–31.

Gómez-Lobo, A. "Plato's Description of Dialectic in the Sophist 253d1–e2." *Phronesis* 22 (1977): 29–47.

Gudeman, Alfred. *Aristoteles ΠΕΡΙ ΠΟΙΗΤΙΚΗΣ*. Berlin: de Gruyter, 1934.

Hackforth, R. "Plato's Divided Line and Dialectic." *Classical Quarterly* 36 (1942): 1–9.

Hallett, P. "Eye Movements." *The Handbook of Perception and Human Performance*. Ed. Kenneth R. Boff et al. Vol. 1. New York: Wiley, 1986. 1–112. 2 vols.

Halliwell, Stephen. "Aristotelian Mimesis Reevaluated." *Journal of the History of Philosophy* 28 (1990): 487–510.

——. *Aristotle's Poetics*. Chapel Hill: U of North Carolina P, 1986.

——. *Plato: Republic 10*. Warminster: Aris & Phillips, 1988.

Jakobson, Roman. "Dialogue on Time in Language and Literature." *Poetics Today* 2.1 (1980): 15–27. Rpt. in *Verbal Art, Verbal Sign, Verbal Time*. Minneapolis: U of Minnesota P, 1985.

Janko, Richard. *Aristotle: Poetics I*. Indianapolis: Hackett, 1987.

Kirby, John T. "Mimesis and Diegesis: Foundations of Aesthetic Theory in Plato and Aristotle." *Helios* 18 (1991): 113–28.

——. *The Rhetoric of Cicero's* Pro Cluentio. Amsterdam: J. C. Gieben, 1990.

Koller, Helmut. *Die Mimesis in der Antike*. Bern: A. Francke, 1954.

Lear, Jonathan. *Aristotle: The Desire to Understand*. Cambridge: Cambridge UP, 1988.

Lloyd, A. C. "Plato's Description of Division." *Classical Quarterly* ns 2 (1954): 105–12.

Maguire, J. P. "The Differentiation of Art in Plato's Aesthetics." *Harvard Studies in Classical Philology* 68 (1964): 389–410.

McHale, B. *Postmodernist Fiction*. New York: Routledge, 1987.

McKeon, Richard. "Literary Criticism and the Concept of Imitation in Antiquity." *Modern Philology* 34 (1936): 1–35. Rev. and rpt. in *Critics and Criticism Ancient and Modern*. 1952. Ed. R. S. Crane. 2nd ed. Chicago: U of Chicago P, 1973.

Minervino, F. *Tout l'oeuvre peint de Seurat*. Paris: Flammarion, 1973 (a translation of *L'opera completa di Seurat*. Milan: Rizzoli, 1971).

Nehamas, Alexander. "Plato and the Mass Media." *Monist* 71 (1988): 214–34.

———. "Plato on Imitation and Poetry in *Republic* 10." *Plato on Beauty, Wisdom, and the Arts.* Ed. J. Moravcsik et al. Totowa, NJ: Rowman & Littlefield, 1982. 47–78.

Nodine, C. F., and D. F. Fisher, eds. *Perception and Pictorial Representation.* New York: Praeger, 1979.

Noton, D., and L. Stark. "Eye Movements and Visual Perception." *Scientific American* 224 (June 1971): 34–43.

———. "Scanpaths in Eye Movements During Pattern Perception." *Science* 171 (1971): 308–11.

———. "Scanpaths in Saccadic Eye Movements While Viewing and Recognizing Patterns." *Vision Research* 11 (1971): 929–42.

Prince, Gerald. "Introduction to the Study of the Narratee." *Poétique* 14 (1973): 177–96. Rpt. in *Reader-Response Criticism: From Formalism to Post-Structuralism.* Ed. J. P. Tompkins. Baltimore: Johns Hopkins UP, 1980.

Ricoeur, Paul. *Time and Narrative.* Vol. 1. 3 vols. Chicago: U of Chicago P, 1984 (a translation of vol. 1 of *Temps et récit.* Paris: Seuil, 1983).

Rimmon, Shlomith. "A Comprehensive Theory of Narrative: Genette's *Figures III* and the Structuralist Study of Fiction." *PTL* 1 (1976): 33–62.

Robinson, R. *Plato's Earlier Dialectic.* Ithaca: Cornell UP, 1941; 2nd ed., Oxford: Clarendon, 1953.

Rock, I. *The Logic of Perception.* Cambridge: MIT P, 1983.

Rosenstock, B. "Rereading the Republic." *Arethusa* 16 (1983): 219–46.

Sayre, Kenneth. M. *Plato's Analytic Method.* Chicago: U of Chicago P, 1969.

Shorey, P. "The Origin of the Syllogism." *Classical Philology* 19 (1924): 1–19.

———. "The Origin of the Syllogism Again." *Classical Philology* 28 (1933): 199–204.

Sörbom, G. *Mimesis and Art: Studies in the Origin and Early Development of an Aesthetic Vocabulary.* Stockholm: Bonniers, 1966.

Stark, L., and S. R. Ellis. "Scanpaths Revisited: Cognitive Models Direct Active Looking." *Eye Movements: Cognition and Visual Perception.* Ed. Dennis F. Fisher et al. Hillsdale, NJ: Lawrence Erlbaum, 1981. 193–226.

Stenzel, J. *Studien zur Entwicklung der platonischen Dialektik von Sokrates zu Aristoteles.* Breslau: Trewendt & Granier, 1917. Second German edition (Leipzig: Teubner, 1931) translated by D. J. Allan as *Plato's Method of Dialectic* (Oxford: Clarendon, 1940).

Verdenius, W. J. *Mimesis: Plato's Doctrine of Artistic Imitation and Its Meaning to Us.* Leiden: Brill, 1949.

Webster, T. B. L. "Greek Theories of Art and Literature Down to 400 B.C." *Classical Quarterly* 33 (1939): 166–79.

II
COLORS
AND MUSIC:
SCIENCE AND
MEDIA TECHNOLOGY

Visible Sounds and Audible Colors: The Ocular Harpsichord of Louis-Bertrand Castel

JOACHIM GESSINGER

The figures of sculpture and painting are placed side by side in space and present the extension of reality in actual or apparent totality. Music, however, can only place before us tones in so far as it makes a body under the spatial condition tremble, setting the same in an oscillating motion. These oscillations only affect art under the aspect that they follow one another; and for this reason the sensuous material generally only enters into music with the *temporal* duration of its movement instead of taking with it its spatial form.

—Hegel, trans. in Osmaston 371–72[1]

Introduction: Diderot's Visit to Castel's Workshop

In his famous "Lettre sur les sourds et muets" (Letter on the Deaf and Dumb), published in 1751, Diderot mentions a visit to the workshop of Louis-Bertrand Castel, a Jesuit priest who was well known for his invention of an ocular harpsichord. Diderot was accompanied by a young deaf-mute who—as Diderot imagined—would appreciate the opportunity to experience music for the first time in his life—that is, through his eyes. Diderot writes:

I led my deaf-mute to Rue Saint-Jacques, to the house where the man and his machine were shown. Ah! Monsieur, you will never imagine the impression he received from both, nor his ideas.

You will agree that it was impossible to tell the deaf and dumb something about the nature and the marvel of the clavichord, and—

49

lacking any idea of sound, the signification of this machine was as incomprehensible for him as the use of our speech-organism. What kind of ideas did he develop? . . .

My deaf-mute thought the genial creator to be deaf-mute himself and that the harpsichord was a medium of communication. Each nuance on the keyboard would have an "alphabetical" value and with the skill of his fingers the player would combine letters to words: the result was a complete discourse of colours. (50)

A "discourse of colours," music perceived by the eyes, offers a new dimension in art and aesthetics and in the theory of signs. This development, however, is the topic of the second part of my essay, where I will follow the debate from the middle of the century onward. For now I want to reconstruct the history of the ocular harpsichord itself—a device that originally was not invented as a tool for discourse analysis.

The Philosophical and Scientific Implications of Castel's Invention

Diderot's "Lettre" and Castel's invention of the ocular harpsichord ("clavecin oculaire" or "Farbenclavicymbel") were contributions to a primarily philosophical and epistemological discussion, yet they indicated an important turn in this discussion: the theories of knowledge and of perceptive physiology were transformed into a *psychology* of art and language.[2]

Castel announced his project for the first time in the *Mercure de France* (1725), followed by a series of articles in the *Journal de Trevoux* ten years later. A summary is also given in his *L'Optique des couleurs* (1740). Castel was a Jesuit priest and a talented mathematician, a natural scientist and an amateur in matters of art. Voltaire praised him as "Euclide-Castel,"[3] but that was before he became familiar with Castel's "Nouvelles expériences," a series of experience descriptions that started with a brief account of the initial idea: "Monsieur, when I published my project of a veritable chromatic music in 1725, my idea was the ultimate consequence of the geometrical thread, of the *analogies* which I—following Athanasius Kircher—had established between sound and light, tones and colors, music and painting or *coloration*," adding, with farsighted modesty, "without any ambition to realize the project myself" (1444).

This tripartite merger—the analogies between the physical nature of light and sound, their perceived forms as tone and color, and the different kinds of artistic performance, music and painting—formed part of a specific theoretical framework that involved aspects of physics, perception, and generation of ideas or knowledge. Before turning to a discussion of these issues, I will provide a brief description of the relationship between musical tones and colors, which are the most exciting aspects of the ocular harpsichord. Castel writes:

> Of the seven or eight tones *ut, re, mi, fa, sol, la, si, ut,* building the musical scale, there are three called elementary tones by musicians, or elementary strings (chords), taking the string for the tone.
>
> The first one, *ut,* is named tonic or bass, because it is the basic tone for all the others. . . . The second tone is *mi,* called third, because it is the third tone in the scale; . . . the fifth tone is *sol,* the quint. From these three tones all the other tones can be derived, they are in perfect harmony. (*L'Optique des couleurs* 69ff.)

Castel believed that the harmonic relations between colors are structured in the same way: "The dark-blue always gives birth of red. Isn't it the chord *ut* that causes retaining the dominant *sol*?" (73).

Castel believed that the musical scale of twelve tones, the basis of modern European music, should have its parallel in the circle of twelve colors, with exactly the same relations between the elements.[4] "Starting with blue, the sequence of colours comes back to blue again, because the blue leads to yellow, the yellow to red, which leads back to blue, with exactly the same nuances as similar tones. And don't tell me that this number of colours and their arrangement is arbitrary" (*L'Optique des couleurs* 169).

	C	H	G	F	E	B	D	
	ROUGE.	ORANGE	JAUNE.	VERT.	BLEU.	POURPRE	VIOLET.	
	se joue de ce demi-cercle en C.	de C en H.	de H en G.	de G en F.	de F en E.	de E en B.	de B en D.	
	45	27	48	60	60	40	80	= 360
1/2		9/16	3/4	1/3	3/4	5/6	8/9 I	
r	e u	t s	i l	a s	ol f	a m	i r	e
	la plus grande réfrangibilité du rouge répond à	celle de l'orange à	celle du jaune à	celle du vert à	celle du bleu à	celle du pourpre à	celle du violet à	
	u	t s	i la	sol	fa	m	i re	

Fig. 1

Table of colors and musical tones.

Castel's assumptions were more daring than anything previously said in favor of an analogy between tones and colors.[5] However, the empirical evidence for Castel's analogy was lacking. It was not clear whether the analogy was based on isomorphic or analogous structures of the objects themselves or of the action they perform on the sensorium, or whether the analogy was a product of nervous or neurophysiological association—of a "Seelenassoziation" (an association of sensations), in the words used in the eighteenth century.

The Epistemological Implications of Different Domains

There were three theoretical domains involved: the theory of the nature of light and sound, the theory of vision and hearing, and the theory of perception and knowledge. And, to a lesser degree, the theory of aesthetics, which at that time was something practiced rather than an elaborated theory.

This distinction of different domains is rather artificial, and I make it only for the purpose of clarifying the historical process. In practice these domains were always interconnected—in different ways, of course, depending on the theoretical status of each domain. There is a significant nonsimultaneity in the development of each domain, and this must be kept in mind if one wants to understand the historical discourse properly. In my diachronic reconstruction this aspect of nonsimultaneity may remain a bit obscure, although I will try at least to turn the attention to asynchronic developments whenever necessary. A new theory of perception, for instance, had to be based on physiological and sensory observations as well as on common norms of aesthetic perception (Wahrnehmungsästhetik). A new theory of perception has not only to accord with the accepted aesthetic practice in painting and music but also with the accepted theories of the physical properties of the perceived objects and the physiological nature of the process of their perception. The title of Batteux's influential 1746 publication, *Les Beaux arts reduits à un même principe* (The Fine Arts Reduced to a Single Principle), indicates the quest to reduce art to the conditions of its perception. When Castel published his *L'Optique* and Diderot his "Lettre," both could relate to a rather well-established, though contested, theoretical foundation on the nature of light, sound, and vision, and to a less developed theoretical discourse regarding the nature of hearing and speaking. The associated epistemological discord was constant, the positions quite clear and firm, but a philosophy of taste was still in its early stages of development.

The Basic Theory: Vibration and Movement

The physiological assumptions underlying Castel's hypothesis were generally known as a theory of vibrations, popularized by Hartley in his *Observa-*

tions on Man (1749). Perception was seen as an interrelation between an object, the medium that exerts the impression of the object on the human sensorium, and the structure of the sensorium itself.[6] Thus light and sound were understood as the same form of movement: sound as vibrations in the air (not *of* the air), light as waves or little "tourbillons" (Malebranche), whirls in a medium called *aether.* Both media produce vibrations of the auditory responding visual nerves, which link the acoustical imprint on the eardrum and the image on the retina with a (frontal) part of the brain called "sensus communis." This interrelation was said to be established by an isomorphic movement, a vibration or oscillation, which Castel called "unisson,"[7] Herder simply "Ton" (*Werke* 19). It was a natural organic movement that made the organism and the sensorium ready to react to external irritations in the form of stronger or weaker vibrations.[8] This was a widely adopted theory and had its roots in the older conceptions of universal harmony (Kircher, Leibniz, Lullus) and the more recent Cartesian geometrical reconstruction of nature.

In the unfolding of his idea of a structural harmony between colors and tones, Castel was much indebted to Newton.[9] After having mentioned his affiliation with Newton himself in his first article in 1725, he became a member of the anti-Newtonian party in France (I will return later to this point when I discuss Castel's new concept of music and painting). Some fundamental physical observations made by Castel on the nature of vision and light, and, at the same time, to related epistemological questions, made him rethink his position on Newton.

Theory of Vision and Theory of Knowledge

In his *Opticks,* first published in 1704 (sections had been written from 1675 onward), Newton separated the physical object *light* (lumen) from *colors* as a category of human sensation:

> If at any time I speak of light and rays as coloured or endued with Colours, I would be understood to speak not philosophically and properly, but grossly, and according to such conceptions as vulgar People in seeing all these Experiments would be apt to frame. For the rays to speak properly are not coloured. In them there is nothing else than a certain power and disposition to stir up a sensation of this or that Colour. (1:90)

This distinction mirrored a clear epistemological position—truly Malebranchian—as his theory of light could be interpreted as a theory of vision. It exerted an enormous influence on similar programs, such as Berkeley's "Theory of Vision" and Goethe's "Farbenlehre." Newton continues:

For as a sound in a Bell or musical String, or other sounding body, is nothing but a trembling Motion, and in the Air nothing but that Motion propagated from the Object, and in the Sensorium 'tis a sense of that Motion under the form of sounds; so Colours in the Object are nothing but a disposition to reflect this or that sort of rays more copiously than the rest; in the rays they are nothing but their dispositions to propagate this or that Motion into the Sensorium, and in the Sensorium they are sensations of those Motions under the forms of Colours. (1:90ff.)[10]

This could be interpreted as a welcome support for older speculations that went much further than the statement of a common physical nature of visual and auditory perception as vibrations—the conjecture of a universal harmony.[11]

Locke's remarks in his *Essay Concerning Human Understanding* (1690) referring to the epistemological issue of this visual-auditory analogy were directed against an actual debate that was at least partly initiated by a suggestion Malebranche had added as an explication to his *La Recherche de la vérité* (1674–78). The French philosopher paralleled the amplitude and frequency of acoustic waves with the wavelike movement of luminous particles[12] and concluded: "We detect the same situation regarding either the light and different colours or the sound and different tones" (3:259).

Locke's criticism in his *Essay* was pungent because Malebranche touched on two major points: the generation of ideas by different perceptions (as part of his theory of knowledge), and the generation of ideas by words (his theory of language): "Simple Ideas," Locke wrote in the fourth chapter of his third book, "are only to be *got by* those *impressions* Objects themselves make on our minds. . . . all the *Words* in the world . . . *will never be able to produce in us the* Idea *it stands for.* For Words, being Sounds, can produce in us no other simple *Ideas,* than of those very Sounds" (425). An equation of visual and auditory perception could not possibly fit into this epistemological framework. "For to hope to produce an *Idea* of Light, or Colour, by a Sound, however formed, is to expect that Sounds should be visible, or Colours audible . . . a sort of Philosophy worthy only of *Sanco Panca,* who had the Faculty to see *Dulcinea* by Hearsay" (425).[13]

I have traced the discussion back to a point where the two different positions regarding the harmony of sound and color (and their analogous perception) had been put forward explicitly. The ensuing debate widened the spectrum of arguments supporting the pros and cons and indicated a significant shift from physics and epistemology to the theory of aesthetics and language.

The Transformation of an Epistemological
Paradox into a Psychological Argument for a
New Theory of Language and Aesthetics

I begin with a short discussion of the different positions held by Locke, Newton, and Berkeley with regard to the epistemological issues of color-tone harmony. Locke offers a new view of the cognitive implications of different perceptions: for the first half of the eighteenth century his blind man (a Cartesian prototype) dominated all debates on visual perception and cognition. It seems rather strange to depend on people who cannot see in order to learn more about visual perception, but if one wants to know which part of knowledge is due to visual perception, one might ask a blind man what he knows—for instance, of forms such as cubes and spheres. (This was the famous Locke-Molyneux hypothesis, which three decades later seemed to have been confirmed by an experiment by Cheselden.) Locke's answer was quite clear: he would *know* nothing at all, unless another sense, the sense of *touch,* could help him. The relationship between vision and touch and the related epistemological issues were the main topic, not only in the English discussion between Locke and Berkeley (who agreed with Locke on this point), but also in the French sensualism of Condillac.

But, Locke continued, no sense other than vision could perceive colors (as no other sense than hearing could perceive sound). Locke's empiricism would not permit him to accept that a blind person could "understand" the color scarlet to mean "the sound of a trumpet" (425).[14] Locke rejects the possibility of synaesthetic understanding.

Newton knew Malebranche's and Locke's opinions very well when he published his *Opticks* in 1704, though we can assume that his reflections had been developed even before Locke's *Essay* appeared. However, he revealed not only, as I quoted before, the common nature of visual and auditory perception as a movement of a physical medium transformed into a neural movement, but he believed that the same mathematical proportions in the circle of colors and in the musical scale had been found "by experiment" (see fig. 2).

Different sectors in the circle show the different proportions: "With the Center O and Radius OD describe a Circle ADF, and distinguish its circumference into seven parts DE, EF, FG, GA, AB, BC, CD, proportional to the seven musical Tones or Intervals of the eight Sounds, *Sol, la, fa, la, mi, fa, sol,* contained in an Eight, that is, proportional to the numbers 1/9, 1/10, 1/10, 1/9, 1/10, 1/16, 1/9" (Newton, *Opticks* 1:114).

At several points Newton makes slightly different calculations, showing, for instance, that the proportions of the distances between colors, resulting from refraction, are "either accurately, or very nearly, as the Cuberoots of the Squares of the length of a Chord, which sound the notes in an Eight" (2:84).

55

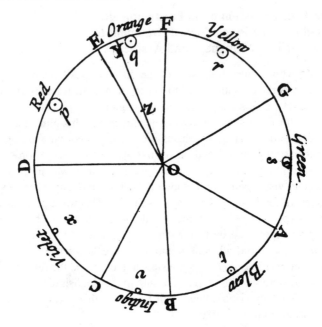

Fɪɢ. 2
Newton's circle of colors.

To give an impression of this analogy of proportion, I refer to the reconstruction by Albert Wellek (see fig. 3), where G (gamma) indicates the lower (bass) limit of the musical space as a fourth transposition of the Dorian mode starting with D.

Newton's musical scale was quite different from the one we use. Not by mere chance did his circle of seven colors match the hexachord structure of the Dorian scale. And Newton himself alluded to other implications of the analogy of proportions when he asked, ''May not the harmony and discord of

Rot	Kress	Gelb	Grün	Blau	Indigo	Violett
d	e	f	g	a	h	c	d
g	a	b	c	d	e	f	g

Fɪɢ. 3
Wellek's reconstruction.

Colours arise from the proportions of the vibrations propagated through the fibres of the optick Nerves into the Brain, as the harmony and discord of sounds arises from the proportions of the vibrations of the Air? For some Colours are agreeable, as those of Gold and Indico, and others disagree'' (2:136).

Thus the trinity of domains: physics, physiology, and aesthetics, similar to the ingredients of the medieval *perspectiva*.[15] This might have been the direction to follow had another theorist of light, George Berkeley, not rejected Newton's hypothesis, confirming Locke's position regarding different cognitive qualities for different senses, at least in regard to vision and touch: ''The extension, figures, and motions perceived by sight are specifically distinct from the ideas of touch called by the same names, nor is there any such thing as one idea, or kind of idea, common to both senses'' (1:222ff.). The auditory sense caused a specific problem: by ear humans can perceive the sound of words and the sound of physical objects. Locke and Berkeley put forward a skeptical view of language, insofar as sounds can only evoke ideas of the words but do not point directly to their referents. On the other hand, words or names of things could evoke the ideas of their referents—that is, what constitutes their *meaning*. (For instance, the reader likely has a much clearer idea of the color scarlet or blue than of the tone G or D.) Berkeley had to admit that sound could evoke an idea of space and distance. But how does it work with colors? Could someone hear colors, as Locke's blind man did? Or, to express it differently, does the physical nature of light and sound, namely vibration or motion, mean that both are perceptible, either by eye or by ear?

Berkeley discusses this question in *Hylas and Philonus*, a dialogue that was more sophistic than Socratic:

> *Hylas:* It is this very motion in the external air, that produces in the mind the sensation of *sound.* . . .
> *Philonus:* What! is sound then a sensation?
> *Hylas:* I tell you, as perceived by us, it is a particular sensation in the mind. . . .
> *Philonus:* How then can sound, being a sensation exist in the air, if by the *air* you mean a senseless substance existing without the mind?
> *Hylas:* You must distinguish, Philonus, between sound as it is perceived by us, and as it is in itself. . . .
> *Philonus:* . . . are you sure then that sound is really nothing but motion?
> *Hylas:* I am. . . .
> *Philonus:* It is then good sense to speak of *motion,* as of a thing that is *loud, sweet, acute,* or *grave.*
> *Hylas:* I see you are resolved not to understand me. . . .
> *Philonus:* It seems then there are two sorts of sound, the one vulgar, or that which is heard, the other philosophical and real.

Hylas: Even so.
Philonus: And the latter consists in motion.
Hylas: I told you so before.
Philonus: Tell me, Hylas, to which of the senses think you, the idea of motion belongs: to the hearing?
Hylas: No certainly, but to the sight and touch.
Philonus: It should follow then, that according to you, real sounds may possibly be *seen* or *felt,* but never *heard.*

(2:181ff.)

Is it possible that Diderot's deaf-mute, visiting Père Castel and his clavecin oculaire, saw Berkeley's real sounds? Is it a privilege for those who cannot hear to perceive the real, the philosophical sounds, and for those who are blind to perceive the real, philosophical light, thereby gaining the "right view" of the world?

These were indeed the proposals made by Diderot in his "Lettre sur les aveugles" (Letter on the blind) and "Lettre sur les sourds et muets." In 1713, however, the near relation between the perception of colors and tones was only a stimulating hypothesis, established on physical and structural analogies and rejected by the leading theorists of knowledge. We had to wait until the third domain (artistic production and its public evaluation) began to interact with philosophy and epistemology. Only then was the intricate relation between the perception of colors and tones realized: the theoretical consequences subsequently became a matter of discourse and a contribution to the question of the translatability of the senses.

From Knowledge to Pleasure:
Voltaire's Commentaries on Castel's "Betrayal"

It is obvious that Castel's 1725 article incited Voltaire to give a historical account of the color-tone analogy in an additional chapter of the first edition of his *Elémens de la philosophie de Newton.* The idea seemed tempting—in spite of the criticism put forward by Locke and Berkeley—because of its implications for the arts. "One can only thank a man who tries to give others new arts and new pleasures," Voltaire wrote in 1738 (22:505). In the edition of 1741 the remarks in favor of Castel ("the genius philosopher") were eliminated, and after 1741 the chapter discussing Castel was omitted. In a letter to Thieriot of April 10, 1738, Voltaire called Castel "un chien enragé" (a fierce dog), "un fou des mathématiques et le tracassier de la société" (a mad mathematician and a plague on society) (Voltaire, *Oeuvres complètes* 80:193). In a March 1738 letter to Rameau, mentioning a dispute between Rameau and Castel, he sneered: "All deaf men of Paris are invited to a concert which has been announced for twelve years. Even the blind are invited, he thinks them to be rather fair arbiters for colours'' (34:438). And in a letter to Montesquieu, Voltaire complained: ''In the meantime the Dutch booksellers have printed my book and the compliments for Castel without telling me, and so this miserable cretin finds himself celebrated after having insulted me'' (43:495).

What happened to evoke Voltaire's anger? Involuntarily, Castel had made a fool of Voltaire when—at the same time that the *Elémens* was in print, which celebrated Castel as a promising propagator of Newtonism in the metropolitan society—Castel published a revision of his first announcement. To be precise, it was a complete rejection of Newton's major theoretical positions. The ''Euclid-Castel'' had turned into a herald of the new philosophy of taste, which we find in the thoughts of Burke, Mendelssohn, and Herder. (Gaston Bachelard tells only half the truth, calling Castel a belated Cartesian philosopher.) Castel had expected to get into trouble, and Voltaire's calumnious commentaries had the foreseen effect that from this time onward nearly all references to Castel's invention except one were unfavorable. Goethe especially was influenced by this criticism, though he shared most of Castel's opinions.

The New Philosophy of Taste Is a Revision of the Classical Theory of Vision

Castel's dissent from Newton originated in a close contact with artists. He turned from calculation (the ''angle'') and began to examine the material of painting, the coloring matter, and the material of music, which included the instruments, principles of composing, and so on, a sort of empiricism that was systematically adopted by the editors of the *Enyclopédie*. Newton's analysis of ''white'' sunlight through prismatic refraction led him to discover the primary colors; as a ''dilettante and technologist'' (Goethe), Castel found his colors directly in nature, in the surface of materials such as earth, leather, and tinted silk. He proposed black as the source of the primary colors blue, red, and yellow.[16] And instead of analysis and separation, he proceeded with synthesis and mixture and produced the circle of twelve colors. These colors could be modified into lighter or darker colors (the famous problem of ''clair-obscure'' in painting), forming a scale of 144 chromatic tones, spanning the twelve octaves (with twelve halftones each) of the musical range.[17]

Castel replaced the prismatic reduction of colors, the camera obscura, with the natural production of colors: ''Everything in nature is completely mixed and nature sets the tone of all the blends. According to the philosophers, nature is very simple, but they ignore the physical simplicity if they reduce it to dull uniformity and metaphysics that excludes any plurality of the parts or of movement. One colour contains all colours, all tones are enclosed in one'' (''Nouvelles expériences'' 1813–14).[18]

The synthetic approach was evidently a betrayal of Castel's philosophical father, namely, Newton, and an adoption of the views of his grandfather, Athanasius Kircher, a mystic suspect in the view of rationalist Enlightenment. In Castel's own words, "The evil results from the fact that until now optics has been a very poor science. One had only known angles and localisations as rules for the eye's judgement, instead of developing refined, delicate optics, perfectly spiritual, which depend . . . on our natural mental dispositions" ("Nouvelles expériences" 1480).

The philosopher and mathematician had turned into a psychologist of art. Consequently, he introduced a new category to the discussion: "There are three types of perception: the intelligence or idea, the sentiment, and the sensation. The philosophers have numbered only two, the idea and the sensation. . . . The idea corresponds with vision, the sentiment with the persuasion of the ear, the sensation with the blind security of touch" ("Nouvelles expériences" 2343ff.). This was the new philosophy of taste, the *sentiment, in nuce,* and the arrangement of the ear as "Mittelsinn," as it would be referred to later by Herder.

To transpose the musical impression into the visual mode, Castel had to reproduce the musical sentiment, which meant not only translating tones into colors but maintaining the two-dimensional structure of music, chord and melody, and its temporal dimension, rhythm and measure. He introduced a new dimension in visual arts, namely, movement—a fascinating, revolutionary idea, but one that was hard to realize.

As one can imagine, all this remained "graue Theorie," conjectures without practical consequences, unless the public had really *seen* his music of colors. If not, the basic theoretical assumptions were worthwhile to Sancho Panza's philosophy. The public knew Castel's ocular instrument only from hearsay. As a consequence, commentators were free to develop their own ideas about the construction and performance of the ocular harpsichord, and the degree of pleasure to be felt. The spatiotemporal structure of music and painting in particular gave rise to controversies, but also to new solutions. Another amateur in musical theory, Jean-Jacques Rousseau, referred to these differences in his "Essay on the Origin of Language" (1749): "There is no kind of absurdity that has not been given a place in the treatment of fine arts by physical observation. . . . The systematizing spirit has confused everything, and presumes, out of ignorance, to paint for the ears and sing for the eyes. I have seen the famous clavichord on which music is supposedly made with colors. It would be a complete misunderstanding of the workings of nature not to see that the effect of colors is in their stability and that of sounds is in their succession" (61ff.).

The Construction of the Tone-to-Color Transposer

In 1743 the natural scientist Johann Gottlob Krüger published an article entitled "De novo musices, quo oculi delectantur, genere" (On new music that pleases the eye). He made some skeptical remarks about the possibility of producing the same sentiment with both tones and colors. He envisioned a new kind of chromatic music with an aesthetic quality different from that of normal music and painting. Yet he had to solve the crucial problem of showing a harmonic set of colors containing the synchronic and the diachronic structure of music. This required, however, a prior solution to the problem of how to produce a simultaneous and permanent changing image composed of a mixture of colors and their sequence.[19]

Castel's instrument exposed small pieces of colored silk when a key was pressed. With this technique it was impossible to mix and change colors at the same time. Therefore, Krüger suggested a completely different construction (see fig. 4). With the keystroke, a sort of diaphragm opens and allows the light of a candle to pass through different colored glasses and lenses. When a chord is represented as several concentric circles, the outer ring is the lowest tone, the inner rings are the higher tones, and in the center there is a mixed color of all tones of the chord. When the standard harmonic sequence, a triad (tonic, third, fifth), is played, Krüger's imaginary audience (or better: spectators) will see a blue outer circle, then a yellow and a red one, and in the center they will see nothing because it is all black (based on Castel's theory of chromatic light. Despite Krüger's efforts to improve Castel's original construction, he remained skeptical.

One of the few enthusiastic comments was published by Georg Philipp Telemann, a well-known German composer, born in 1681, four years before Johann Sebastian Bach. In 1738 Telemann spent some months in Paris, met Castel, and saw his as yet uncompleted instrument. Telemann stressed that only musicians were able to appreciate and understand the underlying principle of the instrument—an important turn in the discussion. Beginning with the tonic C (in the C-major scale) as a fixed basis and a basic color, the musical twelve-tone scale corresponded to the colors blue, celadon, green, olive, yellow, gold, orange, red, carmine, violet, agate, and blue-violet. Castel's spiral tone-color arrangement was aptly described.[20] Yet Castel's interest was not—like ordinary philosophers or scientists—limited to the chromatic scale and the structures of consonances, because music had a second dimension: the melodic movement or the sequentiality, the "soul" of music. Transposed into colors it sounds like this: "Here it is important to expose the colours and to hide them as you like: once blue, then red, later green followed by violet . . ." (Telemann 4).

Could this be a pleasant and harmonic spectacle for the eye? Some critics objected that the eye could not perceive the harmony of sequences of colors as the ear does. The *Encyclopédie* stated: "Adieu la mélodie & l'harmonie" ("Clavecin oculaire" 512). Telemann was convinced that pleasure was a result of mental activity: analyzing and comparing order and disorder perceived

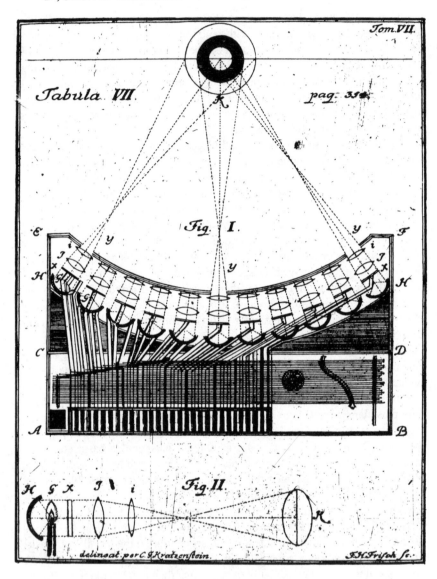

FIG. 4
Krüger's construction of the ocular harpsichord.

either by ear or eye. His limited concept of pleasure was nothing more than the recognition of musical or visual clusters.[21]

Reevaluation of Music and Painting: The Reaction to Castel's New Philosophy of Taste

Still a prophet of Burke's theory of sentiment, the literary critic and philosopher Moses Mendelssohn denied that colors and tones had an equivalent aesthetic quality. In his "Briefe über die Empfindungen" (Letters on sensations), Mendelssohn referred to the old theory of a harmonic sensorium and gave us the keyword that unites physiology and philosophy of taste. "The analysts of the human body have taught you that the nervous vessels build a delicate web of thousands of labyrinthine passages so that in the entire system every piece is linked with the whole and v.v. The degrees of tension are harmonically transmitted from nerve to nerve and never does a modification take place in one part without, as it was, having an influence on the whole. The connoisseurs of art call this harmonic tension the tone" (82).

Like Telemann, Mendelssohn identified two elements as the source of pleasure: the uniformity in the multiplicity (the beautiful) and the correspondence of the manifold (perfection). Then he added something that goes beyond Telemann—the amelioration of our physical situation and sensuous delight: "Divine art of music! You are the only one which surprises us with all kinds of pleasure. . . . The *imitation* of human passions, the artificial connection between the most paradoxical disharmonies: sources of *perfection!* The light proportions of the vibrations: a source of *beauty!* The harmonic tension of all nervous chords a source of sensuous *delight*" (85).

Mendelssohn admitted that it should be possible to discover a similar threefold harmony perceptible by other senses, such as smell, taste, and sight.[22] However, "the ocular harpsichord seems to promise more than it can really perform. I concede to the colours the harmonic blend and variation, source of sensuous beauty. Furthermore the sensual delight, the amelioration of our physical condition can hardly be denied. It is most probable that the nervous parts of the eyes in their harmonic tensions are modified in even the same way as the nerves of the ear. But can a melody be the source of perfection, the imitation of human actions and passions, can a melody of colours bless us with that kind of pleasure?" (86ff.).

Mendelssohn's answer was "no," because passions could be recalled by musical reproduction in our mind, whereas there seemed to exist no similar relation between passions and colors. Furthermore, perceiving colors without forms, shapes, or figures appeared to be impossible. But has anyone yet found a harmony of forms, shapes, and figures? The argument is quite clear: the *form* of music is an inscription in a mental space of time, as structures of harmony, melody, and rhythm. In painting, however, colors are normally perceived simultaneously—time is of minor importance because colors are permanent—but colors have necessarily a spatial dimension. The expression of musical feeling through colors requires a transformation from temporal into spatial structures, from transition to permanence. Yet in Mendelssohn's day there was no aesthetic theory available to handle the timing of colored forms.[23]

Why not try it the other way around, with musical depiction? This task was tackled by the prolific writer and popular philosopher Johann Jacob Engel. In his essay ''Über musikalische Malerey'' (On musical painting), Engel gave a thoroughly designed outline, beginning with a brief semiotic discussion of the differences between music and painting. While colors in a work of art are both conventional signs and imitation of real objects, musical tones can only be imitations, either of real phenomena or their impressions in the mind (''Seele''). Art is imitation of nature: this was the commonly adopted position. In music this imitation is generally imperfect. Sometimes music imitates only qualities of objects perceived by other senses as speed or movement. Engel calls these ''*transcendent* similarities.'' This idea relates Engel's theory of musical painting to those theories of the origin of language that rely on imitation: primary language imitates not the objects of the exterior world themselves but only their inherent transcendent qualities perceived by different senses.

For Engel, the imitation of impressions (or better: sentiments) was the main task of music. And according to this understanding even color can be imitated by music, in his paradoxical formula: ''Even the color is paintable. Because the impression of a soft color is somehow similar to the impression of a soft tone on the soul'' (4:308).[24] The musical sentiment had its complement in the organic movement, often called the inner tone; the physical movement had its equivalent in the inner motion, the emotion (''Gemütsbewegung'').[25]

Sounds are, according to Engel, the most powerful means of producing such vibrations and constitute the subconscious sympathy among living species (animals and humans). The human condition relied on the communication of sounds—sounds of passion, pain, and joy. This is another important reference to the theory of the origin of language, especially to Herder, who wrote, ''The tone of sensation shall transpose the sympathizing creature into the same tone'' (*Werke* 19).

Music was said to paint or imitate the natural succession (or association) of passions. This assertion had its parallel in a linguistic discussion with which Engel was quite familiar: the debate on natural word order or on inversion, the theme of Diderot's ''Lettre sur les sourds et muets'' and of many other writers.[26]

Theory of language, which at that time was mostly discussed in terms of a theory of the origin of language, was not far from Mendelssohn's and Engel's reflections. In the final sections I will discuss the glottogenetic version of language theory.

Psychology of Art and Theory of Language

In his essay on the origin of language, Herder refers directly to Locke's and Diderot's mental experiments of sensual deprivation. Like others, he denied the possibility that Cheselden's blind-born young man could really develop a correct idea of space, form, and color through vision alone and without the assistance of other senses. But unlike Locke's epistemological approach and the French philosophy à la Condillac, hearing (not touch) was Herder's favorite sense: in Herder's terms, the eye was a brilliant but passionless sense, while the ear was the real and first instructor for language during the transitional process from animal to human.

> There is for instance a sheep. As an image it looms before the eye with all things and images and colors on a great canvas of nature. How much is there and how difficult to distinguish! All the characteristic marks are finely interwoven, placed together, and all still ineffable. Who can speak shapes? Who can sound colors? Let him take the sheep under his probing hand. This sensation is more sure and fuller, but it is so full and so obscure, with one thing within the other. Who can say what he is thus feeling? But listen! The sheep bleats! Now one distinguishing mark separates by itself from the canvas of the colors wherein so little was to be distinguished. One distinguishing mark has penetrated deeply and clearly into the soul. "Oh," says the learning beginner, like Cheselden's blind man when given the power of sight, "now I shall know you again—you bleat!" ("Essay on the Origin of Language" 129)

After this reminiscence Herder sketched another primary situation, which contained all the ingredients of former "Gedankenexperimente": a blind (Locke, Voltaire, Diderot), deaf, and dumb subject (Diderot) in an isolated situation (Condillac, Maupertuis):

> So man is a listening, a noting creature, naturally formed for language, and even a blind and a mute man—we understand—would have to invent language if he is not without feeling and is not deaf. Place him at ease and in comfort on a deserted island: Nature will reveal itself to him through the ear. . . . But how poor and how strange would the conceptions be which this mutilated individual could associate with such sounds. (129ff.)

Summary

Finally, I want to highlight the major characteristics of the development in the second half of the eighteenth century: Mendelssohn was convinced that trying to produce the same effect in painting as in music by means of a certain order of colors would be in vain because music was—in contrast to painting—in a perfect degree beautiful. Engel maintained that music could paint colors, yet not perfectly. Both agreed on a harmonic or sympathetic organization of the sensorium. But the equation was no longer valid: the analogous physical nature of light and sound (vibration and movement) and analogous perceptive modes (vibration and movement again) did not *lead* to an analogous aesthetic quality of colors and tones (or: music and painting). The developing theory of language emphasized that each mode of perception had its own cognitive effect, connecting sound, audition, and speech production with the birth of language and language acquisition. The articulated tone was supposed to be the major element of phylogenesis.

So what really was the "discourse of colours" that Diderot's deaf-mute saw when he visited Castel in about 1750? A possible answer is given by Herder in his dialogue "Vom Angenehmen und Schönen" ("Kalligone"), just at the end of the century: "The music makes an inner clavichord sound which is our own innermost nature. . . . Is it possible that what is touched within us is Castel's clavichord showing colours or images?" (*Sämtliche Werke* 77).

In an English report it was said that Castel's harpsichord was built for "philosophical eyes" (Wellek, "Farbenharmonie und Farbenklavier" 368). Diderot named the hero of the "Lettre sur les aveugles" "un vrai philosophe" and said his deaf-mute had more philosophical insight into the nature of tones and language than most of the philosophers before. This was the moment when the new hero from 1750 onward, the deaf-mute, was announced: the hero of the ideologues in France and the preclassic psychology of language in Germany.

If you suspect that the colors perceived by the young deaf-mute were *real* colors in Berkeley's sense, that is, not perceptible by means of the eyes, and thus that both the ocular harpsichord and the deaf-mute might just have been a philosopher's instrument—you might be perfectly correct and join Goethe and the editors of the *Encyclopédie* in their doubt that Castel's ocular harpsichord had ever performed.

Notes

1. "Die Gestalten der Skulptur und Malerei sind im Raum nebeneinander und stellen diese reale Ausbreitung in wirklicher oder scheinbarer Totalität dar. Die Musik aber kann Töne nur hervorbringen, insofern sie einen im Raum befindlichen

Körper in sich erzittern macht und ihn in schwingende Bewegung versetzt. Diese Schwingungen gehören der Kunst nur nach *der* Seite an, daß sie nacheinander erfolgen, und so tritt das sinnliche Material überhaupt in die Musik, statt mit seiner räumlichen Form, nur mit der *zeitlichen* Dauer seiner Bewegung ein" (Hegel 163).

2. For a more elaborate reconstruction of the implications for the theory of language and of the important shifts of focus from 1700 onward see Gessinger, *Auge & Ohr* and "Gedankenfiguren—Sprachfiguren."

3. In a letter to Thieriot from November 18, 1736, mentioning the conflict over Rameau (*Orphee-Rameau*) (34:166).

4. Those relations could be expressed in mathematical proportions (or geometrically), as we find in several publications on optics and acoustics: Newton's *Opticks* (1704), Euler's *Tentamen novae theoriae musicae* (1739), and Diderot's *Principes généraux d'acoustique* (1745).

5. They obscure even an early remark of the later secretary of the Académie Royale de Paris in 1720, de Mairan, who tried to parallelize the distances observed by Newton in his experiments on refraction with the "distances" between different tones, or, more precisely, the length of the strings producing different tones.

6. "All arguments therefore, which prove the Performance of Sensation and intellectual Perception, by means of Vibrations of the medullary Particels, must infer, that muscular Motion is performed by Vibrations also. And conversely, if Vibrations can be shown to take place in muscular Motion, they must also be instrumental in Sensation and intellectual Perception" (Hartley 86).

7. "Les organes se montent à l'unisson, de tout ce qui les affecte d'une manière particulière, pendant un tems. Le mouvement sur-tout d'oscillation ou de tremblement, est facile à apprendre. C'est à-peu-près le mouvement tonique & naturel de tous nos organes, n'y eût-il que le battement du coeur & des arteres, pour leur donner le ton" (Castel, *L'Optique des couleurs* 16).

8. Hemsterhuis, an influential Dutch philosopher and man of letters, believed that the feeling for measure and rhythm was founded in prenatal organic movement, the tactile source provided by the mother's heart ("Lettre sur l'homme"). The importance of a natural disposition for measure in the contemporary theory of music and prose is evident, though Diderot rejected this supposition vividly.

9. This is pointed out by Albert Wellek. From the late 1920s onward, Wellek wrote a series of articles on Castel's invention as well as on synaesthesia in literature and music, in which he provided a great deal of valuable bibliographical information on the topic of this essay.

10. In Newton's theory of the nature of light, colors are defined by two parameters: lightness and darkness of a given color, and the differences between colors. In terms of vibrations, stronger or weaker vibrations of the optic nerves mean lighter or darker colors, and the different speed (promptitude) of vibrations produces different colors (in modern terms: energy and frequency of light).

11. Athanasius Kircher and, after him, Leibniz in his *Nouveaux essais,* had made this daring conjecture. The mutual relations of colors are supposed to be the same as those of musical tones: an equation of proportions. The keywords are rapports

(relations), consonances, and dissonances, and, as a general framework, harmony, indicating the relation to the concept of universal harmony.

12. "Que le son ne se fait entendre que par le moyen des vibrations de l'air qui ébranlent le nerf de l'oreille. . . . Il est certain que les couleurs dépendent naturellement de l'ébranlement de l'organe de la vision. . . .

"Ainsi il en est de la lumière & diverses couleurs comme du son & des différents tons. La *grandeur* du *son* vient du plus & du moins de *force* des vibrations de l'air grossier, & *la diversité des tons* du plus au moins de *promptitude* des ces mêmes vibrations comme tout le monde en convient. La *force* ou l'éclat des couleurs vient donc aussi du plus au moins de *force* des vibrations, non de l'air, mais de la matière subtile; et les différentes espèces des couleurs du plus & du moins de promptitude des ces mêmes vibrations" (Malebranche 3:259ff.).

Voltaire however, in his comment on Malebranche, denied any similarity between visual and auditory perception. After a brief description of the architecture of the inner ear, he continued: "Cet artifice de tant d'organes, et de bien d'autres encore, porte les sons dans le cervelet; il y fait entrer les accords de la musique sans les confondre; il y introduit les mots qui sont les courriers des pensées, dont il reste quelquefois un souvenir qui dure autant que la vie.

"Une industrie non moins merveilleuse lance dans vos yeux, sans les blesser, les traits de lumière réfléchis des objets. . . . Ils peignent dans la rétine les tableaus dont ils apportent les contours. Ils y tracent l'image nette du quart du ciel.

"Voilà des instruments qui produisent évidemment des effets déterminés et très différents, en agissant sur le principe des nerfs, de sorte qu'il est impossible d'entendre par l'organe de la vue, et de voir par celui de l'ouïe" (44:209ff.).

13. In 1699, after the publication of Locke's *Essay*, Malebranche made an important addition to his text from 1678 to clarify his position, or, better, to displace his "natural science" from the suspicious proximity to mere speculation and bad metaphysics. The following statement was given in a session of the Académie Royale on April 4: "On pourroit donc peut-être juger par la suite des couleurs, si elle étoit bien constante, que les vibrations du jaune sont plus promptes que celle du rouge, & et celles du rouge que du bleu, & ainsi des autres couleurs qui se succedent. Mais il me paroît impossible de découvrir précisément par ce moyen ni même par aucun autre, les rapports exacts de la promptitude de ces vibrations, comme on les a découverts dans les consonances de la Musique. On ne peut sur cela que deviner & aller au vraysemblable" (3:260, note).

14. It was exactly this remark that Castel referred to in a nicely arranged experiment designed to demonstrate that this blind man was perfectly right. "Un jour dans une assemblée des gens de l'ésprit où il s'agissoit du clavecin," he reported, "j'avançai un fait que je tiens d'un de mes amis, celebre oculiste, c'est M. de Woolhouze. Cet homme . . . me contoit qu'il avoit vu ou entendu parler en Allemagne d'un aveugle qui distinguoit les couleurs au toucher, & les caractérisoit par rapport au sens de l'ouie." Being aware of the mainly skeptical reaction of his listeners, Castel asked the most skeptical of all: "Quelle couleur il croiroit que cet aveugle eû caractérisée par le son d'une trompette. Le rouge, me repondit-il, & tout de suite par une espece d'acclamation, quatre ou cinq autres voix se déclarent pour la même couleur" ("Nouvelles expériences" 1832).

15. Cf. Lindberg, *Studies in the History of Medieval Optics*.

16. "Les philosophes veulent que toutes les couleurs soient dans le blanc; j'ai mes raisons pour en chercher le vrai origine dans le noir" ("Nouvelles expériences" 1808).

17. He even found an elegant response to the objection that in the circle of colors one returns to blue again after passing green, red, orange, violet, etc., whereas moving along musical scales, one arrives an octave higher and not at the same tone. The solution was something like a spiral color-to-tone projection.

18. The same holds for music: "Ce n'est pas dans une *chambre sourde* à travers un *cornet de sourd* appliqué à un *infiniment petit trou* qu'on juge de la musique . . ." ("Nouvelles expériences" 1829).

19. ". . . accedit quod supra iam monui, musicam omnem esse vel harmonicam vel melodicam. . . . Quodsi igitur iam ultro largiri vellemus, cantum melodicum huius machinae ope oculis posse repraesentari, quid vero fiet de cantu harmonico, a quo maximam, neque sine ratione, suavitatem promittere solent musici? rem enim paullo attentius considerantes inveniemus, sonos sibi coëxistentes, non sigilatim, non separatos, set simul & commixtos quasi percipi" (Krüger 348ff.).

20. There were twelve revolutions corresponding to each of the twelve octaves, which resulted in 144 different colors or tones. Telemann calls this concept "a really new chromatic music," but, as an experienced composer, he should have known that there was neither an instrument that could reproduce twelve octaves nor a human ear that could hear them (the upper limit is far beyond the perceptibility of the human ear).

21. "Daß alles, was den Tact und die Bewegung anbelanget, unter Farben und Klängen gemein seyn werde. . . . Die Klänge gefallen nur durch eine deutliche Verschiedenheit, durch ihre Uebereinstimmung und Vergleichung; Die Farben sind so mannigfaltig als die Klänge, und haben gewisse Uebereinstimmungen. Das Auge kann sie zusammenfügen, ihre Vergleichungen entwickeln und ihre Ordnung und Unordnung empfinden. Diß Empfinden veruhrsachet das Vergnügen und Anreizen in allen Dingen, und das eigentliche Vergnügen der Music besteht in dem, solchen Unterschied augenblicklich, und nach und nach in kurzer Zeit mehrmals zu bemerken. . . . Kurz: Es ist unstreitig, daß diß Farbenspiel ergetzen wird. Denn Music ist nichts anders, als eine Ergetzlichkeit" (Telemann 6ff.).

22. Vision is the cue for Mendelssohn to recall the whole story of visual harmony. A blind man suffers more from a sensory deprivation than a deaf-mute, because the eyes perceive more precisely and their range of perception is much wider. Only minor attempts had been made to discover the harmony of colors, discovered then by the great Newton. But the harmony of colors still lacks an elaboration like that of musical tones, despite Castel's invention.

23. As was in this century, e.g., Kandinsky's presentation of Mussorgsky's *Pictures at an Exhibition,* Schlemmer's *Triadic Ballet,* and Disney's *Fantasia.*

24. The means of a composer are numerous: key, tonic, intervals, melody, movement, rhythm, harmony, pitch, instrumentation, volume.

25. "Alle leidenschaftlichen Vorstellungen der Seele sind mit gewissen entsprechenden Bewegungen im Nervensystem unzertrennlich verbunden, werden durch

Wahrnehmung dieser Bewegung unterhalten and verstärkt'' (Engel 4:312ff.). This ''Gemütsbewegung'' is often visible as physical action such as mime, movements of the arms, shaking of the whole body, etc. And vice versa: organic vibrations produce passions, ''Seelenerschütterungen.''

26. In singing, things change considerably because this kind of music has not only to paint (or depict) objects as sensations but to express the relation between emotion and the outer world. Engel gives a rather strict formulation: ''Nur Ausdruck erreicht den Zweck des Gesanges; Malerei zerstört ihn'' (4:330). Singing is the most vivid, most sensitive, and most passionate form of discourse. Engel gives no explanation of this characterization, but I think he had in mind the dual character of sounds as words or meaningful signs and expression of inner passion.

References

Bachelard, Gaston. *La formation de l'esprit scientifique*. Paris: Vrin, 1947.

Batteux, Charles. *Les Beaux arts reduits à un même principe*. Paris: Durand, 1746.

Berkeley, George. *Works*. Ed. A. A. Luce and T. E. Jessop. 3 vols. Montreal: Nelson, 1948.

Castel, Louis-Bertrand. ''Clavecin pour les yeux, avec l'art de peindre les sons et toutes sortes de pièces de musique. Lettre écrite . . . le 20 Fevrier 1725.'' *Mercure de France* (1725): 2552–77.

———. *Farben-Optick*. Halle: Renger, 1747.

———. ''Nouvelles expériences d'optique et d'acoustique.'' *Mémoires pour l'histoire des Sciences et des Beaux-Arts (Journal de Trevoux)* (1735): 1444–82, 1619–66, 1807–39, 2018–53, 2325–72, 2642–768.

———. *L'Optique des couleurs, fondée sur les simples observations, & tournée surtout à la pratique de la peinture, de la teinture & des autres arts coloristes*. Paris: Briasson, 1740.

''Clavecin oculaire.'' *Encyclopédie ou dictionnaire raisonné des sciences, des arts et des métiers*. Ed. Jean le Rond d'Alembert et Denis Diderot. Paris: Briasson, 1753.

Diderot, Denis. ''Lettre sur les sourds et muets.'' Edition commentée et présentée par Paul Hugo Meyer. *Diderot Studies*. Vol. 7. Genf: Droz, 1965.

———. ''Principes généraux d'acoustique'' (1745). *Oeuvres complètes*. Vol. 9. Ed. J. Assezat and M. Tourneux. Paris: Garnier, 1875–77.

Engel, Johann Jacob. *Schriften*. Vol. 4. Berlin: Mylius, 1801–6.

Erfurt, Jürgen, and Joachim Gessinger, eds. *Schriftkultur und sprachlicher Wandel*. Osnabrück: OBST-Redaktion, 1993.

Euler, Leonhard. *Tentamen novae theoriae musicae ex certissimis harmoniae principiis*. Petersburg: Typographia Acad. Scientiarum, 1739.

Gessinger, Joachim. *Auge & Ohr: Studien zur Erforschung der Sprache am Menschen, 1700–1850*. Berlin: de Gruyter, 1994.

———. ''Gedankenfiguren—Sprachfiguren. Über Denken und Sprechen bei Diderot oder Diskurs über das Essen.'' *Sprachwissenschaft im 18. Jahrhundert*. Ed. Klaus D. Dutz. Münster: Nodus, 1993. 1–13.

Hartley, David. *Observations on Man, His Frame, His Duty, and His Expectations*. London: Leake & Frederick, 1749.

Hegel, Georg Wilhelm Friedrich. *Werke.* Vol. 15. Frankfurt am Main: Suhrkamp, 1986.

Hemsterhuis, François. "Lettre sur l'homme et ses rapports avec le commentaire inédit de Diderot." Texte établi, presenté et annoté par Georges May. Paris, 1772. New Haven: Yale UP, 1964.

Herder, Johann Gottfried. "Essay on the Origin of Language." *On the Origin of Language.* Trans., with afterword, by John H. Moran and Alexander Gode. Chicago: U of Chicago P, 1986.

———. "Kalligone." *Sämmtliche Werke. Zur Philosophie und Geschichte.* Vol. 18. Stuttgart-Tübingen: Cotta, 1830.

———. *Werke.* Herausgegeben von Wolfgang Proß. Band 2: Herder und die Anthropologie der Aufklärung. Darmstadt: Wissenschaftliche Buchgesellschaft, 1987.

Krüger, Johann Gottlob. "De novo musices, quo oculi delectantur, genere." *Miscelanea Berolinensis.* Vol. 8. Berlin: Akademie der Wissenschaften, 1743. 345–57.

Leibniz, Gottfried Wilhelm. *New Essays Concerning Human Understanding.* Trans. Alfred Gideon Langley from *Nouveaux essais sur l'entendement humain,* 1765. New York: Macmillan, 1896.

Lindberg, David C. *Studies in the History of Medieval Optics.* London: Variorum Reprints, 1983.

Locke, John. *An Essay Concerning Human Understanding.* 4th ed. 1700. Oxford: Clarendon, 1975.

Mairan, Jean-Jacques d'Ortous de. "Castel's ocular harpsichord." *Histoire de l'Académie des Sciences et Belles-Lettres, Année 1737.* Paris: Imprimerie Royale, 1740. 61.

Malebranche, Nicolas. *La Recherche de la vérité (1674–1678). Oeuvres complètes,* édité par Geneviève Rodis-Lewis. Paris: J. Vrin, 1964. *The Search After Truth.* Trans. Thomas M. Lennon and Paul J. Olscamp. Columbus: Ohio State UP, 1980.

Mendelssohn, Moses. "Briefe über die Empfindungen." *Jubiläumsausgabe.* Vol. 1 of *Gesammelte Schriften.* Stuttgart: Frommann-Holzboog, 1755/1971. 42–123.

Newton, Isaac. *Opticks or a Treatise of the Reflexions, Refractions, Inflexions and Colours of Light. Also Two Treatises of the Species and Magnitude of Curvilinear Figures.* London: Smith & Walford, 1704.

Osmaston, F. P. B. *The Philosophy of Fine Art.* London: Bell, 1920.

Rousseau, Jean-Jacques. "Essay on the Origin of Language." *On the Origin of Language.* Trans., with afterword, by John H. Moran and Alexander Gode. Chicago: U of Chicago P, 1986.

Schier, D. S. *Louis Bertrand Castel, Anti-Newtonian Scientist.* Cedar Rapids, IA: Touch, 1941.

Telemann, Georg Philipp. *Beschreibung der Augen-Orgel oder des Augen-Clavicimbels, so der berühmte Mathematicus und Jesuit zu Paris, Herr Pater Castel, erfunden und ins Werk gerichtet hat; aus einem Französischen Briefe übersetzet.* Hamburg: Piscator, 1739.

Voltaire, François Marie Arouet de. *Oeuvres complètes.* Ed. Theodore Besterman. 135 vols. Genève: Institute et Musée Voltaire: Slatkine, 1968– .

Wellek, Albert. "Castel." *Musik in Geschichte und Gegenwart.* Kassel: Bärenreiter-Verlag, 1952. 898–99.

————. "Das Doppelempfinden im 18. Jahrhundert." *Deutsche Vierteljahresschrift für Literaturgeschichte* 14 (1936): 75–102.

————. "Farbenharmonie und Farbenklavier. Ihre Entstehungsgeschchte im 18. Jahrhundert." *Archiv für die gesamte Psychologie* 94 (1935): 347–75.

Opera in the Light of Technology

FRIEDRICH A. KITTLER

Although Greek drama underwent a somewhat premeditated renaissance in the form of opera around 1600, Homer's suns did not rise again. The midday light that had shone on the southern slopes of the Acropolis and the theater of Dionysus did not return. On the baroque stage all performances had to adhere in verse and music to an invisible limit, now thoroughly forgotten: the essence and existence of art were determined simply by the finite burning time of the candles that illuminated both stage and auditorium.

A new, technological sun has bestowed on today's audiences endless scenes or infinite melodies, such as Wagner's. In 1876, Wagner (following the London *Lyceum*) had gaslighting installed in the new opera house at Bayreuth, which made possible an unlimited burning time as well as the slow, hallucinatory brightening and dimming of scenery (Hyman 310). Five years later, on October 10, 1881, the Swan United Electric Light Company stepped into the theatrical present: 1,158 current-conducting carbon filaments encased in glass (824 as stage lighting) turned night into technological day at the London Savoy Theater (Technisches Museum Wien 20).[1]

Yet the technological sun changed more than the duration of performances. Its light created—to use Walter Benjamin's words—another world of perception (''Merkwelt''). When on March 12, 1902, Etienne Gaspard Robertson put a current through two carbon rods for the first time, the dazzled audience saw (as the *Journal de Paris* noted) ''at the moment of contact a spark shining with astonishing brightness'' (Technisches Museum Wien 11). In this way, lightning—which had only recently been technologically tamed by Franklin—made a comeback, but in the new, reproducible form (''Machbarkeit'') that would later be embodied in Wagner's god, Donner. On his com-

73

mand, "a powerful flash of lightning" escapes from "the cloud" in *Rheingold.*

Initially it was a matter of extending this artificial flash of lightning from one moment in time to several hours. Carbon rods, just like the old candles, burn down until the increasing distance extinguishes the spark and therefore the arc lamp. But in 1848 designs appeared where the decreasing current itself, in a negative feedback loop, counteracted the increasing distance between the elements, thus ensuring constant distance. Needless to say, this first "endless lightning" struck the one medium that attracted and brought together all the dreams of the nineteenth century: grand opera. The Parisian physicist Léon Foucault, famous not only for measuring the earth's revolution and the speed of light, but also for his experiments in photography and electricity, did the composer Meyerbeer a favor that was to have great consequences: he installed for him the first practical application of the carbon arc lamp. During the premiere of Meyerbeer's *Prophète* at the Grand Opera, Paris, Foucault's electrical sun shed its light on a concave mirror that projected the light from behind onto a transparent silk screen. Thus, a sharply defined circle of light (or rather, since the eyes of the baffled premiere guests were easily tricked, the Sun itself) was suspended high above the opera stage (see Baumann 136–41).

Yet every sun, whether in the sky over Greece or in artificial paradises, contains all the colors of Newton's spectrum. On the picture-frame stage of old (itself the synthesis of several arts) these hues were achieved by paint and dye, that is, by layers of color on scenery and costumes. The audience, as Goethe's dramatic heroes so lucidly explained to them when facing a rainbow, were essentially limited to "seeing what is illuminated, not the light" (*Pandora* 1:958; see also *Faust II* 4695–727). Dazzling sunlight would have simply obliterated man, that idol of classical art. However, in the modern theater, which is the synthesis of arts and media, it is the colors themselves that shine. Goethe's futile refutation of Newton's color theory has been refuted in turn.

The Italian Opera House of Her Majesty Queen Victoria was the scene of the first of many light shows that nowadays link works of art ("Gesamtkunstwerke") as diverse as the Bayreuth Wagner Festival and rock music. Charles Babbage and Michael Faraday were cooperating in London at the same time the friends Foucault and Meyerbeer were active in Paris. While Babbage had constructed the precursor of all modern computers, Faraday had put an end to the age of the candle as well as to his own *History of a Candle* by introducing the one unifying concept we have of electricity, heat and light. Babbage and Faraday must therefore have been "unquestionably the most successful lighting team, from the scientific point of view, which theater history has ever known" (Hyman 311).

During a visit to the German Opera House in 1846, Babbage happened to observe how the gaslights tinged his companion's hat and program red. He immediately turned to scientific experimentation. Much more powerful sources of light than gas—such as limelight or the recently invented carbon arc lamp—were supposed to reproduce this pleasing, accidental effect, make it stronger and more controllable. To this end Babbage placed colored liquids enclosed in glass in front of Faraday's lamps, which then projected the light onto the stage in all its spectral variations. To celebrate this theatrical revolution through the sheer power of technology, Babbage immediately wrote a suitable ballet that simply transformed—or projected—lighting effects into action: an allegory of the British scientist cum dramatist himself (bearing the male name Alethes, or "truthful one") encounters an artificially synthesized rainbow (given the mythological female name Iris) in hallucinatory love. To achieve this, scenery and costumes were entirely white, perhaps for the first time ever in the history of the theater. But this was only so that they could shine in every other color as the characters danced through the cones of projected light until the entire spectrum of Newton's rainbow was truly encompassed or exhausted.

Such is the massive extent to which life and death have come under technological stage direction since Babbage (and his contemporary Wagner). If Iris (in accordance with the script) initially "appears as dead," it is only because blue light falls on her sleeping "form all in white." Conversely, "she seems to be filled with life" precisely to the "measure to which the blue light is gradually turned down and the red light equally gradually turned up" (Hyman 312).[2] Wagner uses the media of light and music in the same way. When the medium of light disappears in *Rheingold* it is to liken the gods, after the loss of their life-giving apples, to mere mortals: according to the relevant stage direction, "a pale fog envelops the stage with increasing density; in it the Gods look increasingly ashen and old." It takes the cunning tricks or special effects of two gods, who unmistakably represent fire and lightning, to make the fog (thereby loosely adapting Babbage) yield to a rainbow-ballet of the blessed. Finally, the medium of music, too, is used in this way when in Wagner's musical dramas generally each crescendo of voice or orchestra coincides with breathing and singing, that is, life, but each diminuendo with death (see Kittler, "Death and Destruction").

Nor did Babbage exclude nature from this death. His ballet begins in crevasses with a dance of all things frozen, which then, through sheer tricks of light, turn into their exact opposites: the ice is turned to fiery rock while the glacier becomes the center of a volcano, which enables the fire spirits to stage, together with the fearless explorer Alethes, their own version of the *Waberlohe*.[3] In view of such optical and pyrotechnical miracles, it is not surprising that the Italian Opera House had two firehoses at the ready during Babbage's ballet rehearsals, or that it was ultimately not prepared to take the risk of staging the premiere. While it may have been possible to insure the theater building against fire, the management argued, the audience was nevertheless irreplaceable (see Hyman 313).

Apparently news had not yet reached London of Wagner's almost contemporaneous project to stage a performance of the *Ring* on a strictly provisional theater stage that was to be as transient as media or projections, which was, in other words, to go up in flames along with the score at the end of the performance. Thus the *Götterdämmerung*—where the "curtain" indeed "falls when the Gods are completely engulfed in flames"—was not preempted. (There is no need to dwell on the great theater fires of Nice in 1880 and Vienna in 1881, as a consequence of which our very own iron safety curtain, first technologically and then politically, was to separate the new electrical illusion energies from their audiences.)

Much less spectacular, but much more difficult to stage than the rainbow of light, was another rainbow: that of sound. Music too has a spectrum, simply because in amplitude and phase every real sound is the sum total of its keynote and its (theoretically infinite) harmonics. Nothing else distinguishes the acoustic profiles of individual instruments or singing voices, even when they all produce the same keynote, the same tone.

But occidental music—much in contrast to the human ear—was not willing or able to know about the rainbow of sounds. With its inception, when an unknown Greek from Asia Minor invented our own vocal alphabet and musical notation system (and probably the coin as well) all at one stroke (see Lohmann), it became possible to notate any sound of a singing voice and any interval of an instrument, but no more than that. It was for good reason that Pythagoras celebrated each integral ratio between tones (as produced by varying lengths of strings) with the word *logos,* the greatest honorific among Greeks. Similarly, intervals, not sounds, were paraded on medieval staves (see Scherer 115–46), because to go further than that, to measure and notate the oscillation ratios within each single note as and when it is produced, was simply a mathematical impossibility.

This union of music and alphabet was not dissolved until the mathematics of differential calculus. In 1739, Euler's "Essay on New Music Theory" replaced the basic concept of the interval with that of frequency. The latter no longer measures the length of strings in space but, conversely, the recurrence of an oscillation in a given time. Since then tones have been nothing but events the human ear perceives as a unified tone precisely and only because their duration is beyond the reach of any scope of perception. Eighty years later, Baron Fourier, departmental prefect and mathematician under Napoleon, laid the necessary foundation for calculating all individual component oscillations in terms of amplitude and phase on the basis of Euler's equation, even in the most complicated composite sounds. Fourier's spectral analysis accomplished for sound what Newton's had done for light. Computability now extended beyond musically well-defined tones to encompass the entire gamut of sounds, down to droning, hissing, and roaring. Since then, sound in general—which may or may not be a composed euphony—has been closely connected to the unifying concept of electricity, heat and light. Today, compact disc covers display computer graphics representing the entire frequency spectrum of the music within.[4] An entirely numerical script has thus finally drawn level with the human ear and has granted it the completely new right to hear sounds wherever musicology and theory of harmony had only ever discerned tonal values.

To save us the trouble of having to include nonintegral multiples of the fundamental tone in our calculation, let us now take, as an example, any sound that is produced by a bass (rather than a bell) (see Stauder 142–58). Naturally, the musical notation system simply prescribes, for instance, the tone E-flat. Yet when an instrument plays E-flat, its harmonics too resound in the form of integral multiples of the basic frequency: E-flat 1, E-flat 2, B-flat 2, E-flat 3, G 3, B-flat 3, E-flat 4, and so on. This is precisely the sequence of tones that the horns add to the double bass in *Rheingold* from the seventeenth bar of the prelude onward. Thus, Wagner might simply have implemented Fourier's new analysis of music in his composition. Of course, the bassoons add the third harmonic B-flat from the fifth bar onward, thereby producing one of those hollow fifths whose "eerieness" imprinted itself "particularly powerfully" on the memory of the "child" Wagner according to the composer's own testimony (*Mein Leben* 37).[5] Of course, the horns lack the seventh harmonic— located somewhere between C and D-flat—simply because no European instrument can produce it. After all, with their natural tone series, Wagner's modern valve horns—whose "introduction" had "unarguably achieved so much for the instrument" (*Tristan und Isolde* VI)—also make reference to those natural horns and times past, which the *Rheingold* prelude as a whole re-creates as the origin itself. Yet nature with its flux and roaring is as distant from the monochords and intervals of the Greeks as it is close to the measuring range of Fourier analyses. Instead of proceeding harmoniously or melodically according to the laws of musical logic, the tetralogy begins by encompassing the entire ambit, that is, the frequency spectrum of a Wagnerian orchestra. At the same time the eerie fifths cast their spell on him, the "adult boy absorbed with voluptuous horror all the various chaotic hues of sound one hears when an orchestra is tuning up" (*Mein Leben* 37).

In the nineteenth century such thrills were considered more suitable for dilettantes or engineers than for would-be composers. This emancipation of sound is maliciously summed up in a comparative formula by Debussy's *Monsieur Croche*—an antidilettante on principle—when he says that Beethoven's orchestra "strikes him as a black and white drawing with a range of select shades of gray," whereas Wagner's orchestra "appeared to him as a kind of colorful, almost evenly applied color paste in which the sound of a violin can no longer be distinguished from that of a trombone'' (53). But since black and white drawings resided above all in books, and select shades of gray in nineteenth-century typography (see Kittler, *Aufschreibesysteme* 94), Monsieur Croche was—despite his musical name and his mockery of Wagner—not dilettante enough to want to return from Wagner's spectrum of sounds to Beethoven's music paper.

"Musicians," Croche continues in the dialogue with Debussy, "only hear music written by schooled hands; that inscribed in nature they never hear. To watch the sunrise is much more useful than to listen to the *Pastoral Symphony*. What is the use of your almost incomprehensible music? Should you not rather eradicate all the parasitical complexities which put us in mind of the intricate mechanism of a safe's combination lock?'' (55). This is the same comparative formula again, only with reversed value. No negative image is better suited than a combination lock to describe the distance from nature of that world of signs that knows only letters or numbers—or elements of an alphanumeric code, to use computer jargon. Such elements were used by schooled musicians to encrypt (like Bach) their own name or (like Berg) a lover's name, while secret services and safe owners use them to minimize the constantly growing risk of access. As regards the procedure of exhausting all the possibilities of a combinatorics to compose fugues or secret radio signals, written music and secret-service cryptography are entirely one and the same.

However, the opposition of nature and code, as presented by Croche, is in itself a cryptogram encoding the novelties of Wagner of all people. In the second act of *Tristan,* Debussy's hopes for the future of music were realized decades before they were even formulated. Wagner supplanted the intricate mechanism of a combination lock with a music that would be inscribed into nature itself.

As we know, the most modern of Wagner's musical dramas is based on a medieval romance. But the reason for this is less well known. Gottfried von Strassburg had scattered cryptograms and anagrams throughout the text of his romance of chivalry, thus emphasizing—as the first vernacular writer in German—the written word itself. Gottfried no longer addressed (as did so many of his chivalrous predecessors) a group of aristocratic earwitnesses. Through anagrams—which are necessarily bound to escape the unaided ear— the scholar or scribe invented a new audience: the literate person or reader.

Wagner's *Tristan* is the revocation of this entire communications system.[6] Tones such as Fourier's take the place of letters, which had—from Gottfried through Gutenberg to Goethe—reigned supreme as literature. In Gottfried's chivalric romance, Tristan and Isolde use their initials, T and I, as a secret code to arrange forbidden nights of passion. Inscribed shavings of wood— almost like Germanic runes—float down a stream to signal when the danger is past. The literate Gottfried scattered exactly the same signs—now as Latin letters—all over his novel in the form of anagrams, thus perfecting the intricate mechanism of a combination lock.

By contrast, in its very plot Wagner's musical drama examines what is meant by listening to the music of nature. At the exact point where the letter code T/I occurs in Gottfried, Wagner puts a tonal equivalent. The second act of *Tristan* opens with an ambivalent, whirring orchestral chord, the decoding of which becomes a dramatic problem. Brangaene interprets it, all too rightly, as the sound of King Marke's bugles. Isolde, on the other hand, is driven by "the impetuousness of her desire" for Tristan "to perceive what she imagines": according to her, it is not "bugles that sound so sweet" but "the gentle trickling of a spring that is murmuring so delightfully." Her erotic-acoustic hallucination thus misconstrues the bugle call (which signals Marke's approach and bids Tristan leave) as a purely natural source of sound, which is itself an invitation to a night of passion. At the price of her doom, Wagner's heroine hears only music inscribed in nature, and this was long before Debussy. She immediately orders Brangaene to give Tristan an agreed-on signal, a sign that no longer has anything to do with Gottfried's anagrams and everything to do with the technological suns of modernity: she puts out the torch, whose light—of course—"fades away gradually," as only the gaslights of Bayreuth can, in order to turn on instead the nocturnal black light of love itself.

It is these new optics and acoustics that conjure up Maurice Maeterlinck, on whose *Pelléas and Mélisande* Debussy was to base his first libretto. After all, King Arkel's fictional medieval realm Allemonde also anticipates Allemagne, Wagner's eternal musical empire.

Certainly, Croche's advice to listen to the music of the sunrise of all things has little meaning in the context of a fin de siècle opera or of the kind of decadence that is visited upon Arkel's family in so mysterious a fashion. To take Croche's advice is left to the songs of the emerging social democracy. Debussy simply got rid of Maeterlinck's opening scene, where the maids in fact watch and talk about a sunrise. Instead, in the final scene the dying Mélisande watches the Sun set through the large window that has been opened at her request. After all, according to Debussy there is "nothing more musical than a sunset; for one who sees and listens with the heart it is the best lesson to be learnt from that book which is rarely read by musicians: the Book of Nature" (178).

The disappearance of natural light makes possible a series of optical shocks that promote the stage lighting to a leading role: the moon in the underworld grotto, the light that shines from nocturnal windows, the torch that reveals to little Yniold the tears on the faces of Mélisande and Pelléas. Maeterlinck—author of a drama about twelve blind men who perish in "the primeval Nordic forest under the infinite starry sky"—replaces not only "the category of action with that of situation" (Szondi 57) but also, and more importantly, man with media technology.

This is why Debussy's opera begins in the darkness of a forest where human beings are faced with everything but cryptograms: they are simply deprived of the faculties of sight and hearing.[7] This is also why the operatic love story ends in complete accordance with the acoustically hallucinatory model of Isolde and Brangaene, rather than setting to music Debussy's doubts "about Wagner's solution," as promised.

> *Pelléas* (embraces Mélisande): Just listen, just listen, my heart is almost choking me . . . Come! Come! . . . Oh! how lovely it is in the darkness . . .
>
> *Mélisande:* I see someone behind us . . .
>
> *Pelléas:* I see no one . . .
>
> *Mélisande:* I heard a noise . . .
>
> *Pelléas:* I hear only your heart beating in the dark . . .
>
> *Mélisande:* I heard withered leaves rustling . . .
>
> *Pelléas:* That is the wind stirring up all of a sudden . . . While we were embracing, it was still . . .[8]

Pelléas is, of course, mistaken when he—unlike his more discerning lover—imagines the steps of a jealous and murderous brother to be the harmless sounds of bodies and natures, in the same way Isolde construes the hostile bugles to be the sound of a spring, or as Wagner's characters in general listen to the breathing of the other members of the cast. Yet it is precisely the impetuousness of erotic desire that once more offers the opportunity to create "in the darkness" what Nietzsche called a "perfect world of hearing" (28). Under such acoustic conditions as would soon be established technologically by the radio play, Debussy was able to compose orchestral tones that are ambivalent to the extent that the fundamental European distinction between tones and noises, music and nature, becomes blurred. On the stage and for acting ears, that which Debussy was later to propose in his essay entitled "Music in the Open Air" becomes reality—"the blowing wind, rustling leaves, the fragrance of flowers would mysteriously concur with the music"—in much the same way as it does in "gramophones," a view expressed in the same essay (49, 67).[9]

But because "a Wagnerian" will not be satisfied with this invisible "orchestral magic," Debussy "ventures" to commend, in addition to the gramophone, its technological twin, "the film as a means of optical animation" (151). Edison's two great innovations, the phonograph and the cinema, thus became the media for and technological basis of modern music. Precisely because the phonograph and cinema—being nontextual recording devices—

endanger the old "love of literature," we still have, according to Debussy, "a means of rekindling an interest in symphonic music in our contemporaries: let us bring together absolute music and film. It is film—the film strip as Ariadne's thread—that enables us to find our way out of this disturbing labyrinth" (248).

"In Wagner," Nietzsche enthused, "everything visible in the world strives to deepen and internalize itself in the audible and searches its lost soul; also in Wagner everything audible in the world strives towards light, in order to appear to the eye, to attain corporeality, as it were. His art always leads him on a double way, from a world as aural spectacle into a mysteriously related world as visual spectacle, and vice versa" (39). Since Nietzsche's prophetic words, the beautiful no longer resides in the incorporeal realm of the imagination. Rather, it is conditional on the senses or the media, which are, physiologically speaking, as distinctly separate as they are technologically interconnectable. Art is reproduced by recording media such as film and gramophone, and transmission media such as television and radio.

Let us take, on the one hand, a perfect world of hearing—without light, but with perfect reverberation and echo—and, on the other, a mysteriously related "world as spectacle"—deadly quiet, but perfectly illuminated. And the media event *Salome,* Wilde's or Strauss's, can begin.

> (A large terrace of Herod's palace, adjoining the banqueting hall. Soldiers are leaning on the balustrade. On the right an enormous staircase, left in the background an old cistern with a green bronze railing. The moon is shining very brightly.)
> *Narraboth:* How beautiful princess Salome is tonight!
> *Page:* Look at the full moon, how strange it looks. Like a woman climbing out of her grave.
> *Narraboth:* She is very strange. Like a little princess whose feet are white doves. One might think she was dancing.
> *Page:* Like a woman who is dead. She glides away slowly.[10]

Every femme fatale is the object of the erotic glances that follow her like spotlights. Salome herself, "like a woman who is dead," uses neither words nor signs except for the dancelike way of walking that distinguishes the heroines of silent films. This is why the men, from Narraboth to Herod, follow her with their eyes and words. But since fin de siècle opera theater is already film theater, a technological spotlight or projector that further automatizes all male projections is suspended above the whole interplay of glances: historically speaking, Salome's moon comes between Foucault's technological stage sun and the Jupiter lamps of future film studios. Therefore, and therefore only, the princess can become its mirror image, that is, a star.

On the old picture-frame stages ("Guckkastentheater") there was never any question of special light sources, if only because candles were the elementary, and equally secret, condition of its existence. The full moon over the Dead Sea was quite a different matter: each time it brightens or fades in Wilde's *Salome,* it is according to the author's directions. This is echoed in the characters' dialogue and in Strauss's composition. Babbage's experiment goes into serial production. And Salome—whose seven veils may or may not be the seven colors of the rainbow—incarnates Nietzsche's perfect world of seeing.

Yet, in the discourse of media technology, a perfect world of seeing can only exist if the characters are simultaneously set off against the contrast or background of a perfect world of hearing. Salome's silent film script is what it is only against the backdrop of Jochanaan's soundtrack. The essentially visible woman is brought face to face with the invisible but essentially audible prophet. The underground cistern where Herod has incarcerated the Baptist achieves an even more technological amplification of the prisoner's voice than could be achieved by any church nave, notwithstanding the fact that naves are, as we know, constructed with the aim of optimizing reverberation of the priest's words. Jochanaan's cistern becomes the horn of a gramophone. What the cursing prophet's invisible voice pits against Herod's drunken visual festivity is quite simply a recording function: Jochanaan reminds Amnesia of its own sinful past.

This confrontation of film and gramophone, of Salome and Jochanaan, can only end tragically. What comes from the prophet's mouth is the word of God; what enters Salome's ear, however, is a mere media effect. Conversely, the femme fatale who is looked at by all men only looks at Jochanaan. After Jochanaan's execution she sings:

> There was nothing in the whole world
> So red as your mouth.
> Your voice was like a vessel of incense,
> And when I looked at you
> I heard mysterious music.
> Ah! Why did you not
> Look at me, Jochanaan?
> You laid over your eyes
> The blindfold of one
> Who wanted to see his god.
> Well, you have seen your god,
> But me, me,
> Me you have never seen.
> Had you seen me,
> You would have loved me![11]

The tragedy thus unfolds between the eye and the ear, between optics and acoustics. A seeing and hearing that still hold on to the God of the Bible (and therefore of the play) are confronted with a seeing and hearing that drive their pure physiology of the senses to the point of synaesthesia. Salome does not hear a single word of Jochanaan's speech because, conversely, just seeing him is music to her ears. When he reiterates all the past sins of the dynasty, her only possible response is (impossibly):

> Speak more, Jochanaan,
> Your voice is like music
> In my ears.[12]

It is a Wagnerian answer. Under media conditions, even articulated speech dissolves into the kind of roar that Herod hears again and again in the sky, or which Brunhilde sends out to Wotan in the finale of *Götterdämmerung*. Yet when the very same Brunhilde reminds Siegfried of their common past, his response is:

> Like a miracle sounds
> What you wonderfully sing,
> But its meaning seems dark to me.
> Your shining eye
> I see bright;
> Your wafting breath I feel warm,
> Your voice's singing I hear sweet.
> But what your singing is telling me,
> Amazed, I do not understand.[13]

Having reached the technological plateau that was for a long time defined by Wagner, operas repeat the same effect over and over again: Siegfried hears breath and music in his lover's voice, but not her epic recapitulation; Pelléas hears Mélisande's heartbeat, but not his brother's footsteps; Salome hears the music of the prophet's voice, but not the message it conveys. At precisely this point—the articulated word and the notated interval of notes—at which all analysis has ended since the inception of the Greek vocal alphabet, modern ears press on. The operatic characters themselves perform a task that is possible for the technological media but not for human ears: a Fourier analysis of their own opera.

Translated by: Anja E. Belz

Notes

1. On Swan's American competitor Edison, who, among other things, lit the Paris Opera, see Clark 86–101.
2. See Babbage's technological stage direction referring to Alethes and Iris (in Hyman 312).
3. The protective wall of fire with which Wotan surrounds the sleeping Brunhilde.

83

4. See, for example, Laurie Anderson, *Mister Heartbreak*. Warner LP 925007–1, 1984.

5. On the "pure fifth sounds" in the first movement of Beethoven's Ninth Symphony, see also Wagner, *Mein Leben* 43.

6. As Nietzsche states with respect to communication systems, in media-technologically plain language, Wagner's art "cannot, as the philosopher can, be embarked on the small boat of written description" (Nietzsche 72).

7. Goland introduces his future wife with the words: "She cannot hear me. I cannot see her face" (see Maeterlinck 6).

8. Pelléas (umarmt Mélisande): "Hör nur, hör nur, mein Herz erstickt mich schier . . . Komm, Komm . . . Oh wie schön ist's in der Dunkelheit. . . ." Mélisande: "Ich sehe jemand hinter uns. . . ." Pelléas: "Ich sehe niemand. . . ." Mélisande: "Ich habe ein Geräusch gehört. . . ." Pelléas: "Ich höre nur dein Herz im Finstern schlagen. . . ." Mélisande: "Ich hörte dürre Blätter rascheln. . . ." Pelléas: "Das ist der Wind, der sich plötzlich regt. . . . Während wir uns umarmten, schwieg er still . . ." (66).

9. "Phonograph's Papa," as Edison was known in his time, thought somewhat differently: "Some people like progressive music, but very, very few," he said in confidence. "The Debussy fanatic thinks that because he loves Debussy, thousands of others must naturally love him too. He would be astonished to discover what a musical island he is living on, one scarcely discernible on the musical map of the world. The whole world wants music, but the whole world does not want Debussy, any more than it wants complicated operatic arias" (Clark 166).

10. (Eine große Terrasse im Palast des Herodes, die an den Bankettsaal stößt. Einige Soldaten lehnen sich über die Brüstung. Rechts eine mächtige Treppe, links im Hintergrund eine alte Zisterne, mit einer Einfassung aus grüner Bronze. Der Mond scheint sehr hell.) Narraboth: "Wie schön ist die Prinzessin Salome heute nacht!" Page: "Sieh die Mondscheibe, wie sie seltsam aussieht. Wie eine Frau, die aufsteigt aus dem Grab." Narraboth: "Sie ist sehr seltsam. Wie eine kleine Prinzessin, deren Füße weiße Tauben sind. Man könnte meinen, sie tanzt." Page: "Wie eine Frau, die tot ist. Sie gleitet langsam dahin" (*Salome* 5–7).

11. "In der ganzen Welt war nichts so rot wie dein Mund. / Deine Stimme war ein Weihrauchgefäß, / und wenn ich dich ansah, / hörte ich geheimnisvolle Musik. / Ah! Warum hast du mich nicht / angesehn, Jochanaan? / Du legtest über deine Augen / die Binde eines, / der seinen Gott schauen wollte. / Wohl, du hast deinen Gott gesehn, / aber mich, mich, / mich hast du nie gesehn. / Hättest du mich gesehn, / du hättest mich geliebt!" (*Salome* 331–39).

12. "Sprich mehr, Jochanaan, / deine Stimme ist wie Musik / in meinen Ohren" (*Salome* 66–67).

13. "Wunder tönt, / was wonnig du singst, / doch dunkel dünkt mich der Sinn. / Deines Auges Leuchten / seh' ich licht; / deines Atems Wehen fühl' ich warm, / deiner Stimme Singen hör' ich süß. / Doch was du singend mir sagst, / staunend versteh' ich's nicht" (*Die Musikdramen* 731–32).

References

Baumann, Carl-Friedrich. *Licht im Theater; Von der Argand-Lampe bis zum Glühlampen-Scheinwerfer*. Wiesbaden: Steiner, 1988.

Clark, Ronald W. *Edison: Der Erfinder, der die Welt veränderte.* Frankfurt am Main: Sozietätsverlag, 1981.

Debussy, Claude. *Monsieur Croche, Sämtliche Schriften und Interviews.* Ed. Francois Lesure. Stuttgart: Reclam, 1982.

Goethe, J. W. von. *Faust II.* Vol. 3 of *Werke: Hamburger Ausgabe in 14 Bänden. Dramen.* München: Beck, 1986. 146–364.

———. *Pandora.* Vol. 5 of *Werke: Hamburger Ausgabe in 14 Bänden. Dramen.* München: Beck, 1981. 332–65.

Hyman, Anthony. *Charles Babbage, 1791–1871: Philosopher, Mathematician, Computer Pioneer.* Stuttgart: Klett-Cotta, 1987.

Kittler, Friedrich. *Aufschreibesysteme 1800/1900.* Munich: Wilhelm Fink, 1985. *Discourse Networks 1800/1900.* Trans. Michael Metteer with Chris Cullens. Foreword by David E. Wellbery. Stanford: Stanford UP, 1990.

———. "Death and Destruction in Wagner's Works." *Programme Book III.* Bayreuth: Bayreuth Festival, 1987.

Lohmann, Johannes. "Die Geburt der Tragödie aus dem Geiste der Musik." *Archiv für Musikwissenschaft* 37 (1980): 172–74.

Maeterlinck, Maurice. *Pelléas und Mélisande.* Stuttgart: Reclam, 1972.

Nietzsche, Friedrich. *Richard Wagner in Bayreuth.* Ed. Giorgio Colli and Mazzino Montinari. Berlin: Carl Hanser, 1967. Vol. 1, part 4 of *Werke, Kritische Gesamtausgabe.*

Salome. Musikdrama in einem Aufzuge nach Oscar Wildes gleichnamiger Dichtung in deutscher Übersetzung von Hedwig Lachmann. Musik von Richard Strauss, opus 54. Orchester-Partitur, Fürstner Ltd., Bramstedt und Boosey & Hawkes Ltd.: London, 1938.

Scherer, Wolfgang. *Hildegard von Bingen. Musik und Minnemystik.* Freiburg im Breißgau: Traute-Hensch, 1987.

Stauder, Wilhelm. *Einführung in die Akustik.* Wilhelmshaven: Heinrichshofen, 1976.

Szondi, Peter. *Theorie des modernen Dramas.* Frankfurt am Main: Suhrkamp, 1959.

Technisches Museum Wien (Technical Museum Vienna), ed. *100 Jahre Elektrotechnik. Zum 100. Jahrestag der Gründung des Österreichischen Verbandes für Elektrotechnik.* Vienna: Eigenverlag Technisches Museum Wien, 1983.

Wagner, Richard. *Mein Leben.* Ed. Martin-Gregor Dellin. Munich: List, 1976.

———. *Tristan und Isolde.* London: Pocket Source, nd.

Wagner, Richard, and Joachim Kaiser. *Die Musikdramen.* Mit einem Vorwort von Joachim Kaiser. Hamburg: Hoffmann and Campe, 1971.

III

THE UNIVERSE AND THE
SELF: MONADS, EYEBALLS,
AND INDIVIDUALS

"Infinitely Repellent Orbs": Visions of the Self in the American Renaissance

RICHARD HARDACK

W e are thus assisted by natural objects in the expression of particular meanings. . . . Did it need . . . this host of orbs in heaven, to furnish man with the dictionary and grammar of his municipal speech?

—Emerson, "Nature" (*W* 1:32)[1]

Introduction

For most American Renaissance transcendentalists, the male self is imagined as a self-contained but permeable orb, which is both an organ of sight and an individual planet with its own orbit. This conception is the result of an American pantheism that imaginatively merges and fragments human and divine bodies into parts, which are themselves, like Emerson's eye, also at times considered wholes. The representation of these orbs and orbits tells us much about the social and taxonomical relationship of the individual to the community, the part to the whole, the particular to the All, in nineteenth-century America. In its most realistic form, political pantheism reflects the isolation of male identity and vision, the imperative that each man merge only with the All and never with other men. As a result, each man needs to maintain himself as a self-contained orb in its own orbit. In its most ideal form, social pantheism allows men to merge their bodies with one another through nature, to exist in a kind of collective, transcendent, and nondifferentiated unity with the All. The American pantheist, the most extreme form of transcendentalist, also seeks scientifically to correlate and unify all particular bodies to types, or to primordial forms, for example, to leaves and spines, and finally globes and orbs. Hence the individual eye, when rendered transparent and transcendent,

89

becomes an orb, globe, or symbol of the All. American pantheists conceive of the globular and the circular as affording a kind of embryonic unified field theory and a chain of being for all bodies. In this essay I present a narrative of what happens to the eye—the orb—in Emerson and Melville. Their version of the American self is manifested as a globular entity, and what happens to that self happens to the eye.

For the pantheist, there is a syntax, what Emerson calls a grammar of municipal speech, inherent in anatomy. The formation of eyes provides a model for the development and relationship of the parts and wholes of all natural bodies, and for the representation of those bodies. By seeing Emerson and Melville in the context of pantheism, and more specifically of Goethe as emblematic pantheist, it becomes possible to trace the logic behind Emerson's idealist merger as a transparent eyeball, a merger that for Melville inevitably leads to the political and social fragmentation of bodies, language, and vision in *Pierre*. At the juncture of the American Renaissance, Emerson's abstract union with nature replaces actual political union for the pantheist. But while the precondition for the unity, uniformity, and democratic equality of the nation is now provided by a model of universal nature and natural science, the effects are political and social. When the body of nature is substituted for the body politic—or the political body—the consequences are played out in the representation of the individual body. What we ultimately discover from Emerson's and Melville's renderings of these body parts is that transcendental pantheism is necessarily undemocratic and cannot be used to bridge the gap, or to create a union, between self as mere body part and self as unified, transcendent orb and political collective. More than a series of puns, these metonymic visual tropes, used by a wide variety of writers to locate identity, reveal how pantheism specifically enables transcendentalists to think they can elevate a body part and the organ of sight into a transcendent model for universal nature and democratic union. But their imagined visual union always leads to its own dissolution; the contradiction of an eye that represents both a visionary vehicle and a self annihilated in the All finally results in an eye that is merely a fragmentary body part.

As evinced by Emerson's self-dividing transparent eyeball and his oft-repeated depiction of his "truncated" society, or by Melville's innumerable amputees, men are parts, particular orbs, seeking to become wholes by merging with an undifferentiated nature, the universal orb. But universal or ideal nature is seamless and does not have body parts: it is globular and all-encompassing, an abstract orb. Individual men, however, always retain their identity as parts, as particular orbs, even when merged into the globular All. One's very identity then comes to be predicated on individual fragmentation, on one's status as part. One becomes this partiality, for in the transcendental outlook individuality is itself partial. In this sense, the body part, the eye, is to the body as the self is to identity.

It is not unusual to see Melville as exposing the limits of Emerson's already strained transcendentalism. But critics have failed to see the degree to which Melville uses the same specific frame of pantheism in his own work, and the extent to which the pseudoscientific, taxonomical, and morphological discourse of "ocular" pantheism determines Melville's political and social response to Emerson's idealism. The idealist use of pantheist models of nature, of nature's globular and "visual" construction, attempts to bypass but ultimately reifies the social and political structures of American society. What is first predicated on the plane of Emerson's universal natural science—in the language of visual pantheism, on universal bodies, and the transparent sphere of the All—is played out and dissolved in the sphere of Melville's political pantheism, in the language of particular bodies, fragmented orbs and orbits. Eyes are foremost the locus of human representation, so it is not surprising that altering the language of visuality changes not just one aspect of the self but all the contingent parameters of that self. By pursuing Emerson's and Melville's visual language we recuperate not just the pantheist's sense of how and why the self is like an eye—along with the discourse of pantheism's natural science, whose crucial resonance has largely been lost to us—but how this formulation generates a series of epistemological effects, particularly concerning the nature of individual and social identity. The individual self-reliant orb cannot exist in the All of nature, nor finally in the whole of society; the price of membership in either unity is the identity of the self, while the price of isolation turns out to be the fragmentation of the self as body.

Goethe and the Anatomy of Vision

Pantheists seek to unify particular bodies to type, or primordial forms—for example, the leaves and spines of Goethe's romantic taxonomy. The morphology of leaves, which will be closely connected to the representation of eyes, is largely imported to America from Germany, along with a redefinition of the relation of man to nature. A vociferous and long-running debate was staged in the American religious and popular press concerning the scientific and philosophical consequences of America's fascination with German natural science. The many polemicists for and against pantheism in America from the 1830s to the 1870s tend to focus both on pantheists' religious reveries with nature and on their predisposition toward theories of natural development or evolution. For Rev. J. M. Manning in "The Strengths and Weaknesses of Pantheism" in *Half Truths and the Truth*, the slippage of the social borders between men begins with the removal of the boundary between God and nature: "The fascination of Goethe arises in [this] way. He did not distinguish between the divine and the simply natural. He animated nature with God" (380–81).[2] This conflation of nature with god is the direct correlative of the new science of German romanticism. According to John Hunt, in *Pantheism and Christianity,* first published as a pamphlet in 1866, modern anatomy, modern theories of order, can be traced to the "unity of Goethe":

> More than ninety percent of the bones in the human skeleton have their homologies recognized by common consent in the skeletons of all vertebrata. The same uniformity recognized in the animal kingdom is acknowledged by botanists to prevail in the vegetable world . . . scientific botanists have adopted the unity of Goethe . . . every flower . . . is a metamorphosed branch . . . subject to exactly the same laws of arrangement as regularly shaped leaves . . . the principle of archetypal order. . . . (362–63)

All parts of these hierarchically developed anatomies are not merely analogous, but homologous. Soon even leaves have eyes. We are on our way to finding a single archetypal body part that can represent or encapsulate the entire body: the eye will become homologous to the self. Goethe is regarded as the founder of modern science, which becomes an Emersonian discourse of human development toward the most complex, yet most rudimentary, organ, one that is nothing but absorbs and represents all. As Manning writes,

> The history of comparative anatomy [and the so-called development theory] cannot be written without reference to [Goethe]. . . . In botany, also, Goethe's work on the Metamorphosis of Plants may be said to have suggested, if it did not originate, what is now the distinctive doctrine and boasted glory of modern science . . . that all plants conform to a single type in their structure; that in their development . . . they only repeat the universal type. . . . The unity of nature was with him a transcendental truth. (198–99)

The separate discourses of comparative anatomy and the unities of nature converge in Emerson, who resituates them in an American context and provides an essentially botanical and visual system of representation for American transcendentalists. For Emerson, all such "development" leads to the eye, which is his final universal type.

American Renaissance writers were familiar with a variety of scientific treatises that proposed that all organic forms were based on universal models and conjured a veritable assembly line of evolution. Robert Chambers, whose 1844 *Vestiges of the Natural History of Creation* establishes the proto-evolutionary theory of development, writes that "the *pitcher,* as this is called, is not a new organ, but simply a metamorphose of a leaf. These facts show

how all the various organic forms of our world are bound up in one—how a fundamental unity pervades and embraces them all'' (197). Such visions of archetypal order and what is endlessly called "the unity of nature" are derived directly from Goethe; through his morphology the plant body is traced backward to the leaf, which as we shall soon see is also an eye or lobe. The human body is in effect evolved into a single organ, an eye, which signifies the coherence of all organic forms. A metamorphose of the self, this eye is not a new organ but the final representation of the fundamental unity of nature, at least until Melville has his say.

A fundamental unity seems also to embrace the naturalists of the American Renaissance. During the nineteenth century, Americans particularly favored circular forms, the globular, the eye. A wide variety of authors in distinct disciplines—writers of treatises of natural science, religious polemics, and even legal tracts—used this same visual language, as exemplified by the following excerpt from *The Panidea,* written in the 1840s by Job Durfee, the chief justice of Rhode Island. According to Durfee, whose work includes a chapter on "Spheres, Sensuous and Supersensuous,"

> Acting through its sensuous sphere, [substance] tends to assimilate all matter to the globular form. . . . It tends from beneath, to reduce all things to the globular form. . . . Of these inconceivably vast masses, that are accumulated in the depths of space, portions may acquire, from the very accumulation, distinct centres, and so separate into orbs, and systems of orbs. So the whole human race, though acted upon by the same assimilative energy, separates into distinct nations and communities. (427)[3]

One enormous orb or globular form, the sphere of the All, is reduced to separate, distinct orbs. In the reverse direction, bodies, individual orbs, merge into larger spheres. Worlds, nations, and selves, and finally the body parts of those selves, are then variations on this globular form, this pan-idea. These globular entities represent the height of the pantheist's taxonomical model, and provide a kind of ur-language and organ; the eye/orb exists before everything but is also the form to which everything develops, the beginning and end of the circle of representation.

The redefinition of God as nature or natural law is coterminous with the redefinition of the models of human and plant anatomy. Under the influence of eighteenth- and nineteenth-century German natural science, those who study nature come to new conclusions about its creation and its transcendent meaning. All of nature now reflects a universal, uniform circularity; and the self that allegedly does not merely reflect but generates that model must then also emerge as universal and circular. This process begins with the linguistic and taxonomic reevaluation of the bodies of nature. In the penultimate chapter

93

of *Walden,* Thoreau goes a bit further off the limb than usual and claims that "in the globe or animal body" literally all forms are constructed from the manipulations of lobes, or leaves; the animal body is itself an orb. We again begin with a Goethean morphology, and here wind up with a universal thaw of the globe's linguistic and material viscera: ". . . the earth expresses itself outwardly in leaves . . . the atoms have already learned this law, and are pregnant by it. The overhanging leaf sees here its prototype. . . . The whole tree itself is but one leaf, and rivers are still vaster leaves. . . . Is not the hand a spreading *palm* leaf with its lobes and veins? The ear may be regarded, fancifully, as a lichen . . . with its lobe or drop. . . . The Maker of this earth but patented a leaf" (204). Thoreau launches into a lengthy (and without this context thoroughly bizarre) digression on the linguistic origin of these leaves, which are themselves ultimately lobes or globes, and the basis for the structure of all matter. From Goethe's morphology of leaves we inevitably reach the all-encompassing orb, moving from atom to earth: "No wonder that the earth expresses itself in leaves. . . . Internally, whether in the globe or animal body, it is a moist thick lobe . . . [*lobos* in Greek] globus, lobe, globe. . . . The very globe continually transcends and translates itself, and becomes winged in its orbit" (205).[4] Thoreau's "translation" is not just linguistic; it produces a literal transformation from leaf to lobe. All leaves are then lobes themselves; the leaf can be converted to a lobe, a globe, an orb. If we compare Goethe's taxonomy and American transcendentalism, we always wind up with, as it were, a single vision. Through the transcendentalists' belief in natural transformation, all objects can be correlated to archetypal forms; once the veil of nature is lifted, everything is translated into an eye. In all natural and social sciences, the maker of all but patented a leaf, a lobe, an orb.

In this same language, Emerson's spheres and orbs of natural and social bodies then serve to situate all individual and social bodies against one another. The redefinition of nature as divine remains inextricable from the conception of man as individual and universal orb. Such a formulation begins with the substitution of nature or natural law for an anthropomorphic god, and ends with the recalibration of man's relation to nature and of his systems of self-representation. In his early lecture on Luther, Emerson already locates Goethe as a representative pantheist: "There has never been since Luther a great man of the first class who believed as he did. . . . All others . . . Newton, Leibniz . . . Goethe have joined Nature to Revelation to form their religion or like Spinoza, Rousseau, Laplace have worshipped like the Indian, Nature alone" (Whicher and Spiller 1:132).[5] Goethe's pantheism, coupled with his taxonomy, helps determine the disposition of the eye in the American Renaissance. According to Emerson's paraphrase of Goethe, "Eyes are better on the whole than telescopes or microscopes. He has contributed a key to many parts of nature, through the rare turn for unity and simplicity in his mind. Thus

Goethe suggested the leading ideas of modern botany, that . . . the eye of a leaf is the unit of botany, and that every part of a plant is only a transformed leaf'' (''Goethe,'' *W* 4:275).

As Emerson unwittingly attests, eyes are indeed ''better on the whole,'' and they provide the organ of simple unity and of all correlation, the seat not of consciousness but of representation. Every object is only a transformed leaf, lobe, or eye. For Emerson, Goethe's taxonomy cannot be separated from his pantheism, nor, as we shall see, the ''simple'' unit and unity of the eye from the archetypal botany supporting it. The ''eye'' of this leaf will appear everywhere in American Renaissance transcendentalism: we have so far only glimpsed the tip of the pyramid. Quoting Goethe, Emerson insists that ''it is in the stomach of plants that development begins, and ends in the circles of the universe'' (''The Sovereignty of Ethics,'' *W* 10:186). Such a process, which either begins or ends in eyes and orbs, epitomizes Emerson's use of Goethe's morphology and ontology; life begins in ''every globe from the remotest heaven . . . from the first principal of growth in the eye of a leaf,'' is built up through vertebrae—''spine upon spine'' as Emerson says—and ends once more as an enormous eye, the very circle of the universe (''Nature,'' *W* 1:40). The orb, which represents the individual, but globular and whole man, is the center of the universe; the transparent, transcendent eye of man and the eye of the leaf represent the first principles, the very genesis, of nature. According to Emerson, in what sounds like a direct paraphrase of Job Durfee's globular pantheism,

> Nature centres into balls,
> And her proud ephemerals,
> Fast to surface and outside,
> Scan the profile of the sphere;
> Knew what they signified,
> A new genesis were here. (''Circles,'' *W* 2:299)

These globular balls, which create and order the universe, always begin with the eye and end with God, forming a closed circle: ''The eye is the first circle; the horizon which it forms is the second; and throughout nature this primary figure is repeated without end. It is the highest emblem in the cipher of the world. St. Augustine described the nature of God as a circle whose centre was everywhere and its circumference nowhere'' (''Circles,'' *W* 2:301). This universe is a circular eye, necessarily ubiquitous, and, like Emerson's mortal eye, it ''forms'' or turns all it sees into uniform, spherical, and thus wholly representative or archetypal objects. (This universe also represents a closed male circle with no reproduction or extinction, only the circulation of preexisting matter.) For the yet-to-be-disillusioned pantheist, these orbs in their concentric orbits, though all representative ciphers, connote only the perfect circles of heaven, and neither a duplicitous mirroring nor a circumscription of the self.

Early on, Emerson transports his transcendental pantheist, as he would soon transport himself, from the enclosure of churches to nature's field of vision:

> When the student of nature, quitting the simplicity and perfectness of natural laws, came into the churches and colleges . . . they there found such gross and unworthy views of [God] as not agreed but contrasted with their own conclusions respecting the cause of Nature . . . the removing of this veil from the creation enabl[ed] man from the little globule in which we are embarked to send his eye so far into the surrounding infinity . . . [bringing] to light the most wonderful proofs of design—beneficial design—operating far and near in atoms and in systems . . . [proving that all things] fluctuate between fixed and impassable limits, that there is no ungoverned orb, no loose pin, no lawless particle . . . planet gravitates to planet and star attracts star, each fulfilling the last mile of its orbit. (McGiffert 175–76)[6]

Such images of divine nature are yoked to this vision of universal orbits. The "governed" orb remains the sign of universal order, planetary unity, and the coherence of parts to wholes. From his globular planet, man casts his transcendent eye onto the universal orbit. Each particle or individual atom bears the same determinant shape and is subject to the same laws as each planetary orb. The orbit is the inescapable circular path of the orb—predictable, coherent, and recursive; each orb creates another orb, a larger version of itself, by following this orbit.

Envisioning an aggregate, system, nation, or globe held in its orbit, the young Emerson preaches that "every atom contributes its part to gravity, and the vast attractions that hold the globe together and keep it in its orbit are made up of the separate attractions of all the atoms" (Bosco 155). The orbits of globes and the gravity of the eye keep the world together, and God or the All resides at the center of any of these circumferences: "Happiness is the sense of well being that results from the soul's health, and there only can all its faculties revolve in their orbit and every inclination keep its place when God is in the centre of the system" (16).[7] For the most, Emerson imagines that the orbs and orbits of the universe will coexist harmoniously: "The sky with its eternal calm, and full of everlasting orbs, is the type of Reason" ("Nature," *W* 1:27). God, or a divinely merged self, resides at the center of a universal circumference, is in fact this universal orb, throughout Emerson's works: his eye holds all the separate atoms, the parts, together. That God is All, and the All of nature is Pan. We must now remember that it is while walking in the woods, beneath the leaves or lobes of trees, under Goethe's and Thoreau's botanical elysium, that Emerson first turns into an organ of sight.

In "Nature"—whose original title was actually "Pan," and all of whose

original references to "Pan" were replaced by "Nature" at publication—
Emerson writes that within the "plantations of god . . . in the woods . . . [I
am] bathed by the blithe air and uplifted into infinite space—all mean egotism
vanishes. I become a transparent eyeball. I am nothing; I see all; the currents
of the Universal Being circulate through me; I am part and parcel of God"
(*W* 2:10–11). In the All of nature, Emerson metamorphoses into the very
model, the ur-organ, of transcendental anatomy. This passage offers not just
Emerson's famous image of the transcendental American self as eyeball, but
the necessary conjunction of such a self with a pantheistic vision of God.
Emerson had unequivocally preached in a sermon that to be nothing and see
all is in fact to *be* God, to be All: he became able to see "not [with] man's
eye, which sees a little, but . . . the eye of God, which sees all" (Toulouse and
Delbanco 127).[8] (In his poem "The Eternal Pan," Emerson even describes
Pan as a deity who "hides in pure transparency": though invisible to the
uninitiated, Pan sees all. For Emerson, as he writes in "The Genuine Man,"
when man is one with the divinity, "where the mind has no low ends . . .
[man] is transparent." Believing that the true poet can at times virtually pass
his hand through his body, Emerson repeatedly asserts that "the Universe is
transparent; the light of higher laws than its own, shines through it" [*JMN*
6:219]. Such transparency, which for Emerson always bears an attendant per-
meability and immateriality, is not merely a form of honesty, but of nonexist-
ence: as Emerson attests, "I am nothing.") At the very outset of Emerson's
Works, the self in fact disappears, is transcended, and then becomes merged
with the All, the Universal Being, as a transparent eyeball or orb. The circular
currents of the Universal Being, that All of Pan, flow through Emerson the
orb. Emerson's transparent eyeball would supplant all traces of Emerson himself; in order to be nothing, not be seen, and see all, he leaves behind all
particularity or individuality, which is absorbed by the body of the universe,
its all-seeing eye. The transition from self to All is foremost one of radical
disproportion, with a body part being elevated to the level of the whole, an
eye replacing the self. Already Emerson has provided Melville with what will
become Pierre's anatomy, not of universal merger, but of bodily fragmentation.

In effect, this image of the transparent eyeball both reifies and disposes
of the truncated man of "The American Scholar," the man in society who is
multiply amputated: "a good finger, a neck, an elbow, but never a man" (*W*
1:83). For this is exactly the operation Emerson performs on himself; to figure
oneself as a transparent eyeball is to leave the individual blind, sighted only
insofar as he individually ceases to exist. Sight, which occludes the I, is then
by its very nature a form of divine fragmentation and inhuman unity; the
body is reduced/enlarged to a single eye, but the eye becomes an entire body.
Emerson's transformation is a form of union with the body of the All, but also

a fragmentation into mere body part; this is why for Melville, and even for Emerson, the pantheist always oscillates between the sublime and the ironic, the divine and the demonological. In the terms of pantheism, the truncated man of society and the sublime poet of nature are rendered parts trying to be wholes: "Once man was all: now he is an appendage" ("Divinity School Address," *W* 1:127). Once man was Pan, now he is only the appendage of the All. In this case, the appendage or organ is the eye, the proposed recompense for a man who once existed before society, who was Edenically All or God, and one with nature: a subject who was simultaneously an object; and the observer who was not split from himself, the man who once could see and be at the same time.

Emerson and the Divine Orbit

In the American Renaissance, the rhetoric of eyes and I's is consistently conflated, and orbs of seeing always remain in flux with orbs of being. But the orb or eyeball does far more than see; it necessitates a field of gravity and a series of orbits around itself. Vision represents not just a way to validate the underlying, a priori connectedness of things—things that for Emerson are all made of the "same stuff"—but a force of attraction and repulsion, and vision itself generates connectedness through what Emerson calls "optical relation." Seeing is never a passive endeavor; it generates being. The eye goes beyond interpreting to "imprisming" and reproducing what is seen. What Emerson calls the "plastic power of the human eye"—the very rhetoric he ubiquitously uses to describe "all-plastic nature"—is the power to absorb and retransmit the external world: nature's unity "seems partly owing to the eye itself" ("Nature," *W* 1:15). But such Emersonian insights into the sublime merger of the I with the All inevitably give way to more horrific or uncanny apprehensions of bodily and visual disjunction.

The American self is systemically seen as an orb that sees and travels in wholly overlapping, or else unique and incommensurate, orbits. That self is either merged with and absorbed by the All or the democratic mass—the self that transcends individuality—or kept inordinately self-reliant and self-contained—the self that never merges, but either remains isolated or, like Ahab, without merging merely accretes other bodies to his. This process of social osmosis is again best reflected in the disposition of Emerson's orbs. For the young Emerson, even before "The American Scholar," it is the unnatural conscription of solitary men to society that generates the bodily projection and fragmentation pantheism would attempt to render a divine merger with the All. In 1838, after delivering lectures on, respectively, "The Doctrine of the Hands," "The Head," and "The Eye and the Ear," Emerson concludes in "The Heart" that "man is insular and cannot be touched. Every man is an infinitely repellent orb, and holds his individual being on that condition. In fact, men are continually separating and not nearing by acquaintance. . . . Best amputate'' (Whicher and Spiller 2:280). Here the eye represents not a unified and regulated All, but one element in a field of universal billiards. Instead of an eye uplifted into ''infinite space,'' the orbs here become infinitely repellent. Each man is a self-contained orb and can bear no impingement without literally losing his globular integrity and falling to pieces. Once the pantheist snaps out of his metaphysical reverie—as he always does, typically as the result of some individual physical sensation, such as digestion, evacuation, or pain—each man's gravitational field, his magnetism, his influence, becomes too strong. He must repel others, especially his family, for when they get too close he absorbs their bodies to his own orbit (or, even worse, they absorb his orbit to theirs; it becomes all the more ironic yet appropriate that Melville insisted that he did not oscillate in Emerson's rainbow, in his ''swing,'' in his orbit). In Emerson's language, men must then separate ''by acquaintance,'' be repelled, and this repulsion is often conceived as an amputation. It tells us much about how to approach the corpus of his contradictory, ''amputated,'' and almost ''untouchable'' works that Emerson also conceives of his own writing in these same terms; he writes to Carlyle that he considers his own compositions ''the most fragmentary result: paragraphs incomprehensible each sentence an infinitely repellent particle'' (Leverenz 42).[9]

American pantheists consistently imagine male bodies as orbiting globes; these animated bodies collide and repel, and by ''acquaintance''—social and physical interaction, or even mere proximity—merge and amputate. For Emerson, men's bodies must then become inverted magnets. Here we see the direct connection for Emerson between amputation and orbs: the fragmented man of society, the walking appendage, is also a repellent orb. To become an orb is then to reach the whole while also being reduced to an amputated part. In this cryptic, almost Lawrencian passage, Emerson further pursues his psychic polarity, a form of merger with the universe: ''The universe is the bride of the soul. A private sympathy is partial. Two human beings are like globes, which can touch only in one point, and, whilst they remain in contact, all other points of each of the spheres are inert; . . . and the longer a particular union lasts, the more energy of appetency the parts not in union acquire'' (''Experience,'' W 3:77). Since each man is the universe, Emerson also avers that if man joins himself to others, ''the stricter the union the less & more pitiful he is.'' In Emerson's version of the American and divine union, merger with men, and even participation in democracy, diminishes the self; any union that unites self with anything less than the universe renders one partial, truncated, and, paradoxically, diminished or amputated.

For the young Emerson, the orb provided a model of universal merger, a way for the self to become whole, and for that globular whole to absorb all variety or discord in a unity that suffers no fragmentation. Emerson had once promised, "There is no revolt in all the kingdoms from the commonweal; no detachment of an individual. Hence the catholic character which makes every leaf an exponent of the world" (*W* 1:201). This leaf remains the model of the lobe or globe, part of the catholic or universal nature of the universe: it should never become detached or lose the universal orbit. For the transcendentalist, microcosmic representation is made possible by the integrity of parts to their extrapolated wholes; each leaf, lobe, or orb represents, is an exponent for, the entire world. But even Emerson eventually discovers that this is the "age of detachment," and the catholic character of the commonweal dissolves. Each individual necessarily becomes a rebel orb, an "ungoverned" orb, a "lawless particle" detached, amputated, and cast out of the universal orbit. It is here that Emerson's circular chain of being also comes undone. Emerson once believed in "the eternal chain of cause and effect which pervades Nature, which threads the globes as beads on a string" ("Immortality," *W* 8:344). These eternal chains tether each individual orb to the universal center. But once the orbit of the I, the coherence of the chain, is lost, each orb careens to chaos: "Let him loosen one moment the invisible link which binds atom to atom which we call *cohesion*—what makes one particle of granite adhere without cement to another particle of granite. . . . Or let snap the chain by which creation holds. . . . Loose the ethereal cord and how would each orb start from its path into a lawless track . . . into pure destruction of all life" (Toulouse and Delbanco 257–58). Once Melville loosens this chain, the orbs begin to spin in ungoverned and unpredictable paths; without the globular forces of gravity and cohesion, without the circular chain of creation, the orb once merged with the All is cut off from life itself.

Not only are these all-encompassing circular images treated as serious scientific models of nature, but, more importantly, they determine the nature of social models for human identity. At their most rudimentary, the individual eye and the transparent eyeball represent the individual body and the mass body of democracy (or the mass body of a divine nature). All of Emerson's self-reliant individuals, whom he calls "repellent orbs," will, as Carolyn Porter suggests, try to see and be in opposition.[10] Despite Emerson's faith in transcendence, the transparent eyeball can never do both at once, and it can never truly exist in society. To avoid merger with the All of society, Emerson merges with the All of nature. Emerson thus desires his orbit to be the universal, but also the only, orbit, to incorporate to itself the All of society. In Emerson's woods and commons, even a second orb would decenter the entire globe. In the transparent eyeball, the seeing eye-orb and the being I-orb (or world-orb) become schizophrenically cross-eyed with one another. Emerson, the all-embracing transparent eyeball who is also a repellent orb, straightforwardly notes in optical terms his fear of the very pantheistic merger he pursues: "I had better never see a book than to be warped by its attraction clean out of my own orbit, and made a satellite instead of a system" ("The American Scholar," W 1:90). (He also asserts that the monomaniac, the man who "fastens his attention on a single aspect of truth," will in effect get caught "in the hoop of [another's] horizon" ["Intellect," W 2:339].) To be too close to another person, another orb, always entails becoming subject to his orbit and what is propitiously known as his sphere of influence. Books and people often exert a kind of organic influence, a botanical/visual magnetism, on the allegedly self-reliant Emerson. Because "of the presence, or the general *influence* of any substance as of . . . a living plant," Emerson imagines a proto-Lawrencian field of nature; this influence parallels the effect of gravity on any smaller globe: "And I can as easily dodge the gravitation of the globe as escape your *influence*" ("The Method of Nature," W 1:216; emphases mine). Influence is a form of gravity, causing the orb to lose its orbit. As Melville puts it in *The Confidence Man:* "For much the same reason that there is but one planet to one orbit, so can there be but one such original character to one work of invention. Two would conflict to chaos" (246–47). More than one character to a book or an orbit "is good presumption there [are] none at all." In the end, individual men can only be body parts to the whole, unified body of the universe; when they orbit near each other, chaos ensues. The world simply isn't big enough for two transparent eyeballs, for it would then become two worlds.

Melville and the Melancholy of Anatomy

According to Rev. J. M. Manning, in his chapter "Pantheism in the Form of Self-Worship," pantheism effectively inverts the natural order of things; man does not see and represent the universe—the universe represents itself through man. To Manning's pantheist, for whom the world comes to consciousness in man, "We human beings are, as it were, but the innumerable individual eyes through which the infinite world-spirit regards itself": we are just a means for the living universe to see and talk to itself (137). It is emphatically not Emerson's eye, but Pan's, the oversoul's or world-spirit's, that sees as a transparent, all-encompassing organ. For Emerson, too, "each person is only a piece of the universe made alive," equally a way for the universe to see itself (*JMN* 10:278). You become a transcendent piece of this living universe, a whole, when you are translated into its organ of over-sight.

Early in his career, Melville both adapts and consciously parodies such Emersonian theories of orbs and identity. In *Mardi,* Melville's deranged staging of Emersonian pantheism, Mohi is asked if he has seen proof of the divinity; he replies, no, "but the whole archipelago has." The world of Mardi is then a pantheistic, collective awareness defining itself and everything in its line of sight: "Mardi is a monster whose eyes are fixed in its head, like a whale's; it can see but two ways, and those comprising but a small arc of perfect vision. Poets, heroes, and men of might are all around this monster Mardi. But stand before me on stilts, or I will behold you not, says the monster" (329). Mardi is a seeing-eye world to the blind men inhabiting it. And it is a living body whose primary shape and function are that of the globular eye. Despite its imperfect field of vision, its ability to recognize only the genius, or the man on the shoulders of giants, Mardi has perceived what one man has not—the unified world, the sum of its parts: " 'Thus,' exclaimed Babbalanja, 'does Mardi, blind though it be in many things, collectively behold the marvels which one pair of eyes sees not' " (302). Though it has two eyes like a whale—a depiction Melville returns to in his meditations on metaphysical circularity and physical wheels and whirlpools throughout *Moby Dick*—Mardi is still a single collective orb. (Each individual orb becomes the Emersonian emblem of that world-orb: a concealed face "expose[d] a solitary eye. But that eye was a world" [*M* 164].) Through the Emersonian mixing of bodies and metaphors, the universal, detachable eye of transcendentalism needs only the tongue of the poet to animate its world. Pantheists accumulate body parts—eyes, kidneys, hands—into a giant being, imagined as either Gaea or a monster that is the world. God becomes an animated, embodied nature, an Emersonian "over-body" whose parts accomplish what man cannot. Melville starts with the same single detachable eye as Emerson: Babbalanja asks, winking: "Can that eye see itself, Yoomy? Taken out of its socket, will it see at all? Its connection with the body imparts to it its virtue." To which Mohi replies, "He questions everything. Philosopher, have you a head?" (*M* 402). For Mohi, the detachable eye of the transcendent postindividual sees what the man in himself cannot see, even as Mardi sees what individual men cannot. At this stage of Melville's career, Mardi is only Emerson's detached and merged orb translated into the larger globe of the world.

While commonly not considered a transcendentalist, Melville is as absorbed by the rhetoric of pantheism—for example, by orbs, fragmented bodies, and merger with a transcendent, divine nature—as Emerson. Melville writes to Hawthorne, "In reading some of Goethe's sayings, so worshipped by his votaries, I came across this, '*Live in the all*.' That is to say, your separate identity is but a wretched one—good; but get out of yourself, spread and expand yourself, and bring to yourself the tinglings of life that are felt in the flowers and the woods, that are felt in the planets Saturn and Venus, and the Fixed Stars" (Davis and Gilman 130–31). (Although Melville finds this proposition absurd, he can never reject such a possibility, and he always oscillates between longing and irony.) In the terminology of Emerson, one of Goethe's votaries, Melville is tempted to spread and expand his body until it becomes the entire world (a move Emerson repeatedly makes, for example, in a dream

in which the protagonist is eating the whole world as if it were an apple).
To the pantheist, men's bodily orbs are also like colliding planets; Melville
frequently depicts planets as men with distinct personalities. These orbs are
consistently invoked in conjunction with the One and the All of pantheism,
and with merging with nature. In *Mardi,* "Saturn, Mercury, and Mardi [were]
brothers, one and all, and across their orbits to each other talked like souls"
(511). Redburn, too, at first experiences a pantheistic reverie, one associated
with Goethe's taxonomy of archetypal and unified bodies, in finding himself
merged with his ship and the orbiting universe. The connection between an
animated anatomy and Pan, the All, is explicitly suggested by Redburn himself, who intimates he is as aware of Goethe's *Metamorphoses of Plants* as
Emerson:

> I think it would not be a bad plan to have a grand new naming of a
> ship's ropes, as I have read, they once had of the classes of plants in
> Botany . . . the various parts of the human body; which, indeed, is
> something like a ship; its bones be the stiff standing rigging, and the
> sinews the small running ropes. . . . Every mast and timber seemed
> to have a pulse in it that was beating with life and joy; and I felt a
> wild exulting in my own heart. . . . Then was I first conscious of a
> wonderful thing in me, that responded to all the wild commotion of
> the outer world; and went reeling on and on with the planets in their
> orbits, and was lost in one delirious throb at the center of the All. (*R*
> 118–19)[11]

A ship that is literally alive, like a living world, is animated by a pantheistic
nature and merges us with the orbit of the All. This is a complicated passage,
but we can trace the pantheist's animation of the inanimate world to the orbiting eye; we begin with the morphology of plants as applied to the inanimate
world, proceed through a merger with nature, and wind up in a deliriously
Emersonian orbit. Redburn first suggests giving his ship a Goethean botanical
classification, translated to human vertebrae. In other words, his living ship
has evolved, and is composed not just analogously, but homologously, to the
human body; such a taxonomical revelation leaves Redburn in pantheistic reverie, in unity, with Goethe's or Emerson's orbiting All of nature. That All is
represented by a self that becomes one throbbing eye/I at the center of a
globular universe that is itself only a giant orb. Until Melville's Pierre, neither
Emerson nor Redburn nor any other pantheist becomes two eyeballs—they all
become a single cyclopean eye at the center of the All. The pantheist's vision
of the sublime then also renders Redburn another version of a transparent orb,
one with a living universe. (And throughout Melville's work, the globular
world is constructed like a specifically throbbing human body. Mardi, in the
"slow, majestic throbbings of its heart, perceptible . . . in the tides of the

lagoon,'' and the innumerable ships Melville consistently describes as living creatures, are "alive to their axes" [*M* 378].) At this stage, Melville still primarily echoes and only playfully parodies Emerson's formulations of the ocular and orbiting self. This stage does not last.

In his earlier works, Melville, like Emerson, pursues merger with a universal or common orbit, and a subsequent union or amalgam of bodies: he, too, imagines as yet no ungoverned orb. But Melville and his characters cannot overcome the repulsion of orbs or bodies, which finally do not bear allegiance even to themselves. As we have seen, much of the rhetoric of bodily or corporal pantheism comes to America through German romanticism.[12] Germans are specifically blamed in the religious press of the day for American transcendentalism and the substitution of nature and theories of development for a god of creation. Melville, too, finds a Germanic scapegoat for a theosophy and body politic gone awry. For Melville, Goethe finally becomes not just the corrupter of youth but the representative corrupter of natural identity, a model not of universal fraternity but of universal fratricide. After his many attempts to become a "soft-social pantheist," to merge into the All of a communal male society, Melville's Pierre rejects Goethe's "corporate pantheism" as a philosophy of ineluctable bodily fragmentation; all through the second half of *Pierre,* male bodies, including Goethe's, are partitioned and amputated rather than unified. After initially dramatizing the possibilities of becoming an enormous eye in *Mardi,* Melville by the time of *Pierre* has rejected Goethe's and Emerson's orbs. Emerson's overdetermined eye-I-orb-orbit configurations effectively implode in the character of Pierre, whose self becomes a part of his own body, an orb-bit. Suffice it to say—as Pierre soon discovers in the dismembered torso of the Titan Enceladus—that what Emerson viewed as the threat of disharmony and rebellion is incarnated in the extremities of our bodies. Pierre's hopes for American democracy literally come apart with his body, a body that cannot merge with or coexist in the orbit of any others.

In a letter to Hawthorne written just before he began *Pierre,* Melville at first associates Goethe's "all feeling" with his own version of natural transparency, and he remembers feeling his legs sending out shoots, his hair feeling like leaves (Davis and Gilman 142). The lobe comes full circle. Melville's next creation, Pierre, also at first seeks "the refuge of the god-like population of the trees. . . . Their high foliage shall drop heavenliness" upon him: with his feet in "contact with their might roots, immortal vigor" will steal into him (*P* 134). Melville and Pierre begin the same process of natural immersion that leads to Emerson's transcendental transformation to all-orb. But, like his creator, Pierre ultimately finds he cannot lose his individual identity to nature without relinquishing the coherence of his body. In his assertion and retraction of his own pantheistic impulses, Melville winds up chiding Goethe for telling a man with a raging toothache to merge with nature and "live in the all." In the very same timbre, Pierre writes on a scrap of paper, one of many scattered on the floor around him: ''Away, ye . . . who once did delude me that . . . pain was only a tickle . . . thou inconceivable coxcomb of a Goethe. . . . Already the universe gets on without thee, and could still spare a million more of the same identical kidney. Corporations have no souls, and thy Pantheism, what was that? Thou wert but the pretentious, heartless part of a man'' (*P* 342). Pierre then cannot escape the somatic fate of Goethe, and of his pantheistic disciple Emerson; in fact, his body is even figuratively dismembered to produce his book. Like Emerson's, Pierre's eye is still the organ of representation itself. With the failure of Goethe's pantheism soon comes the inevitable dissolution of the pantheist orb predicated on male merger with nature. ''A special corporeal affliction now descended like a sky-hawk'' upon Pierre: ''His incessant application told upon his eyes. . . . They became so affected . . . he wrote with the lids nearly closed . . . sometimes he blindly wrote with his eyes turned away from the paper'' (*P* 381). (The following action completes an arc begun in *Omoo,* where nature conspires to mark a scurrilous character with split vision: ''with a villainous cast in one [eye], they seemed suspicious of each other'' [*O* 142]. The lost Melvillean character bears a body at odds with its self, most visibly expressed in the disposition of his eyes.) ''Solitary as at the pole,'' Pierre cannot merge with any collective humanity, and instead finds that even his own body has insufficient gravity to hold itself together: ''But now at last since the very blood in [Pierre's] body had in vain rebelled against his Titanic soul; now the only visible outward symbols of that soul—his eyes—did also turn downright traitors to him, and with more success than the rebellious blood. . . . The pupils of his eyes rolled away from him in their own orbits'' (*P* 383). Emerson's universal or fraternal orbit, the catholic coherence of his commonweal, has been entirely lost. This is the culmination of Goethe's philosophy expressed as the ends of his anatomical systems; more than one orb is traveling in the same orbit, conflicting to chaos. No single, transcendent orb awaits Pierre. Men choose their own conflicting orbits in Pierre's democracy, until finally the parts of these men assume their own orbits as well. When pantheism falls apart, its collapse is represented in the political fragmentation of the body; our ''ungoverned'' eyes see what they will and do not recognize their neighbors in the body. This moment delivers the dramatic resolution of Pierre's life and body; his versions of transparent eyeballs, the very symbols of his soul, cannot even recognize their host. Pierre's dismemberment represents Melville's final rejection of Emerson's organs.

Finally in *Pierre,* what ''time crushed in the egg''—as Pierre later imagines ''crushing [Goethe in his hand] like an egg from which the meat hath been sucked''—suggests that the reproduction of being or orbs incurs violent truncation (*P* 28, 342). For the pantheist, seeing is itself a form of male replication of ideal forms—seeing reproduces being. To be denied sight, as Pierre

105

so emphatically discovers, is in the most Oedipal terms also to be denied progeny. Instead of being all, a universal orb, Pierre winds up not being at all. Pierre simply does not have the orbs to procreate with vision or with bodies. Goethe's eggs or orbs, the balls that more likely be than see, fall victim to Pierre's abstract and finally reflexive rage; this violence represents the very amputation or castration of male orbs Emerson so frequently invokes. (When Emerson loses his eponymous son Waldo, who is imagined to be a part of his own body, he tells Carlyle that he feels as if an eye had been plucked out [Leverenz 65 or Slater 20]. Still paralleling Emerson in *Mardi,* Melville had described a character as "saying that he was quite blind, for some months previous he had lost one eye in the death of his eldest son, and now the other was gone. 'I am childless—henceforth call me Roi Mori. That is, twice blind' " [*O* 254]. Even in later symbolically ridding himself of Emerson in *Pierre,* Melville thus retains the same visual language of the offending eye he wishes to remove. For Melville's men, the act of seeing remains indistinguishable from the process of reproduction.) In *Pierre,* Melville has then staged the rebellion and violent dissolution of Emerson's transparent orb, the self that would merge with and see through the All. Because he cannot see, Pierre cannot be; he can no longer reproduce himself even in writing, nor determine whether it was his vision or his self that was first denied.[13]

Notes

1. All references to Emerson, unless otherwise noted, are indicated by *W* for *Works* or *JMN* for *Journals and Miscellaneous Notebooks.* References to Melville are indicated by *CM* for *The Confidence Man, M* for *Mardi, O* for *Omoo, P* for *Pierre,* and *R* for *Redburn.*
2. For a comprehensive historical introduction to the determinant role natural science played in shaping the epistemology, aesthetics, and literary influence of German romanticism, see Cunningham and Jardine.
3. Obliquely enough, the following passage from Nathaniel West's *The Dream Life of Balso Snell* invokes the same form of globular or unifying pantheism, here in some sense imported from European painters: "If the world is one [everything part of the same thing—called by Picasso "nature"] then nothing either begins or ends. Only when things take the shapes of eaches, everys, anys, eithers [have ends] do they have feet . . . Cezanne said, 'everything tends toward the globular' " (64). The opposing fragmentary rhetoric of pantheism, of wholes gone to parts and whole bodies amputated to bits, is also inflected in the dismemberments of West's *A Cool Million,* and particularly Lemuel Pitkin's loss of his eye: "Then another lucky accident occurred. When Lem bent awkwardly to pick up his teeth, the glass eye that Mr. Hiney had given him popped from his head and smashed to smithereens on the floor. . . . What kind of a pretty boy was this that came apart so horribly?" (114). I would argue that American pantheism provides a kind of missing link between the American Renaissance—e.g., Tocqueville's take

on pantheism in *Democracy in America*—and modernism for writers like West and D. H. Lawrence—e.g., his take on pantheism in "Pan in America." As an impersonal nature is deified and an anthropomorphic god is rejected, natural law continues to appear to the modernist, as it did to nineteenth-century pantheists, as potentially transcendent and unifying, but in practice mechanical and fragmenting

4. In the context of *Walden*'s more "visceral" approach to nature, Thoreau reconfigures Emerson's globe as a lobe directly affected by gravity, by proximity to the globe of the earth; as such it is rendered more material and specific than Emerson's abstract orbs.

5. Leibniz believes in the pantheistic representation of the many in the one, and his monads, filtered through further refinements in natural science, provide a specific basis for much of Emerson's visual rhetoric. Though less frequently cited or vilified than Goethe in the American popular and religious press, Leibniz should be considered an equally relevant source for those interested in reconstructing Emerson's influences. One can consider Emerson's orb a kind of metaphysical monad, an example of what he always designates "unity in variety." Like Emerson's ideal rather than real orb, each of Leibniz's unique monads would still be universally representative and contain in itself the all-plastic power of representation. Of itself, the monad would also resist any influence and develop only according to an internal schema. Leibniz's monad, the ultimate atomic element, remains indivisible and universally reflective; it is effectively shapeless and hence accords with an all-encompassing globular form, and is always a whole and never a part. Like God, this monad is a primary unity; in fact, one might say that Emerson has transformed the monad from being merely representative of divinity to being necessarily divine.

6. In this and other passages from Emerson visuality, as a result of the eye's shape, becomes itself associated with the circular and the globular and with all orbs and orbits.

7. The function of orbs in the framework of transcendentalism is routinely suggested even by non-transcendental writers. Poe, for example, in "Ligeia," uses this same language of eyes, I's, orbs, and orbits to locate the "transcendental" identity of the narrator's wife: "Those eyes! those large, those shining, those divine orbs! they became to me the twin stars of Leda . . . in my intense scrutiny of Ligeia's eyes, have I felt approaching full the knowledge of the secret of their expression—felt it approaching—and so at length utterly depart. And (strange, oh strangest mystery of all!) I found in the commonest objects of the universe, a circle of analogies to that expression . . . a sentiment such as I felt always aroused within me by her large and luminous orbs." Poe's language here reads as a pastiche of Emerson's circular analogies of the universe. In effect, the protagonist who sees transcendent meaning in orbs is always an obsessional monomaniac who uses eyes and circles to wrench determinate meanings from dumb nature. Transcendental images of orbs continue to connote a troubled merger of identity, as Ligeia dies and is supplanted by, or merged with, the narrator's second wife, Rowena. Ligeia's fate also presages that of Pierre, who similarly loses his eyesight as he tries to comprehend and complete his text: "Her presence, her readings alone,

rendered vividly luminous the many mysteries of the transcendentalism in which we were immersed. Letters, lambent and golden, grew duller than Saturnian lead, wanting the radiant lustre of her eyes. And now those eyes shone less and less frequently upon the pages over which I pored. Ligeia grew ill. The wild eyes blazed with a too-too glorious effulgence.'' Finally, when Rowena is literally transformed into the dead Ligeia, the narrator locates her resurrected identity in her eyes, and so ends his tale: "And now the eyes opened of the figure which stood before me. 'Here then at least,' I shrieked aloud, 'can I never—can I never be mistaken—these are the full, and the black and the wild eyes of the lady—of the lady Ligeia.' '' Not merely the window of the soul or the eyes of reason, eyes during the American Renaissance serve to locate the overlap of the impersonal and personal aspects of consciousness and identity. See Mossman 479–92.

8. For "The Genuine Man" see McGiffert 185.

9. The letter to Carlyle can be found in Slater 185.

10. For a compelling reading of the social context of Emerson's depiction of a seemingly unified observer and observed, and the ontological implications of his reified objectivity, see Porter's *Seeing and Being.* Porter's work on the interdependence of vision and identity has informed my approach to this topic throughout this essay.

11. For a fuller discussion of the taxonomic, phallic, and metonymic role of spines—the vertebrate equivalent of leaves in romantic taxonomy—throughout Emerson's and Melville's works, particularly in *Moby Dick,* see Hardack, " 'The Seductive God' '': Pan and Transcendental Individualism in American Literature'' (Diss. UC Berkeley, 1994): 105–93.

12. During the American Renaissance, Germans are alleged to have a special affinity for the Absolute geist of pantheism, derived from "the German madness for the absolute one, the monistic all-in-all'' (see Manning 136). In "German Transcendentalism,'' in the September 1845 issue of *The Christian Examiner,* the anonymous author, warning the orthodox who may be "suspected, on doctrinal grounds, of inclining to Transcendentalism,'' quotes Philip Schaf: "One section of the Hegelian school has produced the latest and most dangerous form of [modern] Rationalism, in which the doctrine of myths and pantheistic hero-worship are made to play so large a part . . . it must be considered that [some German transcendentalism] is rendered so dangerous, just because it has received into itself, pantheistically caricatured to be sure, so many truths of Christianity, for which the old Rationalism had no organ whatever'' (223).

Andrews Norton, in his 1839 *A Discourse on the Latest Form of Infidelity,* writes that "in Germany the theology of which I speak has allied itself with atheism, with pantheism . . . [following] Spinoza, whose argument . . . is simply this, that the laws of nature are the laws by which God is bound, Nature and God being the same'' (11). Norton goes on to denounce the intuitive assumption of unity with nature, and pantheists' attempts to transcend Christian resurrection with what is in effect pagan metamorphosis: "[In] the modern German school . . . [Schleirmacher's] is a system of pantheism, wrought up in a highly declamatory style, in which . . . religion is the sense of the union of the individual with the universe, with Nature, or, in the language of the sect, with the One and All. It is a feeling; . . . it is independent of the idea of a personal God. And the belief and desire of personal immortality are 'wholly irreligious,' as being opposed to that which is the aim of religion, 'the annihilation of one's own personality,' 'the living in the One and All,' 'the becoming, as far as possible, one with the universe' '' (44). Norton conceives of American infidelity as the result of the unchecked influence of German theology. This becoming one with the universe is reflected in the unity of globes and orbs, in becoming an eye that has erased the self and merged with the All.

In "Melville as Novelist," Gustaaf Van Cromphout suggests that Melville, too, is strongly influenced by German philosophy and aesthetics and that his novels are constructed in response to issues raised therein. As a result, Melville's pantheism develops as an extension of his Germanic romanticism, and his fiction develops as an extension of German aesthetics: "As an expression of genius, the novel aims at 'the union of two absolutes, *absolute individuality* and *absolute universality.*' The universe, in other words, is subjectivized to the extent that consciousness becomes universal" (35). This universal consciousness, as well as the "unity of nature," is expressed by the eye, symbol of self/I and the All. Pierre then constructs his body and his text closely on Goethe's model, and both unravel as Goethe disillusions his disciple Pierre.

See also Duban for a brief overview of Norton's anti-Germanic critique of pantheism and Emerson. Also see Van Cromphout's *Emerson's Modernity and the Example of Goethe* for a thorough assessment of Goethe's aesthetic and philosophical influence on Emerson.

13. My thanks to Carolyn Porter, Mitch Breitwieser, and Sam Otter for their comments on earlier versions of this article.

References

Bosco, Ronald, ed. *The Complete Sermons of Ralph Waldo Emerson.* Vol. 3. Columbia: U of Missouri P, 1991.

Chambers, Robert. *Vestiges of the Natural History of the Creation.* 1844. New York: Humanities, 1969.

Cunningham, Andrew, and Nicholas Jardine, eds. *Romanticism and the Sciences.* Cambridge: Cambridge UP, 1990.

Davis, Merrell, and William Gilman, eds. *The Letters of Herman Melville.* New Haven: Yale UP, 1960.

Duban, James. "The 'All' Feeling: Melville, Norton, and Schleirmacher." *English Language Notes* (June 1986): 38–42.

Durfee, Job. "The Panidea." *The Complete Works.* Providence: Gladding & Proud, 1848. 346–463.

Emerson, Ralph Waldo. *Journals and Miscellaneous Notebooks.* Ed. William Gilman and Alfred Ferguson. Cambridge: Harvard UP, 1973.

———. *Works.* Boston: Houghton, 1904.

Hardack, Richard. " 'The Seductive God': Pan and Transcendental Individualism in American Literature." Diss. UC Berkeley, 1994.

Hunt, John. *Pantheism and Christianity*. 1884. Port Washington, NY: Kennikat, 1970.

Leverenz, David. "The Politics of Emerson's Man-Making Words." *Manhood in the American Renaissance*. Ithaca: Cornell UP, 1989. 42–71.

Manning, J. M. *Half Truths and the Truth*. Boston: Lee & Sheppard, 1871.

McGiffert, Arthur, Jr., ed. *Young Emerson Speaks*. Boston: Houghton Mifflin, 1938.

Melville, Herman. *The Confidence of Man*. New York: Signet, 1964.

———. *Mardi*. New York: Signet, 1964.

———. *Omoo*. Chicago: Northwestern UP, 1968.

———. *Pierre*. New York: Signet, 1964.

———. *Redburn*. Middlesex: Penguin, 1976.

Mossman, Tam, ed. *The Unabridged Edgar Allen Poe*. Philadelphia: Running, 1983.

Norton, Andrews. *A Discourse on the Latest Form of Infidelity*. 1839. Port Washington, NY: Kennikat, 1971.

Porter, Carolyn. *Seeing and Being*. Middletown, CT: Wesleyan UP, 1981.

Slater, Joseph, ed. *The Correspondence of Emerson and Carlyle*. New York: Columbia UP, 1964.

Thoreau, Henry David. *Walden*. New York: New American Library, 1960.

Toulouse, Teresa, and Andrew Delbanco, eds. *The Complete Sermons of Ralph Waldo Emerson*. Vol. 2. Columbia: U of Missouri P, 1991.

Van Cromphout, Gustaaf. *Emerson's Modernity and the Example of Goethe*. Columbia: U of Missouri P, 1990.

———. "Melville as Novelist." *Studies in American Fiction* 13.1 (1985): 31–44.

West, Nathaniel. *A Cool Million and The Dream Life of Balso Snell*. New York: Avon, 1965.

Whicher, Stephen and Robert Spiller, eds. *The Early Lectures of Ralph Waldo Emerson*. 2 vols. Cambridge: Harvard UP, 1959, 1964.

"Moral Astronomy": On a Metaphor in Novalis and Its Conceptual Context

KARL MENGES

In my philosophy of everyday life, I have come across the notion of a moral astronomy, in Hemsterhuis's sense, and made the interesting discovery of a religion of the visible universe.

—Novalis[1]

The meaning of this assertion by Novalis in a letter to Friedrich Schlegel of July 20, 1798, is not readily apparent. It gains contours when confronted with a similar passage from the essay "Die Christenheit oder Europa" (1799), whose famous stance against the Enlightenment has long been misread as a conservative if not reactionary statement about the legitimacy of the modern age. Novalis develops a seemingly undialectical juxtaposition between the "meager" contemporary times—existing, despite the "splendor of its discoveries," only on "borrowed light"—and a "yearning" for the "old sky" and its expected reappearance in the poetic concept of a "living astronomy."[2] Within the context of this astronomical metaphor, the "Europa" speech unfolds a triadic perception of history, tracing the various stages of acculturation from an original state of harmony through a phase of enlightened discord and alienation to the reconstructive project of a millennial golden age. Yet belying this seemingly straightforward tale, the speech is in fact a highly differentiated typological account of Western civilization, centered in an assessment of the process and prospects of modernity. It is clear now that the essay is not (or at least not exclusively) a nostalgic restrospective of the "beautiful and resplendent days" of the early Middle Ages, but a skillful poetic exploration of the interlocking historical events that define modernity in terms of the dialectics

111

of the Enlightenment. Oscillating between a critique of modern analytical reason and the expected reorientation of rationality toward the social sphere (with the utopian goal of a universal European peace), the speech reflects the romantics' fear that the edifice of scientific rationality has begun to dominate life to such an extent that the value systems of traditionally accepted norms of social interaction are in danger of being irretrievably lost among the reified interests of competing operational ideologies.

It is not by coincidence that these strictures of enlightened reason are presented within the context of vision. In fact, the allusions to optics are as abundant in early romantic texts as they are indicative for the thrust of Novalis's speech in that they play metaphorically with the self-image of the Enlightenment, which consistently promotes itself in terms of an encompassing visual representation of reality. The terms *enlighten, erleuchten,* and *éclairer* all indicate the discovery and universal preoccupation with vision as the regal sense of a rational modernity. Defining itself dualistically in terms of light and darkness, of the primacy of vision over the secondariness of empirical reality, this dualism and the accompanying reductionism characterize Western thought at least from the seventeenth century on. Although it already inhabits the mind/body dichotomy of the Aristotelian tradition—most succinctly in the medieval notion of an "adaequatio rei et intellectus"[3]—it is not until Descartes that the separation between mind and body accelerates into the concept of a representationist, visual control of reality, with the mind as the "mirror of nature" (Rorty 17ff.). While the Thomistic theorem, in other words, still suggests only an approximation between inner and outer worlds, it is the Cartesian model that exploits the ocular image of the mind's eye in terms of a complete dualism, surveying and controlling through representations whatever occurs in the world outside. Valid knowledge, according to this model, can be obtained only when the mind of that "thing that thinks" ("res cogitans") is trained to "mirror" reality. Separate from the life-world ("res extensa"), it sees itself as reflecting that world, while reflecting on it. The visual metaphor thus suggests a fundamental division between the mind and reality, with the implication that the object always carries some referential liability because truth is merely a function of pure theoretical insight. The term *theoria,* of course, is etymologically linked to the eye, denoting visual contemplation, and a theorem is a doctrine grounded in visual perception. Thus valid knowledge is ultimately nothing but pure vision, unsullied by corporeal concerns, and this position is underwritten by Kant in no uncertain terms.[4]

Representational certainty, then, must be considered one of the central epistemological assertions of the Enlightenment. Initially simply a term designating a concrete subject/object relation, during the eighteenth century *repraesentatio* gains a self-reflective dimension (especially in Leibniz and Wolff) that eventually culminates in Kant's taxonomic notion of representation as the highest and most sophisticated principle of all philosophical inquiry (see Birus 28). It thus evolves from an exterior semiotic designation ("stat aliquid pro aliquo") to an internal operation, centered solely on the mental processes of the self-conscious subject. By virtue of this redefinition, the term no longer regulates existing relationships but creates and shapes them on the presupposition that the capacity of representing something that is past or otherwise not present rests exclusively with the self-reflective subject. The shaping of knowledge is no longer a function of any object-immanent relation but rather the result of mental operations whose constitutive powers are eventually grounded in a new, transcendental philosophy of consciousness. Representation as "Vorstellung" is therefore first and foremost self-representation, which, not by coincidence, is accorded the highest classificatory status of theoretical philosophy in Kant's *Critique of Pure Reason*.[5]

This development confirms what Michel Foucault has described as a major epistemological shift between preclassical thought, with its inclusive and synthesizing ordering system, and the Enlightenment's dismissal of all semiotic correspondences in favor of a new "order of things"—a different "episteme"—of regulatory systems and grammatical taxonomies, promoting exclusively the principle of analytical reasoning over analogical associations.

This order of similitude and resemblance draws to a close with the dawning of the classical age, which, on Foucault's account, starts with Descartes's discrediting of all analogical presuppositions. For Descartes, resemblances are no longer markers of recognition and knowledge but signs of uncertainty and error. They do not deliver clear distinctions between self and other, identity and difference; rather, they remain opaque (literally, they do not reflect light) in their synthesizing disposition and therefore draw the wrath of an enlightened, analytical mind-set that strives to purge all unclear analogies and presuppositions. Because the collecting of resemblances cannot compete with the new method of scientific analysis, similitude is no longer the basis of knowledge but that of error, as Don Quixote finds out to his great dismay (Foucault 46ff.).

This transition is most significantly contained in a new form of linguistic representation that, in its universal reach, takes control of reality with an all-consuming, appropriating force.[6] As language is no longer attached to things, representation becomes a tool of the new paradigm, which, in its universal, transhistorical reach ultimately takes control of reality in an encompassing and appropriating force. The activities of the mind "no longer consist in drawing things together, in setting out on a quest for everything that might reveal some sort of kinship, attraction, or secretly shared nature within them, but, on the contrary, in discriminating, that is, in establishing their identities, then the inevitability of the connections with all the successive degrees of a series. In this sense, discrimination imposes upon comparison the primary and fundamental investigation of difference'' (Foucault 55).

This process, through which Western thought enters the ''age of judgment'' (Foucault 61), involves, most significantly, the displacement of the traditional, ternary concept of signification (between sign, signifier, and signified) in favor of a ''strictly binary organization'' (64), in which the structure of language reflects our logical capacities before any material affectation of our senses. Foucault speaks of a ''duplicated representation'' (63) whose syntax not only mirrors any exterior reality but, in a quasi-transcendental dimension, reflects its very own logical predispositions. Understanding a sentence and thus understanding the world does not simply mean comprehending it as a subjective, representational projection; it means, first of all, understanding it in terms of what is reasonable in or about it. Linguistic representation, then, is defined by the inscription of logic into grammar, which affects signification to the extent that irrational, unreasonable, or magical events are excluded as they are literally beyond comprehension.

It is against this model of representation that the romantics—in a second reordering move—rise up with a vengeance. At issue is no less than the limits of representation, as the sudden loss of its foundational powers leads to an immense fragmentation of knowledge. In the process, language loses its traditional role as the hitherto exclusive carrier of that knowledge. It emerges as an object itself that reacts to its epistemological ''demotion'' with the invention of literature as an exclusively self-referential pursuit. Abandoning its transparency during the classical age, language now reclaims its own structure and density, giving rise to the hope of a rebirth of a linguistic unity not unlike that of the pre-Enlightenment totality of resemblances. Yet where the Renaissance text was ultimately controlled and limited by the primal text of the world, that is, God's creative word, the language of modern literature remains ungrounded, affirming nothing but its ''own precipitous existence'' (Foucault 300), thus wandering with ''no point of departure, no end, and no promise'' (44).

It is no coincidence that Foucault should invoke at this point Hölderlin, Mallarmé, and Artaud as witnesses for this process of linguistic autonomization. Yet he might, more importantly, have included Novalis, whose literary work and accompanying theoretical reflections illustrate the described paradigm shift from a classical to a modern episteme in its literal, that is, precisely its visual, implications. Novalis postulates nothing less than a reorientation of vision, which he circumscribes in terms of a ''moral'' or ''living astronomy.'' This metaphor indicates the need for an alternative epistemological paradigm in which vision or representation are no longer constrained in the enlightened binary structure, but directed beyond the realm of traditional visibility in order to seek out, again, analogies and correspondences as in the preclassical age.

Novalis's astronomical metaphor thus stands as the visual icon of another world, offering an alternative representational model to any rationalistic self-sufficient constraints.

That alternative thrust—specifically, the attempted reversal of the binary representational grid—guides the following attempt to trace the connections between the early romantic critique of the Enlightenment and its aesthetic alternative within the context of German idealism.

Connected with Novalis's critique of vision is a critique of writing and, by implication, of the enlightened book. This is not coincidental. The graphic representation of meaning relies on vision so exclusively that its haptic substitute derives its legitimation only negatively, through a lack of sight. No one who can see reads or writes braille. Writing, then, is such a primary corollary to sight that the age of light and universal vision, not by coincidence, produces books of encyclopedic intentions. Writing becomes the enlightened activity par excellence, and Novalis draws on this phenomenon with his own project of an "Encyclopaedistik" as the attempt to reclaim the idea of universalism from the sole proprietorship of the Enlightenment.

The first step in this reclamation is the denunciation of rationalistic literacy. There is, for example, the scribe in the Klingsohr tale at the end of part 1 of *Heinrich von Ofterdingen,* who is possessed by the encyclopedic intention to record everything as "accurately" as possible. Consequently he writes down everything people tell him, yet his writing does not hold; it vanishes when dipped into a "dark bowl of clear water," held by a "noble, godlike woman." Even more unsettling, if, by chance, a drop of water hits the scribe, "so fielen eine Menge Zahlen und geometrische Figuren nieder, die er mit vieler Ämsigkeit auf einen Faden zog, und sich zum Zierrath um den magern Hals hing" (then a multitude of numbers and geometrical figures fell to the ground. He threaded them diligently on a string and hung it around his scrawny neck for adornment) (1:294).

The scribe's lack of attractiveness obviously stands for the dryness of a book culture that has lost its natural moorings in a semiosis of representational power and calculability. Writing "everything" down with the historiographical intent of creating permanence and universality is therefore canceled out by the disappearance of the inscription and its message. Nothing meaningful can be fixated, because true meaning, apparently, does not reside in presence but in absence, not in order but in disorder. Because order, however, remains a manifestation of the forces of history, a new historiography is needed, one that would disempower its enlightened predecessor while focusing, in a paradoxical task, on that which is present and familiar, yet always escapes definitive representation. At issue, in other words, is that ever evolving but elusive manifold of Being, which cannot be cornered in a representational grid but which needs fantasy, imagination; in short, the transformation into a romantic fairy tale in order to become visible in its hidden presence. "Mit der Zeit muß die Geschichte Märchen werden—sie wird wieder, wie sie anfieng" (Eventually, history must become a fairy tale—it will return to the state in which it began) (3:281).

The scribe's enumerative fixation, then, has far-reaching consequences. It represents the limits of enlightened representation, which, again, does not really represent anything at all. In fact, since it makes things disappear, it renders itself impotent and obscure. And the scribe is the icon of such impotence. He stands for the very condition of denaturation, which is the topic of that most famous Novalis poem, "Wenn nicht mehr Zahlen und Figuren / Sind Schlüssel aller Kreaturen" (When no longer numbers and figures / are keys to all creatures), in which Ludwig Tieck, not by accident, had found the essence, the inner spirit, of his friend's work, expressed in the lightest of manners (1:360).

And yet, the discrediting of the scribe does not extend to a disavowal of representation as such. It only addresses coercive, enlightened writing that cannot pass the water test of permanence, because all texts are intertextual, transitory, multidimensional, and therefore successfully resist arrest. These texts liquefy, mix with others, and thus lose the specificity of their signification—not because they were expressed in writing but because that writing had the universalist ambition of presence. Such writing is as vain as it is in vain, for the pretension of presence invariably dooms all intentional activity, leaving it to its destiny as a play of differences and a sample of infinite dissemination.

This problem of intentionality in speech and writing is addressed most succinctly in the linguistic text "Monolog." Starting with the observation that speaking and writing are very peculiar things and that real conversation is a mere "Wortspiel," Novalis focuses on the tension between representation and its referential truth content (cf. Seyhan 87). In fact, "play" becomes the telling term in an argument that rejects any intentional, content-specific appropriation of language. "Gerade das Eigenthümliche der Sprache, daß sie sich blos um sich selbst bekümmert, weiß keiner" (Precisely that characteristic aspect of language that it is only concerned with itself, no one appreciates) (2:672), which means that no one has as yet realized the fundamentally playful and nonintentional essence of aesthetic articulation. No longer a carrier of preexisting meaning, language is thus redefined as an autonomous entity that produces meaning only in the very act of articulation, by and for itself.[7]

This notion of a nonintentional, self-referential play of differences is at the core of Novalis's philosophy of language, and on its basis he attacks all intentional or representational language as the "the most ridiculous and contradictory stuff": "If someone wants to speak about something specific, moody language makes one say the funniest and most reversed stuff. From this results also the hatred that so many serious people have for language. They notice its arbitrariness but do not notice that the despised chatter is the infinitely serious side of language."[8]

Content-specific speech, in other words, produces nothing but empty chatter, which Novalis identifies even in his own reflection when trying to define the essence of poetry. Such an attempt must, by definition, fail because it approaches something undefinable from an extra-referential, metaphysical position. The conclusion is obvious: "If I believe I have indicated the essence and function of poetry most clearly, I know nevertheless that nobody can understand it, and that I have said something stupid because I wanted to say it."[9]

Intentional speech, then, just like representational writing, corresponds to the gaze in that both try to structure reality from a preconceived notion. That effect is particularly evident in language. Burdened by the representational task of standing for something else when it is supposed to represent only itself, language is forced into a position from which it needs to be liberated, and that liberation Novalis develops with a reorientation of vision. Again, if the eye is the regal sense of the Enlightenment, its ever "purer" visual ideal corresponds to an ever greater material control. That structuring system eventually reaches its limits with the early romantics, whose central insight into the epistemic implications of representation involves rethinking vision as the central metaphor in this paradigm shift.

Critical and even contemptuous of the analytical gaze and its representational tug, Novalis attempts the restitution of the "genuine" ("ächte") conditions through a restoration of true vision. Such vision, as a first consequence, must not be binary as in the closed circuitry of logic and grammatical representation; it must occur, rather, as a free play in recognition of the infinity of all differential manifestations, which are always already beyond the representational grid. Against any one-dimensional fixation, Novalis therefore proposes an oscillating approach, a "Hin und her Direction" (2:117), a floating to and fro in space and time on the conviction that "'nur der rückwärtsgekehrte Blick bringt vorwärts, da der vorwärtsgekehrte Blick rückwärts führt" (only the retrospective vision moves forward, since the straightforward vision leads backward) (3:381).

It is this principle that guides Heinrich von Ofterdingen's looping poetic path, for his individual development—if it is one at all—does not unfold in terms of the usual struggle between individual and world, as the typical educational novel suggests.[10] Heinrich's evolution is marked, rather, by insight and hindsight, both of which are a function of communication, of memories and remembrances, rather than struggle. Conversations—on abstract topics, no less—dominate the novel to the extent that it can be and has been misread as dull for its absence of any developmental tension. Heinrich does not interact with reality in any painful or antagonistic way; he is not being marked or hurt by the reality principle, but wanders childlike through stages that afford him acquaintances with human history in an exploratory "back and forth direction" of restrospective and anticipatory images that set him on the road toward his eventual poetic destiny. On his way he has a variety of exotic encounters that evoke the needed metaphorical pluralism of education over any linear conceptual approach. He experiences the mythical age (Arion-tale, Atlantis), the land of the Morn, the splendors of Arabia, and time and again the beauties and mysteries of nature, as in the tale of the miner, the reflections on history, the conversations on poetry, and the explorations of love. Heinrich's education occurs in images and tales, in painless fiction, rather than in the believable struggle of a realistic educational novel. To that extent, his path follows an alternative route, defined by an alternative representational paradigm. It is not one of confrontation in which the object disappears in the orbit of a declarative, one-dimensional script while its subject succumbs to the domination of the world. Rather, it explores in a conscious construction ("bewußte Setzung") the paradoxical disposition of man who reaches beyond that very construction, aware of the fact that it is at best an approximation of the Absolute, which can never be reached but must still be sought out.

Against the writing of the Enlightenment, then, there is the text of nature, which, in its puzzling simultaneity of presence and absence, of order and chaos,[11] highlights the episode of the book within the book, which Heinrich finds in the cave of the hermit. Although he cannot read it, he recognizes figures of his present life, although "they seemed to come from a different age." The book has no title but mirrors stages of his own life beyond all conventional representation. Its message remains mysterious and yet strangely familiar. Thence the urge to understand, rather than conquer the riddle: "Heinrich war sehr bekümmert, und wünschte nichts sehnlicher, als das Buch lesen zu können, und vollständig zu besitzen" (Heinrich was quite distressed and wished for nothing more intensely than to be able to read the book and to own it altogether) (1:265). Eventually the hermit reveals some of the secrets of the book (which is written in Provençal) while reinforcing others: "I cannot remember exactly what the content was. Only this much I know. It is a novel about the wonderful fates of a poet in which poetry is presented and applauded in multiple contexts."[12]

Provençal, of course, is the Romance and Romantic language that differs most visibly from any enlightened script in that it resists liquidation as it presents a palimpsest, another text behind writing. Reaching beyond any semantic immediacy, the "wondrous" poetic tale reveals itself as an originary language, an arch-écriture that contains and conveys something that is present and yet hidden; it is the "secret word" that, at best, can be glimpsed in the "grammatical mysticism" (3:267) of hieroglyphics and old documents ("Ur-kunden"), with their simultaneously secret and holy messages.

Hidden to the analytical gaze, those secrets manifest themselves in signs and icons. They are present in the book of nature—"Die Welt ist ein gebunde-ner Gedanke" (The world is bound in thought) (3:595)—and can be deciph-ered only by unconventional means. A different language must first be mastered, in appreciation of its playful autonomy, which displaces any inten-tional verdict and in which the "secret word" has supplanted all injurious chiffers and inscriptions.

Here we are confronted with the question as to how to accomplish this transition on a discursive level and without the famous *salto mortale* into the operatic world. A link might be suggested between the new vision and its metaphor, astronomy, and one of the central epistemic concepts of the early romantics, "intellektuelle Anschauung" (intellectual intuition). But first, what defines intellectual intuition, and what is its range in Novalis's philos-ophy?

The starting point must be the epistemologically central *Fichte-Studies* (1795–96), which open with a "Deduktion der Filosofie" (2:117) aimed at a first definition by way of a differentiation between "Reflexion" and "Ge-fühl."[13] Underlying this deduction is an awareness of the limitations, even the secondariness, of thought in relation to life and its agent, feeling, which No-valis unfolds in the following argument:

If philosophy traditionally attempts to establish one encompassing onto-logical principle, a first explanatory cause or simply the Absolute, that process always ends—consciously or not—with the relativization of the very Absolute through the endeavor to represent something that, by definition, resists repre-sentation. Precisely by trying to make the Absolute the object of definitive knowledge, one makes it a relative entity, demonstrating nothing, ultimately, but the finitude of human knowledge. The conclusion is obvious: reflection cannot have a constitutive, defining, and thus definitive function; it cannot be an epistemic ordering system, because it is itself based on something that is more originary and foundational, and that opposite something is non-order, not-knowing, chaos, or feeling.

This argument is central to Novalis's and other romantics' (e.g., Hölder-lin) rejection of Fichte's attempted grounding of consciousness in self-con-sciousness, which as a problem had been already touched on—but not resolved—by Kant. Underlying the problem is the fundamental duality be-tween subject and object as reflected in the corresponding duality between sensory intuition and our cognitive disposition. Kant retains this duality even though he installs the "synthetic unity of apperception," or pure self-con-sciousness, as the "highest principle of philosophy" (*Kritik der reinen Ver-nunft* B 134). His conclusion is that, although pure apperception includes the consciousness of its existence, that existence is still fundamentally precognitive to the extent that all prepredicative manifestations of apperception remain in the dark.

Fichte is trying to overcome this duality. In the *Wissenschaftslehre* (1794), as well as in its various amendments (*Versuch einer neuen Darstellung der Wissenschaftslehre,* 1797, and *Wissenschaftslehre nova methodo,* 1797–99), Fichte argues for a prereflective unity of consciousness by way of intellectual intuition. This he defines as an operation that unites sensory perception and cognitive judgment on the hypothesis that pure consciousness is always already familiar with itself before any concrete articulations. Such familiarity involves three essential suppositions. First, all consciousness of something is, to begin with, self-consciousness. As such, it represents, second, an object in the process of self-reflection, which, third, produces an awareness of a reflecting subject in whose reflection subject and object converge. This reflection of consciousness upon itself is accessible through a reductive operation in which the subject views itself as acting in the process of contemplating its own actions.

Reflection as a self-conscious action is here the key point. It refers to a self-reflective intuition that is not intuition (''Anschauung'') in the Kantian polar opposition to cognition but an intellectual intuition in which the subject is conscious of its viewing itself as the object of an acting or positing subject: ''Die Anschauung, von welcher hier die Rede ist, ist ein sich Setzen als setzend . . . keineswegs aber ein bloßes Setzen'' (The intuition which is at issue here is a positing in the act of positing . . . but by no means a mere positioning) (Fichte 1.4:276).

Fichte describes the intricacies of this concept in terms of an ''in sich zurückgehendes Handeln'' (an active folding back on itself) (1.4:216), in which the subject posits itself by viewing or reflecting (on) itself.[14] The self-reflective action constitutes ''den ursprünglichsten Act des Subjects'' (the originary act of the subject) and as such precedes all other acts of consciousness (1.4:216). This position remains Fichte's epistemological credo throughout; it originates in the early review of Reinhold's *Aenesidemus* (1793), where intellectual intuition is first introduced in terms of the stated priority of an acting (and viewing) consciousness: ''Das absolute Subject, das Ich, wird nicht durch empirische Anschauung gegeben, sondern durch intellectuelle gesetzt'' (The absolute subject, the I, is not given by an empirical observation but positioned by an intellectual one) (1.2:48).

The viewing of the consciously acting subject, then, defines intellectual intuition as a cognitive transcendental unity that binds subjectivity and objectivity together before all empirical concretizations.[15] It is an operation of pure consciousness for which Fichte, time and again (as in the following excerpt from a letter to Schelling), reclaims the conventional prevalence of vision in order to validate its representational priority: "Es kann nicht von einem Seyn . . . sondern es muß von einem Sehen ausgegangen werden. . . . Seyn ist—sich nicht durchdringendes Sehen" (We must not start from Being . . . but from vision. . . . Being is seeing that does not penetrate itself) (3.5:46).

This notion of a prereflective unity of cognition appeals to all romantics because of its universal ambition. Still, it does not escape their critique, which Novalis illustrates with the observation that no judgment can possibly be rendered on anything without a prior unity of perception. If this still sounds very much like Fichte, it is because Novalis, too, searches for a prereflective unity, yet he finds it not in the cognitive part of intellectual intuition (which for him retains Kant's basic duality) but in the entirely different, truly precognitive realm of Being.

Deviating from all idealistic philosophy of consciousness and its visual connotations, Novalis bases his critique of Fichte on the epistemic priority of "Seyn" (2:106), and its sensory agent, "Gefühl." This, as a prereflective given entity, defines the epistemic boundaries of reflection. "Die Filosofie ist ursprünglich ein Gefühl" (Originally, philosophy is a sentiment), and because it is based on feeling, it is secondary; "Die Filosofie bedarf daher allemal etwas Gegebenes . . . Construiren läßt sich Filosofie nicht" (Philosophy, therefore, is always in need of a given) (2:113ff.), in fact, "was die Reflexion findet, scheint schon da zu seyn" (what reflection finds, appears to be there already) (2:112).

Because philosophy, in other words, is always already defined by an immutable Being, it can, at best, hope to describe—or, better, circumscribe—but never identify, let alone construct that Being in its ontological priority. Trying to do that, as all epistemic constitutivism attempts, only inverts the boundaries in that it ignores the fact that "die Grenzen des Gefühls sind die Grenzen der Filosofie" (the boundaries of feeling are the boundaries of philosophy) (2:114), as Novalis states with an almost Wittgensteinian radicality.[16]

Feeling, then, is primary, thus independent and absolute.[17] Furthermore, preceding any teleological reflection, this means that feeling is beyond articulation. The feeling subject experiences itself as being grounded in an Absolute ("Seyn," "Gefühl") that, simultaneously, eludes description. Feeling, furthermore, is mute, it "cannot feel itself," but precisely because of its inarticulate disposition, feeling needs reflection in order to speak up. "Das Gefühl kann sich nicht selber fühlen. . . . Es läßt sich nur in der Reflexion betrachten" (A sentiment cannot feel itself. . . . It can only be contemplated through reflection) (2:114). This means, of course, that if reflection is secondary to feeling as an absolute given or an ontological principle, it is that very feeling that needs reflection in order to articulate, not the principle, but its own awareness of it, to turn outward what would otherwise remain nothing but an inwardly inarticulated sensation.

The question remains as to what constitutes this feeling and, conversely, reflection (2:114ff.). Clearly, feeling as the antonym of thought means not-knowing. Because of that, however, it is dependent on reflection in order to articulate what would otherwise remain an internalized apprehension of that in which knowledge is grounded. Reflecting on that Absolute, then, requires a secondary reflection on the limits of feeling, which allows us to speak eventually of not-knowing in a Socratic sense, that is, with an awareness of the sensitive foundations of knowledge as well as its limitations.

Novalis develops this dialectic between feeling and thought in an "ordo-inversus" doctrine through a literal (visual) reflection on reflection: just as the mirror image involves the inversion of oppositional givens, left and right, so does cognitive reflection produce an inverted image of the object of contemplation. Looking at feeling in a reflective way, therefore, leaves us with a loss of that very feeling, and vice versa: "Wenn das Gefühl Was ist, so ist Reflexion nichts . . . und so umgekehrt" (When feeling is something, then reflection is nothing . . . and vice versa). Or: "Die Reflexion ist Nichts—wenn sie Was ist . . . Das Gefühl ist Nichts, wenn es in der Reflexion Was ist" (Reflection is nothing—if it is something. . . . Feeling is nothing, when it is something in reflection) (2:118). In other words: because "feeling"—even as the origin of all philosophical considerations—"cannot feel itself" (2:114), it must rely on its opposite, thought, for its articulation. Yet as soon as feeling is viewed reflectively, it loses its spirit in such articulated reflection. While it is true, then, that "it can only be considered in reflection," it is also true that "the spirit of that feeling vanishes" (2:114). As a result, feeling and reflection change positions to the extent that reflection, as the identifying agent, seems to be "something and feeling nothing," when in fact it is the reverse: "feeling is something and reflection is nothing" (2:118).

Only the "simple consciousness" falls victim to that inversion, while the "reflected consciousness" (2:118), in a second inversion, mirrors the inverted image in order accurately to reflect the identity of its object, that is, foundational Being. While its presence reaches from the infinite to the finite, the first reflection inverts it, thus assuming priority in that the motion is now directed—with a constitutive ambition—from the finite to the infinite. Yet, Novalis cautions, "Die Filosofie soll nicht mehr antworten, als sie gefragt wird. Hervorbringen kann sie nichts" (Philosophy should not answer more than what she is being asked. She cannot create anything) (2:113). This leaves consciousness with only the option of correcting the "ordo inversus" in a second reflection that will restore the priorities by turning the reflecting ego onto itself, while acknowledging the infinitesimal and only approximative task of representing the Absolute. In such double reflection the subject eventually affirms the limits of its own conscious reach.

It is the dialectical unity of duality generated by the second (knowing or reflected) reflection on feeling that leads us to the Absolute, if only—and this is central—in form of its cognitive relativization. Broken reflexivity, as manifest in literally endless approximations, and not the Fichtean claim of its conscious closure, then, defines Novalis's concept of intellectual intuition (2:116).[18] Feeling has become reflected feeling, and as such it is the object of itself, which means that the most developed form of reflection has been achieved.

Intellectual intuition as that highest form of consciousness involves a reflection on feeling, which remains beyond conceptual clarification. Its object is the Absolute as a negative entity, as something missing (Uerlings 139). Thus, since reflection cannot reach feeling, the activities of intellectual intuition and, with it, of philosophy end, ultimately, as an exercise in modesty.

Just because the Absolute cannot be represented conceptually does not mean, of course, that it does not exist, and furthermore, that it should not be brought to the fore with all the limitations that define self-reflective knowledge. In fact, precisely because it can only be alluded to in a process of infinite mirroring and approximation, it is that very approximate value of the Absolute—no more and no less—that sets the boundaries for all cognitive endeavors. Reflection must admit to its conceptual limitations that allow, at most, for the expression of an "infinite free activity," of "evocations" ("Ahndungen"), or an unending "yearning" ("Sehnsucht") for something that is simply beyond comprehension.[19]

Because of the deficiency of thought, however, and the priority of Being, this yearning for the Absolute remains constant. Because it cannot find fulfillment in the conceptual finitude of reason, it must seek it in the representational infinity of art (see Frank, "Fragmente" 466ff.). For its purpose, especially the "purpose of poetry," is the "elevation of man beyond himself" (2:535), which makes poetry "jene längst gewünschte Erfindungskunst" (that long-wished-for art of invention) (2:454).

The transition from a conceptual to an aesthetic answer, therefore, is by no means an escapist solution to an intractable problem. It is rather the logical conclusion drawn from the recognition of the limits of thought. The insufficiency of reason leads to aesthetics, where its infinite variables and possibilities merge with the eventual idea of a "representation of the unrepresentable," a notion Novalis tries to capture in one of his more famous aphorisms: "The sense for poetry has much in common with mysticism. It is the sense of the unique, personal, unknown, secret, that which needs to be revealed and which will need to be necessarily fulfilled. It presents the unrepresentable."[20]

This poetic idea of representation allows us to focus once more on the initial astronomical reference. We have seen how Novalis interprets the analytical gaze as a function of an epistemological deficit. Against the limited form

of vision, as contained in the modern geocentric world, Novalis, by consequence, posits a limitless, contemplating vision that, reaching into space-time,
no longer separates things but rather unites them in the universe of imaginative
thought. Visual perception is thus reversed: sight is no longer focused on the
finite in an analytical gaze but directed outward, toward infinity, where—as
vision in the sense of anticipation—it carries conceptual and aesthetic implications alike.

Novalis circles this alternative visual paradigm in a variety of metaphors,
one of which is that of a "poetic theory of the telescope" (3:411). This metaphor, which calls on a prototypical instrument of the Enlightenment in support
of metaphysical and poetic legitimation, mediates both reason and anticipatory fantasy. It works on the supposition that changes in perception are not
tied to linear technological innovations but that truly innovative technology
must be linked to imagination, to the extent that discoveries are at least as
much a function of fantasy as of intellect. It is in that context that the telescope
(which had found access already into eighteenth-century theories of the wonderful in Milton, Bodmer, and Breitinger) becomes an "ideal symbol" in its
combinatory power of magical and analytical or technical capabilities.[21] In
fact, it advances to a central epistemological metaphor based on the realization
that true perception is ultimately impossible without a change in vision, without imaginary or poetic help. For imagination truly articulates itself only aesthetically, and it is this conviction of the need of a universal poetization
("Universalpoesie") that drives the early romantic revisitation and revision
of transcendental idealism.

This poetization is consistent. Not through "borrowed light" but only
through "genuine intuition" ("ächte Erfindung"), through a quasi-transcendental imagination, can the limits of analytical philosophy be overcome. That,
however, involves a construction project that Novalis celebrates with the ex-
clamation: "Die Poesie ist das ächt absolut Reelle. Dies ist der Kern meiner
Philosophie. Je poetischer, je wahrer" (The poesy [the poetic] is the truly real.
This is the centerpiece [core] of my philosophy. The more poetic, the more
true) (2:647).

With regard to the astronomical metaphor, this means that astronomy, as
a theory that draws simultaneously from imagination and science, legitimizes
both thought and poetry. It pulls together that which remains divided in conventional ordering in the "chaotic" and poetic space-time of the universe.
Resisting the classical separation of discursive and aesthetic knowledge, and
surmounting the traditional division between aesthetics and perception, Novalis's metaphor of a "moral astronomy" advances a concept of non-Euclidean
science that is driven by mediation rather than separation and is based, metaphorically, on the notion of an encompassing, synthesizing vision rather than
an appropriating analytical gaze.

Trained on the discovery of truth, astronomy thus becomes a playful discipline that describes the credo of the early romantics in the mediation of philosophy and poetry with the elusive goal of evoking the Absolute in the infinity of the universe. This practical task has its epistemological corollary in intellectual intuition. Astronomy must be content, like philosophy, with an ultimate not-knowing. Simultaneously, however, the thematization of not-knowing is the necessary first step beyond enlightened ignorance. Such not-knowing is in fact a dialectical communicative knowledge; it is "true enlightenment," enlightenment of the enlightenment, precisely and only through its broken reflexivity. Two aspects, finally, emerge in these speculations:

First, there is a consistency in Novalis's epistemological considerations that leads him from the rejection of the analytical gaze to a "reflected" reflection in terms of an outward-bound infinitesimal vision as the only legitimate path from the confines of a fractured enlightened reality to a poetic union of infinite connections. This path is thinkable, just like intellectual intuition, only in terms of a radical turn, that is, not through reflection of the finite but through an extension, a double-mirror effect, as it were, and thus as a step beyond the confines of finitude into the realm of the universe.

Second, what emerges as a corollary is the moral imperative of such an inversion, which refers us back to the mention of a "moral astronomy" in the introductory quote. That quote carried a direct allusion to Hemsterhuis, whom Novalis knew through Herder and who fascinated him with his Neoplatonic speculations about the existence of a "moral organ," a concept similar to the notion of "moral sense" in Shaftesbury and others. Hemsterhuis advances his doctrine of this "organe morale" in order to assert the cogency and necessity of moral judgments and decisions. Such judgments emerge in analogy to a generally sensualist position that stipulates that all ideas and judgments derive from external stimulations with which we are in contact through our sense organs. Hemsterhuis posits that certain nonsensory internal affections, such as love and hate, carry the same degree of distinctness as the sensory impressions, which leads him to speculate (in the Lockean sensualist tradition) about the referential connections of such impressions with the outside world. Such affections are manifestations of our consciousness and thus, by necessity, functions of a sensualist epistemology, if the assumption should hold—as Hemsterhuis believes—that all thoughts are manifestation of sensual affections and not the reverse. All internal affections relate to interactions with the world; they carry moral significance and are determined by a "moral organ," to which Hemsterhuis goes so far as to assign specific sensations: "De l'organe moral résultent trois espèces de sensations différentes: celle de motif ou de désir, celle de devoir, et celle de la vertu" (From the moral organ, three different sensations emanate: those of motive or desire, those of duty, and those of virtue) (Hemsterhuis 1:124).

Despite such physiological assertions, for which he was challenged to

125

provide proof by Diderot and others, including his own editor (Hemsterhuis 1:129), Hemsterhuis clings to his concept of the "moral organ," a decision Novalis found truly prophetic: "Hem./s Erwartungen vom moralischen Organ sind ächt profetisch" (Hem./s expectations of the moral organ are truly prophetic) (2:562). And why? The answer—complex and associative as always in Novalis—is generally related to the concept of temporality and time that defines his work generally.

In all his attempts at an evocation or approximative exploration of the Absolute, Novalis never loses sight of the fact that, because we are limited beings ("Mängelwesen"), we will never be able to accomplish this task. Any attempt, therefore, to explore the Absolute always ends with the realization of our essential duality, that is, the fact that we are eternally separated from it. This fact is a function of our temporality, a given of our being creatures of history, yet such relativity is here to be overcome. Overcoming temporality ultimately amounts to a willingness to overcome or to relativize the order of history and life. Drawn out to its radical conclusion, this means nothing less than the necessary displacement of these paradigms through their opposites— chaos and death—not just in terms of a positive reinterpretation of the antonyms but as a radical validation of their inherent moral implications.

Death, in particular, becomes a goal of moral dimensions in that it implies the transcending of temporality. And why is this morally necessary? Because time is the equivalent of displeasure, which defines everyday life; accordingly, overcoming displeasure advances to a moral quest. It is, in fact, the "purpose" of our existence: "Verwandlung der Unlust in Lust und mit ihr der Zeit in Ewigkeit" (Transformation of displeasure into pleasure and with it of time into eternity) (2:667).

To put it differently, what becomes essential is the transcending of life precisely in its everyday temporality, because "wer das Leben anders, als eine sich selbst vernichtende Illusion, ansieht, ist noch selbst im Leben befangen" (whoever views life as other than a self-defeating illusion, is himself still caught up in life) (2:563). Dying, by consequence, becomes an act of "totalization"; it gains, as a "yearning" ("Sehnsucht nach dem Tode") (1:153), a moral distinction.

This moral dimension remains attached to Novalis's notion of an inverted chaos philosophy and its corollary, inverted vision. The experience of a "deficiency of being" ("Mangel an Sein") in the conscious awareness of being always already contained by an Absolute ("Seyn") connects the early philosophical investigations with the later notion of universal poetry ("Universalpoesie"). What unites both is the need to abandon abstract reflection in recognition of the fact that we always already exist in a hermeneutical, "lighted" situational context that cannot be created but can, at best, be explained. The critical juxtaposition of the universality of light and vision with that of its derivative, reflected, or "borrowed" kind makes this abundantly clear.

It is in this context that Novalis eventually speaks of light as the "vehicle of the community—of the universe," adding the question: "Ist dis ächte Besonnenheit in der geistigen Sfäre nicht ebenfalls?" (Is genuine reflection in the spiritual sphere not the same?) (2:619). If this rhetorical question must be answered affirmatively, then it is also difficult to reject the connected statement, "Die Astronomie muß die Grundlage aller Physikalischen Wissenschaften werden" (Astronomy must become the basis of all physical sciences) (3:470), or, shorter yet, "Alle Theorie [ist] Astronomie" (All theory is astronomy) (3:334).

Notes

1. "In meiner Philosophie des täglichen Lebens bin ich auf die Idee einer moralischen im Hemsterhuisischen Sinn Astronomie gekommen und habe die interessante Entdeckung der Religion des sichtbaren Weltalls gemacht" (Novalis 4:255). Translations throughout this essay are my own.
2. "Die Natur fing an immer dürftiger auszusehn, und wir sahen deutlicher gewöhnt an den Glanz unserer Entdeckungen, daß es nur ein geborgtes Licht war, und daß wir mit den bekannten Werkzeugen und den bekannten Methoden nicht das Wesentliche, das Gesuchte finden und construiren würden." Diagnosing a reversal of this trend, Novalis continues: "So währt es fort und es ist leicht zu ermessen, . . . wie unter diesen Umständen die Witterung sich klären und der alte Himmel und mit ihm die Sehnsucht nach ihm, die lebendige Astronomie, wieder zum Vorschein kommen muß" (Novalis 3:521ff.).
3. Aquinas, *Summa Theologiae* 1.16.1: "Quod autem dicitur quod veritas est adaequatio rei et intellectus. . . ." Also 1.21.2: "Respondeo dicendum quod veritas consistit in adaequatione intellectus et rei, sicut supra (1.16.1) dictum est. Intellectus autem qui est causa rei, comparatur ad ipsam sicut regula et mensura: e converso autem est de intellectu qui accipit scientiam a rebus."
4. Kant, *Anthropologie in pragmatischer Hinsicht* 449: "Der Sinn des Gesichts ist . . . der edelste; weil er sich unter allen am meisten von der Betastung, als der eingeschränktesten Bedingung der Wahrnehmung, entfernt . . ."
5. It is this new subjective disposition of *repraesentatio* (which is rendered much more closely in the English or French correspondences of idea or idée than in the German "Vorstellung") that informs Kant's notion of "Vorstellung." Before obtaining insight into the "transcendental application of pure reason," Kant beseeches those who have the interest of philosophy at heart ("denen Philosophie am Herzen liegt") to pay attention to the original meaning of "idea" in order not to confuse it with other "forms of representation" ("Vorstellungsarten"). Thence his decision to give a hierarchical classification ("Stufenleiter") with representation as the highest generic concept of theoretical philosophy: "Die Gattung ist Vorstellung überhaupt (repraesentatio). Unter ihr steht die Vorstellung mit Bewußtsein (perceptio). Eine Perception, die sich lediglich auf das Subjekt, als die

Modifikation seines Zustandes bezieht, ist Empfindung (sensatio), eine objektive Perzeption ist Erkenntnis (cognitio)'' (*Kritik der reinen Vernunft* B 376ff.).

6. Representation, according to Foucault, only emerges with the advent of the classical order. Yet clearly it also defines preclassical knowledge, albeit on a different semiotic basis. Representation, in the Renaissance episteme, denotes the link between signified and signifier through resemblance. In the classical episteme, representation becomes a function of arbitrary convention.

7. Saussure will later describe this play of linguistic differences with important consequences for the poststructuralist debate in his assertion that language is not a treasure trove of definitive signs and meanings but a system of arbitrary signification, ''a series of differences of sound combined with a series of differences of ideas'' (120).

8. ''Will [jemand] aber von etwas Bestimmtem sprechen, so läßt ihn die launige Sprache das lächerlichste und verkehrteste Zeug sagen. Daraus entsteht auch der Haß, den so manche ernsthafte Leute gegen die Sprache haben. Sie merken ihren Muthwillen, merken aber nicht, daß das verächtliche Schwatzen die unendlich ernsthafte Seite der Sprache ist'' (2:672).

9. ''Wenn ich damit das Wesen und Amt der Poesie auf das deutlichste angegeben zu haben glaube, so weiß ich doch, daß es kein Mensch verstehen kann, und ich ganz was albernes gesagt habe, weil ich es habe sagen wollen . . .'' (2:672).

10. As Hegel wryly describes with reference to Wilhelm Meister, ''das Ende solcher Lehrjahre besteht darin, daß sich das Subjekt die Hörner abläuft, mit seinem Wünschen und Meinen sich in die bestehenden Verhältnisse und die Vernünftigkeit derselben hineinbildet und in ihr sich einen angemessenen Standpunkt erwirbt'' (568).

11. The identification of chaos or disorder as the foundation of order marks one of Novalis's most fascinating and timely epistemological observations. Note the following aphorism from the *Allgemeine Brouillon* (1789–99): ''In der künftigen Welt ist alles, wie in der ehmaligen Welt—und doch alles ganz Anders. Die künftige Welt ist das Vernünftige Chaos—das Chaos, das sich selbst durchdrang—in sich und außer sich ist—Chaos^2 oder ∞'' (3:281). Similar entries associate chaos with poetry (1:286), fluidity (3:100), and turbulent processes in general. Such phenomena are precognitive manifestations of the most general term, Being (''Seyn''), which is tantamount to foundational chaos: ''Um das Ich zu bestimmen müssen wir es auf etwas beziehn. Beziehn geschieht durch Unterscheiden—beydes durch These einer absoluten Sfäre der Existenz. Dis ist das Nur Seyn—oder Chaos'' (2:106ff). The proximity of such utterances to contemporary chaos theory has recently been the topic of a most interesting paper by Joyce Walker, who argues that the recursive structure of *Heinrich von Ofterdingen* models iterative and looping processes prevalent in natural, nonlinear dynamics (e.g., 53ff.). It also explains the astounding postmodern texture of the novel, if postmodernism is to be understood here in its broad, yet programmatic resistance to structuring and closure. Insofar as such order is present in the prototypical educational novel *Wilhelm Meisters Lehrjahre,* Novalis's agitated rejection of Goethe's modernity becomes ever more comprehensible in terms of a similarly programmatic ''Anti-Meister.''

12. "Ich kann mich nicht genau mehr des Inhalts entsinnen. Soviel ich weiß, ist es ein Roman von den wunderbaren Schicksalen eines Dichters, worinn die Dichtkunst in ihren mannigfachen Verhältnissen dargestellt und gepriesen wird" (1:265).

13. For a detailed treatment of the conceptual history of "intellektuelle Anschauung" from Kant to Novalis, see lately Frank, "Fragmente" 417ff., 447ff. See also his previous work covering the same ground, here especially " 'Intellektuelle Anschauung': Drei Stellungnahmen zu einem Deutungsversch von Selbstbewußtsein: Kant, Fichte, Hölderlin/Novalis" (in *Die Aktualität der Frühromantik*, ed. E. Behler and J. Hörisch [Paderborn: Schöningh, 1987], 96–126). Frank, in a whole series of seminal publications since 1969, has provided some of the most inspiring impulses to Novalis research in particular and early romanticism in general. His contributions, whose value rests largely with the philosophical illumination of the romantic critique of transcendental idealism, provides essential impulses that still need to be fully incorporated into the discussion. For a most recent survey of research see Uerlings, who also offers innovative interpretions of the interplay among aesthetics, theory, and political philosophy (on intellectual intuition see 136ff.).

14. See 1.4:277ff.: "die Intelligenz schaut sich selbst an. bloß als Intelligenz oder als reine Intelligenz, und in dieser Selbstanschauung eben besteht ihr Wesen. Diese Anschauung wird . . . intellectuelle Anschauung genannt—Ich bediene mich statt des Wortes Intelligenz lieber der Benennung: Ichheit; weil diese das Zurückgehen der Thätigkeit in sich selbst für jeden, der nur der geringsten Aufmerksamkeit fähig ist, am unmittelbarsten bezeichnet."

15. See also the following emphatic description of intellectual intuition as the highest form of consciousness: "Dieses dem Philosophen angemuthete Anschauen seiner selbst im Vollziehen des Acts, wodurch ihm das Ich entsteht, nenne ich intellectuelle Anschauung. Sie ist das unmittelbare Bewußtseyn; daß ich handle, und was ich handle: sie ist das, wodurch ich etwas weiß, weil ich es thue. . . . Jeder, der sich eine Thätigkeit zuschreibt, beruft sich auf diese Anschauung. In ihr ist die Quelle des Lebens, und ohne sie ist der Tod" (1.4:216ff.). Fichte explicitly distances himself from Kant, who never considered intellectual intuition other than a "noumenon" and as such beyond the reach of human intellection. See *Kritik der reinen Vernunft*: "Wenn wir also die Kategorien auf Gegenstände, die nicht als Erscheinungen betrachtet werden, anwenden wollten, so müßten wir eine andere Anschauung, als die sinnliche, zum Grunde legen, und alsdann wäre der Gegenstand ein Noumenon in positiver Bedeutung. Da nun eine solche, nämlich die intellektuelle Anschauung, schlechterdings außer unserem Erkenntnisvermögen liegt, so kann auch der Gebrauch der Kategorien keineswegs über die Grenze der Gegenstände der Erfahrung hinausreichen . . ." (B 308ff.).

16. Cf. Wittgenstein: "The limits of my language mean the limits of my world" (5.6).

17. "Gefühl scheint das Erste—Reflexion das Zweyte zu seyn" (Novalis 2:114).

18. "Das Gefühl giebt . . . der Reflexion zu seinem Contingente den Stoff der intellectualen Anschauung. So wie das Gefühl der Reflexion in Aufstellung seiner ersten

Formen behülflich seyn mußte, so muß die Reflexion, um etwas für sie zu bear-
beiten mögliches zu haben mitwirken—und so entsteht die intellectuale Anschauung'' (Novalis 2:116).

19. ''Durch das freywillige Entsagen des Absoluten entsteht die unendliche freye
Thätigkeit in uns—das Einzig mögliche Absolute, was uns gegeben werden kann
und was wir nur durch unsre Unvermögenheit ein Absolutes zu erreichen und zu
erkennen, finden. Dies uns gegebne Absolute läßt sich nur negativ erkennen,
indem wir handeln und finden, daß durch kein Handeln das erreicht wird, was wir
suchen'' (Novalis 2:269ff.). Against the venerable tradition of reading Novalis in
terms of aesthetic or metaphysical escapism, the notion of approximation, as the
central tenet of his theoretical and poetic writing, finally seems to be taking hold.
This is true, in particular, of the poetic oeuvre, whose aim is not the representation
of some discrete Absolute but rather of that which remains ''unrepresentable'' in
the most literal sense. See lately the valuable survey by Uerlings (106ff.) and his
contrastive description of Novalis's goal as a ''narrative Konstruktion immanenter
Transzendenz'' (229ff.). Although the density of Uerlings' language evokes images of tortuous ''Wissenschaftsdeutsch,'' his concept is of remarkable lucidity.
''Narrative Konstruktion'' refers to the (aesthetic) conceptualization of knowledge beyond conventional ordering systems, while ''immanente Transzendenz''
tries to capture Novalis's corresponding fascination with infinity and its—at
best—approximative representability. Novalis anticipates here the neostructuralist
notion of a disseminative ''play of differences'' (Derrida) as the ever shifting,
thus self-negating manifestation of an Absolute. See Winfried Menninghaus regarding this play: ''reflexion *ist* das Absolute—als 'Medium' eines differentiellen
Spiels ohne festen Grund. So verstanden ist die romantische Theorie des Absoluten als Reflexionsmedium prima philosophia *als* Negation von prima philosophia'' (57).

20. ''Der Sinn für Poesie hat viel mit dem Sinn für Mystizism gemein. Er ist der Sinn
für das Eigenthümliche, Personelle, Unbekannte, Geheimnißvolle, zu Offenbaren-
de, das Nothwendigzufällige. Er stellt das Undarstellbare dar'' (3:685).

21. Thence Stadler's observation as a ''Realität registrierendes und zugleich Realität
setzendes . . . Werkzeug'' (55).

References

Aquinas, Thomas. *Summa Theologiae*. Madrid: Biblioteca de Autores Christianos,
1951.

Birus, Hendrik. ''Zwischen den Zeiten. Friedrich Schleiermacher als Klassiker der
neuzeitlichen Hermeneutik.'' *Hermeneutische Positionen: Schleiermacher, Dil-
they, Heidegger, Gadamer*. Ed. H. Birus. Göttingen: Vandenhoeck, 1982.

Fichte, Johann Gottlieb. *Gesamtausgabe der Bayrischen Akademie der Wissenschaften*. Vols. 1.2, 1.4, 3.5. Ed. R. Lauth and H. Gliwitzky. Stuttgart-Bad Cannstatt:
Frommann, 1965–82.

Foucault, Michel. *The Order of Things: An Archeology of the Human Sciences*. New
York: Random House, 1973.

Frank, Manfred. ''Fragmente einer Geschichte der Selbstbewußtseins-Theorie von

Kant bis Sartre.'' *Selbstbewußtseinstheorien von Fichte bis Sartre*. Frankfurt: Suhrkamp, 1991. 413–599.

———. ''Die Philosophie des sogenannten 'magischen Idealismus.' '' *Euphorion* 63 (1969): 88–116.

Hegel, Georg Friedrich Wilhelm. *Ästhetik I*. Berlin: Aufbau Verlag, 1955.

Hemsterhuis, Frans. *Oeuvres Philosophiques I–III*. Ed. L. S. P. Meyboom. Hildesheim: Olms, 1972.

Kant, Immanuel. *Anthropologie in pragmatischer Hinsicht*. 1798. Werkausgabe XII. Ed. W. Weischedel. Frankfurt: Suhrkamp, 1964.

———. *Kritik der reinen Vernunft* (1781–87). Hamburg: Meiner, 1955.

Leibniz, G. W. *Hauptschriften zur Grundlegung der Philosophie*. Trans. A. Buchenau, ed. with contributions Ernst Cassirer. 3rd ed. Hamburg: Felix Meiner, 1966.

Menninghaus, Winfried. *Unendliche Verdopplung: Die frühromantische Grundlegung der Kunsttheorie im Begriff absoluter Selbstreflexion*. Frankfurt: Suhrkamp, 1987.

Novalis Schriften. Vols. 1–4. Ed. R. Samuel, H.-J. Mähl, and G. Schulz. Stuttgart: Kohlhammer, 1960, 1975, 1981, 1983.

Rorty, Richard. *Philosophy and the Mirror of Nature*. Oxford: Basil Blackwell, 1989.

Saussure, Ferdinand de. *Course in General Linguistics*. New York: McGraw-Hill, 1966.

Seyhan, Azade. *Representation and Its Discontents: The Critical Legacy of German Romanticism*. Berkeley: U of California P, 1992.

Stadler, Ulrich. ''Hardenbergs 'poetische Theorie der Fernröhre.' Der Synkretismus von Philosophie und Poesie, Natur- und Geisteswissenschaften und seine Konsequenzen für eine Hermeneutik bei Novalis.'' *Die Aktualität der Frühromantik*. Ed. E. Behler and J. Hörisch. Paderborn: Schöningh, 1987. 51–62.

Uerlings, Herbert. *Friedrich von Hardenberg, genannt Novalis: Werk und Forschung*. Stuttgart: Metzler, 1991.

Walker, Joyce. ''Romantic Chaos: The Dynamic Paradigm in Novalis's *Heinrich von Ofterdingen* and Contemporary Science.'' *German Quarterly* 66.1 (1993): 43–59.

Wittgenstein, Ludwig. *Tractatus Logico-Philosophicus*. London: Routledge, 1974.

The Dialectic of Romantic Enlightenment and the Psychodynamics of the Hypervisual in Hölderlin's *Hyperion*

HARALD WEILNBÖCK

A pronounced emphasis on visual perception and expression characterizes and defines the cultural development of modernity since the Renaissance. Ramifications of this psychohistoric trend can be found both in the sciences and in the arts. The eighteenth century experienced a particular boost of the visual and inaugurated philosophical and scientific discussions about the functions and the significance of the five senses (Utz 19–39). Friedrich Hölderlin's texts, though not directly engaged in these theoretical discourses, provide a good example of this increased visualization of poetic language and literature. Within the milieu of late-eighteenth-century literary currents, Hölderlin's romantic emphasis on visual language represents the (identical) binary opposite of the Enlightenment's obsession with clarifying vision. Moreover, Hölderlin's writing can be classified as *hypervisual,* as it maintains and even intensifies the Enlightenment's focus on visual investment, but does not engage in its ideological emphasis on optical accuracy or in its empirical and objective framework. Thus, in the romantic vision a more ecstatic and potentially manic mode of visual perception and creation prevails, and at times preoccupies, Hölderlin's *Empedokles* and *Hyperion.* I will focus on the latter text and closely read some passages that highlight this impulse toward a new sort of visual perception and also inaugurate a new creative force. Rather than recounting a plot of incidences or the flow of dialogue mimetically, literature begins to convey images and visual impressions almost purely through figurative and metaphoric language, also including material of the nature of visualizing daydreaming. The technique of intensive visual troping is grammatically assisted by Hölderlin's paratactical style. Thus, his texts have a density and richness of imagery that anticipates impressionistic styles of painting and writing. At times the text displays an almost cinematographic mode of image

132

sequencing. Moreover, in analogy to the *Rückenfiguren* of romantic painter Caspar David Friedrich, the text thematicizes the position of the contemplative onlooker. It often depicts the protagonist contemplating landscapes and looking at nature with a painter's eye. Not only does the visual inspiration produce richness of visual language in its various tropes on a scale from metaphor to metonymy; but the text uses metaphors and allegories that raise the issue of vision itself. For instance, metaphors of the eye, of light, and of colors appear frequently. In this way, Hölderlin's texts represent the psychohistorical condition of hypervisuality, which underlines the aforementioned shift of paradigms in perception and creation, indicating a profound change of the individual's psychosomatic organization.

In this respect Hölderlin is one of the most modern authors of his time. This also is reflected by the history of Hölderlin's reception, which really only began in the twentieth century. The period when the world wars were fought sets the stage for both the Enlightenment's collapse (Horkheimer and Adorno) and the implosion of romantic visuality.[1] It is therefore all the more significant that the reception of Hölderlin's visual mode of writing began and proceeded with some momentum at this time: philosophers as different as Martin Heidegger, Walter Benjamin, and Theodor Adorno referred to Hölderlin's poetic language as a major foundation of their respective concepts of modernity without, however, fully recognizing the momentum of vision as its most powerful component. The particular history of reception indicates that this visual inspiration of modern poetic language has a dark side to it. I argue that vision's dark side of traumatic hypervisuality reflects cultural experiences of fragmentation and indicates an increasing alienation of the self from the perceived world. This applies both to the Enlightenment's supposedly clear vision and to romanticism's imaginative and synaesthetic countervision. *Hyperion* reveals this dark aspect of the visual milieu wherever vision and visual language collapse or turn compulsive, indulging in a symbiotic gaze of fusion and total narcissistic identification with the viewed object. In these instances, the intensified production of visual language coincides with a drop in what I will tentatively call vision's richness and liveliness. The visual mode of interaction and creation acquires a narcissistic dynamic and loses contact with its living environment. The Kantian contemplation (''Anschauung'') generates ''Enlightenment's mirror stage'' (Japp 82)—or, as the psychoanalyst Heinz Kohut would put it: the idealistic self develops a ''mirror transference'' with the world it set out to see and interact with but ultimately fails to reach and get in *touch* with (*Narzißmus* 140).

In this respect, I argue that the emergence of a bourgeois milieu of scientific and artistic visuality needs to be problematized as cultural and psychosomatic hypertrophy of the visual. The visual milieu has to be read as an indication of a long-term psychosocial traumatization, not only of the balance and cooperation of all senses, but also of the functioning of all channels of communication and interaction within the social world. Historically, the up-surge of the visual milieu in the seventeenth century was concurrent with the shift toward different forms of production, social life, and interaction (Habermas).

The text contains two direct indications of visuality as a sign of alienation and social deterioration rather than creative liberation and life-affirming emancipation: First, the intensified sense of vision does not coincide with an increased sharpness and/or richness of perception. Accuracy of perception, of course, cannot be measured by any ontological categories of the so-called reality. Accuracy has to be redefined as richness, multiplicity, and flexibility in relating to whatever is perceived. Richness of perception then means the ability to realize and integrate as many aspects of a real-life situation as possible without losing the minimal cohesion that is necessary for an empathic and purposeful (in whatever way) response on the part of the self. I will attempt to show that the tremendous dynamic of visuality in *Hyperion* originates in a nonrelational and potentially hysterical enthusiasm of projective aestheticization: the view on the outside world is highly projective, idiosyncratically narrowed, and troubled by ambiguities. This perceptual position indicates an impairment of the capacity to interact with and relate to the world in a flexible and responsive manner that is at the same time empathic and delineated.

The second indication of alienation in the visual milieu is that visual language and visual writing appear to be disturbed by experiences of touch. In a curious way, the visual fantasies and metaphors of this text are shot through with motifs of physical contact and touch. In one crucial instance it can be shown how the intense experience of a physical encounter makes the textual process of visual imagination and creation collapse, so that it has to reconstitute itself and rebuild the shattered capacity to envision the world and produce (visual) literature. Touch, the most immediately physical of all senses, can generally count as the opposite of the sense of vision, which is able to operate over great distances and is, in a way, the most nonphysical of all senses. Therefore, the eighteenth-century scientific and philosophical discourse on perception perceives vision and touch as a dichotomy and creates a debate as to which has the higher priority. Around 1800, Enlightenment's accuracy seemed to have won this debate, and vision occupied the highest rank on the scale of senses (Utz 19–39). In Hölderlin's language of poetic visuality, the experience of touch appears to be the repressed other, which, of course, is still desired by the self. Vision is intensified and, as it were, inflated precisely because the visual milieu resists and represses the experience of touch. In a more general perspective, one could refer to Winnicott's psychoanalytic observation of a pediatric phenomenon in which the ''over-activity of the mental function'' in children occurs in tandem with the disturbance of the psychophysical well-being and the "psychosomatic cohesion" of the self. This phenomenon from developmental psychoanalysis can serve as a leading notion for the conceptualization of the visual milieu ("Mind and Its Relation to the Psycho-Soma" 244), as well as the psychosocial mechanisms of this psychosomatic shift of perceptual paradigms. During the earliest stages of child development, a sense of touch is evidently the most important, with deprivation and traumatization in this area likely to impair the development and coordination of all other senses. More specifically in terms of vision and touch, Kohut observes that, "with some patients in mirror transference, the visual realm is over-cathected with investments which focus on this [visual] realm because other modes of interaction (for instance the oral and the tactile) have failed to respond to the child's narcissistic needs" (*Narzißmus* 142).

In Hölderlin's *Hyperion,* both the sense of vision and the sense of touch can be shown to fluctuate between states of manic overstimulation and states of depressive (and protective) numbness and dysfunction. This dynamic defines a cultural situation of general dissatisfaction and alienation regarding both the mode of perception and the mode of interaction with the world of objects. An object-relation milieu of this kind can be described in psychoanalytic terms as tendentially narcissistic, since the experiences expressed in the text resemble the expressions of personal suffering as they appear in accounts produced in psychotherapeutic settings. Since I draw mostly from self-psychology and object-relation theories, these accounts are theoretically situated in a post-Freudian context of sociological psychoanalysis.

On these theoretical grounds, I will define the concept of modern alienation first as a disorder of perception as it becomes more visual, less content-rich and flexible, and fetishistically fixated on certain—mostly visual—stimuli. Second, as perception is impaired, interpersonal (object) relations and the variety of available options for flexible and empathic response to a particular communicative (and political) situation narrow. Narcissistic styles of perception and behavior abound. Varied responsiveness, empathic capacity, and personal demarcation are replaced by an incessant and insatiable tendency toward symbiotic fusion and identification with another person, which is essentially achieved visually. The flip side of this romantic adoration is the fervent denigration of the identification-resistant other. On a different level, this narcissistic fusion or identification can also be established with an abstract and more or less mythic entity, like an idea of fusion and/or homogeneity—for example, the idea of a nation, or the visualized idea of the space of a country, of a race, of nature per se, or of art. Because the milieu of visual perception and visual identification uses, as it were, the world as a screen for a permanent mirror stage, it is inevitably accompanied by a potential for tremendous rage and violence. In mirror transference, aggression is activated whenever the real world does not want to, or cannot, act as an unconditionally reliable point of identification and as an agent of visual mirroring of the gaze of the self and its idiosyncratic imagination (Kohut, "Thoughts on Narcissism"). For this reason, the poetic text of a pronounced visual inspiration shows signs of tremendous and yet repressed aggression.

The way Hyperion experiences and describes his departure from his home island of Smyrna anticipates the visual mode of much of the writing and depicted (inter)action that follows. Despite the active decisiveness of his departure, Hyperion experiences it in a quasi-cinematographic position of a spectator's passivity. Lying motionless and comfortably on the boat, he looks back to his hometown and becomes the imaginative onlooker of his former sphere of life: "In wonderful tranquillity, just like a child who does not know about the next moment, I lay there on the boat, I saw the trees and the mosques of this town, the green paths on the coast, and my usual way up to the Acropolis, this I looked at and I let it go on and on always further."[2] His gaze follows the paths he once went on. The boat in its motion slightly changes the camera angle of his perspective for him, and Hyperion lets this gaze "go on and on always further," like a film does. Hyperion cherishes this position as ultimate childlike bliss. A psychoanalytic reading, however, would add that the childlike bliss of an entirely passive and visual contemplation and fusion is already a little less than ultimate or optimal, since such visual bliss has already sacrificed the more direct and physical modes of interaction. Therefore, instead of having undergone a conscious leave-taking and the work of mourning, the reality of loss dawns on Hyperion with sudden vehemence and as an utter shock once the filmlike images sink into the sea "wie ein Sarg in's Grab" (like a coffin into a grave) (*Hyp.* 2:622). When the film breaks, the visual identification breaks down too, and tremendous fear results.

In accordance with what much of contemporary film theory says about cinematic perception, Hyperion's camera-like gaze is not really very perceptive but almost idiosyncratically selective and highly projective. Simply speaking, what is outside the gaze is less important then what the gazing eye projects onto the outside. On the boat trip to Diotima's home island, Hyperion is again in complete passivity "in Charons Nachen" (in Charon's boat), and he drinks from the "Schaale des Vergessenheit" (bowl of oblivion) (*Hyp.* 2:639). The wheelman tries to show him places, but "ich sah nicht lange hin, und war im nächsten Augenblike wieder in meinen eigenen lieben Träumen" (I did not look at it too long, and in the next moment I was again in my beloved dreams). However, when the mountains of Diotima's home island appear, Hyperion is touched by a "wunderbare[n] Gewalt" (wonderful power): "Mit großem Auge, staunend und freudig sah' ich hinaus in die Geheimnisse der Ferne" (With big eyes, marveling and joyful, I looked outside into the secrets of the far) (2:639). But even in this moment of intense visual perception, there are secrets, things that cannot be seen, that Hyperion focuses on—while at the same time losing his focus into the far. It will become more evident later that, even in loving and interacting with Diotima, Hyperion narcissistically stays in his own "lieben Träumen" or focuses on the "Geheimnisse der Ferne."

While Hyperion's gaze is intense and existentially charged with energy and/or significance, he sees neither very much nor very clearly. In one of many scenes in which he romantically contemplates landscape, he is "verloren in's weite Blau, blick' ich oft hinauf an den Aether und hinein in's heilige Meer" (lost in the far blue, [he] often looked up into the ether and into the sacred ocean) (*Hyp.* 2:585). This intense glance from the tip of the mountain into nature does not seem to expect more than the undifferentiated blue as an all-encompassing visual mode of the world. Therefore, the ocean and the sky become identical and mirror each other. Moreover, both entities, after merging with each other, fuse with the color of the viewing eyes themselves, which in *Hyperion*—whenever their color is specified—are always fair, that is, blue (2:720, 753), or are even explicitly designated as "Aetheraugen" (ether eyes) (2:706, 731). This color leveling anticipates a more general nivelation of all specific objects, which in this contemplating gaze tend to fuse into one big blue cloud of ether. The world is painted quasi-impressionistically, and more than that, in one particular shade of color. It is perceived as if through a blurry blue-filter of a camera.[3] Thus the visual screening serves the narcissistic impulse "Eines zu seyn mit Allem, das ist Leben der Gottheit" (to be one with everything; this is the life of the goddess) (2:585). In this respect, it seems to be more than just a metaphor when in *Empedokles* Pausanias exclaims about his mentor that "himmlisch jugentlich [du] den holden Schein / Von dir auf jedes eigen überstralst, / Daß alle deines Geistes Farbe tragen" (your sublime light falls upon every single thing, so that every one bears your spirit's color) (2:708). In a political context, this kind of intensely projective visuality is likely to inspire a totalizing, if not totalitarian, perspective. However enthusiastically this view might express itself in literature, with respect to the social milieu it implies the contrary of responsive and life-affirming styles of interaction: "Ich liebe dieß Griechenland überall. Es trägt die Farbe meines Herzens. Wohin man siehet liegt eine Freude begraben" (I love Greece everywhere. It bears the color of my heart. Wherever you look a joy is buried) (*Hyp.* 2:637). Here the ecstatically projected vision even turns into an X-ray view. Just as Hyperion in the boat saw the "Geheimnisse der Ferne" (secrets of the far), in this instance he sees something from the past that is "begraben" (buried) under the real, existing world. The fundamental ambivalence of a joy that is attached to buried things goes unnoticed. Diotima expresses this impressionistic impulse for the image and for "Schein" in the immediate context of the denial of death: "Sterblichkeit ist Schein, ist, wie die Farben, die vor unserem Auge zittern, wenn es lange in die Sonne sieht!"

(Mortality is an apparition, it is like the colors that tremble before our eye if it looks into the Sun for a long time) (2:672).

The narcissistic denial of mortality anticipates the neglect not only of the difference between colors but of difference altogether. In another instance of romantic vision from atop a mountain, Hyperion feels that "das kochende Meer der Wooge des Kornfelds gleicht" (the boiling sea equals the wave of the cornfields) (*Hyp.* 2:585). This also applies the other way around: "At noon I was on top of the mountains. . . . Like an ocean the country lay before me from which I ascended; it was a heavenly infinite play of colors . . . and as the Sun of the sky again found itself in the thousandfold change of the light that the earth gave back to it, my spirit recognized itself in the bounty of life."[4] The landscape, which is an infinitely more differentiated sight than the blue sky and the blue ocean, is compared with and finally identified with the ocean. The differentiated landscape, with all its evidence of nature, human life, and culture, is dissolved into ether. It is hymnically perceived and yet reduced to an indistinguishable "Farbenspiel" (play of colors) and a "tausendfache[r] Wechsel des Lichts" (thousandfold change of the light), which refers back to the experience Diotima expressed in her denial of death. In turning from the ocean view toward the contemplation of landscape, it seems as if the spectator on the mountain peak suffers, at the moment the overstimulation of his impressionistic color filter collapses into its identical opposite, the radicalized expressionist vision of "tausendfache[r] Wechsel"—and sees nothing really. The narcissistic isolation of this lonely and yet manic visionary is complete when he deludes himself into believing he is in the midst of life's bounty ("Fülle"), while actually he is at a maximum distance from concrete life and cannot even discern any of its manifestations.

The mirror quality of this form of projective perception and interaction is expressed doubly in the passage just quoted. The Sun is described as finding itself mirrored in its own "tausendfache[r] Wechsel des Lichts," which the world reflects again. In direct analogy to this paradigm of a substanceless but highly energetic mirroring, Hyperion states that his spirit is reflected in what he calls the bounty of life, which he cannot differentiate in the process of perception. This notion of bounty of life, as self-referential and projective as it actually is in this instance, can be psychologically understood as an expression of the desire to achieve a rich and emotionally satisfying mode of object relation. However, due to his narcissistic and manic-depressive disposition, Hyperion appears compelled to shift back and forth between manic overstimulation and profound depression and thus cannot achieve any working relationship. The manic phase is experienced as ecstatic sensation of light and color, and the depressive phase is defined by total darkness, "eine Nacht unsrer Seele, wo kein Schimmer eines Sterns, wo nicht einmal ein faules Holz uns leuchtet" (the night of our soul when not a glimmer of a star and not even a rotten piece of wood gives us light) (*Hyp.* 2:627). Already in mild depression vision is depleted and images fade: "Ich [Hyperion] ließ auch wirklich die Erscheinungen der Welt vorüberziehn, wie Nebel im Herbste" (I [Hyperion] let the appearances of the world really walk past me like the fog of autumn) (2:624). One has to keep in mind that it is not really any capacity for rich and flexible perception that is lost in the autumn fog of depression. What he is missing here is the projective energy of his habitual enthusiastic gaze with which he creates the image through imagination rather than seeing and relating to the world. Therefore, the moments of manic visual ecstasy do not yield any higher level of clarity and differentiated perception than the moments of autumn fog of depression do. In moments of ecstasy "I looked for the highest mountains . . . and my spirit extended over the visible world as if it was his; wonderful! sometimes I felt as if my fire purified and melted the things of the world like gold, and something divine became of it."[5] The ecstatic gaze fuses and melts everything into one entity, just as it did through the concept of ether. Here, this entity, of all things, is gold, which is immediately appropriated, that is, turned into property "als wäre sie sein" (as if it was his). It is precisely because the depressed as well as the manic gaze sees nothing really and relates to nothing really that this optical mode of (non)relating comes with a tendency to take possession of whatever enters its field of vision.

In any political perspective, this viewpoint has worrisome implications. Energetically charged from his ecstatic mountain-view contemplation, Hyperion decides to go down to civilization in order to not only share his enthusiasm but also cure and elevate the allegedly alienated people: "I had been too fortunate in collecting the beauty of nature to not fill the gaps of human life with it. My pitiable Smyrna appeared in the colors of my enthusiasm and stood like a bride."[6] This attempt to provide compensation for the supposed alienation of others formulates itself in a visual mode when it sets out to fill "gaps of human life" with light. The projective gaze turns messianic while it illuminates and enlightens these gaps with the color of its enthusiasm. It closes off, as it were, the independent life of these niches of the unseen, while it projectively turns their reality into his "bride" and his possession. This procedure may count as exemplary of romantic pedagogy in general (Miller). It holds as little promise for any concrete political work as it is capable of concrete perception. Not surprisingly, this enthusiasm does not last long, and with the beginning of the next letter Hyperion again withdraws into his reclusion. He is confined to a narcissistic object-relation mode: he misses "de[n] schöne[n] Trost, in Einer Seele meine Welt zu finden, mein Geschlecht in einem freundlichen Bilde zu umarmen" (the consolation of being able to find one's own world in one's soul and to embrace his own kind in a friendly image) (2:603)—the image of a bride who invariably belongs to the one who owns this perception of her. The recipient of this quasi-marital embrace virtually

139

has the status of a "friendly" mirror image with which the self fuses possessively while the other is not acknowledged as a real person: "Was ich sah, ward ich, und es war Göttliches, was ich sah" (what I saw, I became, and what I saw was divine) (2:591). This mechanism of projective identification performs at the same time the idolization of an object and the aggrandizement of the self.

Already the first few letters of the letter-novel *Hyperion* delineate the visual mode of perception and existence and express some interference from visuality's repressed other, the sense of touch. If we were to look for a topographical trademark for Hölderlin's writing, we would have to choose the position of the lonesome but all-the-more inspired poet on a mountain peak. He casts hymnic glances at the surrounding landscape, from which he is at the same time maximally removed. *Hyperion* begins in this aloof position. The hero stands on the "Höhn des Korinthischen Isthmus" (heights of the Isthmus of Corinth) (*Hyp.* 2:583) and looks down onto the Greek countryside. Already in this very first instance of pronounced visuality, the cloaked and obfuscated desire for a more direct and/or physical contact with the world finds its indirect expression in metaphoric language: "and like the bee among flowers my soul often flies back and forth between the two oceans which on the right and on the left side cool the feet of my glowing mountains. One of the two bays ["Meerbusen," ocean bosoms] should have especially pleased me."[7] Intense visual contemplation produces figurative language about motifs of the body and of physicality: the bosoms of the ocean kiss the red-hot glowing feet of the (male) mountains. The heat of this imagined contact reveals both the intensity of the desire and the tremendous fear of getting in touch with human life, which in the vaguely distanced form of a landscape becomes the subject of the onlooker's almost hypnotic contemplation. The fact that Hyperion here positions himself vis-à-vis and above a pair of "Meerbusen" would suffice for a more traditional psychoanalytic approach to assume the enactment of a reverse scene of breast-feeding in which the reactively subjugated bosoms "cool the feet" of the male mountain. Be this as it may, what is important in terms of object-relation theory is the fact that Hyperion as a contemplative spectator positions himself at a maximum distance from the world in order to be able to enjoy it in his particular mode of visual and solipsistic enthusiasm. He subsequently produces these intensely charged metaphors of physical contact, which represent the other side of his visual position and induce anxiety. Because of this anxiety, the closure of this letter explicitly excludes all other human life: "Forget that there are human beings, beleaguered and endlessly humiliated heart, and return where you came from, into the arms of nature, the immutable, calm and beautiful."[8] Of course, not only human beings but nature itself is really only immutable, calm, and beautiful if one takes the aloof and (an)aesthet(ic)ized position of a distant onlooker who does not bother or cannot bear the less beautiful details and more intense experiences that nature and real interaction with humans have to offer once one gets closer. The spectator cannot bear or perceive his contemporary reality because his most vehement need rests in the past and on a more imaginary level: He aims for the total "return . . . into the arms" of symbiotic merging with an image. The desire for touch is paradoxically experienced in a doubly imaginative way through the visual fusion with a romanticized landscape.

The narcissist's encounter with and confrontation with the real, existing world is inevitable in the end and likely to trigger some form of aggression, which will be directed either toward himself or toward the world. In its overall thrust toward civilizational nemesis and liberation warfare, *Hyperion* reveals a constant propensity toward aggression. This surfaces most clearly and very abruptly in Hyperion's barbed and hateful speech about Germany, which euphemistically went down in literary history as Hölderlin's reprimand ("Scheltrede") of the Germans. On closer examination, this sudden activation of a latent potential of rage also stems from a situation of increased nonvisual closeness with the concrete world. For this passage is the only one in which the German poet Hölderlin writes or has Hyperion write about Germany, but he writes from an ostensibly foreign perspective. After Hölderlin has situated the entire novel in Greece, which he has never visited in person and all the more intensely envisions in literature, he for a brief moment gets in touch with the topic of Germany. Germany, of course, is much closer to the author personally than the setup of the novel admits and, thus, provokes in him a great anger. Hölderlin/Hyperion steps down, as it were, from the aloof position of his mountain view of Greece and gets in touch with the real world, that is, Germany, which cannot easily be deflected through aestheticized visualization. Any close contact with the complexities of the real world is demanding and sends the author into a fit of narcissistic rage. This impulse likens Hölderlin to his hero Hyperion, who gets very impatient whenever he comes too close to the allegedly Philistine people of any Greek village and finally takes refuge in some form of seclusion.

This constant potential for aggression is inherent in a cultural milieu of intensified vision, and in more subtle ways it already expresses itself in the very first pages of the novel. The mountain view of Corinth induces in Hyperion fantasies about the youthful and aggressive Corinthians of antiquity, who distributed and indulged in the wealth of their robberies. Any ethical consideration of this lifestyle of violent appropriation is precluded by visual and imaginative enthusiasm. At the beginning of the second book, Hyperion once again sits on top of a mountain on the island of Salamis. There he engages in what seems to be his daily evening ritual of contemplating the peninsula of Attica, across from Salamis: "There I spend my loveliest hours, there I sit whole evenings long looking across toward Attica, until finally my heart pounds too heavily. Then I take my equipment, go down to the bay, and catch fish.''[9] This sort of contemplation generates an energetic charge that makes Hyperion leave the position of the spectator and catch fish, which does not appear to be a sign of aggression in any troublesome sense of the word. However, the rather belligerent dynamic of this seemingly innocuous ritual of visual contemplation is shown more clearly in the continuation of this scene and/or visual tableau: "I catch fish. Or on my mountain peak I also read about the old magnificent sea battle that was once storming at Salamis in a wild and prudently directed chaos, and then I enjoy the spirit who was able to direct and tame the raging chaos of friends and foes like the rider of a horse.''[10] The contemplative charge breeds visions and fantasies of tumultuous war scenes in which violence seems to be as much an expression of hostility as of an almost erotic comradeship. This romantic aestheticization of warfare and physical violence is inspired by the hidden but hystericized desire of the visually isolated individual to gain a more immediate physical contact and thus physically stimulate the psychosomatic self.

Within romantic topography, the mountain view's identical other side is the subterranean location in the (Platonic) cave. Hyperion fantasizes about withdrawing with Diotima into the "Tiefen der Gebirgswelt" (depth of the mountain world), where "wird das Geheimniß unseres Herzens ruhn, wie das Edelgestein im Schacht, im Schooße der himmelragenden Wälder" (the secret of our heart will lie quietly like the marble in the cave, in the deepest midst of trees that reach for the sky) (*Hyp.* 2:748). The innermost deepness of the symbiotic connection with the cave "reach[es] for the sky" just as the mountain view focused the blue ether. The real world on the surface of the earth constitutes the topographical in-between of the cave and the peak and remains inaccessible to and estranged from the viewer. The visual isolation and imperceptibility of the concrete surface world is complete in both positions: "und [im Schacht] wir werden sitzen am Quell, in seinem Spiegel unsere Welt betrachten" ([in the cave] we will sit at the spring, and in its mirror we will look at the world) (2:748). From the perspective within the cave, the spring outside the cave is said to be surrounded by trees reaching for the sky; here, too, the precinematic view on the world is confined to one's own image and to the blue of the sky's ether.

Themes of visuality and physicality in this text can often be found intertwined in a more elaborate manner than through metaphoric reference. A certain tender physicality already is part of the contemplative experience: the ether gaze into the "far blue" is accompanied by the imagination that "ein verwandter Geist mir die Arme [öffnet'], als löste der Schmerz der Einsamkeit sich auf in's Leben der Gottheit" (a related spirit opens his arms, and the grief of loneliness dissolves into the life of a goddess) (*Hyp.* 2:585). This embrace, strictly speaking, remains a visual and imaginary scene. However, the account ends with the nonchalant mentioning of a clearly physical sensation: "die zarte Welle der Luft mir um die Brust spielt" (a tender whiff of air plays around [my] chest). The position of increased narcissistic needs displays a preference for the physical stimulation through whole-body skin sensation rather then through a specific erotogenic zone and/or a particular physical fantasy. In this manner the physical borders of the fragile core identity are sensually reconfirmed. What for the visual position is the desire for mirroring through the constant and absolutely reliable gaze of the other, on the level of physical sensation the need for perfect "holding" (Winnicott in Hughes 143) is that which potentially escalates into excessive whole-body skin stimulation (Reich 305). In order to be less threatening, this stimulation is not delivered by an actual other but by an abstract and anonymous entity, such as nature: "And when I often lay there under the flowers and took a sunbath in the tender spring light, and while I looked up into the fair blue that encompassed the warm earth, when I . . . sat after a refreshing rainfall when the twigs were still trembling from the caresses of the sky, and when over the dripping forest golden clouds moved. . . ."[11] In this Werther reference, Hyperion is not quite aware that he himself, much more than the twigs, is trembling from the caresses through the dripping forest and through the sunbath, that it is he who feels encompassed and held by the blue ether and the golden clouds, he who needs to be held this way.

There is, of course, nothing per se symptomatic or ominous about sensual fantasies and/or actions of this kind unless they coincide with a cultural and social milieu of profound dissatisfaction and disorientation. Then a culture of vision and tender skin erotics is prone to escalate into masochistic extremes of violent skin stimulation. Empedokles' suicidal leap into the (skin-)burning volcano is one extreme form of this psychosomatic escalation (Reich 305). Hyperion's impulse to engage in warfare, too, follows a psychosomatic dynamic that aims for a suicidal maximum of physical stimulation: "gäb' es eine Arbeit, einen Krieg für mich, das sollte mich erquiken!" (if there was only a task or a war for me, that would refresh me!) (*Hyp.* 2:652). *Hyperion* and *Empedokles* can be read as a sadomasochistic pair of texts expressing two sides of an identical state of psychosomatic alienation. If Empedokles is suicidally and masochistically driven to leap into the volcano, Hyperion turns this aggressive dynamic around and becomes himself the sadistic volcano: ". . . this incredible and magnificent striving. To be everything and all that, like the Titan of the [volcano] Aetna, storms upward from the depth of our being. And yet, who would not rather feel it inside himself, like the boiling oil, instead of admitting that one is born for the whip and for the yoke."[12] The alternative between Empedokles and Hyperion is the sadomasochistic one: between jumping into the burning volcano and fusing with totality, or himself being the volcano and spraying the boiling oil onto others, thus fusing these others with himself. The sense of touch goes rampant in a disturbing way while the sense of vision is inflated to its neurotic primacy and still remains incapable of providing enough mirroring support for the fragile self in order to not be driven into psychosomatic desperation.

Hyperion's relationship with Diotima provides crucial insight into the dynamic of love in these times of increasing visualization. Not surprisingly, Hyperion declares the visual event of seeing Diotima to be the ultimate consumption of his love. He pronounces himself unalienably and fully happy, "wenn auch der heilige Moment, wo ich sie zum erstenmale sie sah, der lezte wäre gewesen" (even if the sacred moment when I first saw her would have been the last) (*Hyp.* 2:643). From this very optical mode of experience Hyperion derives a sense of superiority vis-à-vis his friend Bellarmin, who lives in Germany and who, as Hyperion hastens to stress, has "never seen" her. He distances himself from Bellarmin in a unique and surprisingly antagonistic gesture: "da denke ihres Wesens . . . und denke meiner Seeligkeit! aber vergiß nicht, daß ich hatte, was du ahnest, daß ich mit diesen Augen sah, was nur, wie in Wolken dir erscheint" (contemplate her being . . . and think of my bliss; but do not forget that I had what you only imagined, that I saw with these eyes what appeared to you only as in clouds) (2:644). Hyperion's sudden and unprecedented protestation about the supposed uniqueness and authenticity of his experience of Diotima as opposed to Bellarmin's merely textual experience via the letters he received from Hyperion is odd. There is really nothing—it seems—that Hyperion could possibly lose to Bellarmin, who, in any event, is far away and totally reduced to the function of a mirroring self-object and, therefore, is never granted a single return letter. Rather, Hyperion's protestation reveals his very narcissistic position. For despite his protestations, Hyperion himself is not really able to relate to Diotima in any other way than to contemplate her and imagine her in a quasi-literary manner. In spite of the fact that he actually was with her, Hyperion was not able to break out of his narcissistic shell and experience anything beyond what Bellarmin or Alabanda, his Greek friend, could experience while merely reading or hearing about her. Curiously, this also works the other way around. Just as Hyperion is detached even though he was with Diotima, Alabanda is intensely attached without personally knowing her. Alabanda is going to reject Hyperion's offer to live with him and Diotima because he fears that the visual reconfirmation of his already existing (imaginary) identification with Diotima could become devastatingly intense: "Um Diotimas willen würd' ich dich betrügen und am Ende mich und Diotima morden, weil wir doch nicht Eines wären" (For Diotima I would betray you and in the end kill her and myself because we would not be able to be one after all) (2:756). Tragically, within the narcissistic realm of this doubled double bind, the mode of imaginative literary adoration is the closest one can get to another person.

In this process of literary idealization, metaphors and allegories of the eye and of viewing play a crucial role. Hyperion hymnically exclaims that his heart was devoted to hers, just "wie die Wimper für das Auge da ist" (as the eyelash is there for the eye) (*Hyp.* 2:655). The consumption of this love is total and at the same time totally visual: "und all mein Leben sich hingab in den Stralen des Augs, das sie nur sah, nur sie umfaßte" (all my life was invested into the eye that only she saw, only she comprehended) (*Hyp.* 2:655). This is an entirely self-referential flow of life in that this "eye that only she saw" is actually his own eye in a total fixation on her. Such narcissistic infatuation does not come without an aggressive and/or slightly arrogant potential. "Where is the being that recognized her like I did? In which mirror were the rays of this light collected like in mine? [In which mirror] was she blissfully shocked by her own glory because she did not see herself before she saw herself in my joy?"[13] What is ominous on a linguistic level is the fact that the emphasis on the visual tropes and on the theme of vision appears to propel the breakdown of metaphoric language itself into literal reference, which as a linguistic indication of fragmentation coincides with the breakdown of interpersonal relationships. Therefore, Diotima is a vision rather than a figure already in this initial encounter and thus clearly on her/its way to being expelled from the plot as a real figure in order to become a mere fantasy that will then be all the more enthusiastically idealized in Hyperion's lifelong ritual of literary writing.

In a context of such pronounced visuality, it is worthwhile to take a precise look at the scene in which the romantic lovers actually have some sort of a physical encounter. This encounter must be called coincidental rather than intentional because while Diotima was still fearfully withdrawing, Hyperion found himself completely incapable of approaching her in any intentional manner. He rather "lebt" in "Gedanken an sie" (lived in thoughts about her) (*Hyp.* 2:667), and this is something he would never really stop doing. He imagines her everyday procedures, and as a narcissistic feedback imagines her being lost in thoughts of exactly the same kind: "Daß ja nichts meine Friedliche störe, wenn sie mit süßen Phantasien ihr Herz erfrischt" (That nothing may disturb my peaceful woman when she refreshes herself with sweet fantasies) (2:668). This state of mind is imaginative and visual and, therefore, fundamentally opposed to and threatened by physical contact: "daß ja nichts diese Traube betaste und den erquikenden Thau von den zarten Beeren ihr streife!" (nothing may touch this grape and wipe off the refreshing dew from the tender berries!) (2:668). And yet imaginative visuality unwittingly gravitates toward its other of physicality. However, in the visual milieu, meaningful and concrete action emerges most often in the form of an unconscious and compulsive force that seems entirely beyond intent and control. Hyperion continues: "Thus I dreamed. However, while the thoughts were looking for her

145

within the walls of the house, the feet were looking for her elsewhere, and before I realized it I found myself walking under the arches of the holy forest . . . where I saw her for the first time."[14] While Hyperion's visual imagination precinematically projects fantasies onto the screens of his room's walls, his body, as it were, splits off and his feet sleepwalk him to the place not where he knew he could actually meet Diotima but where he *saw* her first. Since anxiety is felt whenever the body takes over, Hyperion at this point evokes a fantasy of annihilation upon arriving at this place: "jezt ergriff mich eine Gewalt, als trät' ich in Dianen's Schatten, um zu sterben vor der gegenwärtigen Gottheit" (now a force took power over me as if I entered Diana's shadow in order to die before the present goddess) (2:668). This fantasy is placed, as it were, under the negative gaze of the other of light, which is Diana's shadow.

At this stage of Hyperion's move toward the body of the other, the dissociation of body and soul seems to reverse itself, and "die Seele war vorausgeeilt, und hatte die irrdischen Glieder verlassen" (the soul has rushed ahead and has left the earthly members behind) (*Hyp*. 2:668). This self-perception could be called a defensive delusion because it has the soul rush on right before the lovers actually meet and have their first bodily encounter. At the moment of encounter, however, perception and imagination break down completely: "Ich hörte nicht mehr und vor dem Auge dämmerten und schwankten alle Gestalten" (I did not hear anything anymore, and before my eye all figures were shaking) (2:669). The lovers literally and metaphorically run into each other at the place where Hyperion first *saw* Diotima. This can only be explained as coincidence or otherwise imagined as predestination.[15] The physical encounter makes Hyperion lose consciousness completely: "Schwinde, schwinde, sterbliches Leben. . . . Es ist hier eine Lüke in meinem Daseyn. Ich starb, und wie ich erwachte, lag ich am Herzen des himmlischen Mädchens" (Disappear, disappear, mortal life. . . . At this point there is a gap in my existence. I died, and when I reawakened I lay at the heart of the heavenly maid) (2:669). What happened? This phrase at first seems to suggest a very intense physical or even sexual encounter. However, the various scenic depictions of this situation, which are given after Hyperion rose from the dead, are entirely confusing and inconsistent. First Hyperion lies "at the heart of the heavenly maid," which suggests that the couple is actually lying on the ground. A few lines later they seem to be standing: "lag das reizende Köpfchen mir auf der Schulter, lächelte süßen Frieden, und schlug sein ätherisch Auge nach mir auf" (the enchanting little head lay on my shoulder and her etheric eyes looked up to me); and only a little bit later, with the explicit reaffirmation of the standing position, undisturbed visuality sets in again full force: "lange standen wir so in holder selbstvergessener Betrachtung" (we stood long this way in blissful unselfconscious contemplation) (2:669). Here any physicality in this event seems to be denied again.

Hyperion's sensual and perceptive apparatus suffers considerable shock and confusion throughout this process of approaching a moment of physical closeness. First, the physical and the mental, that is, visual, split up completely. Then Hyperion loses consciousness in the moment of touch, and after regaining it (and even in the retrospective of the letter-writing process) he does not seem able or willing to give a consistent scenic visualization and description of the event he experienced. What is given resembles more an experimental superimposition of various points of view or camera angles.[16] It is only when this disruptive and subversive moment has passed completely that the romantic couple safely reenters its state of visual identification and symbiotic fusion: "Laß mich, rief ich, laß mich dein seyn, laß mich mein vergessen, laß alles Leben in mir und allen Geist nur dir zufliegen; nur dir, in seeliger endeloser Betrachtung!" (Let me, I exclaimed, be you; let me forget myself, let all life and all spirit in me fly to you, only to you in blissful endless contemplation!) (2:670).

The experience of touch, however, remains a desired and frighteningly hyperstimulating issue. In a situation that requires Hyperion to hold Diotima, he feels that "und Taumel und Toben war in allen Sinnen, und die Hände brannten mir, wie Kohlen, da ich sie berührte" (a tempestuous frenzy was in all my senses, and my hands were burning like live coals when I touched her) (*Hyp.* 2:647). It is essential to realize that this eccentricity by no means indicates a satisfying and fulfilling life situation—on the contrary. Later Hyperion tells Bellarmin that "when her heavenly head dying from bliss sank down along my bare neck and the sweet lips lay on my pulsating chest . . . Oh Bellarmin, my senses faded and my spirit fled."[17] The writing about this sensuous moment immediately creates tremendous anxiety, and Hyperion continues with an extremely violent metaphor: "ich sehe, wie das enden muß. Das Steuer ist in die Wooge gefallen und das Schiff wird, wie an den Füßen ein Kind, ergriffen und an die Felsen geschleudert" (I see how this must end. The rudder had fallen into the ocean, and the ship is seized by the feet like a child and thrown against the rock) (2:674). This romantic and contemplative couple cannot bear closeness and, therefore, finds justifications to separate again. Diotima sends Hyperion on an educational journey through Europe. Hyperion, choosing a more male version of this avoidance reaction, follows the impulse to wage a war of liberation side by side with a male alter ego and rejoins Alabanda.

After the profound narcissistic mortification of losing the battle, Hyperion is entirely incapable of being with Diotima—the projection of his self-idealization. The melodramatic undertones in which this is expressed give ample proof of the inability to truly mourn her absence. Finally, Diotima does what the whole literary romantic thrust of this *love novel* somehow anticipates her doing: She commits a mysterious form of mental suicide. Even here the text reads quite melodramatically. Hyperion, after effectively equating love with death, especially anything physical about love, and after denying the reality of death at the same time, does not really seem to mind the death of Diotima very much. This is in a sad way consistent, since the woman whom he could not really touch and whom he could not really encounter other than in a visual and quasi-literary way might just as well not be there at all. Thus Hyperion can idealize Diotima all the more in an inspired fashion and write about her— not as a person but rather as an image. Already after his suicidal engagement for the Russian army, it was "dein Bild mit seinem Himmelssinne, hab' ich noch, wie einen Hausgott, aus dem Brande gerettet" (your image with its heavenly sense [that] I was able to save from the fire like a household god) (*Hyp.* 2:750). Likewise, Hyperion wishes that after his death Diotima would walk through the landscape they had enjoyed together, while "und laß . . . dir mein Bild dabei begegnen" (my image would encounter you) (2:734). For the aesthetic and/or visual mind it is the fact that "einen schönen Tod ist meine Diotima gestorben" (my Diotima died a beautiful death) that inspires life: "das ist's auch [der schöne Tod der Diotima], was mich aufweckt, und meine Seele mir wiedergiebt" (it is this [the beauty of Diotima's death] that reawakens me and gives back to me my soul) (2:770). The inability to relate to another person in a sensual and empathic manner inspires this aesthetic and visual mode of existence within one's own literary script. In the cultural milieu of a literary absolute (Lacoue-Labarthe and Nancy), the world and in particular the woman, inasmuch as it constitutes a difference, has to be idealistically adjusted to or aggressively excluded from the writer's own visual image. Since the actual woman is removed from the plot, Hyperion's literary and imaginative productivity can flourish. Therefore he ends the novel on a strangely promising note rather than on a note of mournfulness: "Nächstens mehr" (Next time more of this) (2:782). The curious intensity and even the beauty of romantic vision and light foreshadows the catastrophes that the visual milieu is going to undergo one century later when, during the period of the two world wars, the (visual) reception of Hölderlin will begin.

Notes

1. Visuality and specularization as phenomenon in the context of fascism is discussed by Paul Virilio; by Russell Berman as "the privileging of sight and visual representation" (100); and by Thomas Elsaesser in his fascism formula "to be is to be seen" (50).
2. "Mit einer wunderbaren Ruhe, recht, wie ein Kind, das nichts vom nächsten Augenblick weiß, lag ich so da auf meinem Schiffe, und sah die Bäume und Moskeen dieser Stadt an, meine grünen Gänge an dem Ufer, meinen Fußsteig zur Akropolis hinauf, das sah ich an und ließ es weiter gehn und immer weiter" (*Hyp.* 2:622). All translations are mine unless otherwise indicated.

3. In this context it seems congruent if a recent publication on Hölderlin is composed as a photo collection that, while using impressionistic and pointillistic techniques, attempts to evoke Hölderlin's life and oeuvre as a photographic vision (Straub).

4. "Um Mittag war ich auf der Höhe des Gebirgs. . . . Wie ein Meer, lag das Land, wovon ich heraufkam, vor mir da, jugendlich, voll lebendiger Freude; es war ein himmlisch unendlich Farbenspiel, womit der Frühling mein Herz begrüßte, und wie die Sonne des Himmels sich wiederfand im tausendfachen Wechsel des Lichts, das ihr die Erde zurükgab, so erkannte mein Geist sich in der Fülle des Lebens" (*Hyp.* 2:601).

5. ". . . sucht' ich die höchsten Berge mir auf und . . . regte mein Geist sich im Freien, und dehnt', als wäre sie sein, über die sichtbare Welt sich aus; wunderbar! es war mir oft, als läuterten sich, und schmelzten die Dinge der Erde, wie Gold, in meinem Feuer zusammen, und ein Göttliches würde aus ihnen und mir" (*Hyp.* 2:659).

6. "Ich hatte zu glüklich in mich die Schönheit der Natur erbeutet, um nicht die Lücken des Menschenlebens damit auszufüllen. Mein dürftig Smyrna kleidete sich in die Farben meiner Begeisterung, und stand, wie eine Braut, da" (*Hyp.* 2:601).

7. ". . und, wie die Biene unter Blumen, fliegt meine Seele oft hin und her zwischen den Meeren, die zur Rechten und zur Linken meinen glühenden Bergen die Füße kühlen. Besonders der Eine der beeden Meerbusen hätte mich freuen sollen" (*Hyp.* 2:583).

8. "Ja, vergiß nur, daß es Menschen giebt, darbendes, angefochtenes, tausendfach geärgertes Herz! und kehre wieder dahin, wo du ausgiengst, in die Arme der Natur, der wandellosen, stillen und schönen" (2:584).

9. "Da hab' ich meine liebsten Stunden, da siz' ich Abende lang uns sehe nach Attika hinüber, bis endlich mein Herz zu hoch mir klopft; dann nehm' ich mein Werkzeug, gehe hinab an die Bucht und fange mir Fische" (*Hyp.* 2:637).

10. ". . . fange mir Fische. Oder les' ich auch auf meiner Höhe droben vom alten herrlichen Seekrieg, der an Salamis einst im wilden klugbeherrschten Getümmel vertobte, und freue des Geistes mich, der das wütende Chaos von Freunden und Feinden lenken konnte und zähmen, wie ein Reuter das Roß" (*Hyp.* 2:637).

11. "Und wenn ich oft dalag unter den Blumen und am zärtlichen Frühlingslichte mich sonnte, und hinaufsah in's heitre Blau, das die warme Erde umfieng, wenn ich . . . nach einem erquikenden Regen, wenn die Zweige noch bebten von den Berührungen des Himmels, und über dem tröpfelnden Walde sich goldne Wolken bewegten . . ." (*Hyp.* 2:588).

12. ". . . das ungeheure Streben, Alles zu seyn, das, wie der Titan des Aetna, heraufzürnt aus den Tiefen unseres Wesens. . . . Und doch, wer wollt' es nicht lieber in sich fühlen, wie ein siedend Öl, als sich gestehn, er sei für die Geißel und für's Joch geboren?" (*Hyp.* 2:596).

13. "Wo ist das Wesen, das, wie meines sie erkannte? In welchem Spiegel sammelten sich, so wie in mir, die Stralen dieses Lichts? erschrak sie freudig nicht vor ihrer eignen Herrlichkeit, da sie zuerst in meiner Freude sich gewahr ward?" (*Hyp.* 2:655).

149

14. "So träumt' ich. Aber indeß die Gedanken zwischen den Wänden des Hauses nach ihr spähten, suchten die Füße sie anderswo, und eh' ich es gewahr ward, gieng ich unter den Bogengängen des heiligen Walds . . . wo ich sie zum erstenmale hatte gesehn'' (*Hyp.* 2:668).

15. Because of its lack of clear perception and intent, narcissism has a worrisome tendency to turn into a life-form completely directed by coincidence. As a form of delusional compensation for this arbitrariness, it often finds itself accompanied by a tendency to perceive events as predestined.

16. Winfried Kudszus made the observation that whenever Hölderlin's poetry deals with images and concepts of a more concrete nature, the perspective of representation is confused and shattered and the tone is anxious. Whenever the poetry uses abstract concepts or ideas, the perception becomes stable and the tone more calm. Thus, even the linguistic approximation of a more concrete object(-relation) destabilizes.

17. ". . . ha! wie das göttliche Haupt, sterbend in Wonne, mir am offnen Halse herabsank, und die süßen Lippen an der schlagenden Brust mir ruhten . . . o Bellarmin! die Sinne vergehn mir und der Geist entflieht'' (2:674).

References

Benjamin, Jessica. *The Bonds of Love: Psychoanalysis, Feminism, and the Problem of Domination.* New York: Pantheon, 1988.

Berman, Russell. *Modern Culture and Critical Theory: Arts, Politics, and the Legacy of the Frankfurt School.* Madison: U of Wisconsin P, 1989.

Elsaesser, Thomas. "Primary Identification and the Historical Subject: Fassbinder's Germany." *Cinetracts* 11 (1980): 43–52.

Foster, Hal, ed. *Vision and Visuality.* Dia Art Foundation: Discussions in Contemporary Culture 2. Seattle: Bay, 1988.

Habermas, Jürgen. *Strukturwandel der Öffentlichkeit: Untersuchungen zu einer Kategorie der bürgerlichen Gesellschaft.* Frankfurt am Main: Suhrkamp, 1963.

Hölderlin, Friedrich. *Sämtliche Werke* 17 vols. Ed. Michael Knaup und D. E. Sattler. Frankfurt am Main: Roter Stern, 1982.

Horkheimer, Max, and Theodor W. Adorno. *Dialektik der Aufklärung.* Frankfurt am Main: Fischer, 1969.

Hughes, Judith. *Reshaping the Psychoanalytic Domain: The Work of Melanie Klein, W. R. D. Fairbairn, and D. W. Winnicott.* Berkeley: U of California P, 1989.

Jameson, Fredric. *Fables of Aggression: Wyndham Lewis, the Modernist as Fascist.* Berkeley: U of California P, 1979.

Japp, Uwe. "Das Spiegelstadium der Aufklärung." *Neue Hefte für Philosophie* 18–19 (1980): 79–102.

Kernberg, Otto. *Borderline Conditions and Pathological Narcissism.* New York: Janson Aronson, 1975.

Kleinspehn, Thomas. *Der flüchtige Blick: Sehen und Identität in der Kultur der Neuzeit.* Reinbek: Rowohlt, 1989.

Kohut, Heinz. *The Analysis of the Self: A Systematic Approach to the Psychoanalytic Treatment of Narcissistic Personality Disorders.* New York: International UP,

1971. German: *Narziβmus: Eine Theorie der psychoanalytischen Behandlung narziβtischer Persönlichkeitsstörungen.* Frankfurt am Main: Suhrkamp, 1973.

———. "Thoughts on Narcissism and Narcissistic Rage." *Psychoanalysis of the Child* 27 (1972): 354–64.

Kudszus, Winfried. *Sprachverlust und Sinnwandel: Zur späten und spätesten Lyrik Hölderlins.* Stuttgart: Metzler, 1969.

Lacoue-Labarthe, Philippe, and Jaen-Luc Nancy. *The Literary Absolute: The Theory of Literature in German Romanticism.* New York: State U of New York P, 1988.

Manthey, Jürgen. *Wenn Blicke zeugen könnten: Eine psychohistorische Studie über das Sehen in der Literatur und Philosophie.* München: Fink, 1983.

Miller, Alice. *Am Anfang war Erziehung.* Frankfurt am Main: Suhrkamp, 1983.

Reich, Wilhelm. *Charakteranalyse.* Köln: Kiepenheuer & Witsch, 1971.

Sennett, Richard. *The Fall of the Public Man.* New York: Knopf, 1974.

Shapiro, Barbara. *The Romantic Mother.* Baltimore: Johns Hopkins UP, 1983.

Straub, Rudolf. *Hölderlin als Wanderer: Mit einem Nachwort von Peter Härtling.* Fotographiert und inszeniert von Rudolf Straub. Berlin: Aufbau, 1991.

Utz, Peter. *Das Auge und das Ohr im Text: Literarische Sinneswahrnehmung in der Goethezeit.* München: Fink, 1990.

Virilio, Paul. *Die Ästhetik des Verschwindens.* Berlin: Merve, 1986.

———. *Logistik der Wahrnehmung.* Berlin: Merve, 1986.

———. *The Vision Machine.* Bloomington: Indiana UP, 1994.

———. *War and Cinema: The Logistics of Perception.* London: Verso, 1989.

Winnicott, Donald. *Holding and Interpretation: Fragment of an Analysis.* London: Hogarth, 1986.

———. "Mind and Its Relation to the Psycho-Soma." *Collected Papers: Through Paediatrics to Psycho-Analysis.* 1949. London: Tavistock, 1958.

———. *Playing and Reality.* London: Tavistock, 1971.

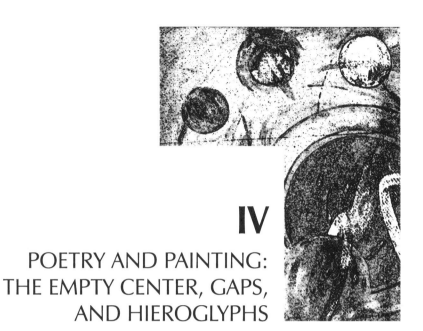

IV

POETRY AND PAINTING:
THE EMPTY CENTER, GAPS,
AND HIEROGLYPHS

Aldo Palazzeschi and Giorgio de Chirico: Decentralized Antitraditional Aesthetics

ANTHONY JULIAN TAMBURRI

Introduction

Aldo Palazzeschi's early works represent a moment in Italian cultural history when the canon, here specifically poetry, came under close scrutiny. For Palazzeschi especially, this scrutiny proved to be twofold; not only did he question the status of that which we may call the *tradizione aulica* (literally, the *courtly tradition;* in general terms, I would suggest, the *dominant culture*), but he also manifested during this period of his literary career a desire to surpass even those who, like himself, questioned the prevailing *tradizione*. Giorgio de Chirico found himself in an analogous situation when he began painting; he, too, reacted to a similar scrutiny in a manner that distinguished him from his many contemporaries (see Lukach; Rubin). Consequently, both artists took one step further than their *rebellious* confreres by not adhering to any organized movements for any significant length of time, thereby situating themselves in a cultural context that deviated greatly from the norm.

In a very (proto)postmodern way, they both lay by the wayside any notion of universality or absoluteness. In this sense, then, one can easily equate such notions to the general notions associated with a postmodern discourse—for example, stability/subversion, hierarchy/anarchy, determinacy/indeterminacy, genital/polymorphous. The rejection of any validity to the notion of "hierarchy"—or, better, universality or absoluteness—is characteristic for those who are, to paraphrase Jean-François Lyotard, "incredul[ous] toward [grand or] metanarratives" (xxiv), for whom, since meaning is "not fixed, not definite, not hardened into a mineral immobility" (Calvino, *Six Memos* 70), their business is not "to supply reality but to invent allusions to the conceivable which cannot be presented" (Lyotard 81).

In this essay we shall see how these two artists, one a writer the other a painter, reacted to traditional artistic performance in an analogous manner. What follows is based on two simple premises: First, discussing Palazzeschi and de Chirico does not necessarily imply a direct, intertextual relationship. Instead, the premise here is one of an epistemological and, perhaps also, ideological commonality—namely, they were two artists coming into their own during an aesthetically turbulent time in Italy. Second, the notion of *language* is not limited to the audio/scriptual aspect of communication, that is, speech; signs, referents, codes, and the like are indeed also visual.

Concerning language and its signifying function, Bakhtin had once discussed the decentralization of the "verbal-ideological world" (258ff.). With regard to what I shall discuss here, I would modify slightly Bakhtin's binomial into a more generalized couplet—the signifier-ideological world—so that the discussion of language decentralization is broadened to one of the signifier, be it verbal or visual. More specifically, then, along the lines of sign-functions, one sees that the two functives of expression and content are no longer in mutual correlation. The content, at this point in time with regard to a noncanonical art form, is different from that of the canon. The sign-function realized in this new process of semiosis is now in disaccord with the dominant culture's expectation of the coding correlation.[1] Another important consideration here is the interpreter's fore-understanding, "drawn from [his or her] own anterior relation to the subject" (Gadamer 262).[2] This notion of fore-understanding is surely a basis for both the sender's generation and the addressee's use and interpretation of signs. That is to say, the sign (or sign-function) is not ideologically neutral. Rather, its use and interpretation are dependent on both the sender's and the addressee's prejudgments.[3] The artist's suspension of direct reference renders the sign and referent more obscure and ultimately allows for aesthetic (i.e., generative and interpretive) manipulation. The sheet of paper or the canvas becomes a "vehicle most suited to conducting critical awareness to an understanding, appreciation, and interpretation of the [art, be it scriptual or visual] of the past."[4] This "work [may ultimately give] embodiment to his theory of [art]" (Marin 53).

In a general sense, then, language—that is, its sign system—cannot be but ideologically invested. As an ideological medium, as it can become restrictive and oppressive when its sign system is arbitrarily invested with meanings by those who are empowered to do so—that is, the dominant culture—so can it become empowering for the purpose of privileging one coding correlation over another (in this case the canon), by rejecting the canonical sign system and, ultimately, denying validity to this sign system vis-à-vis the interpretive act of a noncanonical text.[5] Then, certain ideological constructs are deprivileged and subsequently awarded an unfixed status; they no longer take on a patina of natural facts. Rather, they figure as the arbitrary categories they truly are. All this results in a pluralistic notion of artistic invention and interpretation, which, by its very nature, cannot exclude the individual—author *and* reader—who has (re-)created and developed a different repertoire of signs.

Aldo Palazzeschi's Diverse Verse

Turning our attention to "Chi sono?" (see his *Poemi*), Palazzeschi's first treatise in verse form, we find that his intent of questioning the status of art is implicit in the structure of the poem. It consists of a series of five questions, the first three of which are resolved negatively; highly significant is that each of these three questions represents a different art form: poetry, painting, and music. The result is a refusal to accept the entire cultural inheritance at the beginning of the century. In fact, as did Sergio Corazzini and Guido Gozzano, so now does Palazzeschi rid himself of the traditional label of poet. But in his case he also minimizes those traits that had been main components of the *crepuscolare*[6] movement: "malinconia" and "nostalgia." It is precisely with this rejection that Palazzeschi surpasses his contemporaries in refuting tradition. In the place of introspection he introduces "follia" as the end product of poetry. It is a folly manifested both thematically and stylistically. For folly implies non-sense and irrationality, and in light of all that had preceded Palazzeschi his poetry could only be considered irrational and eccentric in meaning and frivolous in style, especially when compared with one of the more popular, established poets such as a Carducci, a Pascoli, or a D'Annunzio. Consequently, in "Chi sono?" Palazzeschi demonstrates his awareness of the change taking place in the individual's thought process at the beginning of the twentieth century. This awareness, along with a strong desire for change, is manifested in his forceful reaction to the literature of his time, a reaction illustrated by his constant diversion from tradition, evident especially at this time in both his poetry and his prose.[7]

The final two questions of "Chi sono?" lead to the definition of his new role. It is here, in his fourth answer, that some have perceived an ambiguity: the "lente / dinanzi al . . . cuore / per farlo vedere alla gente" (lens / in front of [his] heart / in order to show it to people). While it is true that an initial impression may be that of introspective poetry, it is also highly possible to consider the statement, in relation to that which follows, a prelude to his self-definition; it is a simple expression of candor as he now bestows on himself the label of "saltimbanco" (mountebank, acrobat; hence, artist-acrobat). Indeed, in so doing he makes his first explicit statement against the canon; and within a year's time he will publish his *L'incendiario,* a collection of poetry that contains, among others, poems that express—both metaphorically and literally—an acute awareness of poetic deviation: for example, "L'incendi-ario" and "E lasciatemi divertire."[8]

Palazzeschi's move away from traditional verse writing did not take place, however, only after 1909; even his earliest compositions manifest hints of a turn in another direction. Although most critics tend to classify Palazzeschi's early poetry as *crepuscolare,* there are those who consider him one of the "più autentici innovatori del Novecento italiano" (most authentic innovators of the Italian twentieth century) (Güntert 86). Güntert, in fact, places Palaz-zeschi "spiritualmente vicino a . . . Pirandello" (spiritually close to . . . Piran-dello), since both writers "vivono, ciascuno alla sua maniera, il dramma dell'idealismo europeo, rendendosi conto che il pensiero non raggiunge altro che se stesso, incapace di cogliere l'immediatezza della vita e del presente" (live, each in their own way, the drama of European idealism, realizing that thought reaches only itself, being incapable of grasping the immediacy of life and the present) (70). In reference to the tone and atmosphere of Palazzeschi's initial poetry, Güntert also speaks in terms of a "clima di stanca monotonia" (climate of tired monotony) (66). It is a climate of monotony, or better, a suspension of time, frequent in numerous poems of this period. The majority of these poems, especially those of *I cavalli bianchi,* appear devoid of any emotion, be it on the part of the poet-protagonist or of the characters within. In fact, as Palazzeschi does in numerous poems of this period, this suspension of time and emotion is efficaciously rendered by the constant use of similar words and phrases, if not the repetition of identical verses at different intervals throughout the same poem, which, in turn, leads to the suspension of reference for which the signifier is separated from its traditional signified. Thus, any sense of emotional or physical dramaticity is lacking. Actions and colors are mollified, and the image is often seemingly devoid of any inherent meaning. Such is the case with the following two poems of similar titles:

THE PASTEL OF SLEEP

Violet flames rise in the thick mist
that forbids the view of the sea.
Slowly the sea whispers.
One hears the madman's moan.
Yellow flames rise in the thick mist
that forbids the view of the sea.
Stronger the sea whispers
and covers the madman's moan.
Swift light flames rise,
swift in the thick mist.
The madman is not heard anymore.[9]

THE PASTEL OF BOREDOM

From the dark of the thick thick mist
cypresses black shadows shine through
sponges of mist.
And from far away slowly rocking
comes the sound of an almost spent bell.
Farther and farther still
a train passing by roaring.[10]

Another short, enigmatic poem similar to the two cited above is "Diaphragm of Evanescences":

From the darkest windows
a light violet mist shines through
a most subtle light.
And one hears the dying notes
of the slowest of dances.
From the windows one sees
light flying white tunics passing by
of dancing couples.[11]

The "folle" (madman) of the first poem is rendered completely motionless, while the "coppie danzanti" (dancing couples) of the third seem to move in slow motion; and a conclusion of the visual image of the "treno" (train) in the second poem is heightened by the presentation of a very faint aural motif. Highlighted therefore are the colors, as there seems to exist an overriding concern with them as an expressive element rather than merely a descriptive one. There is a conscious attempt in each of these poems to avoid any form of conventional mode of communication, and the effect of these early verses is, in this regard, a negative one. These early compositions indeed prove to be fine examples of *non-sense* verse, which seem at this point to be headed more toward the metaphysical school rather than the futuristic one.[12] This opacity or lack of communication is a narrative technique Palazzeschi employed often and with great effect in many of his lyrical and prose compositions during these early years of his literary career. And while it is true that at this point the violent dynamics of the incendiario and the tomfoolery of the saltimbanco have yet to be developed, Palazzeschi is nevertheless already well on his way toward the acquisition of an *ars poetica* that deviates from the canon. Significant, therefore, is the appearance of the "folle" in "Il pastello del sonno," for as we have already seen, "follia" will soon appear as one of the two major components of Palazzeschi's aesthetics.[13]

The softened tone of this early poetry, due to its lack of dramaticity and its "stanca monotonia," indeed anticipates the fixity of the metaphysical object, which is apparent not only in "I prati di Gesù" (*Poemi* [1909]), as Bigon-

159

giari has already demonstrated (75), but also in earlier poems such as "Le fanciulle bianche," "Ara Mara Amara," and "Oro doro odoro dodoro" (*I cavalli bianchi* [1905]). One finds simple, realistic images presented by the artist in an enigmatic, inexplicable situation. In "Le fanciulle bianche," for example, if we try to resolve the problem of who or what the "gente" (people) or the "fanciulle bianche" (white girls) represents, we find ourselves hard pressed for an answer. Indeed, many of Palazzeschi's early compositions beg such questions without ever offering convincing or even satisfactory answers. The same is also true for "Il passo de le Nazarene," a poem constructed around a continuous to and fro of two groups of nuns:

THE NAZARENES' WALK

White Nazarenes, black Nazarenes.
From the river to the banks
the convents have been looking at each other for a long time,
they look at each other with the eye of old friendship
the little towers, one white the other black,
the nuns meet in the evening,
in the evening at sunset.
They meet twice, the white ones and the black ones,
on the bridge, on the bridge that joins the two convents,
it joins them for so long because of an old friendship,
the little towers observe each other laughing,
one white and the other black,
the nuns meet in the evening,
in the evening at sunset.
The little churches open at sunset,
the nuns quickly appear and file onto the bridge;
they meet in the middle,
they bow, the white and the black ones,
they each proceed to the small church to extend salutations:
they say a short prayer there
and quickly return to the bridge.
Again they meet in the middle,
the lines bow, the white and the black one,
the nuns meet in the evening,
in the evening at sunset.[14]

Indeed, the entire structure of the poem is founded on a symmetry of parallels and oppositions.[15] Consistent is the chromatic opposition of white and black of the Nazarenes and the towers of their convents. Analogous also are the syntactical and lexical repetition one finds throughout. The nuns, white and black, constitute a chromatic analogy in the "piccole torri, una bianca e una nera" (little towers, one white and the other black), just as the convents themselves seem to mirror each other as "si guardan da tanto i conventi, / si guardan con occhio di vecchia amicizie" (the convents have been looking at each other for a long time, / they look at each other with the eye of old friendship), with the insistence on the reciprocal verb. Except for lines six and seven (repeated three times in the manner of a refrain), all other images seem to have a double in this poem: two types of nuns, two towers, two convents, two churches, two encounters, two bows. The only single element in the poem is the bridge, the obvious meeting point of both groups of nuns.[16] As in other poems, here too the question "So what does it all mean?" comes to mind, especially because the poem does not achieve closure; Palazzeschi leaves his reader with an allusion of an ongoing action. Thus we find in this poem images—lest we forget that the etymology of *image* is *imitari,* to imitate reality!—of a "reality," which, once set side by side, do not seem to present a logical representation of what might be normally perceived as reality.

These are just a few of the many poems Palazzeschi wrote during this period, poems that emanate an aura of ambiguity if not inscrutability, especially when the reader attempts to ground them interpretatively according to his or her previously gathered intertextual knowledge:[17] he or she is now confronted with unfamiliar codes and "key words" (Eco, *Role of the Reader* 26).

Giorgio de Chirico: Uncentralized Painting

Notwithstanding the difference of a few years—Palazzeschi's *Lanterna* appeared in 1907, and de Chirico's first paintings appeared in 1908—it is possible to find analogies between the two artists in the early paintings of Giorgio de Chirico. *The Convent on the Mountain* (1909) seems to present a realistically portrayed scene, yet its meaning is not at all easy to interpret. Pairs of nuns march forward up a path, at the end of which sits a convent.[18] But we do not actually see the convent; we see only its bell tower. Likewise, we see only the backs of the nuns, as they appear as black figures systematically situated on the canvas. Also, we realize that the convent is located on a slope of a mountain and not, as one might initially infer from the title, on the top of a mountain. Thus we have an inconclusive visual narrative, as details such as facial expressions, the convent itself, and the surrounding terrain are all lacking. As a consequence, therefore, lacking also is de Chirico's *narrative responsibility;* he does not offer his observer all the necessary information—that is, details and descriptions—needed to "get the point" (Brilliant 18).[19] Precisely because it is the observer who, by assimilating such details and descriptions, usually supplies the thought processes of the participants in a visual narrative (18), de Chirico makes this virtually impossible for the observer of his texts. His *irresponsibility* as narrator thereby immobilizes his observer's imagination and creates a blank, which here is actually concretized

161

in the text. Looking at the painting as a whole, we see that the path forms a diagonal between the bottom left and the upper right corners. In tracing its imaginary complement, from the lower right to the upper left, we find that the center of the painting actually constitutes an empty space. In Iserian terms, this space represents "suspended connectability in the text," which eventually increases the constitutive activity of the reader/viewer. And while Iser does not refer to actual blanks in the text, their respective functions are similar; they cause the reader/viewer to pause and reflect on what he or she has just read or viewed (198).

At this point we can return briefly to Palazzeschi's poetry, where we find a similar, rhetorically generative phenomenon of the empty center at work: this is especially true for the poetry Palazzeschi wrote before the publication of his 1910 collection *L'incendiario*.[20] In "Il passo de le Nazarene," the bridge on which the nuns meet obviously constitutes a center. It is the meeting point and moment of pause for the two groups of nuns. But, as we have already seen, the poem does not achieve any form of closure; signification remains suspended, and the reader is left with the image of an endless to and fro of the nuns. Thus Palazzeschi, like de Chirico, leaves his reader with an inconclusive verbal narrative from which the reader cannot readily construct any logical meaning precisely because Palazzeschi does not offer the information the reader needs to "get the point." As in de Chirico's *The Convent on the Mountain,* here too we can speak in terms of concretized Iserian blanks. The bridge, which constitutes a meeting point and moment of pause for the nuns, represents in an analogous manner a hermeneutical meeting point and moment of pause for the reader, whose expectations are suddenly interrupted and whose interpretive connectability is thus suspended. Hence the reader's act of signification is halted by the empty center that is literally in this poem, the bridge on which the nuns meet.

This empty center as an unsatisfactory constitutive blank was already present in numerous poems of Palazzeschi's *I cavalli bianchi.* "La voce dell'oro," "Oro, doro, odoro, dodoro," and "La vasca delle anguille" are just three of a number of poems with analogous empty centers. In the first and third poems the center is represented by a supposed or desired object that the reader does not positively know exists. In "La voce dell'oro" it is the supposed "tesoro" (treasure) at the bottom of the "pozzo" (well) situated at the center of a circle of "cipressi" (cypresses). The people dare not enter the circle to approach the well. Instead, they listen from afar for the "lamento: / la voce dell'oro" (moaning: / the voice of gold).[21] Likewise, in "La vasca delle anguille" people stand, with fishing rods poised, around a deep "vasca delle anguille" (eel pond) with the hopes of catching the "grosse . . . buone . . . anguille" (big . . . good . . . eels) they believe—"si dice" (it is said)—live in the pond. In both cases these short poems present a series of realistic images that, when strung together, offer a confused message, at best, with an enigmatic central image—both literal and figurative—in the "pozzo," "tesoro," "vasca," and "anguille."

"Oro, doro, odoro, dodoro," on the other hand, offers a more curious and challenging situation for the reader. The poem opens with the following lines:

> At the end of the long avenue is a giant niche
> that is bordered by high cypress trees.
> The statue was removed a long time ago.[22]

and closes in the following manner:

> There are at the base
> four men wrapped in black capes.
> They look at each other in silence,
> they don't move a finger.[23]

What we find is an object, the "nicchia gigante" (giant niche), in a multicentered position. The first center is represented by the "viale profondo" (long avenue), at the end of which is the niche. Surrounded by the "alti cipressi" (high cypress trees), the niche finds itself in a second centered situation. Similarly, the four men at the base of the niche constitute a third centered position. As Palazzeschi presents a multifold layering of the centering of an object in this poem, he also, willy-nilly, further problematizes the situation of the center. In the previous poems mentioned, Palazzeschi offered his reader the semblance of a centered focal point—that is, the "pozzo," "tesoro," "vasca," and "anguille." Here, instead, he offers his reader an actual empty center, as the "statua fu tolta nei tempi lontani" (statue was removed a long time ago). This said, we can take the centering one step further. For the niche itself, more than the centered object, is another centralizing agent, whereas the statue, or better, the absence thereof, constitutes the centered object. This empty center (the missing statue), immobilizing as it seems to the "quattr'uomini" (four men) who stand "in silenzio, / non muovon un dito" (in silence, / they don't move a finger), is, in an analogous manner, a halting impediment also for the reader, who must now increase his or her constitutive activity—pause and reflect on what was just read—since his or her expectations have not been satisfied and his or her interpretive connectability has been interrupted.

Returning now to de Chirico, we can approach in a similar manner two more of his early paintings: *The Enigma of the Oracle* (1910) and *The Enigma of the Hour* (1912). In the first painting we find its center occupied by a brick wall that complements the foreground, it too constructed of bricks only. To the right of the wall, peering over a black curtain, is a white head, which, according to Soby, "sets the key for a malaise which can neither be explained nor shaken off'' (17).[24] To the left of the wall, peering out over a hillside down to the sea, is a human figure, seemingly headless.[25] Thus it appears that the one figure might complement the other. Keeping in mind the general malaise of the fin de siècle, we might consider such malaise—an unsettling feeling toward the unknown—symbolized by the separation of the two figures. For while the Böcklinesque figure peers out toward the sea—a common metaphor for the unknown—the white head is situated in an alcove, shut off by a curtain. An eventual reintegration of these two figures, on the other hand, might be suggested by de Chirico's unusual perspective. In considering his orthogonals from the left side of the painting, we see that they meet at the center of the brick wall. Here we find a curious component of the painting. At the point of intersection of these lines there exists a faded area on the wall, and this area forms a diagonal from the upper right to the lower left. Following this diagonal, we see that it, in turn, is contiguous with the shoulder of the head behind the curtain and the feet of the peering figure. Finally, we find in this painting a structural device already apparent in *The Convent on the Mountain*. Here, too, the center of the painting consists ever more prevalently of a blank space—constituted primarily by the brick wall—which is both a symbol of the painter's thought process and an invitation for the observer to contemplate the text further.

The Enigma of the Hour presents similar characteristics. Here, too, de Chirico deviates from traditional perspective. For while on the one hand he adopts lines that bring the observer's eyes to a central vanishing point in the painting, there is another set of lines—and figures—that leads the observer off the canvas.[26] Initially the painter's line of vision seems to be centrally situated, but on closer observation one sees that it is instead slightly off to the left. This is evidenced by the columns of the upper walkway, the window in the archway on the left, and the archways themselves. Characteristic of de Chirico, we find the sun shining in from the left side of the canvas and a subsequent shadow cast by the figure to the left of the fountain. This all culminates in the dark figure in the archway to the left of center: a figure of a man who seems to be moving haltingly away from center. This move away from center—a common focal point of traditional perspective—thus figures as a deliberate renunciation of the canon; as such, it also creates a problem for the observer.

Such a problem is compounded by two other characteristics of the painting. The human figures present complement those of the preceding painting, with the exception that here we find three, who are all gazing in different directions. As was already mentioned, the dark figure peers off to the right. The small figure in the walkway peers down toward the bottom left of the canvas, also away from the center, while the white figure in the square faces the center archway.[27] The different direction in which each figure faces is now contrasted by the lines of the fountain in the center of the square. Thus one finds again the repetition of an empty space at a point that traditionally constituted the focal point of a visual narrative. The orthogonals of the fountain lead to the center archway, which, here, similar to the center of the two preceding paintings, constitutes a blank. Consequently, here too the observer's *reading* process is immobilized.

Finally, there is the question of titles in many of de Chirico's paintings. Of the three presented above, the last two especially are of relevance to the difficulties in interpreting the paintings. Indeed, in earlier times—the Middle Ages and the Renaissance especially—illustrations were often subordinate to the text; that is, the written word held the privileged position.[28] Or, in the case of visual art, titles of paintings were merely descriptive of those paintings to which they were appended. In de Chirico's case, however, the titles, while still subservient to the visual narrative, aid in creating an aura of inscrutability. Thus, the "enigma," the puzzling characteristic of these paintings, lies in the very fact that the "enigma"—to which the title refers—is absent. The painter does not present a *concrete* puzzling image; that is, we the observers have yet to witness the more dramatic paintings of the large, empty squares and the patchwork mannequins of the 1910s with which we readily identify de Chirico today. The confusion is thus born out of the presentation of something that seems, simultaneously, both real and unreal, coupled then by the author/painter's choice of title—a veritable *con*fusion due not only to the real and unreal in the visual representation, but also to the combination of an ambiguous visual communication situation with an ambiguous verbal one.

A Tentative Conclusion

As was evident in the first section of this essay, the seemingly unresolved ambiguity is similar in Palazzeschi's early poetry. The short scenes taken from reality are presented to the reader within a suspended state of time and action. It is indeed precisely this state of animation—quasi-motionless while also lacking expressions of sentiments and emotions—that implants an aura of inscrutability into many of these early compositions. They are common descriptions of normal events whose element of surprise lies in the fact that there is not any surprise. The poet simply presents the images, whereas it is the reader's task to form an impression. It is an efficacious attempt, if not his early realization, of negative *non-sense* verse writing, or, in de Chirico's case, of *non-sense* painting. Through their upheaval of traditional representation at the beginning of the twentieth century, both artists deprivilege narrative and coherent textuality in favor of liberating the signifier from an extrinsic signifying force.[29] The reduction of the image (sign) to thing (object) renders it (image) equal only to itself (object) and therefore places it in a state of signification perennially *in potentia,* a form of unlimited semiosis.[30]

In fact, with regard to Palazzeschi's later moment of his conscious decision to move away from traditional poetics ("Chi sono?"), it is important to keep in mind that the notion of art in general at the turn of the century was questioned by many. To be sure, it was a critical moment in art when the writer and painter, in questioning the status of art, expressed such a temperament formalistically in the art work by privileging dissonance and non-sense, and thereby refuting a definitive image of the individual and the artist. And while the artistic maturity of both Palazzeschi and de Chirico is not represented by the works examined above—Palazzeschi still in search of his voice of the scoffing, ridiculing poet we find later in the *L'incendiario* (1910); or de Chirico still to develop into the painter of the fragmented scenes of mannequins and large, empty squares—it is clear that their respective directions were soon to deviate radically from the norm.

The emergence and subsequent acceptance of this and other valid acts of semiosis—the latter due in great part to the postmodern influence of the breakdown of boundaries and the mistrust in absolutes—had contributed to the construction of a more recent heteroglossic creative (and reading, of course) culture in which the "correct language" (Bakhtin 270), and therefore correct process of interpretation, is deunified and decentralized. In this instance, then, if all "languages" are "masks[, and no language can] claim to be an authentic and incontestable face," so no one reading process is "incontestable" and many can be considered valid. The result is a "heteroglossia consciously opposed to [the dominant] literary and/or visual language" (273), for which marginalization and subsequent invalidation of other[31] texts and other types of readers become more difficult to impose and thus less likely to occur.[32]

Thus, perhaps an appropriate way to conclude would be to borrow again from Lyotard and Calvino. For if the literary/artistic experience for Palazzeschi and de Chirico—be it from the perspective of the reader/viewer or the writer/painter—is "a combinatorial game that pursues the possibilities implicit in its own material" (Calvino, "Cybernetics and Ghosts" 22)[33] and not one of "reality" in its absolute, we might conclude that both Palazzeschi and de Chirico put "forward the unpresentable in presentation itself; . . . that which searches for new presentations"; so that the "text [an artist/writer creates], the work he produces are not in principle governed by preestablished rules, and they cannot be judged according to a determining judgement, by applying familiar categories to the text or to the work. Those rules and categories are what the work of art is looking for. The artist and the writer, then, are working without rules in order to formulate the rules of what *will have been done*" (Lyotard 81). In an analogous manner, so does the reader of these same texts work without rules, establishing, as he or she proceeds, similar interpretive rules of what *will have been read*. The reader must now proceed to recodify and reinterpret the seemingly arbitrary—that is, noncanonical—signs in order to reconstruct a mutual correlation of the expressive and content functives, which, in the end, do not violate his or her intertextual knowledge. Moreover, such an act of semiosis relies on the individual's time and place and is therefore always new and different with respect to its own historical specificities vis-à-vis the dominant culture—that is, the canon.

Thus it is, in the final analysis, a dynamics of the conglomeration and agglutination of different voices and reading strategies that, contrary to the hegemony of the dominant culture, cannot be fully integrated into any strict semblance of a monocultural voice or process of interpretation. The utterance, therefore, will always be polyvalent, its combination will always be rooted in heteroglossia and dialogism, and the interpretive strategies for decoding it will always depend on the specificities of the reader's intertextual reservoir. For the modernist reader, then, one rooted in the search for existing absolutes (read here, the canon-makers), the writer/artist's sign system may appear inadequate, perhaps even contemptible, if not also contemptuous. For the postmodernist reader, instead, one who is open to, if not in search of, new coding correlations, the writer/artist's sign system may appear significantly intriguing, if not on occasion rejuvenating, as these texts may indeed present a sign system consisting of manipulated sign functions that ultimately (re)define the sign. To be sure, then, in defense of a fluctuating early-twentieth-century Italian category of creative works, one may recall Lyotard's "incredulity toward metanarratives" (xiv), late-twentieth-century's increasing suspicion of narrative's universal validity, for which artistic invention is no longer considered a depiction of life—or, stated in more ideological terms, artistic creation is no longer executed or performed according to established rules and regulations. Rather, it is a depiction of life as it is represented by ideology (Davis 24), since ideology presents as *inherent* in what is represented that which, in actuality, is *constructed* meaning (Hutcheon 49).[34]

Notes

1. For more on sign-functions see Eco, *A Theory of Semiotics* 48–62.
2. See Gadamer and his notion of the hermeneutical circle in *Truth and Method.* As has been pointed out by Berstein, the hermeneutical circle has proven important also for understanding the sciences (131–38). Significant, then, with regard to the oscillation between parts and the whole are, first, Feyerabend's "anthropological method," for which "each block of information is a building block of understanding," only to be "clarified by the discovery of further blocks" (251); and second, the process Geertz considers a "continuous dialectical tacking between the most local of local details and the most global of global structures in such a way as to bring both into view simultaneously" (69).
3. For more on prejudgments see Gadamer 234–75.

4. Here I borrow from, and slightly modify, Marin's notion of "contemporary painting" and its *ragion d'essere*. For while Marin limits his remarks to contemporary
painters, I believe both Palazzeschi and de Chirico were already engaging in the
embodiment of theory in their art.

5. See, e.g., Volosinov: "A sign does not simply exist as a part of reality—it reflects
and refracts another reality. Therefore, it may distort that reality or be true to it,
or may perceive it from a special point of view, and so forth. Every sign is subject
to the criteria of ideological evaluation (i.e., whether it is true, false, correct, fair,
good, etc.). The domain of ideology coincides with the domain of signs. They
equate with one another. Wherever a sign is present ideology is present also.
Everything ideological possesses semiotic value" (10).

6. The *crepuscolare* (twilight) poets were those whose works embodied a disintegration of the Italian nineteenth-century traditional *ars poetica*. Their works signaled
the end of a tradition by using the very same aesthetic tools to embody such a
break.

7. For Palazzeschi's early prose I have in mind his unusual epistolary and journalis-
tic novel, *:riflessi,* and his more successful futurist novel, *Il codice di Perelà,
romanzo futurista,* now available in English as *Man of Smoke.*

8. The Italian word *incendiario* (incendiary) carries both a literal and metaphoric
meaning. An incendiario can be either (if not both) an arsonist in the literal sense
or an incendiary in the more metaphoric sense of one who makes trouble. To be
sure, Palazzeschi embodies both.

9. "S'innalzano fiamme di viola ne la nebbia densa / che vieta la vista del mare. /
Lento il mare sussurra. / Il gemito s'ode del folle. / S'innalzano fiamme gialle ne
la nebbia densa / che vieta la vista del mare. / Più forte il mare sussurra / e il
gemito cuopre del folle. / Rapide s'innalzano fiamme leggere, / rapide ne la nebbia densa. / Il folle non s'ode più" (*I cavalli bianchi*). (All translations are mine
except where otherwise noted.)

10. "Dal bigio de la nebbia fitta fitta / traspaiono cipressi ombre nere / spugne di
nebbie. / E di lontano dondolando lento / si viene un suono di campana quasi
spento. / Più lontano lontano lontano / passa un treno mugghiando" (*I cavalli
bianchi*).

11. "Da vetri scurissimi / leggera una nebbiea viola traspare / finissima luce. / E
s'odon le note morenti / dei balli i più lenti. / Si vedon dai vetri / leggere passare
volanti le tuniche bianche / di coppie danzanti" (*I cavalli bianchi*).

12. Palazzeschi's adherence to Italian futurism, à la Marinetti, lasted approximately
five years—from 1909 to 1914, when he publicly severed himself from Marinetti's movement. For more on Palazzeschi's futurism, see my *Of "Saltimbanchi"
and "Incendiari."*

13. This is the only poem in which "folle" or any derivation thereof appears before
the publication of "Chi sono?" The significance of such a motif at this early
time, a moment in which Palazzeschi is situated in a phase of experimentation in
search of his own poetic voice, is that it figures as a seed for his eventual poetics
of the saltimbanco. For more on Palazzeschi's *ars poetica,* see my *Of "Saltimbanchi" and "Incendiari"* 24–66.

14. "Nazarene bianche, Nazarene nere. / Del fiume a le rive / si guardan da tanto i conventi, / si guardan con occhio di vecchia amicizia / le piccole torri, una bianca e una nera, / le suore s'incontran la sera, / la sera al crepuscolo. / Due volte s'incontran, le bianche e le nere, / sul ponte, sul ponte che unisce i conventi, / gli unisce da tanto per vecchia amicizia, / le piccole torri si guardan ridenti / una bianca e una nera, / le suore s'incontran la sera, / la sera al crepuscolo. / Le piccole chiese al crepuscolo s'aprono, / ne sortono leste la suore ed infilano il ponte; / nel mezzo s'incontran, / s'inchinan le bianche e le nere, / si recan l'un l'altre a la piccola chiesa al saluto: / vi fanno una breve preghiera / e leste rinfilano il ponte. / Di nuovo nel mezzo s'incontran, / s'inchinan le file, una bianca e una nera, / le suore s'incontran la sera, / la sera al crepsucolo" (*Lanterna*).

15. For more on the symmetry in this poem, see Mariani 226–27 and Savoca 51–55.

16. At this point I would depart from Savoca's reading of this poem. Here he considers even the bridge duplicated, since "ponte" is repeated a second time—"sul ponte, sul ponte che unisce i conventi" (on the bridge, on the bridge that joins the two convents). He then goes on to state that only " 'two times' is not repeated, but only because it contains the double in its meaning, and it is therefore the symbolic key to the composition, in which nothing is unique, and every gesture, every thing, every word is an object of duplication." Instead, I would see this poem as Palazzeschi's early attempt at formulating his philosophy of *controdolore,* especially his notion of reversibility of life's experiences, for which opposites meet and individuals may indeed have different experiences. In this sense, the bridge is very important as a *single* element: it figures as the meeting place of opposites, and as such it therefore recalls Palazzeschi's later image of the circle. See his manifesto, "Equilibrio." With regard to the importance of his three manifestos as explanatory texts of works that preceded them, I have discussed the importance of reading Palazzeschi retroactively in *Of "Saltimbanchi" and "Incendiari"* and in "Aldo Palazzeschi's *:riflessi.*"

17. I have in mind Eco's notion of "inferential walks" in *The Role of the Reader:* "The reader [is] encouraged to activate [a] hypothesis by a lot of already recorded narrative situations (intertextual frames). To identify these frames the reader [has] to 'walk,' so to speak, outside the text, in order to gather intertextual support" (32).

18. I do not wish to suggest a direct intertextual relationship between these two artists simply because there are nuns in both de Chirico's painting and Palazzeschi's poem. I make the analogy between de Chirico and Palazzeschi for reasons apparent throughout the essay: they both represent a mode of artistic expression that is diametrically opposed to the canon.

19. Brilliant goes on to say that "visual narratives in ancient art . . . depend on the closeup description of persons and events, as did the great histories of Herodotus and Thucydides. So, too, did the ancient romances, that marvelous invention of the Hellenistic world" (18). His discussion concerns visual narratives in ancient art, a period in which "semantic fields" (Eco, *Role of the Reader* 26) were generally codified and the reader/observer could then be sure of a promised ending. The situation is radically different with the modern artist, especially one like de

Chirico, who is painting at a time when the canon, both literary and artistic, is situated in a precarious state.

20. For more on Palazzeschi's early poetry in general, see my *Of "Saltimbanchi" and "Incendiari"* 67–126.

21. Indeed, Palazzeschi further complicates his narrative situation with the incongruent coupling of "lamento" with "la voce dell'oro."

22. "In fondo al viale profondo è la nicchia gigante / ch'è cinta dagli alti cipressi. / La statua fu tolta nei tempi lontani" (*I cavalli bianchi*).

23. "Vi sono alla base / quattr'uomini avvolti nei neri mantelli: / Si guardan fra loro in silenzio, / non muovon un dito" (*I cavalli bianchi*).

24. Rubin expresses a similar notion concerning de Chirico's overall subversion of classicism: "By turning it [classicism] inside out, he communicates the singular malaise of modern life" (59). Lukach also speaks of a contrast between Renaissance and twentieth-century perspectives (37).

25. See Soby also for de Chirico's debt to Böcklin (16–17).

26. With regard to de Chirico's lack of interest in central perspectives, see Lukach 37.

27. With regard to these last two figures, we should not ignore a certain intertextual recall of those in *The Enigma of the Oracle*. The broad-shouldered figure in the square echoes the headless figure peering down toward the sea, while the small figure in the walkway—here, too, only head and shoulders—peers down, away from center, to a corner of the canvas. Instead, we readily perceive a curious difference in the color of each new figure, now the opposite of its predecessor, as is also the direction in which these two new figures gaze.

28. In an Italian context, one immediately recalls the illuminated manuscripts of Dante and Boccaccio.

29. In an attempt to bring a fairly rigorous form of semiotics to the interpretation of the figurative arts, Bryson first spoke in terms of "discursivity" and "figurality" in *Word and Image:* "By the 'discursive' aspect of an image, I mean those features which show the influence over the image of language. . . . By the 'figural' aspect of an image, I mean those features which belong to the image as a visual experience independent of language—its 'being as image' " (6). What he seems to do here is take the bipartite notion of sign as consisting of signifier and signified and apply it to the figurative arts, what he calls the "painterly sign," for which signifier and signified are now transformed into the "figural" and the "discursive." One may, semiotically speaking, question the need to distinguish one type of sign (i.e., linguistic) from another (i.e., painterly) if the discourse remains on a cognitive level and not one of physiological perception, which would, of course, require such a distinction.

30. In this regard, Peirce's definition of the sign is a pertinent pre(inter)text to what I state here: "A sign or *representamen,* is something which stands for something in some respect or capacity. It addresses somebody, that is creates in the mind of that person an equivalent sign, or perhaps a more developed sign. The sign which it creates I call the *interpretant* of the first sign. The sign stands for something, its *object.* It stands for that object, not in all respects, but in reference to a sort of

idea, which I have sometimes called the *ground* of the representamen'' (228). *Caveat lector:* What I have in mind here, as is implied in Peirce's *"ground* of the representamen,'' is that any reader's response in any semiotic process must be, to some degree or another, content/context sensitive.

31. I use the adjective *other* here as an umbrella term to indicate that which has not yet been canonized—i.e., considered a valid category—by the dominant culture. Of course, for our own immediate reference, here, one may read, for instance, MLA or, in the case of Italian poetry and other art forms, the mind-set of the Italian Academy, be it in Italy or abroad. Or, if already accepted, such art forms have been so in a seemingly conditional and a somewhat sporadic manner, namely, when it is a matter of convenience on the part of the dominant culture.

32. This is, for Bakhtin, dialogized heteroglossia. A word, language, or culture undergoes dialogization ''when it becomes relativized, de-privileged, aware of competing definitions for the same things'' (427). Only by ''breaking through to its own meaning and own expression across an environment full of alien words and variously evaluating accents, harmonizing with some of the elements in this environment and striking a dissonance with others, is [a word—or, for that matter, language, or culture] able, in this dialogized process, to shape its own stylistic profile and tone'' (277).

33. That is, ''writing,'' for Calvino, ''is purely and simply a process of combination among given elements'' (''Cybernetics and Ghosts'' 17), while reading, or better, ''the spirit in which one reads is decisive: it is up to the reader to see to it that literature exerts its critical force, and this can occur independently of the author's intentions'' (26). (This essay was first delivered in 1967 and subsequently published in Italian, in his volume of collected essays, *Una pietra sopra.*) Indeed, here Calvino echoes notions similar to his ideological confrere, Roland Barthes. One need only think back to Barthes's notion of the death of the author and his concept of text divided into the categories of readerly and writerly.

34. I would like to thank Victoria De Mara and John Kirby, friends and colleagues, for their acute readings of an earlier draft of this essay.

References

Bakhtin, Mikhail M. *The Dialogic Imagination.* Trans. Caryl Emerson and Michael Holquist. Ed. Michael Holquist. Austin: U of Texas P, 1981.

Berstein, Richard. *Beyond Objectivism and Relativism: Science, Hermeneutics, and Praxis.* Philadelphia: U of Pennsylvania P, 1983.

Bigongiari, Piero. ''Il 'correlativo soggettivo' di Palazzeschi.'' *Poesia italiana del novecento.* Milan: Saggiatore, 1978. 75–96.

Brilliant, Richard. *Visual Narratives: Storytelling in Etruscan and Roman Art.* Ithaca: Cornell UP, 1984.

Bryson, Norman. *Word and Image: French Painting of the Ancien Régime.* Cambridge: Cambridge UP, 1981.

Calvino, Italo. ''Cybernetics and Ghosts.'' *The Uses of Literature.* Trans. Patrick Creagh. New York: Harcourt, 1986. 3–27.

———. *Una pietra sopra.* Turin: Einaudi, 1980.

————. *Six Memos for the Next Millennium.* Trans. Patrick Creagh. Cambridge: Harvard UP, 1988.

Davis, Lennard J. *Resisting Novels: Ideology and Fiction.* London: Methuen, 1987.

Eco, Umberto. *The Role of the Reader: Explorations in the Semiotics of Texts.* Bloomington: Indiana UP, 1979.

————. *A Theory of Semiotics.* Bloomington: Indiana UP, 1976.

Feyerabend, Paul. *Against Method: Outline of an Anarchistic Theory of Knowledge.* London: New Left Books, 1975.

Gadamer, Hans-Georg. *Truth and Method.* New York: Crossroad, 1988.

Geertz, Clifford. "From the Native's Point of View: On the Nature of Anthropological Understanding." *Local Knowledge: Further Essays in Interpretive Anthropology.* New York: Basic Books, 1983. 55–70.

Güntert, Georges. "Palazzeschi e la giocondità." *Paragone* 262 (December 1971): 62–88.

Hutcheon, Linda. *The Politics of Postmodernism.* New York: Routledge, 1989.

Iser, Wolfgang. *The Act of Reading. A Theory of Aesthetic Response.* Baltimore: Johns Hopkins UP, 1978.

Lukach, Joan M. "De Chirico and Italian Art Theory, 1915–1920." *De Chirico.* New York: Museum of Modern Art, 1983. 35–54.

Lyotard, Jean-François. *The Postmodern Condition: A Report on Knowledge.* Trans. Geoff Bennington and Brian Massumi. Minneapolis: U of Minnesota P, 1984.

Mariani, Giuseppe. "Crepuscolari e futuristi: contributto a una chiarificazione." *Critica Letteraria* 2.4 (1974): 187–300.

Marin, Louis. Interview. *Flash Art* 127 (April 1986): 52–55.

Palazzeschi, Aldo. *I cavalli bianchi.* Annotated by Adele Dei. Florence: Cesare Blanc, 1905. Parma: Zara, 1992.

————. *Il codice di Perelà, romanzo futurista.* Milan: Edizioni futuriste di "Poesie," 1911. Milan: SE, 1991.

————. "Equilibrio." *Lacerba* 3.4 (January 1915): 28–31.

————. *Lanterna.* Annotated by Adele Dei. Florence: Stab. Tipografico Aldino, 1907. Parma: Zara, 1987. 15–18.

————. *Man of Smoke.* Trans. Nicolas Perella and Ruggero Stefanini. New York: Italica, 1992.

————. *Poemi.* Florence: Cesare Blanc, 1909.

————. *:riflessi.* Florence: Cesare Blanc, 1908. Milan: SE, 1990.

Peirce, C. S. *Principles of Philosophy. Collected Papers.* Ed. Charles Hartshorne and Paul Weiss. Vol. 2. Cambridge: Harvard UP, 1960.

Rubin, William. "De Chirico and Modernism." *De Chirico.* New York: Museum of Modern Art, 1983. 55–80.

Savoca, Giuseppe. *Eco e Narciso: la ripetizione nel primo Palazzeschi.* Palermo: Flaccovio, 1979.

Soby, James Thrall. *The Early Chirico.* New York: Dodd, 1941.

Tamburri, Anthony Julian. "Aldo Palazzeschi's *:riflessi.* Toward a Notion of a 'Retro-Lector.' " *American Journal of Semiotics* 7.1–2 (1990): 105–24.

―――. *Of "Saltimbanchi" and "Incendiari": Aldo Palazzeschi and Avant-Gardism in Italy.* Madison, NJ: Fairleigh Dickinson UP, 1990.

Volosinov, V. N. *Marxism and the Philosophy of Language.* Trans. Ladislav Matejka and I. R. Titunik. Cambridge: Harvard UP, 1986.

Myth, Invisibility, and Politics in the Late Work of Paul Klee

KATHRYN E. KRAMER

On July 19, 1937, the exhibition *Degenerate Art* (*Entartete Kunst*) opened in Munich. Organized by a division of the Reich Ministry for Public Enlightenment and Propaganda, *Degenerate Art*'s presentation of officially outlawed art was sensational and derisive: hundreds of recently confiscated works by avant-garde German artists were accompanied by scornful, mocking commentary and often implicitly ridiculed by the disrespectful exhibition design. The intention was not only to proclaim what kind of art would no longer be condoned under the National Socialists but also to shock the German public into the recognition of the vast aesthetic and moral superiority of the approved art that was on display concurrently at the House of German Art, just across the park from the *Degenerate Art* exhibition. This exhibition, *Great German Art,* was opened by Adolf Hitler himself on July 18, 1937. The works in this exhibition conformed to an aesthetics based on rather sentimental imitation of classical ideals and were intended to provide an inspirational and reassuring contrast to the exotic deformities abounding in *Degenerate Art*.[1]

Paul Klee was represented by seventeen works in the *Degenerate Art* exhibition, a fairly high number for a single artist. One of these works, *Swamp Legend* (1919, Landesmuseum, Hannover, Germany), was hung on the infamous ''dada wall.'' Here Klee's work was aligned—or, better, misaligned—with works by Kurt Schwitters, title pages from *Der Dada* magazine, and a statement by Georg Grosz from a poster for the 1920 *First International Dada Fair*. From a Nazi perspective, to be positioned among dadaists was to be particularly vilified. In *Mein Kampf* and a 1934 speech, Hitler had singled dada out as especially degenerate, due no doubt to Berlin dada's communist sympathies and its satirical characterizations of him. Indeed, the classification of Klee as a dadaist was not wholly inaccurate, since Klee did associate himself with the movement and its activities from 1917 to 1919; but except for this brief flirtation Klee was never really a political animal, preferring—or at least promoting—the role of the rather remote, contemplative artist.[2] To be associated with dadaist anarchism in 1937 was quite troubling considering the nature of Klee's Nazi-induced Swiss exile, which dated from December 1933. A native Swiss, though a German citizen, Klee was unable to apply for Swiss citizenship until he had lived in Switzerland for five years. In 1937 he still had almost two more years to wait and was therefore an intellectual refugee with the daunting prospect of deportation under increasingly stringent Swiss immigration rules (Werckmeister, *Paul Klee in Exile* 40). Klee had no intention of placing his potential Swiss citizenship in jeopardy with overt, inappropriate political action in a country that harbored suspicions of avant-garde art and traces of nationalism similar to fascist Germany's. Also in 1937, Klee had not yet recovered from the severe complications he suffered the year before from the onset of scleroderma, a disease that would prove fatal in 1940. For almost half the year, his energies were focused primarily on convalescence and his art.

Beginning in 1937, when he had recuperated sufficiently to work again, Klee's art manifested a radical change in form and content, initiating the period of his late style (1937–40). A group of paintings begun while Klee was convalescing in Ascona, Switzerland, from September through November 1937 embody this stylistic change: the predominant modes of the previous two decades, such as the fantasy landscapes suffused with the aura of fable (as in *Swamp Legend*), the lyrical abstractions of colored squares, and the precise geometric compositions based on pedagogical models Klee developed at the Bauhaus, were largely if not wholly abandoned in favor of a vocabulary of freely drawn glyphic marks fluctuating between the ideographic and the figurative and scattered across the field of colored squares, as in *Peach Harvest* (1937, Guggenheim Museum, New York) (fig. 1). Many of the titles applied to the works in this new, glyphic style invoke the archaic myths and rites associated with them, such as *Bacchanal with Red Wine* (1937, Private Collection, Switzerland), *Landscape on the Way to Hades* (1937, Munson-Williams-Proctor Institute, New York) (fig. 2), *Lemon Harvest* (1937, Private Collection, Switzerland), and *Fragments of a Region Long Since Past* (1937, Düsseldorf Museum of Art, Germany). A familiar explanation for Klee's stylistic conversion throughout the scholarship on his final Swiss period is that his serious illness and the isolated nature of his exile (he never traveled abroad after settling in Switzerland and received only a few visitors) resulted in a sustained and heightened autobiographical investigation that inevitably led into the recesses of the self and thus to the enigmatic symbols, chimerical figures, and the tenor of myth.

In *Paul Klee in Exile,* Otto Werckmeister acknowledges Klee's illness and lonely exile as backdrops for a new mode of expression, but he also proposes another explanation for the fresh stylistic direction by describing the late work as a response to the cultural policies of National Socialism. This response, couched in what Werckmeister calls "crypto-mythic figuration," allowed Klee to reflect the aberrations and absurdities of National Socialism through the invention of monstrous mutations, the perverse denizens of a demonic otherworld straight out of the darkest of myth. Werckmeister identifies crypto-mythic figuration in the contemporaneous works of Lipchitz, Ernst, Tanguy, Miró, and Moore. Along with Klee, he writes, these artists share in that new, ambivalent pictorial culture of modernism, full of dark fascination with destiny, which historically coincides with the demise of democracy in Europe, the Great Depression, and the rise of fascism, culminating in the Spanish Civil War (33). As an antifascist strategy, crypto-mythic figuration allowed German artists in precarious states of exile to contribute to the international cultural opposition to National Socialism without appearing to be activist. Crypto-mythic figuration, then, was tailor-made to Klee's innate reluctance to make his art political as well as to the constraints of his Swiss residency.

Werckmeister's account of the factors contributing to Klee's politicization in 1937 is a convincing enumeration of quite enough stimuli to politicize even the most unpolitical: the condemnation of German art policies by Christian Zervos in the first 1937 issue of *Cahiers d'Art;* the German bombing of Basque in May; the increasingly virulent antifascism in the work of Picasso, whom Klee much admired; Klee's conspicuous place in the *Degenerate Art* exhibition; the subsequent confiscation in August of 102 of his works in public collections; and the devotion of the entire summer 1937 issue of *Cahiers d'Art* to Picasso's *Guernica* (*Paul Klee in Exile* 32). To this list I would add the codification into laws of the political and racial policies under which Klee was dismissed from his professorship and the subsequent appointment of "politically correct" personnel throughout the German universities, around the time of the opening of the *Degenerate Art* exhibition (Fischer-Defoy 16–17).

I would also agree with Werckmeister's recognition of a mythic element in Klee's putative "political" aesthetics. This essay builds on his assertions by specifying the role of myth in Klee's work from 1937, demonstrating that this role is not only to reflect the apocalyptic mood of Europe in the 1930s but also to function as a response to the Aryan myth constructed by National Socialism. In order to make this claim, a recapitulation of archaic Greek myths' use in the 1930s is necessary.

The chthonic myths of archaic Greece are extremely old myths that describe chaos, the engendering of the earth, the powers of nature, and the underworld realm. Chthonic myths are the stories of gods, such as Dionysus, who know violent derangement, pain, and death and who were celebrated in fertility rites that ecstatically invoked their various dismemberments, flayings, and passions. By contrast, Olympian gods of classical Greece, such as Apollo, products of a later cultural stage in Greece, lived a safe, elevated distance from suffering and pain. The Olympians represent the abstractions of universal harmony and order, while chthonic gods represent elemental powers of nature. Though the Olympians supplanted the chthonic gods, these old gods remained nonetheless vital forces in Greek culture, continuing as objects of worship in the Eleusinian and Orphic mysteries. And, of course, chthonic presences command Greek tragedy: their emergence as irrationality, monstrosity, incest, bloodlust, and patricide and their ultimate subjugation by rational Olympian forces is the antagonistic yet necessary and beneficial struggle described by Nietzsche in *The Birth of Tragedy.*

Throughout the 1930s, the surrealists resorted more than ever before in their writing and painting to the myths of both preclassical and classical Greece. As Whitney Chadwick asserts in *Myth in Surrealist Painting,* André Breton sensed a need in the 1930s to cull "guiding principles" from a group of both chthonic and Olympian myths as a means to clarify surrealist explorations of the unconscious and therefore to continue surrealism's potency as an international movement (1). According to Breton's logic, the myths created through automatism could be placed on a continuum with the Greek myths and thereby gain a definitive tradition. A manifest and venerable tradition would attract more surrealist "adepts" through a greater accessibility and also validate surrealist myth as an effective opponent against the contemporary fascist and imperialist myths that Breton felt were promoting a perilous overemphasis on rationality in Western culture. However, Breton did not conceive of the use of Greek myth by surrealism to be a means toward overt antifascist gestures; its use was merely as a tool dedicated to the wider dispersal of surrealist techniques. Only art dedicated to the liberation of the mind through these techniques could truly bring about political change. Breton's sometime ally among the British surrealists, Herbert Read, termed this kind of political engagement a "politics of the unpolitical," which for him "does not mean to be without politics: every attitude that is more than egoistic is to that extent social, and a social attitude is a political attitude" (334).

Georges Bataille vehemently disagreed with Breton's ambivalent attitude toward political action as well as his pallid use of Greek myth. Their political and philosophical differences were clearly marked with Bataille's founding in June 1936 of *Acéphale,* a journal zealously devoted to promoting archaic, chthonic myth and thereby to fomenting in society an explosion of orgiastic behavior, even ritualistic sacrifice. The acephalic man was the emblem of the journal's enterprise: a figure out of archaic Mediterranean legend, the acéphale had no head or phallus; he lived in a perpetual state of irrationality and dis-

177

memberment—a perpetual state of sacrifice—which for Bataille meant a state of absolute freedom. Throughout the pages of *Acéphale,* Bataille is not vaguely but decidedly antifascist and especially anti–National Socialist, repeatedly stating that the evocation of the instinctive, the unformed, and the demonic would constitute an "insurrection of the lower forces" that would unmask the Nazis' appropriation of the Olympian and their denial of the chthonic in their creation of the Aryan myth and, through this exposure, help to destroy the psychological grasp of the Nazi regime ("Propositions" 17–21). For example, in an article appearing in the January 1937 issue of *Acéphale,* Bataille disparages the mythography of Nazi cultural minister Alfred Rosenberg's *Myth of the Twentieth Century* (1932), which ostracized the chthonic gods from a Nordic-Greek pantheon as non-Aryan pollutants of the Greek cosmogony. Bataille wrote, "when Rosenberg expresses repulsion for the gods of the Earth . . . that do not have as their immediate goal the constitution of force, he expresses beyond a shadow of a doubt the repulsion of National Socialism itself" ("Nietzsche et les fascistes" 3–13). The July 1937 issue of *Acéphale* was devoted to Dionysus and continued the exhortations to address and overwhelm National Socialism with Dionysian ecstasy.

For Bataille, however, acephalic man and archaic myth were not merely counterexamples to Aryan man and Nazi myth. He was not suggesting, in a Bretonian manner, that their thematization would somehow figure forth an antifascism that would dialectically engage with fascism. The revolution against fascism that Bataille envisioned could not take place by Hegelian means: the insurrection of the lower forces could not be a conventional revolution of the masses, because in the end that revolution would only result in the replacing of one order with another. The acephalic enterprise was devoted to perpetual revolution, to continual destruction, to an extreme *heterogeneity* in the face of fascism's extreme *homogeneity*—an enterprise more like an unending sacrificial ritual than a revolution. Taken to its ultimate conclusion, acephalic activity involved a permanent dispersal of power and ultimately death—but an "impossible" death, one that is ongoing, undying.[3] As a totem of this activity, the acéphale embodies, as described by Allan Stoekl, "the very death of representation, control, thought" (195).

Is the acéphale, then, a totem for the death of ritual, necessary to bring about in the face of myth's lethal propulsion of Nazism? The acéphale *is* paradoxical—a mythological figure that represents a state of impossibility. However, for Bataille, the acéphale represents "ritually lived myth," myth in its purest state *as* myth: that state of sacrifice that exists before myth is staticized and employed as a totalizing, constitutive force ("The Sorcerer's Apprentice" 232). Thus, the heterogeneity over which the acéphale presides should not be thought of as nihilistic. Rather, this heterogeneity "informs" a realm of formlessness that inspires the homogeneous realm to attempt its representation, something that will always be an elusive but nonetheless liberating act.[4]

I would now like to explore Klee's inscription of myth in the glyphic in the paintings begun in Ascona as outlined above. In doing so I hope to open up a debate about the operations of Klee's late work in the arena of the political aesthetics of the 1930s and to set the stage for these operations' further theorization.

In an early diary entry describing his creative method, Klee writes, "I place myself at a remote starting point of creation, whence I state *a priori* formulas for men, beasts, plants, and all the whirling forces" (*Diaries* 345). Indeed, Klee's entire oeuvre and its accompanying written theory reveal attempts to delineate the points and the processes from which form generates itself in order—to paraphrase the famous opening statement from his *Creative Credo* (*Schöpferische Konfession,* 1918)—not to reproduce the visible but to render visible (*Das Bildnerische Denken* 76).

This "remote starting point of creation," then, preexists the visible for Klee and may be characterized as heterogeneous along the Bataillean lines. Lyotard recognizes the heterogeneous quality of Klee's description of the process of representation and links the artist's theories about reproducing out of that "remote starting point of creation" to what he calls the "figure-matrix" (224–39). It is worthwhile to examine Lyotard's discussion of the figure-matrix because it both illuminates the limits of representation as proposed by Bataille and also directly addresses Klee's own work at these limits.

As he develops the concept in *Discours, figure,* Lyotard suggests a dual nature for the figure-matrix. As a site of a creator's "originary phantasy," the figure-matrix is the generator of his or her internal phantasms; it is also a force that transgresses the visual field as invisibility: the figure-matrix "does not allow the minimal putting into *opposition* demanded by its spoken expression, or the minimal putting into image or form presupposed by its plastic expression. Discourse, image, and form miss it equally, as it resides in the three spaces together" (278). Lyotard maintains that a good artist does not try to depict his or her "originary phantasy"; this would communicate only to those who may have similar "phantasmatics." Rather, an artist with a truly critical relationship to his or her fantasy produces from within the figure-matrix, representing its processes. Lyotard recognizes that the statements Klee makes throughout his critical essays and pedagogical notes regarding creation, origination, process, and visibility/invisibility indicate a "good" critical relationship to his figure-matrix. Klee's works themselves, however, lag behind Klee's theories in the 1920s, representing for Lyotard a "bad" expressive relationship to the figure-matrix in their explicit attempts to portray fantasies. *Swamp Legend,* with its title alluding to a primordial ooze and the "Loch-Ness-like" creature emerging from the murky townscape, is an example of this kind of

179

fantasy illustration. In the late work, Lyotard sees a much more consistent relationship between Klee's theory and art, so that in works such as *Peach Harvest* (fig. 1) and *Landscape on the Way to Hades* (fig. 2), where the glyphic marks are not quite figures and not quite written characters, discourse and figure are together within the visual field. This imbrication evokes a translinguistic state that exists between an original phenomenon and the language that evolves to refer to that phenomenon; the simplistic device of expressing this state in figures of monsters out of the depths, as in *Swamp Legend,* no longer applies.

What is also operative in the glyphic works of 1937 is an extreme fragmentation of form underlaid by grids of colored squares that act as rational substructures ordering the dispersion of the marks. One may recognize in them an interplay between the homogeneous (the grids) and the heterogeneous (the glyphs) and thus a formal representation of the space of ''ritually lived

Fig. 1

Paul Klee, *Peach Harvest (Pfirsisch-Ernte),* 1937. Watercolor and charcoal on chalk- and glue-primed paper mounted with linen strips on paper; paper support and linen strips: 55.2 × 43.5 cm (21¾ × 17⅛ inches); paper mount: 64.1 × 49.9 cm (25¼ × 19⅝ inches). Solomon R. Guggenheim Museum, New York.

180

FIG. 2

Paul Klee, *Landscape on the Way to Hades,* 1937. Oil on canvas; 18⅝ × 28⅞ inches.
Munson-Williams-Proctor Institute, 310 Genesee Street, Utica, NY 13502.

myth''—true myth, as recounted by Bataille. In ''The Sign in Klee,'' Albert
Cook characterizes a similar nonspecific, mythic space in the glyphic works:
while titles may refer to myths, the free-floating signs do not seem to identify
any particular myth and therefore operate simultaneously as ''schemas for
mythical entities'' *and* indecipherable inscriptions, which allows them to ''triumph'' over any specific myth, to ''remain submythic while being super-
mythic'' (374).

The titles of these works generally key their readings to chthonic myths—
or, more precisely, to chthonic rituals referring to Dionysian rites—as in *Bacchanal with Red Wine;* to rituals of death, as in *Legend of the Nile* (1937,
Kunstmuseum Bern, Switzerland) and *Landscape on the Way to Hades* (fig.
2); and to fertility festivals, as in *Lemon Harvest* and *Peach Harvest* (fig. 1).
Thus the works in which Klee most completely satisfies his theory of ''render-
ing visible'' are pressed into referential service to chthonic myth in the end.
They are exactly contemporaneous with Bataille's acéphale, which also lent a
''chthonicity'' to his ideas about the operations of the heterogeneous.[5] Certainly for Bataille, chthonic myth offered a means to recover myth from Nazi
misuse: it offered figures radically other to those of Nazi myth, and it was
closer to ''ritually lived myth'' than to the mostly tragic myths to which Breton's wing of surrealism resorted. Klee's use of chthonic myth in the Ascona

181

pastels seems to operate similarly to Bataille's acephalic enterprise: he does not so much offer well-defined "counter-myths" that would operate oppositionally to Nazi myths and thus reflect their horrors (such as the surrealists' mythological iconography of minotaurs, sphinxes, and furies tended to do); rather he represents suggestive but unspecific mythic rituals, fraught with potentiality, with heterogeneity.

How might an attempt to formulate illegible signals of myth function as a political gesture in the 1930s? This endeavor goes beyond the cryptic in the sense that Werckmeister describes the term "crypto-mythic," as a smokescreen; it is *literally* cryptic, an attempt at the "impossible": to depict/write a state of invisibility/indecipherability. The result of this gesture was an extremely private visual language that offered a "scopic regime" that challenged National Socialism's mimetic reproductions of its dangerous myths.[6] More importantly in terms of political efficacy, however, Klee's "opaque" visuality highlights the irony of National Socialist visuality: after the Nazis' imposition of *an* absolute, public communicability and *a* community governed by their scopic regime, the illusion of a utopian collective subjectivity is forever shattered. Communication and community must henceforth be continually interrupted in order to prevent the devastation that the assumption of total unity could bring. In other words, heterogeneity must rule.[7] As attempts to communicate the experience of invisibility, Paul Klee's hermetic pictures of chthonic dispersion and fragmentation may be considered not as a retreat before persecution and censorship for the purposes of self-preservation but as a means to communicate a radical, alternative form of representation in the face of Nazism.

Notes

1. For an in-depth presentation of the events and issues surrounding the 1937 *Degenerate Art* exhibition, see Barron.
2. For an account of Klee's early political activities, see Werckmeister, *Making of Paul Klee's Career.*
3. The phrase "politics of the impossible" was used by Bataille in the letter written to Jérôme Lindon in 1962 (*Oeuvres complètes* 3:519–20). Besnier relates this expression to Bataille's politics of the 1930s in "Georges Bataille in the 1930s."
4. Strauss develops Bataille's attempts to define heterogeneity and formlessness in "The Inverted Icarus."
5. It is certainly possible that Klee was familiar with *Acéphale,* since Bataille had published an article by Georges Limbour about his art in the journal *Documents,* which he cofounded and edited from 1929 to 1931.
6. I employ the term *scopic regime* by way of Jay's "Scopic Regimes of Modernity." Metz originated the term in *The Imaginary Signifier.*
7. On the problem of how art and politics can work to keep public space open and relatively undetermined, see Carroll.

References

Barron, Stephanie, ed. *"Degenerate Art": The Fate of the Avant-Garde in Nazi Germany.* Los Angeles: Los Angeles County Museum of Art, 1991.

Bataille, Georges. "Nietzsche et les fascistes." *Acéphale* 1.1–2 (January 1937): 3–13. Paris: Jean-Michel Place, 1980.

———. *Oeuvres Complètes.* Vol. 3. Paris: Gallimard, 1976.

———. "Propositions." *Acéphale* 1.1–2 (January 1937): 17–21. Paris: Jean-Michel Place, 1980.

———. "The Sorcerer's Apprentice." *Visions of Excess: Selected Writings, 1927–1939.* Ed. and with an Introduction by Allan Stoeckl, Carl R. Lovitt, and Donald M. Leslie, Jr. Minneapolis: U of Minnesota P, 1985. 223–34.

Benjamin, Walter. "The Work of Art in the Age of the Mechanical Reproduction." *Illuminations.* Trans. Harry Zohn. New York: Schocken, 1969. 217–51.

Besnier, Jean-Michel. "Georges Bataille in the 1930s: A Politics of the Impossible." *Yale French Studies* 78 (1990): 169–80.

Breton, André. "Political Position of Today's Art." *Manifestoes of Surrealism.* Trans. Richard Seaver and Helen R. Lane. Ann Arbor: U of Michigan P, 1972. 212–33.

Carroll, David. "Community after Devastation." *Politics, Theory and Contemporary Culture.* Ed. Mark Poster. New York: Columbia UP, 1993. 159–96.

Chadwick, Whitney. *Myth in Surrealist Painting: 1929–1939.* Ann Arbor: U of Michigan Research P, 1980.

Cook, Albert. "The Sign in Klee." *Word and Image* 2 (1986): 363–81.

Fischer-Defoy, Christine. "Artists and Art Institutions in Germany 1933–1945." *Oxford Art Journal* 9 (1986): 16–28.

Jay, Martin. "The Scopic Regimes of Modernity." *Vision and Visuality.* Ed. Hal Foster. Seattle: Bay, 1988. 3–28.

Klee, Paul. *Das Bildnerische Denken.* Basel: Schwabe, 1964.

———. *The Diaries of Paul Klee: 1898–1918.* Trans. Pierre Schneider et al. Ed. Felix Klee. Berkeley: U of California P, 1964.

Lyotard, Jean-François. *Discours, figure.* Paris: Klincksieck, 1971.

Metz, Christian. *The Imaginary Signifier: Psychoanalysis and the Cinema.* Trans. Celia Britton et al. Bloomington: Indiana UP, 1982.

Read, Herbert. *Selected Writings of Herbert Read.* London: Faber & Faber, 1963.

Stoeckl, Allan. "Truman's Apotheosis: Bataille, "Planisme," and Headlessness." *Yale French Studies* 78 (1990): 181–205.

Strauss. Jonathan. "The Inverted Icarus." *Yale French Studies* 78 (1990): 106–23.

Werckmeister, Otto Karl. *The Making of Paul Klee's Career: 1914–1920.* Chicago: U of Chicago P, 1989.

———. *Paul Klee in Exile: 1933–1940.* Himeji City, Japan: Himeji City Museum of Art, 1985.

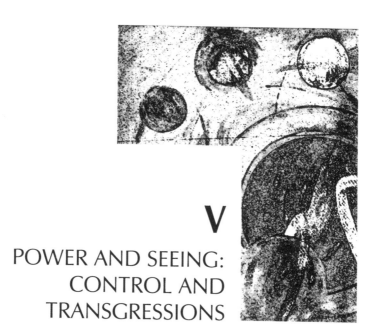

V

POWER AND SEEING:
CONTROL AND
TRANSGRESSIONS

The Eye's Mind: Henry James's *The Sacred Fount* and Vladimir Nabokov's *The Eye*

KAREN JACOBS

Realism's Specular Mirror

In *Signatures of the Visible,* Fredric Jameson untangles the structural components through which realism maintains its representational hold:

> "Realism" is a peculiarly unstable concept owing to its simultaneous, yet incompatible, aesthetic and epistemological claims, as the two terms of the slogan, "representation of reality," suggest. These two claims then seem contradictory: the emphasis on this or that type of truth content will clearly be undermined by any intensified awareness of the technical means or representational artifice of the work itself. Meanwhile, the attempt to reinforce and to shore up the epistemological vocation of the work generally involves the suppression of the formal properties of the realistic "text" and promotes an increasingly naive and unmediated or reflective conception of aesthetic construction and reception. . . . Yet no viable conception of realism is possible unless both of these demands or claims are honored simultaneously, prolonging and preserving—rather than "resolving"—this constitutive tension and incommensurability. (158)

Jameson's division of realism into aesthetic and epistemological modes—or form and content—can be compared with the components of Cartesian spectatorship, a model of spectatorship that repeatedly has been described as hegemonic in Western thought up until this century.[1] The Cartesian spectator's visual perception produced by the body (i.e., binocular vision) can be opposed to the representations of that perception comprehended by the mind; the negotiation between the embodied, literal eyes of perception and "the mind's eye"

187

in the Cartesian model, like the negotiation between form and content in the realist text, involves suppression of the purely mechanical, material operations of optics on the one hand, and of the relativistic potential of vision's contingency on individual observers on the other. The "constitutive tension" Jameson identifies with the simultaneity of aesthetic and epistemological modes in realism can be seen as equally sustained in the Cartesian model, as Richard Rorty, for example, defines it: "In Descartes's conception—the one which became the basis for 'modern' epistemology—it is *representations* which are in the 'mind.' The Inner Eye surveys these representations hoping to find some mark which will testify to their fidelity" (45). It is the elision of these discrete stages of perceiving, representing, and recognizing the world of objects that marks the Cartesian spectator's transcendent, universal view. The enormity of that view, as Paul Ricoeur puts it, entails "a vision of the world in which the whole of objectivity is spread out like a spectacle on which the *cogito* casts its sovereign gaze" (236). The subject of that gaze, critiqued, as Martin Jay has summarized it, as an "ahistorical, disinterested, disembodied subject entirely outside of the world it claims to know only from afar" (10), has been described as a monocular "mirror of nature" (Rorty 45), associated with the detached objectivity of science and the transcendence of a "god's-eye view."

What is so striking about these various attributions is how closely they resemble, or indeed, could be said to describe, the narrator of realist fiction, who invisibly presides over the fictive world it represents as transparently available to it. As Mark Seltzer defines it, the realist narrator's detached posture conceals the mechanisms of power implicit in its sovereign view: "Perhaps the most powerful tactic of supervision achieved by the traditional realist novel inheres in its dominant technique of narration—the style of 'omniscient narration' that grants the narrative voice an unlimited authority over the novel's 'world,' a world thoroughly known and thoroughly mastered by the panoptic 'eye' of the narration" (54). Seltzer is borrowing from Foucault here, alluding to the "society of surveillance" and the techniques of supervision the realist novel internally represents, practices, and, as a social form itself, perpetuates. If we are willing to see the transcendent Cartesian spectator and the omniscient realist narrator as both historically overlapping and theoretically contingent, understanding the realist narrator as the virtual embodiment of the assumptions of Cartesian spectatorship, we can raise questions about how far those "tactics of supervision" continue to obtain as each of those traditions is eroded. That is, as the Cartesian spectator's posture of neutral detachment is increasingly denaturalized and subjectivized at the beginning of the twentieth century, and the realist novel is gradually overtaken by the rise of modernism, how does "the eye in the text" renegotiate its relation to forms of knowledge and power?[2]

One way of initially thinking about this question is to turn to a subgenre of realism, detective fiction, in which the deployment of this "eye" defines its operations, and in which narrative omniscience is modified or problematized. Detective fiction, to the extent that it is motivated by the exposure of a "truth"—the revelation of criminal acts—focalizes and hyperbolizes the relation between narrative envisionment and knowledge by bridging the detached distance of traditional realism. Detective fiction disrupts the aesthetic and epistemological balance sustained by realism by emphasizing the *forms* of knowing and the difficulties of access to the truth; and it revises the coincidence of subject positions through which the reader and realist narrator collude. These defections work to construct, against an omniscient, detached, disinterested gaze, a visual model that reveals its proximate interestedness, its desire, its compromised access to objective "truth," its inherent perversity.

In detective fiction the narrative landscape is transformed from transparency to translucency, in which the realist narrator's unmediated access to objects is deferred in a temporary suspension of a realist contract normally restored at the end. The panoptic powers of an omniscient narrator typically are concentrated in the person of the detective, with the difference that those powers themselves become the subject of scrutiny, rather than the invisible medium in which the text unfolds; the resulting surplus of "evidence" and corresponding interpretive excess it produces will retrospectively be ordered, with clues either privileged as truth or discarded as false leads. In detective fiction, then, as D. A. Miller has argued, "Whether one has an overabundance of signs, or an excess of unattached meanings, the easy equatability of sign and meaning has been troubled" (479). But in detective fiction the initial undecidability of signs, and the linguistic or aesthetic excess with which it is associated, is always recontained, like the crime itself, through the production of the criminal, the "truth," and the restoration of social order. This "depletion of signifiers," as Miller puts it, produces coherence through the exile of excess and restores the narrative world to transparent availability.

In addition to disrupting realism's balancing act between aesthetics and epistemology at this structural level, detective fiction redefines the detached, omniscient posture of the realist narrative's "gaze." In literary texts, of course, such a gaze is a linguistically constructed, representational one and comes into being through the reader's identification with or visualization of the narrator's view. In this sense, we might think of the realist narrator and the reader as coextensive, the realist narrator functioning as a kind of proxy for the reader. Slavoj Žižek's description of the function of filmic proxies with whom viewers identify is a useful way of conceptualizing this textual relation: "Such a logic of fascination by which the subject sees in the object (in the image it views) its own gaze, i.e., by which, in the viewed image, it 'sees itself seeing,' is defined by Lacan . . . as the very illusion of perfect self-mirroring that characterizes the Cartesian philosophical tradition of the subject's self-reflection'' (43).[3] For Lacan, such a relation is an ''illusion'' because it elides the antinomy between the eye and the gaze. As Žižek summarizes, ''The eye viewing the object is on the side of the subject, while the gaze is on the side of the object. When I am looking at an object, the object is always already gazing at me, and from a point at which I cannot see it. . . . The whole point of Lacan's argument is to oppose to the self-mirroring of philosophical subjectivity the irreducible discord between the gaze qua object and the subject's eye'' (35). Whereas in realism this antinomy is dissolved by positing two ''eyes'' or subject positions that align the reader with the narrator, detective fiction offers quite different terms by establishing forms of identification between the reader and characters' delimited views. Just as the reader of detective fiction attempts to mimic the detective's gaze, however ineptly, the detective tries, as his or her most valued epistemological technique, to identify with the gaze of the criminal, to see as the criminal sees, in order to solve the crime. The detective, then, and by extension the reader, aligns himself or herself with a gaze that is on the side of the object; as Žižek puts it, ''such a coincidence of gazes,'' as opposed to the subject's viewing eye, ''defines the position of the pervert'' (37).

Detective fiction thus breaks up ''the illusion of perfect self-mirroring'' that defines the operations of Cartesian spectatorship in conventional realist narration; and it undermines the forms of knowledge on which those models depend in still other ways. Knowledge in detective fiction is revealed as contingent rather than omniscient, relying as it does on the successful interpretation of signs; as the detective's eponymous instrument, the magnifying glass, and favored technique, identification, make clear, only the intimately proximate, interested gaze will solve the crime. In these ways, then, though hardly exhaustively, the narrative techniques of detective fiction replace the transcendent Cartesian spectator with varying forms of subjectivization. Compared with the supervisory functions that Seltzer identifies with realism's omniscient prerogatives—its ''unlimited authority'' over ''a world thoroughly known and thoroughly mastered by the panoptic 'eye' of the narration''— detective fiction overlooks far more circumscribed horizons, thereby compromising the sovereign, regulatory force through which the realist text has been linked with the social order. Moreover, by problematizing realist narrative authority—dislocating its attendant knowledge and mastery, and the equatability of signs and meanings—detective fiction seems to anticipate many of the innovations associated with modernist practice.

While I am not arguing that detective fiction should be understood as a precursor to modernism in any strict sense, I am suggesting that modernist texts regularly employ many of its conventions and strategies. If these conventions are not what makes modernism ''modernist'' precisely, they do provide relatively stable windows into some of the revised forms of spectatorship modernism embraces, as well as some of their linguistic and ideological consequences. We can trace such limited forms of indebtedness in the two modernist texts I will be looking at here, Henry James's *The Sacred Fount* (1901) and Vladimir Nabokov's *The Eye* (1930), for each is derivable, to a differing degree, from the detective genre. *The Sacred Fount* portrays the relentless inquiry of James's narrator into the particulars of others' erotic lives through his pursuit of clues about possible sexual relations. In its rather spectacular failure to expose a definitive ''truth,'' to disclose the ''crime'' of unsanctioned sexual activity, *The Sacred Fount* abjures the gesture of recontainment that controls excess in detective fiction; instead, the text's embrace of that excess can be seen as part of an early formulation of modernist paradigms and practices. The omnipresence of the obsessive, voyeuristic gaze in James becomes the vehicle for an extended critique of the possibility of the detached, disinterested, omniscient vision of the Cartesian spectator and the supervisory force with which it is associated. Making implicit the subjectivized viewer James anatomizes through the self-reflexive model of surveillance it presents, Nabokov's *The Eye* provides a test case through which to consider that viewer's relation to the tactics of supervision associated with realist techniques of representation. In *The Eye* the narrator's repeated attempts to discover the identity of the man who turns out to be himself can unquestionably be contextualized within the ''fantasy of surveillance'' said to characterize the realist narrator's position; but his failure to do so confronts us with a model of panoptic power the stability and success of which appear to be infinitely deferred. By simultaneously offering us a fractured model of the subject and defining the contexts which that subject inhabits as arbitrary extensions of it, *The Eye* fundamentally challenges any neat equation of that subject's narrative authority with disciplinary structures.

From Crystal Cage to Crystal Palace: Henry James's *The Sacred Fount*

Beginning at the train station from which the unnamed narrator is conveyed to a weekend party at the fashionable estate, Newmarch, *The Sacred Fount* devotes itself to the narrator's attempt, as Rebecca West has trenchantly put it, ''to discover whether there exists between certain of his fellow-guests a relationship not more interesting among these vacuous people than it is among sparrows'' (107–8); he never does. In this elaborate parable and parody of failed spectatorship, equivocal artistry, or triumphant voyeurism, depending on one's point of view, the narrator's scrutiny of the erotic relations of his fellow guests exposes nothing so much as the politics of the gaze itself as an issue. The social world of Newmarch functions as a highly regulated, self-contained social laboratory, a "crystal cage" (200) in which the narrator can test, through dedicated observation, his vampiristic "law"—that one romantic partner unknowingly drains the youth, beauty, or intelligence from the "sacred fount" of the other, a lover whose painful knowledge of the sacrifice is mollified by love. He derives the theory from the case of the Brissendens and the way the older Grace has apparently sapped the youth from the much younger, but now older-looking, Guy—or, as he is generally referred to, "poor Briss." Using the Brissendens as his model, he tries to determine whether the formerly acute May Server is responsible for the dramatic improvement of the formerly stupid Gilbert Long; since each is unmarried, the social consequences of discovering such a relation are potentially more serious than those attending his perception of the Brissendens. The narrator's method for testing his hypothesis rests on his own observations and those of several others whom he takes selectively into his confidence; the novel, then, consists almost entirely of talk, in a series of partial collaborations between the narrator and his satellites, whose contributions can be taken either as corroborating testimony or as the joint outcome of the narrator's influence and their suggestibility. The narrator's accumulation of "evidence," punctuated by egoistic outbursts at his own perceptual prowess, culminates in a lengthy contest of conclusions with Grace Brissenden, his primary confidant, at the close.

The narrator's unsavory prurience and his inability definitively to substantiate his theory or arrive at a "truth" have been taken by many critics not only to prove his unreliability but to discredit the posture of detached observation itself in an attempt "to annihilate the distinction between subjective and objective reality" (see Cameron 159 and Porter 34–35). This seems to me the right approach, given that attempts to "resolve" or decode *The Sacred Fount* into an unambiguous narrative, a detective story that finds its man, tend to devolve into the same kinds of obsessive exercises in conjecture and inference of which the narrator himself appears guilty (see Blackall, Moon, Reany, Bysshe Stein, or Tyler). Beginning with the position that *The Sacred Fount*'s narrator "contaminates" his objective posture with subjective contents, I will examine precisely how the distinction between "subjective" and "objective" reality is eroded. *The Sacred Fount,* I will argue, can be read as a virtual anatomy of subjectivization, offering, in the place of a detached, neutral observer, a highly unstable self-reflexive erotics of viewing, able to deliver "knowledge" only about the viewing subject itself; it thus operates as an elaborate send-up of the disinterested narrative postures of realism and Cartesian spectatorship.[4] *The Sacred Fount* ultimately replaces the providential eye, epitomized by the Cartesian camera obscura as a model for visual verisimilitude,[5] with one more closely identifiable with the Marxist reformulation of it, in which the camera obscura, as ideological machine, comes to constitute equally both seers and the world seen as sites of mediation. The novel thus stands as something of a watershed in James's fiction in that he uncovers potentialities in the observer—those of narcissistic distortion and violence—that he attempts to contain in the three works of the major phase.

The representation of Newmarch as a crystal cage, suggesting at once transparency, material value, and incarceration, is a figure both for individual perceivers, each caught and looking out from his or her own "cage" and available to the scrutiny of others, and also for the privileged social community of Newmarch as a whole, imprisoned in a network of social expectations and conventions and operating on the imperative, as the narrator puts it, "to be really what we looked" (157). That *The Sacred Fount* operates within this metaphor of panoptic confinement, rather than producing it at the end as its means of recontainment and resolution, suggests that mechanisms of internalized social regulation are already in place. Inside that "cage," other central external symbols—social order and power, the law and the state—are reassigned to internal agency. In place of the law, that "objective" standard of social consensus the detective works to enforce, the narrator divines what he deems to be a "natural" law of human relations that does not so much restore order as posit a manifestly unjust one, dictating gain at another's expense; though he attributes the agency of his law to higher forces, it is clearly of his own invention. The figure of the "crystal palace" (205), by which the narrator metaphorizes the edifice of his thought, also relocates an external image of state power to the solipsistic interior, transforming him into a kind of all-seeing monarch in a world in which the individual imagination is sovereign. While in his conceptions of "natural law" and "palace of thought" the narrator attempts to situate power at the perimeters of a social world he observes as from a great height, neither actually escapes its determinations; indeed, it is on the strength of his assurance that he and his fellow guests share consistent and legible social behavior—or, to put it differently, internalized forms of self-regulation—that he can base his faith on their readability. He can thus abjure the ignoble "detective and the keyhole" as his means of substantiating his theory in favor of "psychological evidence" (66).

If the social world of Newmarch offers itself, as the narrator would have it, transparently to his gaze, it is because he is of that world, not outside it. But there are really two sides to the notion of transparency and readability—it requires both an objective seer and an unmediated world of objects to work—and both sides of the equation are called into question by *The Sacred Fount*. About halfway through the novel, the narrator expresses the ideal of transparency, during a tableau in which all of Newmarch's guests are assembled:

> I think the imagination, in those halls of art and fortune, was almost inevitably accounted a poor matter. . . . I said to myself during dinner that these were scenes in which a transcendent intelligence had after

193

all no application, and that, in short, any preposterous acuteness might easily suffer among them such a loss of dignity as overtakes the newspaperman kicked out. We existed, all of us together, to be handsome and happy, to be really what we looked—since we looked tremendously well; to be that and neither more nor less, so not discrediting by musty secrets and aggressive doubts our high privilege of harmony and taste. We were concerned only with what was bright and open, and the expression that became us all was, at worst, the shaded but gratified eye, the air of being forgivingly dazzled by too much lustre. (156–57)

To fulfill the requirement "to be really what we looked," the narrator suggests, requires both a measure of willful blindness on the part of an observer—the suspension of "transcendent intelligence" and "preposterous acuteness"—and a heroic self-discipline on the part of its objects to achieve the depth that surface requires—to eradicate "musty secrets and aggressive doubts." Paradoxically, then, transparency, in order to participate in the class aspiration for a "dazzling" surface to fully represent depth, demands a vision stripped of its powers of penetration, one that is alive only to the effects of social convention and not its causes. This static and openly limited model of vision, so well expressed by the image of "the shaded but gratified eye," already curtails the purview of the Cartesian model; even the exiled newspaperman, who might seem the best candidate for that model, is backed by the interpretive power of the imagination rather than by objective apprehension as the potential means to peel back surfaces in the text. It is presumably by calling on a perception measurably augmented by the imagination that the narrator is enabled to say about Lady John, "I could mark these emotions, and what determined them, as behind clear glass" (102). Our choice then, is between two forms of "transparency"—either the shaded eye, which refuses depth, or the imaginatively assisted eye, which produces it. And what is the imagination if not the receptacle for the accumulated knowledge of the social world, the tool of social regulation itself?

The problematization of transparency is reflected in the text's iconography, in which varying metaphors of light predominate. Against the "light of reason," which illuminates the Cartesian model, *The Sacred Fount* emphasizes instead its subjective aspects. Thus, when the narrator's confidants refer to the "great light" shed by his idea, his "torch in darkness" (64), they are also following his "burning" obsession, associated with destruction and desire; later, the narrator describes his arrival with a sense of certainty as a "flight into luminous ether" (255), a figure suggesting rather intangibility and ephemerality. And finally, the narrator describes light as part of the crucible in which he forges his particular brand of perception: "I shall never forget the impressions of that evening,'' he reports, ''nor the way, in particular, the immediate effect of some of them was to merge the light of my extravagant perceptions in a glamour much more diffused'' (156). Illumination in the text, then, perpetually reminds us of this subjective admixture of impression and perception, and of its metaphoric affiliation with the destructive element of fire.

Throwing light on a subject, it becomes clear, is an insufficient guarantor of knowledge, too, because of the way characters are said habitually to screen themselves with others. The narrator understands Lady John to be Gilbert Long's ''screen,'' who masks the real woman who has lent him her wit (36); he believes Gilbert Long to be the screen that produces ''the appearance of a passion'' for Lady John (106); and so on. If the narrator believes some characters function as screens who block his perceptual access, others seem to work as projection screens who, mirrorlike, reflect him back to himself. In a scene in which both sorts of screening are in play, the narrator lectures Lady John about the ''use'' she is making of her ''screen'': ''Will you allow me to say frankly that I think you play a dangerous game with poor Briss, in whom I confess I'm interested? I don't of course speak of the least danger to yourself; but it's an injustice to any man to make use of him quite so flagrantly''; later, he complains of the way she is ''sacrificing'' him (175, 178). If anyone is ''playing a dangerous game'' with others without their knowledge, it is of course the narrator, who uses the rhetoric of sacrifice to outline his plans for poor Briss and others later in the text. In the same vein, the narrator's charges of, for example, Grace Brissenden's ''simplified egotism'' (71) or Lady John's ''extravagantly vain'' ways seem like ''transparent'' instances of self-description.

The narrator's expectation of a transparent social world, of a *crystal* cage, is doomed to failure because access to that world is so complexly mediated; if he chooses to see more than the superficial vision that ''the shaded but gratified eye'' promises, he surveys a field refracted by opaque and specular screens obscuring alike subjects and objects. As if to acknowledge his tenuous positioning there, the narrator frequently imagines himself as the potential object of another's gaze. In such a moment of self-consciousness, he reflects, ''I daresay that . . . my cogitations—for I must have bristled with them— would have made me as stiff a puzzle to interpretive minds as I had suffered other phenomena to become to my own'' (92). Elsewhere the prospect of becoming a visual object appears less hypothetical; while watching people from a balcony, he wonders ''if, in the interest of observation, I mightn't snap down the electric light that, playing just behind me, must show where I stood. I resisted this impulse'' (201–2). By imagining himself in this way, the narrator seems temporarily to occupy the perverse position that Žižek describes, where, ''as a stratagem to evade his constitutive splitting, the subject itself

assumes the position of an object instrumental to the enjoyment of the Other''
(36). But it is not a position he lingers in for long; instead, the narrator prefers
to adopt the pretense, if not precisely the methods, of a detached scientific
observer. As he puts it in a typical moment, ''however slight the incident and
small the evidence, it essentially fitted in'' (202). The possibility of such a
reversal, however, serves as a nagging reminder of the precariousness of the
sovereignty of the narrator's gaze and the position it aspires to outside of its
objects in the social world.

So far I have been looking at what might be called structural problems
that attend the process of observation in *The Sacred Fount*—those that would
constitute any social ''laboratory,'' such as Newmarch, or any particular observer. The construction of subjects and objects through a network of social
conventions; the ''contamination'' of pure perception with impressions and
the imagination; the intervention of mediating ''screens''; the self-reflexivity
of projection; the potential reversibility of subject and object positions—these
difficulties are each of a different order than the purely solipsistic or idiosyncratic problems epitomized by the (inconclusive) accusation of madness lev-
eled at the narrator at various points in the text. Such a division of perceptual
variables into the inherent and the contingent raises the question of the extent
to which the narrator can be taken as a representative or merely as an excep-
tional observer within *The Sacred Fount*. By turning now to those subjective
modes that seem peculiar to the narrator alone, let me begin by considering
one of the only real ''incidents'' in the text—the analysis of the painting
referred to as *The Man with the Mask,* which the narrator, May Server, Gilbert
Long, and Ford Obert collectively examine. As a static object, the painting
affords a less mercurial interpretive ground than the changeable human behavior the narrator and others mainly try to perceive; and because we are afforded
four simultaneous but independent views, we can begin to distinguish collective from individual interpretive problems. The painting normalizes perceptual
(and textual) indeterminacy among the characters and for the reader, and pa-
thologizes, by contrast, the mechanisms by which the narrator attempts to
control it as he aims to achieve and maintain certainty.

The painting *The Man with the Mask* depicts the ''pale, lean, livid face''
of a young man, in old-world black dress, holding a mask in one hand; it is,
the narrator assures the group, ''the picture, of all pictures, that most needs an
interpreter'' (55). The painting promises to work as a kind of textual anagram,
as it materially brings together internal and external points of reference. It
initially functions as a lightning rod for interpretive controversy:

> ''Yes, what in the world does it mean?'' Mrs. Server replied. ''One
> could call it—though that doesn't get one much further—the Mask
> of Death.''

196

"Why so?" I demanded while we all again looked at the picture. "Isn't it much rather the Mask of Life? It's the man's own face that's Death. The other one, blooming and beautiful—"

"Ah, but with an awful grimace!" Mrs. Server broke in.

"The other one, blooming and beautiful," I repeated, "is Life, and he's going to put it on; unless indeed he has just taken it off."

. . . "And what does Mr. Obert think?"

He kept his eyes on [Mrs. Server] for a moment before replying. "He thinks it looks like a lovely lady."

"That grinning mask? What lovely lady?"

"It does," I declared to him, really seeing what he meant "it does look remarkably like Mrs. Server." (56)

Unable to agree on the most basic affective features of the painting—Is the mask "blooming and beautiful" or displaying "an awful grimace"? Is the man removing or putting on the mask?—the group, though never with complete consensus, tries to "resolve" the elements in the painting by assigning to them external sources; the mask is identified as May Server, the face is later declared that of poor Briss. And indeed, the text adds a certain weight to these designations: later the narrator will describe the "terrible little fixed smile" (148) he believes May Server to use as a ruse to cover up her depleted intellectual resources as a "grimace" that becomes "blurred as a bit of brushwork spoiled" (133) from the strain of keeping it up; the "pale, lean, livid face" fits comfortably with other characterizations of the enervated poor Briss.

But, of course, to read the painting in this way creates far more interpretive problems than it solves. On the one hand, the painting can be seen to take up the question of social masks in the novel, expressing the problem of reading them, distinguishing them from a subject's "authentic" face, and of adducing their directionality—Are they revealing or concealing a hidden depth? On the other hand, the painting seems to work as an encoded materialization of the narrator's theory, in which the haggard donor of the sacred fount holds, in Dorian Grey fashion, the improved face of its recipient; but the novel's positioning of poor Briss and May Server in these respective roles will not quite fit, since each of them is designated a loser in the game of amorous transfusion—only Grace Brissenden's face, presumably, should fit the mask held by poor Briss. Finally, we can view the painting as an image of the sympathy that the narrator believes he has discerned between poor Briss and May Server, as victims; but, of course, that reading squares poorly with the opposition suggested by the imagery of face versus mask. The indeterminacy of the meaning of the painting offers itself, inevitably, as a figure of interpretative indeterminacy in the novel at large. Even the "coincidence" that the face and mask in the painting happen to resemble not one, but two of Newmarch's guests goes nowhere—attempts to decode the coincidence lead only to duplicating the game of speculation and inference that is the narrator's questionable method. The painting, like the narrative at large, suffers from a *surplus* of meanings, each of which is only partially substantiated and, therefore, partially adequate; ultimately, the possible meanings of the painting fade and the incident takes its place as just another observational opportunity for the narrator.[6] For all concerned, then, a gap opens up between seeing and knowing, both because the object itself is internally ambiguous, its meaning unavailable to straightforward apprehension, and because those meanings the groups brings to bear on it are so clearly extrinsic—despite their alleged resemblance, May Server and poor Briss were not the actual models for the painted figures.

The painting provides an object lesson in the power of multiple mediating screens to complicate and defer the meaning of aesthetic objects, establishing indeterminacy as the perceptual norm. As such it strikes a cautionary note that replays itself when, in an inversion of the interpretive process applied to *The Man with the Mask,* the narrator transforms the people of Newmarch into the stuff of painting by, in other words, aestheticizing them. But the narrator's aestheticizing practices, among the other subjective forms he brings to bear, have the effect not of exposing indeterminacy but of covering it over. As he gazes at May Server shortly before viewing the painting, the narrator describes her: "She might have been herself—all Greuze tints, all pale pinks and blues and pearly whites and candid eyes—an old dead pastel under glass" (51); at dinner, the narrator compares poor Briss with an "old Velasquez" (158); later, he views his "opposed couples balanced like bronze groups at the two ends of a chimney-piece . . . playing a part in [his] exhibition" (182–83). The aesthetic terms in which the narrator renders his observations are both transformative and appropriative, as the objects of his gaze are recast as the products of his imagination. The aestheticization of the operations of his own intelligence completes this process, in which the objects of his scrutiny, not merely objectified, are internalized as the "creatures" of his imagination. As the narrator reviews his theory at the piano recital, he deems May Server to be "still the controlling image for me, the real principle of composition" (167) in his mental creation; or, as he puts it still more strongly, "To see all this was at the time, I remember, to be as inhumanly amused as if one had found one could create something" (104). If we are tempted, as many critics have been, to understand this process merely as an account of artistic genesis, we should note that sight is equated here only with the *possibility* of artistic creation. At most we should read the narrator's perversely "inhuman amusement" as a parody of the artistic process and recall that, despite his reliance on the rhetoric of aestheticization, his goal is the acquisition of knowledge, not the creation of a product—and even in this he fails.

Just as the aestheticization of the narrator's gaze and its objects confronts

198

us with the subjective powers of mind, the veiled eroticism of that gaze confronts us insistently with the desiring, observing body. The narrator's "anxiety" and "absurd excitement" (94), his "mystic throb" (127), grow with his "ridiculous obsession" (89), leaving him "groan[ing] . . . as if for very ecstasy" (216). As he puts it to Ford Obert, explaining his desire to escape the excesses of Newmarch, "You excite me too much. You don't know what you do to me" (215). The narrator also projects sexual content onto the objects of his scrutiny, as becomes clear in his description of poor Briss in an encounter with his wife: "As a response to her," the narrator relates, poor Briss displays "the gush of the sacred fount. . . . [I]t rose before me in time that, whatever might be, for the exposed instant, the deep note of their encounter, only one thing concerned me in it" (198–99). Finally, the narrator's own "sacred fount" threatens to erupt into an image of bodily pleasure, as he describes his attempt to penetrate May Server's secret: "But if, though only nearer to her secret and still not in possession . . . so it equally came to me that I was quite near enough, at the pass we had reached, for what I should have to take from it all. She was on my hands" (134). That the narrator's eroticism, however, remains self-referential and confined to voyeuristic pleasure is made clear by his admission to himself: "It would have been almost as embarrassing to tell [the other men] how little experience I had had in fact as to have to have had to tell them how much I had had in fancy" (101); the narrator likes only to watch.

In his 1918 essay "On Narcissism," Freud describes the autoerotic origins of narcissism and its linkage to early forms of libidinal development in which "the libido withdrawn from the outer world has been directed onto the ego." He defines the narcissistic state that follows in this way:

> In [the mental life of primitive peoples and of children] we find characteristics which, if they occurred singly, might be put down to megalomania: an over-estimation of the power of wishes and mental processes, the "omnipotence of thoughts," a belief in the magical virtue of words, and a method of dealing with the outer world—the art of "magic"—which appears to be a logical application of these grandiose premises. (32–33)

It is striking how nearly the narrator's own characterization of his adventure anticipates Freud's 1918 account of narcissism. The narrator tells us,

> I had positively encountered nothing to compare with this since the days of fairy-tales and of the childish imagination of the impossible. *Then* I used to circle round enchanted castles, for then I moved in a world in which the strange "came true." It was the coming true that was the proof of the enchantment, which, moreover, was naturally

never so great as when such coming was, to such a degree and by the most romantic stroke of all, the fruit of one's own wizardry. I was positively—so the wheel had revolved—proud of my work. I had thought it all out, and to have thought it was, wonderfully, to have brought it. (128–29)

The narcissist, then, confronts a world believed to be of his own making or "the fruit of [his] own wizardry," where thought is credited with a productive power that acquires proprietary value as "my work"; and this sense of production and ownership profoundly informs the text's representation of seeing and knowing. Understanding his own vision as a form of "currency," the narrator consistently conceives of the materials from which he constructs it in terms of value and exchange.[7] The result of the narrator's narcissism, then, is a vision that commodifies, as regularly as it aestheticizes and sexualizes, its objects. The narrator's vampiristic "law," of course, is the prototype of this relation. Taking her cue from the narrator, Grace Brissenden elaborates that law:

> "One of [romantic pair] always gets more out of it than the other. One of them—you know the saying—gives the lips, the other gives the cheek."
>
> "It's the deepest of all truths. Yet the cheek profits too," I more prudently argued.
>
> "It profits most. It takes and keeps and uses all the lips give." (80)

The same thing—taking, keeping, and using—could be said of the narrator's obsessive desire to see and know; as he himself puts it, "The obsession pays, if one will; but to pay it has to borrow" (23). In this same vein, the narrator describes the theoretical woman whose losses account for Gilbert Long's gain as an empty display window who has "put up the shutters and closed the shop" (35, 37); in yielding to Ford Obert's request for information, the narrator responds " 'What, if I do,' I asked with an idea, 'will you give me?' . . . 'And what then,' I went on, 'will you take from me?' " (205); and in the narrator's final conversation with Grace Brissenden, he wonders, "I might pay for her assurance, but wasn't there something of mine for which *she* might pay?" (242). While the other characters may "exchange" matters of more substance, for the narrator vision functions as the chief currency in this economy; unsubstantiated, it threatens to be deprived "of all value as coin" (313). For even though this narcissist persists in the fantasized "joy of determining, almost of creating results" (214), he seems to require the confirmation, or at least the appreciation, of others to legitimize his "creation."

The language of economic exchange in *The Sacred Fount* makes explicit the pattern of instrumental use to which the narrator puts nearly all his fellow guests, always trying to get better than he gives. Ultimately that language points to the sort of violence the narrator felt constrained to avoid early on, before his imagination, having internalized its aesthetic "objects," became his sole standard of value. We can see this shift decisively take hold in his final confrontation with Grace Brissenden, in which his vision has to survive in a now-competitive marketplace. Threatened by the immanent destruction of his "crystal palace" at the hands of her rival theory, he explains: "There was no point at which my assurance could, by the scientific method, judge itself complete enough not to regard feeling as an interference and, in consequence, as a possible check. If it had to go I knew well who went with it, but I wasn't there to save *them*. I was there to save my priceless pearl of an inquiry and to harden, to that end, my heart" (296). It is significant and characteristic that the narrator recurs to the detached posture of the scientific method and its repudiation of feeling at the same moment he imbues his inquiry with a subjective criteria of value as the "priceless pearl." The rhetoric of sacrifice, too—"I wasn't there to save *them*"—is clearly far from disinterested, suggesting rather the desperate maneuverings of a man attempting to salvage the fruits of his labor. As he puts it elsewhere, "I couldn't save Mrs. Server, and I couldn't save poor Briss; I could, however, guard, to the last grain of gold, my precious sense of their loss, their disintegration and their doom; and it was for this I was now bargaining" (273).

As we have seen, the narrator, far from employing the disinterested methods of an objective science, adds his distinctive stamp to the structural elements of perceptual indeterminacy that are globally attributed in the text. The forms of aestheticization, sexualization, and commodification he practices threaten collectively to obscure the confrontation with interpretive indeterminacy initially staged by the painting *The Man with the Mask*. Each of these modes, moreover, is easily subsumed under the rubric of the narcissistic "fairy-tale" to which the text finally if obliquely alludes, the Orpheus myth, a story in which Orpheus's gaze becomes an instrument of violence because Orpheus sacrifices his bride, Eurydice, to the underworld for the sake of a knowledge tentatively linked to art. As a means at once of acknowledging and disowning this violence, just as he did with Lady John's "use" of poor Briss earlier in the text, the narrator attributes agency elsewhere, projecting onto Grace Brissenden a gaze that is really the outcome of his own methods. About Grace Brissenden's analysis of May Server, he says that it "had the effect of relegating to the dim shades the lady representing it, and there was small soundness in her glance at the possibility on the part of this person of an anxious prowl back . . . [T]o mention her had been to get rid of her" (246). Relegating May Server "to the dim shades," the narrator makes Grace Brissenden the vehicle for the "glance" that will prevent Server's "anxious prowl back.'' *The Sacred Fount*'s invocation of the Orpheus myth at this late stage in the text holds out the promise of a resolution of sorts by organizing its perceptual elements into a coherent narrative, but it forecloses on that resolution, first, by representing it as projection, and second, by failing to recuperate the violence represented by the sacrifice of May Server through the production of reliable knowledge. In a way, *The Sacred Fount* remains most faithful to the end of the Orpheus story, in which the singer is torn to pieces by a group of angry Maenads; ''go[ing] utterly to pieces'' (297) himself at Grace Brissenden's hands, the narrator takes the possibility of narrative coherence and interpretive resolution with him.

As the narrator's theory and, indeed, his very sense of himself as a subject come apart at the seams, so too do his two dominant perceptual fantasies—that of the transparency of the social world and that of his narcissistic construction of it. The notion of transparency the narrator began with, in which he expected the world to reveal itself ''as behind clear glass,'' is now revised to express the absence of meaning rather than its accessibility; as he complains to Grace Brissenden, '' 'We put it, the whole thing, together, and we shook the bottle hard. I'm to take from you, after this,' I wound up, 'that what it contains is a perfectly colorless fluid?' '' (261). Later he appeals to her sense of mercy for his imaginative labors: '' 'Remember,' I pleaded, 'that you're costing me a perfect palace of thought!' . . . she replied 'Oh, those who live in glass houses—' '' (311); the cliché expresses both the narrator's culpable vulnerability—he ''shouldn't throw stones''—and, by neatly deflating his ''crystal palace'' to a ''glass house,'' turns the perceptual tables on a narrator now left humbled and exposed, fallen from his sovereign heights and restored to the field of the social order below. Finally, the narrator's narcissistic belief that he inhabits a world of his own making is likewise discredited; Grace Brissenden clarifies the ''horrors'' the narrator sees: '' 'It isn't, perhaps, so much that you see them—' I started. 'As that I perpetrate them?' She was sure now, however, and wouldn't have it, for she was serious. 'Dear no—you don't perpetrate anything. Perhaps it would be better if you did!' '' (299). Having been thus summarily divested of both omniscience and omnipotence, the narrator implies that his own ''sacred fount'' has run dry—''I didn't after all—it appeared to be part of my smash—know the weight of [poor Briss's] years,'' he confesses, ''but I knew the weight of my own. They might have been a thousand . . .'' (318). It is important to see that, however drastically reduced he appears, the narrator has merely taken his place as a normative viewing subject here. The subjective excesses peculiar to the narrator, really only extreme versions of those by which all subjects are constructed in the novel, deluded him into believing that the visible world was openly available to him; upon his dethronement, he, like the reader, must confront the layers of mediation that keep the possibility of a stable, objective knowledge of that world always at arm's length.

To put it somewhat differently: *The Sacred Fount* expresses the difference between, and brings into conflict, the Cartesian and Marxist versions of the meaning of the "machine" they each transform into visual metaphor, the camera obscura. "For Descartes," as Jonathan Crary describes it, "the images observed within the camera obscura are formed by a means of a disembodied cyclopean eye, detached from the observer. . . . Founded on the laws of nature (optics) but extrapolated to a plane outside of nature, the camera obscura provides a vantage point onto the world analogous to the eye of God" (47–48). This is the sort of eye—albeit outside of the social rather than the natural world—that *The Sacred Fount*'s narrator has aspired to embody, and it is precisely this providential visuality that the text exposes as solipsistic delusion. In its stead the text offers a model closer to Marx's conception of the camera obscura as a figure for the operations of ideology, in which both the inverted image the machine produces and the viewer's apprehension of it are understood to be mediated as historical productions.[8] By representing not just the narrator but the social world he observes equally as "sites of mediation," *The Sacred Fount* comes to resemble the camera obscura as ideological machine.

The linguistic consequences of a model that mediates visual access in this way are substantial for the novel as a whole. To return to "the poor banished ghost," May Server, in her incarnation in the Orpheus myth, we can see this connection drawn out when the narrator tells us, "To mention her had been to get rid of her" (246). Substituting speech for sight in this formulation of what is solely visual violence in the original tale, the narrator makes an equation that aptly describes the text's operations. In the absence of the knowledge it has as its aim in *The Sacred Fount,* vision can yield only talk—endless accounts of itself that seem to merge with the process of perception itself. Because none of the accounts attains the status of truth, retrospectively ordering the excess of meanings produced, the language of vision acquires a surplus value, mimicking the gap between signification and meaning that obtains for visual perception. Language, then, to the extent that it mediates all accounts of vision, becomes the ultimate subjective form by extending the gap between sign and meaning in the visual realm to the linguistic medium in which it is expressed.[9] The narrator conveys something to this effect in his final interview with Grace Brissenden: "It could *not* but be exciting to talk, as we talked, on the basis of those suppressed processes and unavowed references which made the meaning of our meeting so different from its form. We knew ourselves—what moved me, that is, is that she knew me—to mean, at every point, immensely more than I said or that she answered" (272). Sight and its "excitements" could easily be substituted for speech in this formulation, which closely resembles the narrator's account of perception assisted by the imagination, which he offered early on. In this same vein, Grace Brissenden's accusations to the narrator in their final interview—"You see too much" and "You talk too much" (261, 262)—wind up as virtual equivalents. We can see the process of indeterminacy overtake the purely linguistic figure, "the sacred fount," by observing the series of meanings that accumulate around it: as a metaphor for "life force," the visual imagination, sexuality, and, through its etymological link with font, for language, *The Sacred Fount* produces and circulates meanings rather than designates a privileged origin.

The political dimensions of the observer's gaze in *The Sacred Fount*—its potential for narcissistic distortion and violence—are addressed both within the confines of the novel and, by analogy to the obligations of authorship in relation to its narrative materials, in the structural innovations of James's later works. In *The Sacred Fount,* the narrator's pursuit of possibly compromising investigations without the knowledge or consent of his objects is provisionally declared "wanting in taste" (45) or "none of one's business" (69); as he tells Ford Obert, as a result of his methods "Our hands are not clean" (212). Such considerations point not to the fact of mediated vision itself, about which, presumably, nothing can be done, but to its uses and applications in relation to its objects. The problem for James, then, is to find a way to reconcile the claims of "expressional curiosity and expressional decency" (374), as he puts it in his "Prefaces," to honor his own moral imperatives about the "treatment" of his subject matter by constraining the observer's potential for instrumental violence—to emerge himself, that is, with clean hands. In his preface to *The Ambassadors,* the work written immediately after *The Sacred Fount,* we can see these considerations at work in James's repudiation, though initially in strictly formal terms, of first-person narration as "a form foredoomed to looseness." By being rendered in the third person, James tells us, "Strether, . . . encaged and provided for as 'The Ambassadors' encages and provides, has to keep in view proprieties much stiffer and more salutary than any our straight and credulous gape are likely to bring home to him, has exhibitional conditions to meet, in a word, that forbid the terrible *fluidity* of self-revelation" ("Prefaces" 371–72). We can see how some of *The Sacred Fount*'s iconography has been reformulated in this conception, where the "crystal cage" that transparently contained its narrator has been refined into a more opaque material; "encaged" and thus protected from our "straight and credulous gape," Strether is represented as better able to perform his obligation to maintain the text's "stiff proprieties" and to escape "the terrible *fluidity* of self-revelation" or exposure. By instituting such proprieties and "exhibitional conditions," the reader rather than the narrator (or the author) has been reconstituted as their potential violator, whose prurient gaze is now exiled to the outside of the text.

This displacement of observational agency is echoed in James's preface to *The Golden Bowl,* but here authorship is singled out as the probable transgressor of the text's proprieties. He comments:

> I have already betrayed, as an accepted habit . . . my preference for dealing with my subject matter, for "seeing my story," through the opportunity and the sensibility of some more or less detached, some not strictly involved, though thoroughly interested and intelligent, witness or reporter, some person who contributes to the case mainly a certain amount of criticism and interpretation of it. . . . Anything, in short, I now reflect, must always have seemed to me better—better for the process and the effect of representation, my irrepressible ideal—than the mere muffled majesty of irresponsible "authorship." ("Prefaces" 376–77)

The "muffled majesty of irresponsible 'authorship' " suggests, of course, the prerogatives of the traditional realist narrator, whose irresponsibility derives, we must suppose, precisely from its invisibility, its "*muffled* majesty." Whether protecting against the alleged "expressional curiosity" of reader or author in his later works, James not only follows his preference for "some more or less detached . . . witness or reporter" but, in his final two works, multiplies his narrative centers, arguably to obviate the dominating force inevitable in a single perspective; in so doing, he provides a clear alternative to realist omniscience. In *Wings of the Dove,* the "successive centres" or "represented community of vision" ("Prefaces" 353, 355) work to disperse and democratize visuality in the novel, furthering "the author's instinct everywhere for the *indirect* presentation of his main image" (359). The absence of such precautions is figured as a species of violence that inevitably recalls those of *The Sacred Fount.* James explains: "It is as if, for these aspects, the impersonal plate—in other words the poor author's cold affirmation or thin guarantee—had felt itself a figure of attestation at once too gross and too bloodless, likely to affect us as an abuse of privilege when not an abuse of knowledge" (356). As the painting she specularly confronts gradually replaces Milly Theale as a visible presence in the novel, James secures us from the "abuses," which might range from aestheticizing her dying body to "coldly and bloodlessly" viewing her with detachment; along with the reader, he is reduced to "watching her, as it were, through the successive windows of other peoples' interest in her" (359), a strategy in which the subjective stakes or "interests" of others are made, often chillingly, clear (see Veeder and Griffin).

We can begin to see the experiments in form that have led critics to designate the works of late James as modernist as an outcome of his perspectival commitments, those that undermine the conventional status of an omniscient, transcendent model of viewing in favor of openly subjectivized forms. In its most extreme version, in *The Sacred Fount,* the formal consequences of this move are not structural so much as semiotic, in which the indeterminacy of viewing finds its correlate in the disruption of signification itself rather than in the multiplication of delimited perspectives that characterizes the later works; to this extent, *The Sacred Fount* seems the most properly modernist of the works of the major phase. Equally importantly, James's meticulous construction of this protomodernist "eye" involves a crucial renegotiation of the relations to knowledge and power with which the omniscient and penetrating eyes of realist and detective fiction are normally invested. Successful neither as a sovereign representative of the social order nor as the more humble policing agent, the private eye, James's narrative eye rather is private in the more literal sense of the word, primarily subject *to* internalized laws rather than enforcing them objectively. Such an internalization of social order and power obviates the need for, or, arguably, the possibility of, the dramatic restoration of the law that provides conventional closure in detective fiction. Instead, the regulatory outcome of that internalization is most clearly defined in the self-reflexive character of the instrumental violence associated with the narrator's gaze: as James's use of the Orpheus myth instructs us, the narrator himself is as much a victim of his attempt to expose social transgression as are the objects of his unremitting scrutiny. Moreover, because the internalized social order personified by the narrator's gaze acquires such a subjective character, it can lead only to the spectacle of social chaos narrowly averted in *The Sacred Fount.*

The Vitreous Orb: Vladimir Nabokov's *The Eye*

So far I have been focusing on how the discrediting of Cartesian spectatorship and its omniscient claims to knowledge in James intersects with and makes possible dislocations in the signifying functions of language; and I have briefly considered the ways these revised epistemological forms square with the tactics of supervision associated with realist techniques of representation. While a full consideration of "the fantasy of surveillance" upheld by realist narration and the intricacies of its imputed relation to societies that are "increasingly dominated by institutions of discipline, regularization, and supervision" (Seltzer 52)[10] is beyond the scope of my discussion here, I would like to extend some of the questions involved in such a consideration with respect to a single modernist text, in which the relations of surveillance to the sociopolitical world are center stage and are framed in what might be called a post-Cartesian epistemological universe. In what can be only a provisional analysis of the larger question of the degree to which modernism's many narrative eyes stand in for regulatory social forces, I want to ask how the subjectivized forms of viewing represented in *The Eye* inflect its treatment of surveillance as a narrative and possibly social tool. Written in Berlin in 1930, eleven years after his family's flight from Bolshevist Russia, Nabokov's *The Eye*[11] chronicles the adventures of its Russian émigré narrator in the Berlin of the mid-1920s. Although, as he coyly assures us in his 1965 foreword, Nabokov claims to be "indifferent to social problems . . . to community life and to the intrusions of history," and that his books "are blessed by a total lack of social significance" (ii, iii), the text's representation of an expatriate community preoccupied with its possible infiltration by communist agents, no matter how shaped by paranoia, is inescapably historically situated; moreover, as a linguistic artifact alone, the text is inevitably subject to "historical intrusions" of social significance.

We first meet *The Eye*'s narrator while he is an inexperienced tutor in a household with two young boys. After he is beaten and humiliated by the husband of Matilda, a family friend with whom he has been having an affair, he commits suicide. Following his "death," he inhabits a phantom world produced, he believes, by the undiminished activity of his thought and imagination, which nonetheless resembles the world he has left in every particular. This universe is populated by a family of fellow émigrés that lives in his apartment building on 5 Peacock St.—Evgenia, her husband, Khrushchov, and her sister Vanya, with whom the narrator is infatuated, as well as a group of their friends who are their constant visitors. Amongst them is the mysterious Smurov, also in love with Vanya, about whom the narrator becomes more and more curious. The balance of the novel is devoted to the narrator's attempt to discover the true identity of Smurov through a series of probing and secretive investigations of increasingly contraband evidence of others' views of him. The text's eventual disclosure that the narrator is Smurov himself transforms this already phantasmatic detective story into a more self-reflexive exercise, in which the surveillance of another bleeds into the search for self-knowledge, in an ongoing quest for an elusive sense of substantiality. Surveillance takes several forms in the novel: as an atmosphere of paranoid vigilance against possible spies, in the narrator's self-conscious observance of his own activities, and in his ongoing investigations of Smurov.

The world of illusion that the narrator believes he has imaginatively constructed after his suicide, complete with the "themes" (22) of his recovery that he develops, suggests a parallel with the illusory world of fiction and its construction—in this sense, the text can be taken as an extended metaphor for authorship. Like Nabokov, his narrator situates himself at the periphery of an "invisible world that lives in words" (33), which he comes to consider subject only to his cognitive whims for its laws of operation:

> Hosts and guests at 5 Peacock Street move before me from light to shade, effortlessly, innocently, created merely for my amusement.

... Whenever I wish, I can accelerate or retard to ridiculous slowness the motions of all these people, or distribute them in different groups, or arrange them in various patterns, lighting them now from below, now from the side. . . . For me, their entire existence has been merely a shimmer on a screen. (89–90)

Like the narrator of James's *The Sacred Fount,* Nabokov's narrator's narcissistic fantasy that the world is of his own making, "a shimmer on a screen" of his own projection, initially works to expose the solipsistic delusion underlying subjective perception. The notion of a world dependent solely on the operations of the individual mind for its substance is repeatedly problematized in the novel, through the often unwelcome intrusion of materials independent of the projecting self, or what might be termed the "real." Thus, upon learning that Vanya is engaged to another man, rather than being "at [his] dream's disposal, [his] dream-cornered prey" (29), the narrator tells us: "I grew heavy, surrendered to the law of gravity, donned anew my former flesh, as if indeed all this life around me was not the play of my imagination, but was real" (69). In the same way that the intrusion of Vanya's separate desires breaks up his illusion of mastery, the story the narrator tells Vanya about his heroic escape from Russia is disrupted by the observation of Mukhin, her fiancé, that the railroad enabling his escape had never been built; the narrator's invented narrative is described as a "marvelous soap bubble" (50), now burst. Yet just as the intrusions of the real can discredit apparently self-made worlds, they can also legitimize them. Although the narrator tells us that he used to tease his employer, the bookseller Weinstock, because he "was convinced that he was being regularly watched by certain persons, to whom he referred, with a mysterious laconism, as 'agents,' " he later reports: "Most remarkable of all was that once . . . a person he knew fairly well, a friendly, easygoing, 'honest-as-God fellow' (Weinstock's expression), really turned out to be a venomous Soviet sneak" (26, 43). The fact that the fictions the characters embrace can be intruded upon by materials external to themselves that change their status suggests a comparable vulnerability for the fictive standing of the novel and its relation to the outside world from which it draws. Such intrusions suggest the bifurcated, permeable nature of fictive forms, whose self-enclosed hermeticism is always crisscrossed by external references that are potentially independent of the narrative. There are always, then, these two parallel levels operating in *The Eye*—the synchronic universe within the text, and diachronic negotiation between the text and the world outside it.

The text makes explicit reference to these dual ontological levels in its opening sentence, in which the narrator explains that his émigré experience began "in the early twenties of two spans of time, this century and my foul life" (3); but following this introduction, the first, historical, span of time is allowed to fade into the background, upstaged by a more localized dualism, which is spatial rather than temporal. That is, the text shifts its focus, from distinguishing the historically general from the particular, to separating the seeing self from the perceiving other. This reorientation toward a definition of the subject can be seen as a related foray into the problem of ontology, since we need to arrive at a notion of the subject in order to situate it in both an individual register and as a subject of history. But *The Eye,* I will argue, makes the process of distinguishing self from other an elusive affair; instead of producing a stable distinction that would allow for a viable conception of a "subject of history," the text arrives at a more self-reflexive, impenetrable ontology. That ontology posits a multiple, fractured subject whose relation to the world outside resists definition because it is, itself, so internally unstable. By designating the notion of a subject of history as an arbitrary fiction even as it repeatedly evokes it, *The Eye* at once acknowledges the subject's relation to a world outside itself and defines it as unknowable. The narrator of *The Eye,* then, by obsessively trying to situate a man who turns out to be himself, unquestionably participates in the "fantasy of surveillance" said to characterize the realist narrator's position; but his failure to do so derails the easy equatability between his own panoptic powers and those of the "institutions of discipline, regularization, and supervision" narrative authority is thought to represent in realism.

Prior to the narrator's suicide, the seeing subject and perceiving object are represented as at least tentatively distinct. But just as the narrator, plagued by self-consciousness, complains that "even in sleep I did not cease to watch over myself" (7), his description of his young students—"his pupils"— standing by, "one on my right, the other on my left, imperturbably watching me" (10), allows their object gaze to be transformed into an image of self-scrutiny by playing on the dual meaning of "pupils." After the narrator's "death," subject/object relations shift in the novel as he comes to view himself and his personal history with a comparable degree of detachment. "Ever since the shot—that shot which, in my opinion, had been fatal—I had observed myself with curiosity instead of sympathy, and my painful past— before the shot—was now foreign to me" (27). Following the shot, too, the narrator begins to pursue his interest in Smurov, who "made a rather favorable impression on me those first evenings" (33), but whom also, based on his "air of mystery," he comes to suspect as a spy (43). As the narrator accumulates more and more "images" of Smurov, he resolves to try to identify the "true Smurov," to engage, despite the difficulties, in the "classification of Smurovian masks" (54).

I could already count three versions of Smurov, while the original remained unknown. This occurs in scientific classification. Long ago,

Linnaeus described a common species of butterfly, adding the laconic note *"in pratis Westmanniae."* Time passes, and in the laudable pursuit of accuracy new investigators name the various southern and Alpine races of this common species, so that soon there is not a spot left in Europe where one finds the nominal race and not a local subspecies. Where is the type, the model, the original? Then, at last, a grave entomologist discusses in a detailed paper the whole complex of named races and accepts as the representative of the typical one the almost two-hundred-year-old, faded Scandinavian specimen collected by Linnaeus; and this identification sets everything right. (53–54)

The problem with this "scientific" approach, as the narrator describes it, is its fundamentally arbitrary designation of the original, depending on the credentials of the designator rather than any properties inherent to the object. Even if one could arrive at first cause, a "primary Smurov," the text suggests, our comprehension of it would be hampered by its mediated character. About the image of Smurov that Marianna, a friend of the Khrushchov's, holds, the narrator tells us: "To define this image accurately, however, I would have had to be familiar with Marianna's entire life, with all the secondary associations that came alive inside her when she looked at Smurov—other reminiscences, other chance impressions and all those lighting effects that vary from soul to soul" (55). Such a subjectivized image, one should think, is an unreliable standard for truth.

As the images the narrator accumulates of Smurov multiply—making of him a brutal officer to Marianna; a shy, inexperienced youth to Evgenia; a bridegroom to Uncle Pasha; a spy to Weinstock; a "sexual lefty" and kleptomaniac to Roman Bogdanovich; an absurd poet to Vanya—the possibility of designating a "true" Smurov seems arbitrary at best and, at worst, an impossibility. At the end of the novel, after the conflation of the narrator's identity with Smurov's, he admits to the futility and the irrelevance of trying to construct a unified, or even a privileged, version of himself. Following his encounter with Kashmarin, the assailant who provoked his suicide at the beginning of the novel, he tells us,

Kashmarin had borne away yet another image of Smurov. Does it make any difference which? For I do not exist: there exist but the thousands of mirrors which reflect me. With every acquaintance I make, the population of phantoms resembling me increases. Those two boys, those pupils of mine, will grow old, and some image or other of me will live within them like a tenacious parasite. And then will come the day when the last person who remembers me will die.

> A fetus in reverse, my image, too, will dwindle and die within that last witness of the crime I committed by the mere fact of living. (103)

The narrator's contention that there is no self apart from others' images of it insists on the dependency of those partial fragments on an external world to exist at the same time that it foregrounds their vulnerability to change. Such a contingent model of the self suggests that, to whatever degree the narrator's world is of his own making, it has to compete with those constructed by others. Such an atomized vision of simultaneous and arbitrary worlds finds its correlate in the equally arbitrary model of history that the narrator promotes. Repudiating that "wholesale trade in epochs and masses" better known as the "science of history" in Marxist parlance, he declares: "It is silly to seek a basic law, even sillier to find it. . . . Everything is fluid, everything depends on chance, and all in vain were the efforts of that crabbed bourgeois in Victorian checkered trousers, author of *Das Kapital,* the fruit of insomnia and migraine" (27–28).

In place of the behavioral predictability promised by such explanatory "laws" of history, *The Eye* seems to propose a more ethereal, chaotic model, epitomized by Weinstock's séances, in which Lenin puts in appearances alongside less celebrated ghosts; Caesar, Mohammed, and Pushkin send messages along with "a dead cousin of Weinstock's" (38–39). This metaphysical logic informs more worldly encounters as well. The narrator explains, for example, "Once, in the downstairs hall, I happened to hold the door for [Khrushchov,] and his mispronounced German 'thank you' (*danke*) rhymed exactly with the locative case of the Russian word for 'bank'—where, by the way, he worked" (29–30). Meaning, such an encounter suggests, while based on the arbitrary and coincidental, is no less reliable for its patently subjective origins. The kinds of truths such encounters yield, however, are so idiosyncratic that they cannot extend beyond their particular contexts; instead, they dissolve, like Lenin's ghost, into the text's insubstantial atmosphere. Based on the séance as an alternative "historical model," we can infer that the external world, defined as just an unstable extension of the subjectivized self, includes both contexts that the narrative began with—"the early twenties of two spans of time, this century and my foul life." In the hall of mirrors that constitutes *The Eye,* it would appear that there is nothing outside the reflections of self and other to qualify as an independent social world.

The narrator begins, following his suicide, to contemplate a world seen as an extension of his own thought, but he is unable to locate himself within it. In his attempt, however, he comes to occupy two opposed visual positions; in Lacanian terms, he embodies the "constitutive splitting" that characterizes the antinomy between the eye and the gaze. By offering us this fractured model of the subject at the same time as defining the contexts that subject

211

inhabits as arbitrary extensions of it, *The Eye* reframes the way we must conceive of the subject's relation to the historical arrangements that might be thought to constitute it. It is not that *The Eye* will not acknowledge that the subject is situated in a world outside itself, but rather that it defines the process of designating a privileged version of it as an inexact science, as unknowable. The operations of the narrator's supervisory eye, then, are confined to trying to discover the subject of "institutions of discipline, regularization, and supervision" rather than furthering, as a source of power themselves, their aims. Perhaps this far more modest project stands behind Nabokov's claim that his books are "blessed by a total lack of social significance." At the end of *The Eye,* the narrator tells us: "I have realized that the only happiness in this world is to observe, to spy, to watch, to scrutinize oneself and others, to be nothing but a big, slightly vitreous, somewhat bloodshot, unblinking eye" (103). Unlike the pristine, idealized eye of the detached Cartesian subject, this openly embodied eye, veins and all, insists on its subjective roots, and their potentially far-reaching perceptual consequences.

Notes

1. See, e.g., Jay 3ff. and Rorty 38.
2. While there is a large literature attempting to evaluate whether modernism challenges or is the handmaid of the status quo, the question has not, to my knowledge, been raised in light of the techniques of spectatorship and related epistemology.
3. Žižek is talking about nostalgic film here, and the way viewers "see themselves seeing" in the innocent, naive gaze of the filmic proxy, but this is arguably only an extremitized version of a standard process of identification.
4. For a discussion of Henry James's adaptation of his brother William's pragmatism in specifically perceptual directions, and particularly his work on consciousness and subjectivity outlined in *The Principles of Psychology,* see Ryan 75–88.
5. The camera obscura is an image-producing device, typically consisting of a darkened enclosure with an aperture through which the external world is projected, in inverted form, on one surface of the interior.
6. It is interesting to compare the function of this painting with the Bronzino in which Milly Theale recognizes herself in *Wings of the Dove.* Rather than making of visibility an interpretive problem and a potentially indiscreet window into the secrets of others, the Bronzino becomes the ultimate icon of discretion. By making the identification between Milly and the painting so physically and psychologically complete, it can functionally substitute for her in the narrative, while her dying body is secured from the vulgar prurience of others' gazes. The painting critically assists in James's preference, expressed in his preface, for the "*indirect* presentation of his main image.*" Milly confronts the painting, seeing "the face of a young woman, all magnificently drawn, down to the hands, and magnificently dressed; a face almost livid in hue, yet handsome in sadness and crowned with a

mass of hair rolled back and high, that must, before fading with time, have had a family resemblance to her own. The lady in question, at all events, with her slightly Michaelangelesque squareness, her eyes of other days, her full lips, her long neck, her recorded jewels, her brocaded and wasted reds, was a very great personage—only unaccompanied by a joy. And she was dead, dead, dead. Milly recognized her exactly in words that had nothing to do with her. 'I shall never be better than this' '' (144).

7. Agnew has noted this language of exchange quite clearly (89–90). But unlike Agnew, who sees this rhetoric in the larger context of consumer culture in James, I think it is important to see it as part of an interrelated network of subjective forms that mediate the narrator's gaze.

8. As Mitchell has shown, the viability of the camera obscura as a metaphor for ideology has been contested; the definition I offer here is based on Mitchell's interpretation (174ff.).

9. Rowe makes a similar point, though with a different derivation of cause; for Rowe, the indeterminacy of language reflects the difficulties of the artist trying to write him- or herself into being in a language whose meaning is dependent on ambiguous social codes.

10. For an excellent discussion of the politics and power in and of the realist novel, see Seltzer's ''Postscript. Reading Foucault: Cells, Corridors, Novels.'' See also Miller.

11. The book's original title was *Soglyadatay;* Nabokov tells us that it is ''an ancient military term meaning 'spy' or 'watcher,' neither of which extends as flexibly as the Russian word. After toying with 'emissary' and 'gladiator,' I gave up trying to blend sound and sense, and contented myself with matching the 'eye' at the end of a long stalk'' (i).

References

Agnew, Jean-Christophe. ''The Consuming Vision of Henry James.'' *The Culture of Consumption: Critical Essays in American History, 1880–1980.* Ed. Richard Wightman Fox and T. J. Jackson Lears. New York: Pantheon, 1983. 66–100.

Blackall, Jean Frantz. *Jamesian Ambiguity and* The Sacred Fount. Ithaca: Cornell UP, 1965.

Bysshe Stein, William. ''*The Sacred Fount* and British Aestheticism: The Artist as Clown and Pornographer.'' *Arizona Quarterly* 27 (1971): 161–72.

Cameron, Sharon. *Thinking in Henry James.* Chicago: U of Chicago P, 1989.

Crary, Jonathan. *Techniques of the Observer.* Cambridge: MIT P, 1990.

Freud, Sigmund. ''On Narcissism.'' *Collected Papers.* Ed. Ernest Jones. Trans. Joan Riviere. Vol. 2. New York: Basic, 1959. 30–59.

James, Henry. ''Prefaces.'' In *The Art of Criticism: Henry James on the Theory and the Practice of Fiction.* Ed. William Veeder and Susan M. Griffin. Chicago: U of Chicago P, 1986.

———. *The Sacred Fount.* Introd. Leon Edel. New York: Grove, 1953.

Jameson, Fredric. *Signatures of the Visible.* New York: Routledge, 1990.

Jay, Martin. "Scopic Regimes of Modernity." *Vision and Visuality.* Ed. Hal Foster. Seattle: Bay, 1988. 3–28.

Miller, D. A. *The Novel and the Police.* Berkeley: U of California P, 1988.

Mitchell, W. J. T. *Iconology: Image, Text, Ideology.* Chicago: U of Chicago P, 1986.

Moon, Heath. "Saving James from Modernism: How to Read *The Sacred Fount.*" *Modern Language Quarterly* 49.2 (1988): 120–41.

Nabokov, Vladimir. *The Eye.* New York: Vintage, 1990.

Porter, Carolyn. *Seeing and Being: The Plight of the Participant Observer in Emerson, James, Adams, and Faulkner.* Middletown, CT: Wesleyan UP, 1981.

Reany, James. "The Condition of Light: Henry James's *The Sacred Fount.*" *University of Toronto Quarterly* 31 (1962): 138–51.

Ricoeur, Paul. *The Conflict of Interpretations.* Trans. Don Ihde. Evanston: Northwestern UP, 1974.

Rorty, Richard. *Philosophy and the Mirror of Nature.* Princeton: Princeton UP, 1979.

Rowe, John Carlos. "The Authority of the Sign in James's TSF." *Through the Custom House.* Baltimore: Johns Hopkins UP, 1982.

Ryan, Judith. *The Vanishing Subject: Early Psychology and Literary Modernism.* Chicago: U of Chicago P, 1991.

Seltzer, Mark. *Henry James and the Art of Power.* Ithaca: Cornell UP, 1984.

Tyler, Parker. "*The Sacred Fount:* 'The Actuality Pretentious and Vain' vs. 'The Case Rich and Edifying.' " *Modern Fiction Studies* 9 (1963): 127–38.

West, Rebecca. *Henry James.* New York: Holt, 1916.

Žižek, Slavoj. *Looking Awry: An Introduction to Jacques Lacan through Popular Culture.* 2nd ed. Cambridge: MIT P, 1992.

"Teichoscopy" in the Wall Novels of Peter Schneider and Uri Orlev

JEFFREY GARRETT

Unusual sensations accompany the experience of peering over or peeking through a wall at something on the other side: heightened excitement and attentiveness; a sense of voyeuristic security and power; alternatively, feelings of longing, separation, impotence, and deprivation. Walls not only structure space in a physical sense, they also mediate human perception by changing the psychological context of observation. This mediation is significant for literary interpretation, since if mental imagery is a "mimesis of perception" and the visible world therefore "the ultimate source of verbal images" (Collins xxvi, 21), then we would expect some reflex of wall-mediated perception in literary discourse where walls are significantly present. Reclaiming an old literary term but refitting it with new meaning, these properties might aptly be called "teichoscopic," from the Greek word *teichoscopia* "wall-viewing."[1] In two works of recent literature in which the motif of the dividing wall is central, Peter Schneider's *Der Mauerspringer* (1982) and Uri Orlev's *Haii Berehov Hatziporim* (1981), we find just such a wealth of teichoscopic imagery, that is, metaphorical language linking walls with optical devices, such as lenses, mirrors, and the human eye, and also plot structures, which can be elucidated with reference to optical relationships.

On the face of it, surely, nothing would appear less promising than an association of walls, which by their nature are obstructions, and optical devices, which ideally let things through. But consider for a moment the marked morphological and pragmatic similarities between the two. Both are relatively thin, hard membranes of human creation "thrown in the way" (*objectus*) of "apertures" or openings.[2] Both are products of a shared intent by their creators to structure by separation potential interactants into discrete groups of

215

"ins" and "outs," watchers and watched, controllers and controlled. Indeed, it can be argued that wall constructions and optical devices are morphologically identical: wall constructions consist of walls and openings; optical devices consist of openings surrounded by walls. Our differing perceptions of them and our attribution of each to a different conceptual class has more to do with commonly held views of their associated functions—obstructed versus enhanced vision—than with any fundamental structural differences. In fact, I will argue, even these functional differences are questionable. Both "obstructions" and "enhancements" are filters of sensual input.

But let us return to walls and their effect on vision. Any appreciation for the psychophysiological aspects of wall use must proceed from an understanding of visuality that goes beyond a geometric and physical "science of vision" as conceived of roughly from Aristotle to Kant. It must include a recognition that the mind does not so much *receive* reality through its senses as it *constructs* it, and that this reality construction is never independent of the technical means by which images reach the observer (Collins 33). In Western intellectual history, the recognition of this fact is traceable to the early nineteenth century, as Jonathan Crary describes in his recent book, *Techniques of the Observer: On Vision and Modernity in the Nineteenth Century.* Crary relates how the camera obscura, in use since the Renaissance as a means of "capturing" reality by employing a small, lensless aperture in an otherwise walled-in and darkened cabinet, by 1800 had become a dominant philosophical metaphor, defining the way perception and, indeed, science as a whole were conceptualized (29). An explicit comparison of the human eye with the camera obscura, for example, was central to Kepler's theory of the retinal image (37–38). As Crary reminds us (42), Locke also explicitly likened the human mind to the "dark room" of the camera obscura. In the chapter of his *Essay Concerning Human Understanding* (1690) entitled "Of Discerning, and Other Operations of the Mind," Locke suggests that within everyone there is a dispassionate and monadic "mind" examining images that transparent senses have "let in": "For, methinks, the understanding is not much unlike a closet wholly shut from light, with only some little opening left, to let in external visible resemblances, or ideas of things without; would the pictures coming into such a dark room but stay there, and lie so orderly as to be found upon occasion, it would very much resemble the understanding of a man in reference to all objects of sight, and the ideas of them" (2:xi, 17).

Prior to 1800, then, the dominant perception of the camera obscura's role in the constitution of meaning was that of an implicitly clear and translucent mediator, an honest broker of exterior reality dividing "an undifferentiated expanse of the world outside" and "an observer . . . isolated, enclosed, and autonomous within its dark confines" (Crary 34, 39). It was only later, as Crary shows, under the influence of Goethe's *Farbenlehre* and Schopenhauer's reception of Goethe's physiological optics, that the contribution of the "corporeal subjectivity of the observer"—and of this observer's instruments—became recognized as co-constituents of perception and, ultimately, of meaning (69, 85). Increasingly, the camera obscura came to be regarded not as guarantor of objectivity, as it had been until 1800, but as a co-formative, active collaborator in the creation of perceptions and worldviews, as an enhancer of but also a distorter of visual impressions. Hegel, for example, saw in the inverted images created by the camera obscura not a faithful reproduction of the real, but instead an "inverted world" ("verkehrte Welt"), in both senses of the term. Marx, Bergson, Freud, and others saw in this instrument, which the eighteenth century had regarded as the "site of truth," instead a "model for procedures and forces that conceal, invert, and mystify truth" (Crary 29, 30).

With this historical background, we can now shift our attention from walls as parts in architectural and optical systems to their role in structuring literary space. We will see that here, too, they function as constrainers and conditioners of perception, that by no means do they remain inert, simply blocking off some scenes from view and letting others through.

When Peter Schneider's *Der Mauerspringer* (The Wall Jumper) was published in Germany in 1982, it was hailed by many critics as the "endgültige Beschreibung" (definitive description) of the Berlin Wall (Herzog 210). Yet Schneider's book goes far beyond being a mere static description of this monolithic symbol of German division. Colin Russ's characterization in a *TLS* review of the Berlin Wall as the novel's main "character" comes closer to capturing its active, intrusive influence on the perceptions of the many figures whom Schneider introduces, completely out of proportion to its simple, albeit brutal facticity. Birgit Frech's recent dissertation on literary treatments of the Berlin Wall confirms that at least for many contemporaries, it functioned mainly as a psychological barrier, not a physical one: "Die Mauer *wirkte* auf westlicher Seite, als sei sie das unüberwindbare Hindernis, tatsächlich war sie aber, da undurchsichtig, eine vornehmlich psychologische Barriere" (From the western side, the wall seemed to be the insuperable obstacle, but in fact, by blocking vision, it was primarily a psychological barrier) (24). "Die Mauer regt auf, sie verwirrt, macht ratlos" (The wall disturbs, confuses, perplexes) (121).

In light of the foregoing discussion, it should come as no surprise that Schneider's novel is rich in scopic and specular imagery that seeks to capture the sensory deprivations and distortions attributable to the Wall. Early in the novel, for example, we read how for those in the West the Wall had gradually erased all direct perception of Berlin's other half, reflecting back instead only the West's own image: "The view East shrank to a view of the border complex and finally to a group-therapy absorption with the self: for Germans in the West, the Wall became a mirror that told them, day by day, who was the fairest one of all'' (*Wall Jumper* 12).[3] At other moments in Schneider's novel, the Wall seems to admit impressions from the East that are mirror images of reality as one experiences it in the West, but, like mirror images or those projected within the camera obscura, they are precisely reversed.[4] Neither in East nor in West Berlin, for example, does the Wall or its electronic extensions succeed in disrupting television reception, and this leaves TV as a kind of chink or peek through it. By flipping back and forth between two channels, one East and one West, the narrator describes how he obtains two identical but opposite versions of the news. The same phrases of the same language are used in both news broadcasts, but to exactly opposite effect. In the West, ''Der Nachrichtensprecher weist darauf hin, daß diese Bilder seit Wochen nicht in den Ostmedien zu sehen sind'' (The newscaster says that such footage hasn't been shown in the Eastern media for weeks) (28). And in the East, ''Der Sprecher weist darauf hin, daß diese Bilder in den Westmedien nicht gezeigt werden'' (The newscaster notes that these pictures are not being shown in the Western media) (28). In the moment the narrator turns off the TV while the newscaster from the East is speaking, the two discordant realities seem to overlay one another for a brief moment in a single virtual image: ''Wie ich den Fernseher abschalte, sehe ich für den Bruchteil einer Sekunde den Schatten des Kollegen vom Westprogramm; dann wird die Mattscheibe grau'' (For a split second, as I turn the television off, I see the shadow of his West channel counterpart; then the screen goes gray) (28). As Russ writes, ''The moulders of opinion manufacture mirror images, contradictory yet similar,'' of external reality (814). Schneider at one point refers to network producers in East and West as ''laughably alike'' (118). Each is nothing but the distorted image of the other. In German, this pair of mirror images has been lexicalized as *deutsch-deutsch,* ''that most melancholy of German neologisms'' (Russ 814), in which the hyphen between the two halves of the word seems to perform the same separating, yet conjoining, function orthographically as the distorting lens/mirror of the Wall does physically and optically.

The Wall's teichoscopic distortion of perception is so systematic that, in time, it is no longer perceived consciously: ''Uns ist zur Gewohnheit geworden, [die Stadt Berlin] nur halb wahrzunehmen und dennoch diesen Bildausschnitt zum Ganzen zu erklären'' (It has become our habit to see [the city Berlin] only half, but nevertheless to declare this fragment of an image the whole) (Hammer 9). This is very much in keeping with the intent of the two German states, each of which elevated the illusion to dogma. But a subliminally sensed dissonance between state-propagated illusions and intuited reality leads many of Schneider's characters to react in ways that, on the face of it perhaps, appear irrational, but in fact are attempts to rectify perception of the world on the Wall's other side and make what is half—perceptually, at least—whole again. The first strategy Schneider holds out as a way to defeat the optics of the Wall is to become a *Grenzgänger,* or "boundary-walker," a compulsive peripatetic constantly on the move back and forth through the Wall. This is what the narrator does himself: "Mißtrauisch geworden gegen die hastig ergriffene Identität, die ihm die beiden Staaten anbieten, findet er seinen Ort nur noch auf der Grenze" (Having come to mistrust the hastily adopted identity that both states offer him, he feels at home only on the border) (23), for it is only on the border that the Wall does not interpose itself between subject and object. An alternative strategy is that chosen by Herr Kabe, the "wall jumper" of the novel's title, who repeatedly vaults the Wall— and in so doing succeeds quite literally in "over-coming" it. Suspended over the wall for seconds at a time, he can view both East and West with unrefracted clarity. This is the meaning behind Herr Kabe's otherwise inexplicable "fifteen leaps." Far from being grounds for psychiatric treatment (which is what is ordered for him in both the East and the West), his *Wallsprünge* are heroic acts of an individual who subconsciously refuses to surrender his sanity to official dogma, a distortion of reality mediated by the optical qualities of the border wall. The same is true of the other "disturbed" figures in *Der Mauerspringer,* all of whom strive with manic singleness of purpose to neutralize the sensory deprivations and distortions caused by the Wall by passing through it or over it (Frech 122). A final irony is that even now, after the Wall has been removed physically, its afterimage, the "Mauer im Kopf" or "wall-in-the-head," the now famous expression Schneider coined in this novel, continues to confound the clarity of vision between East and West. Of it Schneider observed prophetically, seven years before the actual destruction of the Wall: "It will take longer to tear down the wall in our heads than any wrecking company will need for the wall we can see" (119). This psychological reflex is strikingly similar to what Goethe describes in the *Farbenlehre:* the retinal afterimage we "see" even after an object itself is no longer physically visible and which retains a certain psychological reality for the observer (337).

Schneider's representation of the Berlin Wall brings to mind yet another famous barrier in literature: the mirror of Lewis Carroll's *Through the Looking Glass.* It, too, is simultaneously an immutable and yet magically permeable border separating and connecting two disparate realities. Both of these literary "walls" combine dioptric and catoptric optical qualities—they both refract and reflect—like imperfectly functioning one-way mirrors.

The treatment of visuality in Schneider's *Der Mauerspringer* often leaves open to question just what sense organ is doing the seeing, the physical eye or "the mind's eye," making of the Berlin Wall at once a physical as well as a metaphoric filter of experience. In another work, Uri Orlev's juvenile novel *Haii Berehov Hatziporim* (*The Island on Bird Street*), the role of the wall surrounding a Jewish ghetto in Poland during World War II appears much more tangible and immediate. But here, too, appearances are deceiving and hide a wealth of complex relationships. To gain a full appreciation of this complexity, we must first add to the interpretative framework constructed so far a retrospective look at the development of walls as sociopolitical tools and then consider the implications for visuality.

In his treatise on the invention of the modern prison, *Discipline and Punish,* Michel Foucault traces how walls were transformed from relatively straightforward dividers between groups into complex tools of social management, paralleling what he calls "the formation of the disciplinary society" (209) in Europe during the seventeenth and eighteenth centuries (219). He describes the transition in the sociopolitical use of walls from an instrument to effect a "massive, binary division between one set of people and another" to something infinitely more subtle, a means to fashion "multiple separations, individualizing distributions, an organization in depth of surveillance and control, an intensification and a ramification of power" (198). The typical walls of the earlier age had been the great city fortifications of the Middle Ages, in all their physicality, and the utterly impermeable walls surrounding leper colonies. The former kept that which was not wanted out, the latter formed part of a "practice of rejection, of exile-enclosure," keeping the unwanted locked in (198). By contrast, the most characteristic use of walls in the seventeenth and, especially, eighteenth centuries was for the purpose of segmentation, individuation, and dissymetric surveillance of populations in times of plague. Foucault describes the measures enforced by military authorities in France during plague outbreaks in the late seventeenth century to assign individuals in small groups to rooms with windows, where they would show themselves at intervals to the local syndics on inspection tours (195–97). In terms of Foucauldian political technology, this marked the discovery of how to exploit both the occlusive properties of walls *and* the properties of wall openings to perfect an instrument of surveillance. In this we see an evolution of the wall from a crude "binary" partition to a more carefully differentiating and individuating instrument of social control.

The ultimate refinement of this wall technology, elevating it from the social and physiological to the psychological plane, came with Jeremy Bentham's panopticon, which the English philosopher first introduced in 1786 in the course of twenty-one letters from Russia, published in London and Dublin in 1791 (*Bentham Reader; Works*).[5] In its original form, Bentham's panopticon was a rotunda-shaped building offering an unobstructed view from a central tower into hundreds of rooms or cells arranged radially around it. Bentham lavished special attention on the creation of protected, monodirectional lines of sight: "By blinds and other contrivances, the keeper concealed from the observation of the prisoners, unless where he thinks fit to show himself: hence, on their part, the sentiment of an invisible omnipresence.—The whole circuit reviewable with little, or, if necessary, without any, change of place" (*Bentham Reader* 96).

In *Discipline and Punish,* Foucault observes that it is this disruption of two-way observation, "dissociating the seeing/being seen dyad" (202), that is the sine qua non for the functioning of the panopticon. It alone is capable of inducing in the prisoner Bentham's "sentiment of an invisible omnipresence." As Foucault writes, the "anxious awareness of being observed," regardless of whether or not the subject is actually under observation, coupled with the fear of punishment in the event of observed misbehavior, ultimately leads to a displacement of the relationship between observer and observed from the interpersonal plane to one located solely within the person of the prisoner: "A real subjection is born mechanically from a fictitious relation. . . . He who is subjected to a field of visibility, and who knows it, assumes responsibility for the constraints of power; he makes them play spontaneously upon himself; he inscribes in himself the power relation in which he simultaneously plays both roles; he becomes the principle of his own subjection" (202–03).

From this analysis of Bentham's apparatus of control, Foucault extracts the underlying principle of "panopticism," a form of domination that functions, like its namesake, "as a pure architectural and optical system" (205). For Foucault, panopticism is the fundamental method for the exercise of political control, not only in dictatorships but in all modern states: "We are much less Greeks than we believe. We are neither in the amphitheater, nor on the stage, but in the panoptic machine, invested by its effects of power, which we bring to ourselves since we are part of its mechanism" (217).

Against this background of Benthamite-Foucauldian wall technology, we may now turn our attention to the Nazis' use of walls, thereby also setting the stage, both in a historical and a psychosocial sense, for Orlev's novel of the Warsaw ghetto. As early as 1933, Karl Kraus called attention to an especially perverse aspect of Nazi language use: the "rejection of the figurative" and, accompanying this, the "revindication" of the literal meaning of certain— usually very violent—idiomatic expressions.[6] By this he meant that when a Nazi politician used the phrase "an eye for an eye and a tooth for a tooth," or spoke of rubbing "salt in the wounds" of an opponent, there was no rhetorical hyperbole intended: it was meant quite literally (122).

Recall now our discussion of Foucauldian panopticism, that is, the progressively subtler use of wall technology for the effective social disciplining of populations, yielding ultimately the "panopticisms of every day" (223). In this process, visible mechanisms—walls and like structures—are gradually replaced by their invisible, "figurative" equivalents: laws, social conventions, other "systems of micro-power" (222); ultimately by *mentalities,* the most effective barriers of all.

The Nazis' construction of walled-in ghettos to isolate the Jews of Eastern Europe reverses this process and represents, in a Krausian sense, a clear revindication of the Benthamite panopticon. The "insuperable asymmetries" (Foucault 222) of panoptic constructions lost the abstract, immanent quality they had acquired over the years and became, once again, concrete (in both senses of the word).

It is in this setting, the Jewish ghetto of a city within Nazi-occupied Poland, that Uri Orlev has situated the action of several very successful, largely autobiographical juvenile novels. *Haii Berehov Hatziporim,* published in 1981, was soon translated from Hebrew into over a dozen world languages and won significant literature awards in Holland, Germany, Poland, and the United States, as well as in its country of origin, Israel.[7] It describes the miraculous survival of Alex, an eleven-year-old Jewish boy, within the ghetto of a large Polish city, even after the Germans had emptied it of its inhabitants.

As explained above, the society of the ghetto represents the reconcretization of the panoptic metaphor. As set forth in Bentham's own theoretical writings and realized here by the Nazis, docility and industry were instilled in the ghetto population by a combination of surprise inspection and draconian punishment. The prohibitions against locking doors, keeping radios, and often against speech itself, coupled with all that is observed from the watchtowers and found out by spies and informers, ensured that information flowed in only one direction: to the oppressors. In the panopticon, there is no place to hide. Young Alex learns this painfully during a surprise "selection," a kind of muster used to separate those who would stay in the ghetto to work from those who would be transported to the death camps, when he and his father are quickly ferreted out from their hiding place among bales of rope. They had probably been betrayed by an informer (18).

In what is no doubt a fantastic departure from historical reality, Alex nonetheless escapes (with his father's pistol no less) and holes up in an upper story of a ruined house, the back of which overlooks the ghetto wall: "The view from Number 78 was as irresistible as the house itself. . . . The entire length of the street behind the house was divided by a high brick wall that was topped by broken glass. Beyond it you could see the houses on the Polish side. They were so close that you could almost reach out and touch them, but they belonged to a different world" (27). This disparity between physical distance and perceived distance is a teichoscopic refraction caused by the ghetto wall. In the author's introduction, Orlev says of the Polish children whom Alex can see on the other side that "although they seem so near, they are as far away . . . as were the nearest inhabited lands from Robinson Crusoe's island" (xi). The truth is, of course, that they not only *seem* near, they *are* near. Once again, as in Schneider's *Der Mauerspringer,* we observe how a wall defines psychological space in ways quite independent of its physical function as a divider.

In time, Alex, like his hero, Robinson Crusoe, creates an "island" for himself on the third floor of this house, where he succeeds in accumulating some of the trappings of normal life. But since Alex's isolation is not geographical, like Crusoe's, but sensory, his efforts are devoted in far greater measure than Crusoe's to redressing the asymmetry of the "see/being seen dyad"—indeed, to reversing this asymmetry in his favor. It helps, of course, that in the ruined building no stairs lead up to the broken third floor where he has his hiding place, so no one anticipates its use as a hiding place. Also, by chance, his hiding place is "protected on all sides" from view: "No one could see onto it, neither from inside the house nor from any of the other houses on the street" (57). Crucial to Alex's triumph over the Nazi oppressors, however, is his discovery of an air vent, which becomes his viewing site. Peering through the vent, he can observe events on the other side of the wall without himself being seen. This ad hoc viewing device bears a remarkable resemblance to the shaded blinds designed by Jeremy Bentham for the wardens of his panopticon—and it functions just as effectively. In Orlev's novel, of course, the air vent/peephole is placed at the disposal not of the warden, but of the prisoner, and soon it is employed as an instrument to effect a reversal of visual domination. Alex's hideout *cum* observatory allows him to become invisible to the potentially annihilating power of the state.

In a scene that dramatically illustrates this reversal of the line of sight and the shift of power this brings about, Alex observes, from his hiding place, the uprising of the surviving Jews of the ghetto (96–105). Two rebels flee to the ground floor of Alex's ruined house, but they are immediately discovered by a German soldier, who prepares to finish them off. Alex observes this drama securely from above: "They couldn't see me from where they were standing." Almost casually, Alex shoots the German, who "still had a look of surprise on his face when he spun around and fell." Alex admits the two rebels into his haven and explains to them the incredible: that they cannot be seen (98–99).

Much of Orlev's novel relates how Alex perfects and expands his anti-panopticon. On one of his forays into the depopulated world of the ghetto (84), he finds a pair of binoculars, which allows him to survey everything on the other side of the wall in minute detail: "Often I carefully opened the air vent, took the binoculars, and looked through them at the Polish street across the wall. . . . It took a while, but after a couple of weeks I knew every grown-up and child in the Polish street" (87). He peers "right into" the doctor's office across the way, observes the habits of the "crazy woman," and checks her wall clock when he wants to know the time. He even comes to know the precise habits of the police. "I saw other things too that once, if I had just been running down the street, I would not have paid attention to" (93). This heightening of sensual acuity, reminiscent of the accounts by "interiorized observers" from within the camera obscura vis-à-vis an exterior world (Crary 34), is a direct consequence of Alex's successful reversal of panoptic asymmetry.

Ultimately, the visual domination of his environment allows Alex to neutralize the physical effects of the wall altogether, to find and pass through its secret openings, to beat up the Jew-baiting bully Yanek he had watched from his observation post and to escape back to his hideout, and even to court Stashya, the pretty girl he had spied on as she did her homework. Through all of these direct interactions, Alex closes the "breach between tangibility and visuality" (Crary 19), which is an inevitable by-product of using any kind of optical mediation. In a way, Alex's triumph, like that of Schneider's "wall jumper," alleviates the alienation brought about by the panoptic modern state and represents a return to the position of the individuated but empowered observer/citizen of the Enlightenment. In the case of Orlev's hero, however, the rollback of modern visuality goes even further, ultimately back to the Renaissance ideal of fusion between knower and known.[8] That the "triumphs" recorded in both novels are completely fantastic does nothing to vitiate this analysis, for both works are literary expressions of rebellion against the sensory oppression of walls and can therefore claim a reality of their own, a reality that represents a historical force at least as powerful as the walls they describe.

Notes

1. *Teichoscopia* was the title given by the scholiasts to the third book of the *Iliad*. It is a reference to the safe and elevated vantage point atop Troy's Skaian Gates used by the city's elders for viewing the events on the battlefield. "Come over where I am, dear child," Priam calls to Helen, "and sit down beside me, to look at your husband of time past, your friends and your people" (Homer 104).
2. Cf. the use of "objective" to refer to the lens of a camera, telescope, or microscope.
3. "Der Blick nach drüben verkürzte sich zu einem Blick auf die Grenzanlagen und schließlich zum gruppentherapeutischen Selbsterlebnis: die Mauer wurde den Deutschen im Westen zum Spiegel, der ihnen Tag für Tag sagt, wer der Schönste im Lande ist" (*Mauerspringer* 13). All translations are taken from Leigh Hafrey's translation of *The Wall Jumper.*
4. The German word for this, interestingly, is *spiegelverkehrt*—literally, "mirror reversed."
5. Foucault not only deals with Bentham's work extensively in *Discipline and Punish* (200–209) but also was instrumental in preparing the first modern French edition of Bentham's *Le Panoptique*. Foucault contributed an insightful foreword to this edition in interview form, entitled "L'Oeil du pouvoir" (The Eye of Power).

224

6. It is clear that the Nazis' rejection of the figurative closely parallels their attitude towards abstract painting and other forms of nonrepresentational art.

7. All quotations from *Haii Berehov Hatziporim* are taken from the English translation by Hillel Halkin, *The Island on Bird Street.*

8. As Cassirer wrote of the culture of the Renaissance, "Every sensory perception is an act of fusion and reunification. We perceive the object, we grasp it in its proper, genuine being only when we feel in it the same life, the same kind of movement and animation that is immediately given and present to us in the experiencing of our own Ego" (148).

References

Bentham, Jeremy. *A Bentham Reader.* New York: Pegasus, 1969.

———. *Le Panoptique.* Paris: P. Belfond, 1977.

———. *The Works of Jeremy Bentham, Published under the Superintendence of His Executor John Bowring.* 11 vols. Edinburgh: W. Tait; Simpkin, Marshall, 1843.

Cassirer, Ernst. *The Individual and the Cosmos in Renaissance Philosophy.* Trans. M. Domani. Philadelphia: U of Pennsylvania P, 1972.

Collins, Christopher. *The Poetics of the Mind's Eye: Literature and the Psychology of Imagination.* Philadelphia: U of Pennsylvania P, 1991.

Crary, Jonathan. *Techniques of the Observer: On Vision and Modernity in the Nineteenth Century.* Cambridge: MIT P, 1990.

Foucault, Michel. *Discipline and Punish: The Birth of the Prison.* Trans. Alan Sheridan. New York: Vintage, 1979.

Frech, Birgit. *Die Berliner Mauer in der Literatur: Eine Untersuchung ausgewählter Prosawerke seit 1961.* Pfungstadt: Ergon, 1992.

Goethe, Johann Wolfgang von. *Naturwissenschaftliche Schriften.* Ed. Dorothea Kuhn and Rike Wankmüller. Hamburg: C. Wegner, 1955. Vol. 13 of *Werke.* Ed. Erich Trunz. 15 vols. 1948–60.

Hammer, Manfried, ed. *Das Mauerbuch: Texte und Bilder aus Deutschland von 1945 bis heute.* Berlin: Oberbaumverlag, 1981.

Herzog, Werner. "Absurde Anfälle der Ordnung." *Der Spiegel* 25 May 1982: 210–13.

Homer. *The* Iliad *of Homer.* Trans. Richmond Lattimore. Chicago: U of Chicago P, 1962.

Kraus, Karl. *Die dritte Walpurgisnacht.* 2nd ed. Munich: Kösel, 1955.

Locke, John. *An Essay Concerning Human Understanding.* Ed. John W. Yolton. 2 vols. London: Dent, 1964.

Orlev, Uri. *Haii Berehov Hatziporim.* Jerusalem: Keter, 1981.

———. *The Island on Bird Street.* Trans. Hillel Halkin. Boston: Houghton Mifflin, 1984.

Russ, Colin. "Divide and Misrule." *Times Literary Supplement* 30 July 1982: 814.

Schneider, Peter. *Der Mauerspringer.* Darmstadt, Neuwied: Luchterhand, 1982.

———. *The Wall Jumper.* Trans. Leigh Hafrey. New York: Pantheon, 1983.

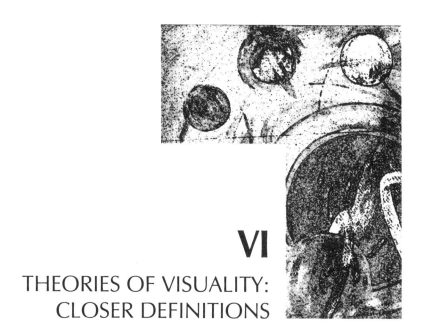

VI
THEORIES OF VISUALITY:
CLOSER DEFINITIONS

Visual Citations: Walter Benjamin's Dialectic of Text and Image

AZADE SEYHAN

Wer seinen Zoll dem Bilderschatz der Masse nicht en-
trichtet, muß scheitern. [Whoever does not pay his dues to
the picture treasury of the masses is bound to fail.][1]

—Walter Benjamin (4:349)

Walter Benjamin's critical studies of history and literature are strongly informed by his sense of passages, borders, and thresholds—in other words, those topoi that highlight events and ideas in the singular moment of their formation or transformation. Benjamin names this interest in the topography of mythical or historical border areas and cultures "Schwellenkunde" (science of thresholds) (5:147). The critical principles of Benjamin's "Schwellenkunde" are operative in the contiguities he proposes between the secular and the profane, antiquity and baroque, baroque and modernity, the verbal and the visual, and also in the phantasmagoric zones between dreams and awakenings each epoch experiences. The zone of passage between image and text has been a constant object of Benjamin's critical gaze. In this border territory he has consistently observed the translation and projection of the two terms into one another. Images are often seen as a text to be deciphered, whereas texts are just as frequently read as visual phenomena.

The interaction of the terms *text* and *image* results in a third term, *allegory*. Allegory, in turn, functions as the central trope of Benjamin's critical interests, which form an interdisciplinary network connecting politics, history, art, literature, film, philosophy, and street signs. In the space-time continuum of allegory, Benjamin marks the coextensivity between the image and the script, the visual and the verbal. His practice of criticism draws its force not

229

so much from intellectual transparency as from the exemplary images it recalls. "Das ursprüngliche Interesse an der Allegorie ist nicht sprachlich sondern optisch" (The original interest in allegory is not verbal but optical), writes Benjamin in "Zentralpark" (Central Park) (1:686).

"Zentralpark" is a central text on Benjaminian allegory. Although it is ostensibly a reading on Baudelaire, its more than forty-five loosely connected fragments are observations on allegory. Furthermore, the text illustrates Benjamin's iconoclastic act of reading history. It is only when the narrative of the world is translated into the allegorical mode that it becomes readable. "Das von der allegorischen Intention Betroffene wird aus den Zusammenhängen des Lebens ausgesondert" (That which is affected by the allegorical intention will be separated from the contexts of life), writes Benjamin. "Es wird zerschlagen und konserviert zugleich. Die Allegorie hält an den Trümmern fest. Sie bietet das Bild der erstarrten Unruhe" (It is simultaneously destroyed and conserved. Allegory holds onto the ruins. It presents a picture of frozen unrest) (1:666). Thus, allegory is both an image maker and a breaker of the passages of time (or history). It captures the unrest, conflict, and breakage that inform historical junctures and projects reconfigurations of the remains of shattered time. Allegory is a privileged term in Benjamin because, like the works of art that always point beyond their time and place, it is a transformative and open-ended figural force. As a mediating term between image and text and between destruction and preservation, it transforms and translates the memory it touches.

Thus, allegory "freezes" as imagistic script that which is lost to the ravages of time. In his very readable (and visual) book *Ways of Seeing,* John Berger, whose many essays on seeing and looking are inspired by Benjamin's critical insights, defines *image* as

> a sight which has been recreated or reproduced. It is an appearance, or a set of appearances, which has been detached from the place and time in which it first made its appearance and preserved—for a few moments or a few centuries. Every image embodies a way of seeing. Even a photograph. For photographs are not, as is often assumed, a mechanical record. Every time we look at a photograph, we are aware, however slightly, of the photographer selecting that sight from an infinity of other possible sights. (9–10)

This definition highlights the re-presentational status of all images. It recalls the German romantic theorist Novalis's observation that "ganze Repraesentation beruht auf einem Gegenwärtig machen—des nicht Gegenwärtigen" (all representation rests on making present what is not present) (3:421). In other words, representation is the act of re-presenting what once was, a presentation of absence in signification, which necessarily assumes perspectivism and interpretation. In the "Erkenntnistheoretische Vorrede" (Epistemo-Theoretical Prologue) to the *Ursprung des deutschen Trauerspiels* (Origin of the German Tragic Drama), Benjamin draws a theoretical distinction, albeit an idiosyncratic one, between knowledge ("Erkenntnis") and truth ("Wahrheit"). Knowledge is characterized by the concept of possession ("Besitztum"); truth, on the other hand, cannot be possessed. It can only exist as self-representation ("ein Sich-Darstellendes"). Thus, unlike knowledge, truth is "unpossessable and impossible to present. . . . This impossibility of *presentation* leads in Benjamin's thought to the designation of truth's proper mode as *representation [Darstellung]*" (Cowan 113–14). Therefore, the truth index of an image is realized in its representability, that of a text in its readability.

Like Berger, Benjamin confirms the nonmimetic, representational status of all images, including photographs. In the essay "Kleine Geschichte der Photographie" (Short History of Photography), Benjamin's allegorical sensibility questions the completeness and impartiality of the photographic image. What fascinates the beholder of the photograph, argues Benjamin, is not the captured "reality" but the telltale signs that signify contingency and link the photographic image dialectically to the beholder's present (2:371). Photographs neither presume nor preserve meaning. Meaning can only be the result of reading/interpreting the image. In a similar vein, Roland Barthes argues that photographs cannot gain access to a "true language" by merely reproducing natural facts; they need to be subjected to criticism in order to become part of a category of knowledge (101). Thus, neither image nor language is mere signs; rather, each signifies and, therefore, demands interpretation. "Die Sprache gibt niemals *bloße* Zeichen" (Language never gives *mere* signs) (2:150), states Benjamin.

The act of signification requires the activity of translation or "transpositing" ("Übersetzen"). The site of this activity houses allegory, which compensates for the lack of correspondence between concept and word by its imagistic memory. Allegory is the regulative trope of this activity, as it compensates for the lack of correspondence between concept and word by its imagistic memory. Allegory consistently points to hidden meanings that demand to be recovered from historical sites. When this meaning is recovered, it fragments and multiplies into many meanings that require translation and interpretation. "Allegoricists, like alchemists," writes Susan Buck-Morss in her discussion of Benjamin's *Trauerspiel,* "hold dominion over an infinite transformation of meanings" (173). The idea that translation and interpretation are not mere commentaries on a work of art but rather its completion and perfection is one of the central tenets of the early romantic school in Germany. Benjamin, whose dissertation *Der Begriff der Kunstkritik in der deutschen Romantik* (The Concept of Art Criticism in German Romanticism) set the critical tenor of his later work, is intellectually much indebted to the theories

231

of literature articulated by the romantic critics. Benjamin's studies on translation constitute part and parcel of his "Schwellenkunde." Like allegory, interpretation marks a site not of direct transmission but of transformation. In a rigorously theoretical essay, "Über Sprache überhaupt und über die Sprache der Menschen" (On Language in General and on the Language of Humans), Benjamin states:

> Translation is the transportation of one language into another through a continuity of transformation; continuities of transformation, not abstract domains of equation and similarity, traverse the translation.
>
> The translation of the language of things into that of humans is not only a translation of the silent into the vocal, but it is also a translation of the nameless into the name. It is also the translation of an incomplete language into a more complete one, which is nothing other than knowledge. (2:151)[2]

Once again, Benjamin's notion of translation as an empowerment of language recalls the early romantics' concept of language "zur zweiten Potenz" (to the second power), a concept used to designate poesy or the transformative power of figural language. Following in the footsteps of the German romantic critics, Benjamin expanded the purview of literary and art criticism, reaching out to take in politics, history, philosophy, advertisement, and film. Thus, criticism—also a science of border crossings in Benjamin—became indicative of the larger project, which could be renamed as the simultaneous completion, self-representation, and critique of the work of art. The readability of art, history, and culture through the praxis of critical reflection is one of the central paradigms of literary modernity.

Although the argument about whether postmodernity represents a radical break from modernity or an expanded version of it will never be satisfactorily settled, it is safe to assume that both movements resulted in a progressive erasure of the boundaries that separated the arts and literature from other modes of knowledge and practices of everyday life. Until the theory debates of the 1980s, the paradigm of literary study was informed by a dichotomy between the works of the canon and those of popular culture. With the advent of poststructuralist theories of discourse and representation, which demonstrated the socially and ideologically conditioned nature of all linguistic constructs, the opposition between canonical and noncanonical texts became untenable. The practice of literary criticism expanded to include the investigation of all manifestations of material culture, from comic strips and hard-rock lyrics to videos and highway billboards. In other words, the boundaries of the literary work dissolved, and it was subsumed by the larger cultural context where literature would be one among several signifying systems.

The expandability of the boundaries of the aesthetic realm is closely related to an insight of Martin Heidegger's that sheds light on a pervasive characteristic of the modern age. In "Die Zeit des Weltbildes" (The Age of the World Picture), Heidegger provides a clue to a comprehensive notion of modernity: he maintains that the decisive moment in the transition to modernity was not the transformation of the "world picture" but rather the transformation of the world into a picture: "The fundamental event of the modern age is the conquest of the world as picture" (134). This picture is not a mimetic representation of the world but a construct of the representing subject. As a result, the truth of both art and science is not an intrinsic value to be revealed but rather a representational model. The objectives of modern scientific research can only be attained when "truth has been transformed into the certainty of representation" (127). This radical shift from the perception of an "objective" world to its subjectively constructed reality brings in its wake a keener awareness of the problem of representation. The realization that the equation between word/image and concept is neither definitive nor resolvable validates an allegorical sensibility that questions and contests the representational certainty of so-called truths, of knowledge, and of ideologies. Thus, the allegorical mode of inquiry has generated provocative questions about how we represent the history of our culture and has refashioned our practice of criticism and, most significantly, literary criticism as a form of cultural critique.

In this context, Benjamin's analysis of topographies of history, memory, and dream re-present collective cultural pasts in new constellations that link them with the present, if only transcendentally. Of particular interest to the present investigation is Benjamin's astute analysis of the emblematic role of language and other signifying systems in the cultural map of modernity. Benjamin regards language not necessarily as a medium of communication but rather as a critical mode of signification, a historical reservoir of meanings, or a museum of inscriptions where both the great and the forgotten actors and events of history are displayed. He decodes cultural history by an analysis of its visual traces. As his much quoted "Über den Begriff der Geschichte" (Theses on History) illustrate, these traces form a discontinuous series, a configuration of fragments that cannot really be read in a linear or logical order, as traditional historiography would have it. "Benjamin was convinced of one thing: what was needed was a visual not a linear logic," writes Buck-Morss. "The concepts were to be imagistically constructed. . . . Nineteenth-century objects were to be made visible as the origin of the present, at the same time that every assumption of progress was to be scrupulously rejected" (218). Benjamin interprets these fragmented, disrupted, and figural traces of collective memory in terms of the present. Often these interpretations are couched in the language of dreams and dream interpretation. "Die heterogensten Zeitelemente stehen . . . in der Stadt nebeneinander" (The most heterogeneous elements of time stand next to each other in the city), writes Benjamin in the *Passagen-Werk* (Arcades Project). "Wer eine Stadt betritt, fühlt sich wie in einem Traumgewebe, wo auch einem Geschehnis von heute das vergangenste sich angliedert" (Whoever enters a city feels himself to be in a dream web, where the most remote past attaches itself also to an event of today) (5:546).

This register of dream associations serves as an affirmation of the allegorical spirit of history. Dreams tell a fragmented story; they narrate by free association. Benjamin rewrites and recontextualizes history by stripping images of events from their "once upon a time" frame and reconfiguring them in dreamlike associations that reflect the images forgotten in the subconscious of the present, a present that Benjamin calls the "Jetztzeit" (time of the now). Benjamin, as Norbert Bolz and Willem van Reijen convincingly argue, assumes the role of the "politischer Traumdeuter der Geschichte" (political dream interpreter of history) (75). The political rehearsal of this psychoanalytic practice yields the "Logik der historischen Erkenntnis" (logic of historical knowledge) (76). In this sense, Benjamin's *Passagen-Werk,* for example, is "eine Reise durch die leibliche Innenwelt der Masse, die schläft und deren Empfindungen sich in der Traumsprache von Mode, Reklame und Architektur chiffrieren" (a trip through the corporeal inside world of the masses who sleep and whose sensations are encoded in the dream languages of fashion, commercials, and architecture) (76). Thus, modernity, as the authors argue, is nothing but the "geschichtsblinde Traumform der Zeit" (history-blind dream form of time) (76). As a political psychoanalyst and image interpreter, Benjamin has to interrupt the dream, conjure forth its images by re-membering the shattered dream pictures. Remembering happens at the moment of awakening. Thus, memory (or history) is a practice of relating the dream fragments (of the past) to the present. Similarly, the study of the fragmented images of dreams is an act of transforming memory, of the translation of the past into the present. Bolz and van Reijen add:

> Benjamin conceives of dreams as a collective form of remembering where the "film" of the past is shown in its most shortened form. His historical materialism is nothing other than the political dream interpretation of these historical pictures. However, those concepts that constitute the historical object of knowledge cannot be gained from the dream of the past itself. . . . Benjamin's political dream interpretation interrupts the dream and makes it readable—that is to say: relevant to the present. (77)[3]

Unlike the psychoanalyst who attempts to access the subconscious by deciphering the dream rebus, Benjamin seeks in the collective dreams of a generation the picture of its material culture. He translates the psychoanalytic reading of dreams into an experience of material history. "Vexierbilder als

Schematismen der Traumarbeit hat längst die Psychoanalyse aufgedeckt'' (Psychoanalysis has long uncovered rebuses as schematisms of the dream work), Benjamin observes, ''wir aber sind mit solcher Gewißheit der Seele weniger als den Dingen auf der Spur'' (but we are more on the track of things than of the soul) (5:281). Another key term closely linked to dream and allegory is memory. ''Wenn es die Phantasie ist, die der Erinnerung die Korrespondenzen darbringt, so ist es das Denken, das ihr die Allegorien widmet. Die Erinnerung führt beide zu einander'' (If it is fantasy that presents remembrance with correspondences, then it is thought that dedicates it allegories. Remembrance leads both to one another) (1:669), writes Benjamin in ''Zentralpark.'' Thus, memory unites thought and imagination in an association of images.

The reciprocity between image and script—the latter, according to Benjamin, retains the last vestiges of the mimetic craft of language—is astutely recalled in Benjamin's ''Über den Begriff der Geschichte.'' Here Benjamin lets history cite history. These citations require no quotation marks. They are evoked as images. For the purposes of the present argument, I would like to tease out the implications of some of Benjamin's theses on history. They provide a productive line of inquiry into the dialectic of word and image in Benjamin's interpretation of the ''dreams'' of history, a dialectic that is programmed to ''freeze'' the images of conflict in history. The series of such framings is intended to shock the reader (of history), to wake one forcefully out of one's dream and enforce a review of the past in the waking life of the present. The operative force in the structure of this argument is the notion that ''historical memory affects decisively the collective, political will for change'' (Buck-Morss ix).

The first thesis presents the picture of a marionette in a Turkish costume who wins every game of chess no matter who the opponent. The marionette sits at a table that appears, through a trick of a system of mirrors, to be transparent from all sides (1:693). In effect, however, a dwarf who is an expert at chess sits hidden under the table and directs all the moves of the puppet, whom Benjamin calls historical materialism. Thus, historical materialism has to take theology into its service if it hopes to win the game, that is, to chart the course of the present material life. In this game theology can no longer be visible, although it is a necessary structure of a tradition of knowledge that now has to be redesigned for modern praxis. Thus, the traditional image has to be shattered and swept under the table. It can no longer operate as an image (of gods, priests, churches), so it must become a hidden voice or a language that gives instruction and advice. The shattered image is reconfigured as an invisible index of intellectual force. Historical materialism invests the fragmented material signs of history with renewed representational significance. As Benjamin states in *Ursprung des deutschen Trauerspiels,* ''jede Idee enthält das Bild der Welt. Ihrer Darstellung ist zur Aufgabe nichts Geringeres gesetzt, als dieses Bild der Welt in seiner Verkürzung zu zeichnen" (every idea contains a picture of the world. The assignment given to the representation of the idea is nothing less than a drawing of this image of the world in its condensed form) (1:228). Image not only represents but also imparts information. Therefore, the production of images furnishes a power base for the producers, who, in the course of history, have been the ruling classes.

"Das wahre Bild der Vergangenheit *huscht* vorbei" (The true picture of the past *flits* by) (1:695), states the fifth thesis. Here Benjamin maintains that if we cannot capture and read these images in terms of their meaning for the present, as cautionary tales, they will be irrevocably lost: "Denn es ist ein unwiderbringliches Bild der Vergangenheit, das mit jeder Gegenwart zu verschwinden droht, die sich nicht als in ihm gemeint erkannte" (For it is an irretrievable image of the past that threatens to disappear with each present that does not recognize it as one of its own) (1:695). The images of the past and the present have to be interwoven to produce a readable text. Once again, images (the dream text of history) have to be translated into words. The allegories of the past remain *in potentia* until actualized in decoding and reading. The recontextualized script of history is drawn from multiple writings, times, and cultures that enter relations of dialogue, contestation, and conflict with one another. The sixth thesis expands on the idea of retrieving the past for present use: "Vergangnes historisch artikulieren heißt nicht, es erkennen 'wie es denn eigentlich gewesen ist.' Es heißt, sich einer Erinnerung bemächtigen, wie sie im Augenblick einer Gefahr aufblitzt" (To articulate the past historically does not mean to recognize it "as it actually was." It means to wrest a memory as it flashes up in moments of danger) (1:695). By objecting to Ranke's historicism, Benjamin urges an investigation of the uses of the past for a present fraught with danger. A conscious recall of the relevant images of history is a call to arms by the historical materialist. It has often been observed that this image of wresting memories from the continuum of history evokes the specter of the impending threat of fascism in Nazi Germany. If at such moments memory cannot be revitalized for the present, then the cumulative effect of experience and knowledge is invalidated.

One of the most memorable images of reading history is etched in the ninth thesis, which depicts the angel of history. The angel faces the past, littered with catastrophic events. It would like to stop and redeem the losses of history, but it cannot. The storm from paradise has the angel in its hold and is pushing it relentlessly toward the future, to which its back is turned. The storm Benjamin names "progress." This powerful picture articulates his damning view of modernity's worship of progress, a concept that has successfully evaded critical evaluation. In the thirteenth thesis, Benjamin elaborates on his criticism of an uncritical view of human progress: "The notion of the progress of humanity cannot be separated from the notion of its steady progression through a homogeneous and empty time. A critique of the notion of this progression has to be the basis of the critique of the notion of progress itself'' (1:701).[4] This critique is provided by the historical materialist, who challenges the fixed images of a given history, defies the ''once upon a time'' complacency of the historicist reading, and ''blasts open'' the continuum of history (1:702). In this act of destruction, the actual power of the past is recouped for the ''Jetztzeit.'' Like the early romantics, Benjamin uses historical citation in a way that renders the cited transcendental; in other words, the citation becomes the site of the possibility of knowing the present. However, the second moment in the art of citation for Benjamin is its destructive character, which recalls the fragmenting function of allegory. An effective quotation does not affirm, but rather ''blasts.'' In an essay on Karl Kraus, Benjamin states that the artful quotation simultaneously redeems and punishes. Citing means calling the word by its real name, thus stripping it violently from its fossilized context and referring it to its origin (2:363). Similarly, the historical materialist cites history in order to shatter it and harness its primordial power as revolutionary vision. In one of the most comprehensive and rigorous studies on Benjamin's ''Theses on History,'' Ralf Konersmann argues that in Benjamin's concept of citation, reading and blasting open are practically identical operations. The knowing reader interrupts the linearity of the text, which is analogous to the regular passage of historical time, in order to highlight and evaluate those fragments acquired by the interruption (68–69).

Thus history is no longer the object of contemplation but a paradoxically empowering destruction that alone enables a revolutionary reconstruction of history. Benjamin's concern is not the factuality of history but the power of the possible. This power is actualized in images that are retrieved from history and reconfigured in language and script. Benjamin sees reading history as an allegorizing process where cultural objects are shattered into discontinuous images and assembled in such a way that marginalized or forgotten events and objects are salvaged in a new configuration. The allegoricist ''must highlight the seemingly inconsequential details of any given larger structure because they have been ignored in the larger process whereby the dominant class ascribes truth value to its ideologically inspired version of history'' (Jennings 26).

The imagination of historical materialism discovers that which did not happen as picture or image in the virtuality of history. In other words, it imagines the not-yet-written scripts of the film of history. The validation of the allegorical inheres in the understanding that representations of so-called historical facts imply a loss in their account of what actually happened. Representation is always fragmentary and thus reveals a predisposition toward the allegorical. When language can no longer impart its spirit, it tends to transform itself into picture. "Geschichte zerfällt in Bilder, nicht in Geschichten" (History decomposes into pictures, not stories) (5:596), observes Benjamin. Thus, the real lessons of history are reclaimed through its pictures, which transmit the power of the past to the present. As representations they communicate what is not given to communication. Elsewhere, Benjamin makes a similar statement when he observes that "die sprachlichen Gebilde, so auch das Wort, teilen eine Mittelbarkeit mit und symbolisieren eine Nicht-Mittelbarkeit" (verbal images, like the word, communicate a communicability and symbolize an incommunicability) (6:15).

The validation of the imagistic finds its confirmation in Benjamin's accounts of the power of film. The reel is the allegory of the real. Unlike bourgeois art, film is not the object of theoretical judgment or speculation but of practical exercise. The bombardment of images characteristic of film confirms and conforms to the discontinuous moments of modern life. Benjamin sees film as a new region of consciousness and as a key to the logic of historical knowledge, for it affords a spectral analysis of everyday life. It helps the subject situate itself in history by letting it see that history and by offering alternative scripts of history at every temporal level. Like allegory, film is the site of the image-language. Like the filmic image, allegory can be cut, preserved, edited, and reproduced. The allegorical imagination narrates a fragmented history that subverts illusions of totality: "Majestät der allegorischen Intention: Zerstörung des Organischen und Lebendigen—Auslöschung des Scheins" (The majesty of the allegorical intention: the destruction of the organic and living—extinguishing appearances) (1:669–70), writes Benjamin in "Zentralpark." The ruling classes, however, always try to project an image of unity, harmony, and continuity. They present a picture of apparent order, like the kaleidoscope in a child's hand, which transforms, by every turn of the hand, one ordered set of images into another one. The order simulated is merely a pastiche of the history of ruling-class styles. Masquerading as a universal rule, this image of truth holds out against the chaos of history. Benjamin declares that the kaleidoscope has to be smashed (1:660). This declaration definitely recalls the image of blasting open the continuum of history. It is one more visual citation that simultaneously aims at destruction and salvation.

Benjamin employs visual citations in the interest of historical explanation. In this sense, the interpretive practice of the historical materialist challenges the historicist, who views history as a closed or "once upon a time" event where various moments are seen as causally linked to one another. In the retrieval of the images from the past for purposes of decoding the present, Benjamin illustrates the radical operation of memory. In an essay on photography in *About Looking,* John Berger explains how this mode of operation remembers traces of the past in its diverse points of communication with the culture of the present:

There is never a single approach to something remembered. The remembered is not something like a terminus at the end of a line. Numerous approaches and stimuli converge upon it and lead to it.
Words, comparisons, signs need to create a context for a printed photograph in a comparable way; that is to say, they must mark and
leave open diverse approaches. A radial system has to be constructed
around the photograph so that it may be seen in terms which are
simultaneously personal, political, economic, dramatic, everyday and
historic. (66–67)

Benjamin draws on the romantic practice of citing radially (and associatively),
whereby the past is evoked not to enshrine it but in such a way that it becomes
the historical condition for the possibility of the knowledge of the present.
Like Nietzsche, Benjamin does not want to view history as a secular relic.
Instead, the relic is transformed by allegory or in allegory into citable and
recyclable material. In this recitation, "Das Gewesene tritt mit dem Jetzt blitz-
haft zu einer Konstellation zusammen" (at the speed of lightning, the past has
merged [present-perfect tense] with the now into a constellation) (5:576). The
following questions are posed in Benjamin's reading of the discourse of modernity: How is power transmitted at thresholds? How does the waking life
gain access to the energy of dreams? To whom do the lessons of history properly belong—to those who view them as a closed chapter or to those who can
salvage them by forcefully stripping them away from their familiar contexts?
In response to these questions, Benjamin implicitly proposes the idea of a new
mythology, a concept reminiscent of early romanticism's well-known project.
In an age poised on the thresholds of unsettling change that put the crisis of
representation once more on the critical agenda, the romantics argued that the
myths of the past could no longer provide answers to current problems. Their
"new mythology" would be an act of redemption through memory. It involved a search for conceptual models of understanding in the past. The finds,
however, could no longer be useful in their ancient cast. They had to be fragmented, re-collected, and synthesized anew to be useful in the modern age.
Thus, they were no longer objects of nostalgia but of potential cultural re-
newal. Similarly, for Benjamin, "archaic images are no longer mythic, but
'genuinely historical,' when they refer to real historical possibilities, and become capable thereby of charging even the most commonplace, secular phenomena with political significance" (Buck-Morss 249).

Although Benjamin's complex and paradoxical ideas can never be fully
clarified by any one critical approach, his allegorizing of early romanticism's
literary methodologies remains a consistent marker of his writing. The concept of the world as a text that does not cease beyond the library; the act of
criticism as one of complement, completion, and correction; the investigation

into the representational nature of knowledge; and an understanding of allegory as a trope that most radically problematizes the notion of reference—these are the visible critical legacies of romanticism in Benjamin's work. Therefore, I take issue with Buck-Morss's dismissal of academic discussions that situate Benjamin's philosophical orientation in the critical tradition of early German romanticism (222). To be sure, Benjamin reads German romantic criticism selectively, that is, in the fragmenting mode. He salvages the conceptual energy of this critical discourse and (re)dresses its conservatively clad images in revolutionary garb. Benjamin even defines representation by the scientific metaphors of early romanticism. Novalis, for example, sees knowledge as a dialectical relation of critical analysis and poetic synthesis. Benjamin illustrates the labor of representation ("Darstellung") in terms of a chemical process, "im Sinne der Chemie . . . als die Erzeugung eines Stoffes durch einen bestimmten Prozeß, welchem andere unterworfen werden" (in the sense of chemistry . . . as the production of a material by a certain process to which others are subjected) (1:109). The labor of allegory is similarly an effort to analyze (by fragmenting and blasting open) and resynthesize (reconfiguring as another image).

In this allegorizing process, the fragmented memories of historical consciousness are captured in dialectical images and re-viewed in contemporary contexts. This process also implies rereading history as an artwork. Like a work of art, which is infinitely perfectible in the romantic setting, history can be infinitely empowering if its decaying myths are shattered, thus releasing its reformative and revolutionary power.

Notes

1. All translations from the German are mine.
2. "Die Übersetzung ist die Überführung der einen Sprache in die andere durch ein Kontinuum von Verwandlungen, Kontinua der Verwandlung, nicht abstrakte Gleichheits-und Ähnlichkeitsbezirke durchmißt die Übersetzung.

   "Die Übersetzung der Sprache der Dinge in die des Menschen ist nicht nur Übersetzung des Stummen in das Lauthafte, sie ist die Übersetzung des Namenlosen in den Namen. Das ist also die Übersetzung einer unvollkommenen Sprache in eine vollkommenere, sie kann nicht anders als etwas dazu tun, nämlich die Erkenntnis" (2:151).
3. "Benjamin begreift den Traum als kollektive Erinnerungsform, in der der 'Film' des Vergangenen in äußerster Verkürzung abläuft. Sein historischer Materialismus ist nichts anderes als die politische Traumdeutung dieser geschichtlichen Bilder. Doch die Begriffe, die den historischen Gegenstand der Erkenntnis konstruieren, sind aus dem Traum des Vergangenen nicht zu gewinnen. . . . Benjamins politische Traumdeutung unterbricht den Traum und macht ihn lesbar—und das heißt: auf die Gegenwart beziehbar" (77).

4. "Die Vorstellung eines Fortschritts des Menschengeschlechts in der Geschichte ist von der Vorstellung ihres eine homogene und leere Zeit durchlaufenden Fortgangs nicht abzulösen. Die Kritik an der Vorstellung dieses Fortgangs muß die Grundlage der Kritik an der Vorstellung des Fortschritts überhaupt bilden" (1:701).

References

Barthes, Roland. *Mythologies*. Trans. Annette Lavers. New York: Hill & Wang, 1972.

Behler, Ernst. *Irony and the Discourse of Modernity*. Seattle: U of Washington P, 1990.

Benjamin, Walter. *Gesammelte Schriften*. Ed. Rolf Tiedemann and Hermann Schweppenhäuser. 7 vols. Frankfurt am Main: Suhrkamp, 1972–89.

Berger, John. *About Looking*. 1980. New York: Vintage, 1991.

————. *Ways of Seeing*. London: BBC & Penguin, 1972.

Bolz, Norbert, and Richard Faber, eds. *Antike und Moderne: Zu Walter Benjamins "Passagen."* Würzburg: Königshausen & Neumann, 1986.

Bolz, Norbert, and Willem van Reijen. *Walter Benjamin*. Frankfurt am Main: Campus, 1991.

Buck-Morss, Susan. *The Dialectics of Seeing: Walter Benjamin and the Arcades Project*. Cambridge: MIT P, 1989.

Cowan, Bainard. "Walter Benjamin's Theory of Allegory." *New German Critique* 22–25 (1981–82): 109–22.

Heidegger, Martin. "The Age of the World Picture." *Questions Concerning Technology and Other Essays*. Trans. William Lovitt. New York: Garland, 1977. 115–54.

Jennings, Michael W. *Dialectical Images: Walter Benjamin's Theory of Literary Criticism*. Ithaca: Cornell UP, 1987.

Konersmann, Ralf. *Erstarrte Unruhe: Walter Benjamins Begriff der Geschichte*. Frankfurt am Main: Fischer, 1991.

Nägele, Rainer, ed. *Benjamin's Ground: New Readings of Walter Benjamin*. Detroit: Wayne State UP, 1988.

Novalis [Friedrich von Hardenberg]. *Schriften*. 4 vols. Ed. Paul Kluckhohn and Richard Samuel. Stuttgart: Kohlhammer, 1960.

Writing and the Nature of the Supernatural Image, or Why Ghosts Float

CHRISTOPHER COLLINS

The boy's brother had been bitten by a vampire. I knew that, but I wasn't prepared for his return that windy night while the boy tried to sleep in his tall-windowed upstairs bedroom. He had grieved for his brother those weeks after the funeral and was now so happy when this smiling figure appeared outside his window. They seemed both happy. I was terrified. The brother outside the curtained window, his white shirt billowing in the wind, his eyes and mouth intently smiling, kept moving closer to the window. But he wasn't walking. There was nothing at all to walk on out there, only wind and a dull moonlight. The camera now showed the boy sitting upright in his bed, calling his brother's name, then switched back to the window where his brother kept hovering and looming. How big was he? I asked myself as my flesh crawled under the sheets, the TV at the foot of the bed propped up on the Butcher edition of Aristotle's *Poetics*.

This was a cheap trick, I said to myself, a mere superimposition of shots, but I couldn't deny that this scene in the film version of Stephen King's *Salem's Lot* had somehow struck a primal chord in my psyche and had done this not so much by the plot as by the visual image of a dead boy, like a thought in his brother's mind, reappearing out of nowhere. The night air was *nowhere* in that no details, such as trees, clouds, or other houses, served as a ground on which this figure was defined. The night, like a mind with no thought except one, the returning dead boy, yielded no clues as to the size and distance of the figure. We like to have these clues when we perceive our world, and we usually find them provided. Figures normally have about them certain spatial reference points: identifiable background objects that the figure partly occludes, and identifiable foreground objects that may partly occlude the figure.

242

The curtained window could have served the latter purpose. I could have used it to place the revenant n feet outside it, but the photography had superimposed the two images in such a way that the contours of the boy and of the tall, curtained window were blended. The apparition was never clearly outside the window, and, as it loomed closer, it seemed to pass effortlessly into the bedroom, the strange, moonlit wind still blowing its hair and clothes. And then it faded and was instantly replaced by an ad for antiperspirant and then by a series of other carefully chosen anxiety-relief products.

A cheap trick, I said with a shudder, and zapped the screen. But it did its work so well. The figure of the dead, vampirized boy had been entirely detached from the space he entered. The gravity that draws all earthly objects downward had had no effect on him. If this scene had been scripted differently, if this dead boy had appeared to his brother in a terrestrially grounded manner—walking on a street, for example—he would have been optically grounded as well: the viewer's eyes could estimate the distance on the horizontal plane on which the two vertical characters were standing. Without the magic of cinematography the visitant would have to show some evidence of his unearthly provenance. He might have come hollow-eyed, a member of the "living dead," bared his lengthened canines, spoken horrors, or otherwise revealed his supernatural character.

The filmic medium made possible the visual depiction of a kind of floating we have all come to associate with a ghost or some other unearthly entity. But was this always the case? If those phenomena identified as disembodied spirits have always floated in the air, then humankind has had to wait for millennia for technology to produce a true depiction of ectoplasmic behavior. Were the ancient storytellers, epic singers, dramatists, and poets bumbling along, striving to get it right, and failing to do so for technical reasons? Before I try to answer these questions, let us consider some of the older ways in which revenants were depicted.

A Typology of Ghostly Gestalts

In another age the dead boy might have returned to the sound of moans and rattled chains. As prisoners come from some underworldly oubliette, ghosts were considered temporary escapees from hell or purgatory who, weak and weighted down with shackles, walked with a somnambulistic gait and shunned the light of day. King Hamlet's ghost proved to be insubstantial, but he did not seem so to the eye. As a dramatis persona, he was obliged to "stalk" the battlements of Elsinore and in Shakespeare's theater must have looked like any other kingly figure. He had therefore to depend on language to appall his son:

> But that I am forbid
> To tell the secrets of my prison-house,

I could a tale unfold whose lightest word
Would harrow up thy soul, freeze thy young blood,
Make thy two eyes, like stars, start from their spheres,
Thy knotted and combined locks to part,
And each particular hair to stand on end,
Like quills upon the fretful porpentine.
But this eternal blazon must not be
To ears of flesh and blood. (*Hamlet* 1.5.13–22)

This ghost is not hauled on cables from the roof, but walks upon the stage like other actors. He does not use language to describe directly what it is like to be in the purgatorial hereafter—that is, what it is like to be a ghost. Instead, resorting to *omissio,* he describes the horripilating effects he would produce if he appeared to his son in his true supernatural form. "O, horrible! O, horrible! most horrible!" (1.5.80).

Theatrical performance has always been an oral art form in which visually embodied speakers orally mime personae and represent their meanings. If they must mime supernatural visitants, the audience must try to ignore the clearings of the throat, the shufflings of the feet, and the mechanisms that may sometimes be required to hoist them into hovering attitudes.

This was not the case with oral diegesis. A character in a play could diegetically report uncanny offstage events like Oedipus's vanishing into the earth at Colonus and leave the details to the imagination of the audience. A reciter of a passage from an epic could describe the strangest of events— theophanies, metamorphoses, dream-visions—and expect the audience to visualize all these on the inner epic stage of the imagination.

The function of ground in the representation of figure is of special importance when that figure is what we call "supernatural." When the medium is mimetic in the theatrical performance mode, this figure must appear in the same mise-en-scène as the other "natural" figures. Unlike the cinematographer, who precisely controls the shifts and fixations of visual fields, the dramatist must present a common space shared by all actors and open to the visual inspection of the audience. This scenic factor always provides the same degree of grounding for portrayed figures, be they ghostly or flesh and blood. When the medium is diegetic in the oral recitation mode, the figures represented in the tale may fly about, transform themselves, or otherwise defy the assumed rules of nature, *but the teller is grounded.* The figures described are absent, *but the describer is present.* He or she therefore remains a stable object of visual attention to the audience and even in the dark is auditorily located in space and situationally contextualized as the teller of this marvelous narrative.

Traditional mimesis and diegesis are thus forms of what we may call "outer imaging." That is, they are social occasions in which a group comes together to enact or assist in an enactment of a precomposed series of events.

Spirit folk, when they do appear in such a setting, are invested with a degree of ordinary humanity. "Jeder Engel ist schrecklich" (Each angel is terrible), says Rilke, but this was not always so:

> Where are these days Tobiae,
> since one of the most radiant of them stood by the simple front door,
> a little disguised for the journey and no longer
> fearsome . . .[1]

Supernatural beings once could lay aside their alien character and, like the angels that visited Abraham and Tobias and the gods that visited Baucis and Philemon, assume ordinary appearances and ordinary needs: they walked and were thus grounded by their contact with the ground. This ground-groundedness is a mark of the outer-imaged supernatural figure as represented in an oral culture through the social medium of ritual and drama.

Inner imaging occurs without social controls. One sort of inner imaging is private recollection (or anamnesis), the everyday act of recalling visually imprinted data from our past experience. If we recall this morning's breakfast (an example philosophers seem fond of using) we may conjure up the bowl of cereal, but we may also be aware of the glass of juice, the table, even the entire room. A figure, in other words, emerges from anamnestic memory fully encompassed by a recollected ground, though this peripheral field is likely to recede into vague contours and colorless surfaces. Kant and Coleridge spoke of this bidden imagery as the work of the reproductive imagination.

Productive imagination, which the Greeks called *phantasia*,[2] is based on stored memory data but does not reproduce recognizable episodes of past experience. Unbidden figures appear in unfamiliar contexts and on grounds that are not as detailed as those that environ recollected figures. The metamorphic images that appear to us in dreams owe their degree of verisimilitude to their relation to an environment that we can inspect by turning our mind's eye toward it as though it, too, were stocked with potential figures. That is, dream figures have dream grounds, though both are unstable and therefore less available to fixated examination. Reverie, unlike dream, is a phantasia that is at least partly willed. Deciding to visualize a situation, we must try to suppress interferent visual input, so we turn our gaze away from distracting objects, unfocus our eyes, or close them altogether. If this visualization is purely visual (without auditory, kinesthetic, or proprioceptive elements, for example), we try to fixate the contours of an *idealized* figure, idealized because if it were a remembered figure, this would be an act of anamnesis, not phantasia. We may, more or less, succeed in this image formation, but it is not likely that we can supply this conjured figure with a ground, for to be aware of a ground we must shift our attention from the figure, and when we do so the figure will quickly degrade and need to be effortfully reconstructed.[3]

The third type of phantasia is hallucination, a waking fantasy in which unbidden imagery is projected eidetically into physical space. A featureless ground—for example, a dimly illumined room, a foggy street, a blank blue sky, a dark night, or an empty seascape—may serve as a projection screen for an inner image that may appear suddenly and just as suddenly disappear. If it persists, it may be because it has become accidentally connected with a perceived but misinterpreted object; a shadow pattern, for example, randomly projected on a child's bedroom wall may seem to be a hideous face or a menacing figure. A hallucination may even be triggered by entoptic causes, such as small particles within the aqueous humor of the eye projected outward into the visual field. Horatio confidently diagnoses King Hamlet's ghostly form as an entoptic illusion—''A mote it is to trouble the mind's eye'' (*Hamlet* 1.1.112). In all cases of hallucination, the secondary determining factor is the hallucinator's interpretation of the apparently perceived data. The virtually universal human fear of death and of the dead guarantees that a good number of these extraordinary episodes will be interpreted not merely as *un*natural, but as *super*natural. The equally universal memorialization of dead loved ones will also suggest that these revenants have a message to convey to the person to whom they appear.

The fourth variety of phantasia is literate, or writing-cued, imaging. Unlike mimesis and diegesis, this is a private action, the decoding of a group of words and the production of a mental image in response to them, a progression from the visual perception of graphemes to the visual imaging of what the words, composed by these written characters, signify. The only visual interference possible to this process of visual imaging is the appearance of those words on the page. In an age before standardized print, the chirographic peculiarities of the text could distract the visual centers of the brain from the imaginal signifieds to the graphic signifiers; illuminated manuscripts, not to mention pattern poems, forcefully drew attention to the written surface as an object, not only as an instrument, of visuality. (William Blake's engraved poetry, which I will touch on briefly below, represents a late example of chirography that lends itself to a peculiar form of visual imaging.) These exceptions notwithstanding, standardized print since the late sixteenth century increased the transparency of graphemic signifiers and enhanced the production of imaginal signifieds. In short, movable type not only made general literacy possible but created a new advance in phantasia, which we might term "typographic imaging." Figure 1 summarizes the foregoing.

The fourth variety of phantasia is of special interest to us, but before we return to an examination of it we need to consider a psychological phenomenon that, I would suggest, has great bearing on the written representation of the supernatural.

IMAGINAL MODE	FIGURE-GROUND RELATION
OUTER IMAGING	
mimesis: drama and ritual ("showing")	fully grounded performance
diegesis: recited narration ("telling")	fully grounded, present teller of ungrounded, absent events
INNER IMAGING	
anamnesis: reproductive imagination	figures on partially supplied grounds
phantasia: productive imagination	
1. *dream* (subconscious phantasia)	deficient grounds
2. *reverie* (preconscious phantasia)	more deficient grounds
3. *hallucination* (conscious phantasia)	unbidden images projected on environment (enhanced by ganzfeld conditions)
4. *literate imaging* (artificial phantasia)	figures projected on imaginally absent grounds (ganzfeld simulation)
a. chirographic	" " with foregrounded writing
b. typographic	" " with transparent writing

FIG. 1

Solitude and the Ganzfeld Phenomenon

The boy was alone when his brother appeared outside his window, floating in a strange light and at some indeterminate distance from the windowpane. (I was alone too and, by devilish coincidence, in *my* bed.) Solitude seems to be a facilitating circumstance for ghostly encounters.[4]

Another circumstance of such sightings is a condition of visual deficiency.[5] Such conditions include visual deprivation (darkness, blindness, closed eyes), homogeneous visual fields (fog, blue sky, etc.), and randomized visual fields (scenery with monotonous features, like deserts, or with ever changing features, like the surface of the sea). These are conditions conducive to inner imaging, for if the mind is long deprived of perceivable figures it begins to project its own imaginable figures. It follows that persons whose business it is to confront such imagery, whether they interpret it as internal or external manifestations, will seek out such conditions through meditation or travel.

These conditions are, in various degrees, conditions of sensory deprivation. The effects of *visual* sensory deprivation were first studied by psychologists in the 1930s after solitary airplane pilots began to report that, during night flights and while passing through extensive cloud cover, they lost their spatial orientation, the angle and direction of the flight relative to the ground, and, most disturbing, they sometimes experienced hallucinations. Radar had not yet been developed, and under these conditions the visual cues that help our stereoptic, earth-grounded species to gauge size and distance were absent. All these pilots had to see beyond themselves was a homogeneous field, or *ganzfeld*, a uniform ground without figures—nothing to satisfy the needs of an optic system that had been evolved to pick out the figures of prey and predator from visually neutral ground. This system, hungry for sensation but unable to find external stimulation, simply projected its own phantasms into this ganzfeld.

These pilots were not all Saint-Exupérys. Their business was not visionary or poetic, and the consequences of producing a lucid dream in the cockpit of a single-engine plane could be fatal (as perhaps it was for Saint-Exupéry himself on his final *vol de nuit* in 1944). Rilke was solitary but fortunately on solid ground when he projected his own inner figure on the ganzfeld of the night sky:

ENTRANCE

Whoever you are, step out into the evening,
leaving your room behind you, where you know everything;
yours is the last house before the far expanses,
whoever you are.
Using your eyes, that wearily can hardly
free themselves from the worn-out threshold,
you slowly raise a black tree up
and place it on the sky: slender, alone.
And you have made the world. And it is great
and like a word that in the silence ripens.
And as your will encompasses its meaning,
your eyes tenderly release it. . . .[6]

Rilke's was a deliberate act of the productive imagination, a celebration of the depictive power of the mind to use a ganzfeld as an empty canvas. In his journal Coleridge recounts a somewhat different ganzfeld experience:

A pretty optical fact occurred this morning. As I was just returning
from Fletcher's, up the back lane and just in sight of the river, I
saw, floating high in the air, somewhere over Banks's, a noble kite. I
continued gazing at it for some time, when, turning round, I saw at
an equi-distance, on my right, that is, over the middle of our field, a
pair of kites floating about. I looked at them for some seconds, when
it occurred to me that I had never before seen two kites together, and
instantly the vision disappeared. It was neither more nor less than
two pair of leaves, each pair on a separate stalk, on a young fruit tree
that grew on the other side of the wall, not two yards from my eye.
The leaves being alternate, did, when I looked at them as leaves,
strikingly resemble wings, and they were the only leaves on the tree.
The magnitude was given by the imagined distance, that distance by
the former adjustment of the eye, which *remained* in consequence of
the deep impression, the length of time I had been looking at the kite,
the pleasure, etc., and [the fact that] a new object [had] impressed
itself on the eye.[7]

The visual information Coleridge had to work with was deficient in a very
particular way: it lacked clear depth cues. Without an ability to assess these
objects' distance from him and without a companion to correct his hallucinatory misperception, he could not assess their size, and without size discrimination the blurred perception of alternate leaves was assimilated into the
pleasurable visual memory of the two birds in hovering flight. This hallucination used the ganzfeld of the sky but was triggered by actual, though misinterpreted, percepts. His Ancient Mariner, after weeks of physical, as well as
sensory, deprivation, had a vision of a ghost ship that emerged out of the sky,
untriggered by a percept:

> There passed a weary time. Each throat
> Was parched, and glazed each eye.
> A weary time! A weary time!
> How glazed each weary eye,
> When looking westward, I beheld
> A something in the sky.
>
> At first it seemed a little speck,
> And then it seemed a mist;
> It moved and moved, and took at last
> A certain shape, I wist.
>
> A speck, a mist, a shape, I wist!
> And still it neared and neared:
> As if it dodged a water-sprite,
> It plunged and tacked and veered.

249

The behavior of this ship in a totally becalmed sea resembles that of a *musca volitans* (a "flitting fly," an entoptic speck), a mirage effect connected perhaps to the "glazing" of the eyes.

Against a bright sky, mysterious travelers float and hover, dark forms against the light. In the night, equally mysterious beings glimmer with their own light (cf. the will-o'-the-wisp and, in Coleridge's poem, the "water-snakes"). In the darkness of Blake's "forest of the night"—perhaps planted with quickly ripening Rilkean word trees—a terrifying Tyger burns brightly, a creature fabricated in those kindred ganzfeld voids of "distant deeps" and "skies."

Language and Hallucination

Dark forms isolated in a field of light, fiery forms self-illumined in darkness. Words projected on silence, words set against the differences of words unspoken: words, too, float in their own kind of ganzfeld. But words actually spoken are contextualized by a particular speech event. In an oral setting—the mimesis of drama, for example, or the diegesis of storytelling—such words have an addresser and one or more addressees, plus an audience of spectators who serve as "superaddressees," as Bakhtin would call them. The determinate intervening space between them, not to mention the more or less detailed environment that encloses them, tends to anchor the purely imaginal promptings of the words within a perceived, socialized space. No hearer of such words confronts a ganzfeld in solitude. This is no dream, no reverie, no hallucination.

The reader of a book is in a situation quite different from that of a hearer of speech, a situation in many ways resembling that of a hallucination. Encountering writing-cued imagery is a solitary activity. When we read we try to block out incidental sensations. We want a quiet place, a comfortable chair or bed. We want, in short, a kind of sensory deprivation in which only one perceptual channel is open, the eyesight we use to read the page. But this graphemic visuality is effaced by another visuality: our ocular organs move saccadically to follow lines of written characters, but our mind's eye "sees" visual signifieds. As the perceived book recedes as an object, imagined shapes appear and disappear. Some are vividly colored, others only edges and outlines. We change visual perspectives as though transported from one position to another. Scenes fade into darkness, and new scenes emerge delineated in some kind of mental light.

Literate imaging, in human evolution a relatively recent manipulation of consciousness, is an inner imaging and, as such, shares some aspects with dream and reverie. Unlike dream, however, the figures it forms lack distinct grounds: we cannot (unless we stop reading or reread earlier passages) shift our mind's eye about this imaginary space as we find ourselves doing in dreaming. It is also distinct from reverie, if by reverie we mean a self-determined phantasia: the absence of a detailed ground in which these figures are visualized is reverie-like, but we are always apprized of the fact that we are encountering an *other* here, not of our own making.

The imagery we form while reading is most like a hallucination in three ways: first, it is experienced by a solitary person; second, figures appear in partial or complete ganzfelds; and third, these figures are unbidden images. Let me comment briefly on these areas of resemblance. (Note: I will direct these remarks to the reading of texts produced in standard typography, but what I say is applicable to chirographically styled or produced texts mutatis mutandis.)

Imagery is formed by a solitary person. Images that we form in reading a text are privately produced and therefore, like hallucinations, essentially unique events. Since the verbal cues we read are rarely specific, the image one person forms in response to a descriptive phrase is necessarily somewhat different from the image someone else might form. Even when the same person responds again to the same set of words, the image might well be slightly different. Like a hallucination, it happens in a circumstance in which no one else is present to corroborate or correct one's imaginal construction. Because mental imagery is impossible to monitor directly from the outside, it is a reader response that most literary theorists find difficult (and therefore inconvenient) to discuss.

Figures appear in partial or complete ganzfelds. That is, *while* we imagine a word-cued figure we do not imagine its peripheral context. We know that A has entered the already described room B, but, while we picture A, we construct a only very general notion of B from memory. Bound as we are to the sequence of the words, we can only imagine what the current words ask us to imagine. Consequently, A will always appear foregrounded and momentarily detached from her setting. As I pointed out in *Poetics of the Mind's Eye* (97–109), the imagination has no peripheral field when it responds to verbal cues. It fixates what it ''sees'' in what would correspond to a foveal (or macular) field. This means that when it forms the image of a figure, it is not simultaneously able to image the ground on which it appears. Words may prompt us to imagine some detail of B—a lamp in the corner, for example—but when we form this image *this becomes a figure,* and all else, including the human protagonist A, becomes momentarily a *ground.*

Figures are unbidden images. Writing is a communication from an other. I choose to encounter the image-cues in a book I open, but I have not determined what these images are or how they are serially arranged (unless of course *I* wrote the text). I myself must transform the graphic signs into my own mental images, but in respect to visuality my collaborative responsibilities stop there. These images are someone else's images, generated by someone else's variable mixture of reproductive and productive imagination. But in the act of reading, as I witness the unfolding of these images, I am not concerned with the author's role in this process. I cannot afford to be distracted by questions of authorial intention or technique: my job is to assist at the manifestation of these autonomous wraiths that I choose to believe in for the duration of this reading experience.

In these three respects, then, typography leads me to simulate the experience of hallucination. Most printed texts do not take advantage of this resemblance by thematizing the inner imagery of phantasia; in fact, most struggle against what I propose is the inherent tendency of the medium to evoke the phantasmagoric. On the contrary, most printed texts seem to offer themselves as representing collectively verifiable reality. But those texts that do represent the envisioning of uncanny figures have the advantage of an exceedingly apt medium.[8]

I began with a description of a single ghostly manifestation. I now turn to several contrasting examples that will show how language organizes groups of ghosts.

Ghostly Processions

One of the problems with mortality is being forgotten after death. One of the privileges of immortality is being able to continue to affect the lives of the living—as an intercessor before a god, as a tutelary spirit, or simply as a local nuisance. Such immortality ensures that one's history continues within the ongoing context of the living. If it does not continue as an active presence, one's life story becomes fixed within a single set of episodes, dwindling in detail like last year's snows and framed by an ever darkening, ever widening margin of oblivion. Then, if one is recalled at all, it is, as it were, as a separate entry is located in a biographical dictionary—one in a long series of entries arranged in an order no more personally meaningful than the alphabet.[9] The historical/biographical context of a person's life is to that person what a peripheral ground is to a figure. A group of decontextualized ghosts cannot constitute a social unit but merely a collection of isolates.[10]

Homer describes this state of isolation in the eleventh book of the *Odyssey*. Odysseus has followed Circe's advice and sailed to the land of the Cimmerians on the misty shores of River Ocean. There he has sacrificed and poured blood into a pit in the sand. Soon the dead make a rush for the temporarily revivifying blood, but he keeps them in order. Only one ghost at a time is permitted to taste the blood and to respond to his questions. This is not a charitable distribution of food to the starving dead but a search for certain pertinent facts concerning his future. He must speak with the soothsayer,

Teiresias, but in the course of this archaic Greek séance he interviews a number of other ghosts (or "souls," *psuchai*) as well.

The first three that Odysseus interviews (Elpenor, Teiresias, and Anticleia, his mother) appear one after the other, but these three dialogues all belong within Odysseus's context. But nearly 40 percent of the rest of the text dealing with revenants is devoted to a procession of famous women whom Persephone sends forward (lines 225–330, apparently an interpolated set piece of mythology, a kind of Ballad of Dead Ladies). These women have no connection with Odysseus or to one another and are there simply, it would seem, to satisfy his curiosity. (He apparently liked to hear a good story as well as tell it.) Each came, one at a time, for her taste of blood: "They came on in succession [*promnestenai*] and each one / Declared her lineage. I asked questions of them all" (233–34).

This procession of ghosts, the first three and then the famous women, appears to him visually as ordinary living individuals. He knows they are dead and he learns that they cannot be embraced, but, even though Anticleia tells him that the dead twitter and flit like birds on their way to the underworld, these do not do so now. They behave like a crowd of famished persons kept at bay by a distributor of emergency food relief. They can fear the sword (48), they can sit down (142), and they can walk (150). Though the Cimmerian atmosphere is dim and murky, they do not hover in the air or suddenly manifest. They are rather like a company of actors miming the dead.[11]

Virgil in the *Aeneid* imitated the oral-diegetic style of Homer, but he was clearly a writer producing a text for solitary readers. The passage that most corresponds to Homer's procession of famous dead women is a procession of destined-to-be-famous, not-yet-reborn men. These are the visible forms of souls waiting their turn in the underworld to be born and grow up to become leaders of the Roman state. Anchises, Aeneas's recently deceased father, first gives him a point-by-point lecture on the spiritual substrate of the universe (*ordine singula pandit* [6:723]), then takes him and the Cumaean Sibyl through the midst of this noisy gathering to a small rise of subterranean earth from which Aeneas "could read down the long line and learn their faces as they came toward him" (*unde omnes longo ordine posset / Adversos legere et venientum discere vultus* [6:754–55]). Unlike Odysseus with the procession of women, Aeneas does not interact with these spirits, and neither he nor his father forms this crowd (*turba*) into a line. These spirits are pointed out as presenting themselves in vignettes, in *tableaux (pas encore) vivants,* that resemble figures from Roman mural art—in, but not of, the same pictorial space. This assemblage, at first a noisy bustle of persons, becomes a silent procession only after the three viewers take their positions and begin to read. It is almost as though the very act of reading them as lines of writing silences them and marshals them into ranks.

Virgil's otherworldly humans are, like Homer's, ground-grounded beings. Though most major divinities in all cultures seem to have the power to go anywhere (and, in order to do so, are able to fly), disembodied human souls were not commonly conceived of as able to rise weightlessly from the earth. Plato's Socrates in the *Phaedrus* (245c–253e) speculates that the heavens are the prenatal abode of souls, but Aristophanes' ridicule of such uranian notions in *The Clouds* demonstrates the presumably commonsense view that human souls before birth, as well as after death, are—or should be—earthbound. Yet Aristophanes was fighting against an increasingly powerful tide of belief in cloudlike psychical behavior. By the first century B.C. the geographer Alexander Polyhistor could declare, "The whole air is full of souls."[12]

Once it was believed that the sky was psychically inhabitable, all sorts of hoverers could be up there. Paul of Tarsus, whom some have called the "second founder of Christianity," urged the Ephesians to remember that their "fight [was] not against flesh and blood, but against the rulers, against the authorities, against the world-potentates [*kosmokratoras*] of darkness, against spiritual evils in the heavens [*en tois epouraniois*]" (Eph. 6:12, New English Bible). Luther, who kept his own counsel when it came to apostolic texts, substituted *hupouraniois* and translated the questionable phrase as "mit den bösen Geistern *unter dem Himmel*" (with the evil spirits under the heaven). As a man who threw inkwells at *böse Geister,* he presumably had a fair notion of where they lurked. When the King James's translators chose to style this phrase "spiritual wickedness in *high places,*" their lack of cosmic specificity indicated that by the sixteenth century the "heavens" had gotten superlatively higher and were associated now with the City of God atop the spheric garrisons of his angelic warriors. They preferred to imagine devils and their hag paramours as confined to lower flight patterns. "Fair is foul, and foul is fair: / Hover through the fog and filthy air," chant Macbeth's three witches (*Macbeth* 1.1.10–11) in another publishing venture dedicated to James I.

In the pre-Copernican cosmos, blessed souls were imagined to dwell above the sphere of the fixed stars (though Dante has some of them meet him on lower spheres for anagogic reasons). Damned souls and, according to some, souls undergoing purgation were imagined under the earth. But the sublunary vault of sky was the special space of ghostly visitors from other worlds.

William Blake's strange doggerel poem "With Happiness Stretchd Across the Hills" describes a visionary walk he took in the autumn of 1801 along the country road between Felpham and Lavant in Sussex. In this poem the sky at first seems to dominate the scenery ("a blue sky spread over with wings"), but soon the winged traffic descends into the landscape and populates it with fairy elves, little devils, God himself, silver angels, golden demons, and then a three-person procession of the dead:

> . . . my Father hovering upon the wind
> And my Brother Robert just behind
> And my Brother John the evil one
> In a black cloud making his mone
> Tho dead they appear upon my path. . . . (13–17)[13]

These three separate figures appear hovering single file, but their relation to the path is ambiguous. Later (line 81) he says they "march before" him. Also, their relation to this spirit-thronged visual field is visually complicated. They do not seem to appear out of a ganzfeld; here the one potential ganzfeld, the sky, is already imprinted with "wings," and soon everything below it is packed with winged, hovering beings.

Blake's ghosts, and his spiritual beings generally, do not float on vacant grounds, though they sometimes come perilously close to the "margin of Non Entity."[14] Like the words entangled in the flowing script that stretches out to the empty margins of his engraved pages, his imagined figures struggle in a plenitude of other figures, both those imagined and those actually perceived in the interlinear spaces as tendrils, tangled roots, soaring birds, and human shapes. The ghostly beings he asks us to imagine are therefore always partly implicated in the foregrounded field of his handwriting and, so, represent the literate imagination prior to standardized movable print. They are neither the plodding revenants of the oral imagination nor the airy floaters that typography helped to conventionalize, but an intermediate species such as we encounter in Dante's *Commedia*.

One final example of a ghostly procession is "The Magi," a poem by W. B. Yeats, which he annotated thus:

> [I] looked up one day into the blue of the sky, and suddenly imagined, as if lost in the blue of the sky, stiff figures in procession. I remembered that they were the habitual image suggested by blue sky, and looking for a second fable called them "The Magi." . . .

THE MAGI

> Now as at all times I can see in the mind's eye,
> In their stiff, painted clothes, the pale unsatisfied ones
> Appear and disappear in the blue depth of the sky
> With all their ancient faces like rain-beaten stones,
> And their helms of silver hovering side by side,
> And all their eyes still fixed, hoping to find once more,
> Being by Calvary's turbulence unsatisfied,
> The uncontrollable mystery on the bestial floor. (318)

This is, the poem tells us, a persistent mental image: a set of three figures appearing and disappearing in a ganzfeld that is a "blue depth of sky." But how "deep" is this field? Where does the sky begin and end? If we cannot be sure of this, we can never know how large or how distant these figures are. Detached from their featureless ground, they seem to loom. And "hovering side by side," not overlapping, the figures cannot be used one for the other to gauge relative distance or size. (See Pound's "The Return," in which ancient gods return "one, and by one" and waver like separate snowflakes in the wind.)

Their manner of manifesting and their restless, yet outwardly affectless, demeanor conform to what we in the tradition of the typographic imagination recognize as the behavior of returning ghosts.[15] Unsatisfied with the death of the God-Man (and presumably their own deaths), they yearn for a new birth—perhaps also to be recontextualized in history, to escape the fate of floating in the literate "mind's eye," and to become once again grounded on that "bestial floor" where, as the old paintings depicted them, they long ago knelt beside shepherds and angels who seemed then as weary of flying as the magi do now.

A Late Conclusion

To be haunted by floating ghosts is to be haunted by images of the flight of time. We are alive to see or imagine the illustrious dead because we have come late into the world and now have only our own conclusion to await. Like Alfred de Musset in his "Prologue to *Rolla*," we say, especially now as the conclusion of the second millennium slouches toward us out of the future, that we were born too late in a world too old. We are late and fear the moment of conclusion at which we will become forever "the late ———."

It is more than a curious coincidence, I believe, that speculation on the aging of the world first began to possess the mind of Europe just as movable type began multiplying written texts.[16] The mechanical linearity of print intensifies the temporality of language, and the groundlessness of the separate images that print evokes narrows the world it represents to a phantasmagoric procession as strait and as straight as the arrow of time.

As readers haunted by the spectral images of the typographic imagination, our past is all behind us, our present is a narrow "now," and our future rushes toward us, dwindling, as a text does, toward its rapid conclusion. We too float through our life as we float through the lines of print. The magi that Yeats projected into the ganzfeld of the sky represented himself and us. We, like them and him, are the "unsatisfied ones." The ghostly forms we imagine, these UFOs (Ungrounded Floating Others) are actually displaced images of ourselves. Like the magi, we yearn for the beginning of a new cycle of cosmic time and for a consciousness reincarnated on some "bestial floor," to reexperience our own nativity in a fully grounded world.

256

It is no wonder that the typographic imagination projects its anxiety about time onto floating images and yearns to revert to the visual plenitude of an oral culture. This was the utopia of Keats's ''Hyperion'' and ''Grecian Urn,'' Goethe's ''Classical Walpurgis Night,'' Yeats's Byzantium and pre-Christian Ireland. ''Aber Freund!'' Hölderlin reminds himself and us in ''Brot und Wein'': ''Wir kommen zu spät. Zwar leben die Götter, / Aber über dem Haupt droben in anderer Welt. / . . . / Aufwärts stiegen sie all'' (We come too late. Although the gods live, / but over the head above in another world. / . . . / upwards they all rose) (97–98, 113).[17]

Notes

1. ''Wohin sind die Tage Tobiae, / da der Strahlendsten einer stand an der einfachen Haustür, / zur Reise ein wenig verkleidet und schon nicht mehr / furchtbar. . .'' (*Duino Elegies* 2.1.3–5). Translation is mine.

2. The Greeks did not, however, grant this power of *phantasia* any artistic function. For a discussion of this issue see my *Reading the Written Image* 28–31, 44, and 125.

3. See Kosslyn, *Image and Mind* 234–39. For a discussion of what he calls the ''mental matrix'' of the imagination see his *Ghosts in the Mind's Machine* 65–66.

4. This does not always seem to have been the case. In other times and other cultures groups of persons have reported seeing phenomena that they interpreted as ghostly, but in our culture it is most likely that such reports will be those of single informants.

5. See my *Poetics of the Mind's Eye* 142–67, especially 156–57.

6. ''Eingang / Wer du auch seist: Am Abend tritt hinaus / aus deiner Stube, drin du alles weisst; / als letztes vor der Ferne liegt dein Haus: / Wer du auch seist. / Mit deinen Augen, welche müde kaum / von der verbrauchten Schwelle sich befrein, / hebst du ganz langsam einen schwarzen Baum / und stellst ihn vor den Himmel: schlank, allein. / Und du hast die Welt gemacht. Und sie ist gross / und wie ein Wort, das noch im Schweigen reift. / Und wie dein Wille ihren Sinn begreift, / lassen sie deine Augen zärtlich los. . . .'' The title of this poem from *Das Buch der Bilder* may be translated ''Beginning'' or ''Initiation,'' but the spatial paradox of going out in order to go in is preserved by ''Entrance.''

7. Entry no. 1668 (November 1803) from *The Notebooks of Samuel Taylor Coleridge*.

8. By comparison, film, like theater, is less well suited, since the eyes of the spectator are free to move at will from central figure to peripheral ground.

9. In Masters's *Spoon River Anthology* the table of contents lists the names of the dead who speak from their graves not in the order of their placement in the book but in the order of an old-fashioned town directory—*alphabetically*—an arbitrary arrangement that underscores an isolation in death that consummates their isolation from one another in life.

10. This appears to be the lonely fate of the departed as it is viewed from the perspective of the living, whose task it is to preserve the memory of the dead and through

257

various rituals "keep them company." Comedic transformations of this loneliness portray the dead as enjoying the company of their contemporaries. Dante's *Commedia* is a sublime version of this in its depiction of the communion of saints in the *Paradiso*.

11. See the afterworlds of Shaw's *Man and Superman* and Sartre's *No Exit*, in which the resemblance to the condition of the living so astonishes the newly dead and makes a point about the living.

12. Quoted by Dodds in *The Greeks and the Irrational* 111. Dodds regards this shift upward as due to the influence of Pythagoreans and Stoics and concludes that from then on "there was no future for *necyomanteia* in the ancient world" (111). These were openings into the world of the dead used for the sort of séance that Odysseus arranged in Cimmeria. The underworld (*hupo ges*) was already for Plato in the *Phaedrus* mainly a place of purgation (249a7); as such, there was no point in petitioning its inmates. True, Virgil's Platonic soul-realm was subterranean, but perhaps it had to be to fit his Homeric design. See also Macrobius's *Commentary on the Dream of Scipio* 1.10.9–15.

13. Included in Blake's letter to Thomas Butts, November 22, 1802, in Blake, *Complete Poetry and Prose* 692. This poem closes with the celebrated "fourfold vision" passage.

14. *The Four Zoas: Night the Second* 35, line 17 (page 319 in Blake, *Complete Poetry and Prose*). I speak here of his poetry, but his paintings have similarly filled-in grounds.

15. For Yeats, all imaginal phenomena, recollected images as well as ghostly apparitions, seem to have had this common characteristic of floating: "Her [Maude Gonne's] present image floats into the mind" ("Among School Children" 25); "Before me floats an image, man or shade, / Shade more than man, more image than a shade" ("Byzantium" 9).

16. See Donne's "An Anatomie of the World" (1611). Milton's early (1628) Latin poem "Naturam non pati senium" opposed the deteriorist position.

17. Translation provided by editor.

References

Avant, Lloyd L. "Vision in the Ganzfeld." *Psychologica Bulletin* 64.4 (1965) 246–58.

Blake, William. *The Complete Poetry and Prose of William Blake*. Ed. David V. Erdman. Garden City, NY: Anchor Doubleday, 1965.

Bundy, Murray Wright. *The Theory of Imagination in Classical and Medieval Thought*. N.p.: U of Illinois P, 1927.

Coleridge, S. T. *The Notebooks of Samuel Taylor Coleridge*. Ed. Kathleen Coburn. Vol. 1. New York: Pantheon, 1957.

———. *Poetical Works*. Oxford: Oxford UP, 1978.

Collins, Christopher. "Figure, Ground, and Open Field." *New York Quarterly* 10 (Winter 1972): 118–26.

———. "Groundless Figures: Reader Response to Verbal Imagery." *The Critic* 51.1 (Fall 1988): 11–29.

———. "The Moving Eye in Williams's Earlier Poetry." *William Carlos Williams:*

The Man and the Poet. Ed. Carroll F. Terrell. Orono, ME: National Poetry Foundation, 1983. 261–85.

——. *The Poetics of the Mind's Eye: Literature and the Psychology of Imagination.* Philadelphia: U of Pennsylvania P, 1991.

——. *Reading the Written Image: Interpretation, Verbal Play, and the Roots of Iconophobia.* University Park: Pennsylvania State UP, 1991.

——. *The Uses of Observation: Correspondential Vision in the Writings of Emerson, Thoreau, and Whitman.* The Hague: Mouton, 1971.

Dodds, E. D. *The Greeks and the Irrational.* Berkeley: U of California P, 1951.

Donne, John. "An Anatomie of the World." *The Complete English Poems.* Harmondsworth: Penguin, 1986. 269–83.

Farah, M. J. "Is Visual Memory Really Visual? Overlooked Evidence from Neuropsychology." *Psychological Review* 95 (1988): 307–17.

Farmer, E. W., J. V. F. Berman, and Y. L. Fletcher. "Evidence for a Visuo-spatial Sketch-pad in Working Memory." *Quarterly Journal of Experimental Psychology* 38 (1986): 675–88.

Finke, Ronald A. *Principles of Mental Imagery.* Cambridge: MIT P, 1989.

Gibson, James J. *The Perception of the Visual World.* Boston: Houghton, 1950.

——. *The Senses Considered as Perceptual Systems.* Boston: Houghton, 1966.

Goethe, Johann Wolfgang von. *Faust, Part Two.* Translated with an Introduction by Philip Wayne. Harmondsworth, Middlesex, England: Penguin, 1959, "Classical Walpurgis-Night," (Part II, Act II) pp. 106–56.

Groner, Rudolf, et al., eds. *Eye Movements and Psychological Processes: International Views.* Hillsdale, NJ: Lawrence Erlbaum, 1983.

Hillman, James. *The Dream and the Underworld.* New York: Harper, 1979.

Holt, Robert. "Imagery: The Return of the Ostracized." *American Psychologist* 19 (1964): 154–64.

Homer. *The Odyssey.* Oxford: Oxford UP, 1980.

Horowitz, Mardi J. *Image Formation and Cognition.* 2nd ed. New York: Appleton, 1978.

Kaufman, Lloyd. *Sight and Mind: Introduction to Visual Perception.* New York: Oxford UP, 1974.

Klinger, Eric, ed. *Concepts, Results, and Applications.* Vol. 2 of *Imagery.* New York: Plenum, 1981.

Kosslyn, Stephen. *Ghosts in the Mind's Machine: Creating and Using Images in the Brain.* New York: Norton, 1983.

——. *Image and Mind.* Cambridge: Harvard UP, 1980.

Kosslyn, Stephen, C. B. Cave, D. A. Provost, and S. M. von Gierke. "Sequential Processes in Image Generation." *Cognitive Psychology* 20 (1988): 319–43.

Lessing, G. E. *Laokoon oder Ueber die Grenzen der Malerei und Poesie. Gotthold Ephraim Lessing. Werke.* Ed. Uwe Lassen. Hamburg: Hoffmann und Campe, 1963.

MacDermot, Violet. *The Cult of the Seer in the Ancient Middle East: A Contribution to Current Research on Hallucinations Drawn from Coptic and Other Texts.* Berkeley: U of California P, 1971.

Macrobius, Ambrosius Aurelius. *Commentary on the Dream of Scipio.* New York: Columbia UP, 1952.

Masters, Edgar Lee. *Spoon River Anthology.* Urbana: U of Illinois P, 1972.

Milton, John. "Naturam non pati senium." *The Poetical Works of John Milton: With Translations of the Italian, Latin and Greek Poems from the Columbia University Edition.* London: Oxford UP, 1958.

Monty, Richard A., and John W. Senders, eds. *Eye Movements and Psychological Processes.* Hillsdale, NJ: Lawrence Erlbaum, 1979.

Nicholas, John M., ed. *Images, Perception, and Knowledge.* Papers deriving from and related to the Philosophy of Science Workshop at Ontario, Canada, May 1974. Boston: Reidel, 1977.

Ong, Walter. *Orality and Literacy: The Technologizing of the Word.* New York: Methuen, 1985.

Paivio, Allan. *Imagery and Verbal Processes.* New York: Holt, 1971.

———. "Images, Propositions, and Knowledge." Nicholas 47–71.

Paivio, Allan, and Ian Begg. *Psychology of Language.* Englewood Cliffs, NJ: Prentice-Hall, 1981.

Pick, Herbert L., Jr., and Linda P. Acredolo. *Spatial Orientation: Theory, Research, and Application.* New York: Plenum, 1983.

Plato. *Lysisor, Friendship. The Symposium. Phaedrus.* New York: Heritage, 1968.

Richardson, Alan. *Mental Imagery.* London: Routledge & Kegan Paul, 1969.

———. "Voluntary Control of the Memory Image." Sheehan, *Function* 109–31.

Rilke, Rainer Maria. *The Duino Elegies.* New York: Harper, 1972.

———. *Sämtliche Werke.* Frankfurt am Main: Insel Verlag, 1959.

Sartre, Jean Paul. *No Exit (Huis Clos): A Play in One Act.* Trans. Stuart Gilbert. New York: Knopf, 1947.

Segal, Sydney J., ed. *Imagery, Current Cognitive Approaches.* New York: Academic, 1971.

Shakespeare, William. *Hamlet, Prince of Denmark.* Cambridge: Cambridge UP, 1985.

Shaw, Bernard. *Man and Superman: A Comedy and a Philosophy.* London: Constable, 1931.

Sheehan, Peter W., ed. *The Function and Nature of Imagery.* New York: Academic, 1972.

———. "Visual Imagery and the Organizational Properties of Perceived Stimuli." *British Journal of Psychology* 58 (1967): 247–52.

Sheikh, Anees A., ed. *Imagery: Current Theory, Research, and Application.* New York: John Wiley, 1983.

Sheikh, Anees A., and John T. Shaffer, eds. *The Potential of Fantasy and Imagination.* New York: Brandon, 1979.

Shepard, Roger, and L. A. Cooper. *Mental Images and Their Transformations.* Cambridge: MIT P, 1982.

Solomon, Philip, and Jack Mendelson. "Hallucinations in Sensory Deprivation." West 135–45.

Talmy, Leonard. "How Language Structures Space." *Spatial Orientation: Theory, Research, and Application.* Ed. Herbert L. Pick Jr. and Linda P. Acredolo. New York: Plenum, 1983. 225–82.

Vernon, J. *Inside the Black Room: Studies in Sensory Deprivation.* London: Souvenir, 1963.

Virgil. *The Aeneid.* Translated into English prose with an introduction by W. F. Jackson Knight. Baltimore: Penguin, 1956.

West, Louis Jolyon, ed. *Hallucination.* New York: Grune & Stratton, 1962.

Wilner, Eleanor. *Gathering the Winds: Visionary Imagination and Radical Transformation of Self and Society.* Baltimore: Johns Hopkins UP, 1975.

Yeats, W. B. *Collected Poems.* New York: Macmillan, 1933.

Yuille, John C., ed. *Imagery, Memory, and Cognition: Essays in Honor of Allan Paivio.* Hillsdale, NJ: Lawrence Erlbaum, 1983.

INDEX

Abstract art: as mimesis of a concept, 37
Acéphale, 177–78
Adler, Hans, 19n. 11
Adorno, Theodor: influence of Hölderin on, 133
Aesthetic theory: Classical Greek origins of, 29–39
Aleatory art, 38–39
Alexander Polyhistor, 254
Allegory: and signification, 231; Walter Benjamin's theory of, 15, 229–31
American Renaissance transcendentalism: influence of German natural science on, 92–93; redefinition of human and plant anatomy, 93–94; rhetoric of eyes/use of visual language, 5, 89, 93, 98–101, 107n. 7
Anagrams, 78
Anamnesis (reproductive imagination), 16, 245, 247
Aristophanes: *The Clouds,* 254
Aristotle: and *diairesis,* 32–33; and *diaphora,* 40n. 13; *Metaphysics,* 40n. 13; and mimesis (imitation), 32–33, 40n. 10; narrative theory, 29; *Poetics,* 32–33; *prattontes,* 34; *Rhetoric,* 40n. 14; six *meré* of tragedy, 32, 33; *sunthesis pragmatôn (muthos),* 34, 35; typology of aesthetics, 29, 32–38
Ars poetica, 168nn. 8, 13
Art: abstract, 37; aleatory, 38; Classical Greek theories of, 29–39; impact of science and media technology on, 4; psychology of, 65

Babbage, Charles, 74–76
Bachelard, Gaston, 59

Bakhtin, Mikhail M., 171n. 32, 250; and decentralization of verbal-ideological, 9, 156
Barthes, Roland, 171n. 33, 231
Bataille, Georges, 11; and acéphale, 177–79, 181; antifascism, 178; and chthonic myth, 181; "politics of the impossible," 182n. 3
Batteux, Charles: *Les Beaux arts reduits à un même principe* (The Fine Arts Reduced to a Single Principle), 52
Baudrillard, Jean, 18n. 7
Benjamin, Walter, 19n. 11; on allegory, 15, 229–31; on angel of history, 236; *Der Begriff der Kunstkritik in der deutschen Romantik* (The Concept of Art Criticism in German Romanticism), 231; distinction between knowledge and truth, 231; on dreams and dream interpretation, 233–34; on historical citation, 237; on historical materialism, 235, 238; on history as allegorizing process, 237; influence of Hölderin on, 133; influence of romantic critics on, 231–32, 239–40; "Kleine Geschichte der Photographie" (Short History of Photography), 231; on language, 233–34; on lighting of opera, 73; on memory, 235; *Passagen-Werk,* 15, 234; on power of film, 238; "Schwellenkunde" (science of thresholds), 14, 15, 229; and text-image interaction, 229, 230, 235; on translation, 232; *Ursprung des deutschen Trauerspiels* (Origin of the German Tragic Drama), 231, 235–36; *Yber den Begriff der Geschichte* (Theses on History), 233, 235–38; "Zentralpark," 15, 230, 238

Bentham, Jeremy: panopticon, 13–14, 220–21
Berger, John, 238; *Ways of Seeing,* 230
Berkeley, George: *Hylas and Philonus,* 57–58; rejection of Newton's color-tone hypothesis, 57; "Theory of Vision," 53
Berlin Wall: literary treatments of, 217; teichoscopic distortion in *Der Mauerspringer* (Wall Jumper), 217–18
Berstein, Richard, 167n. 2
Bigongiari, Piero, 159–60
Blake, William, 246, 250; "With Happiness Stretchd Across the Hills," 254–55
Blumenberg, Hans, 17n. 4
Bolz, Norbert, 234
Breton, André, 11, 177
Brilliant, Richard, 169n. 19
Bryson, Norman, 3, 35–36, 170n. 29
Buck-Morss, Susan, 231, 233

Cahiers d'Art, 176
Calvino, Italo, 171n. 33
Camera obscura, 192, 203, 212n. 5, 216–17
Carroll, Lewis: *Through the Looking Glass,* 219
Cartesian model, 6, 112
Cartesian spectatorship, 12–13, 187–88; and realist narrator, 188
Cassirer, Ernst, 225n. 8
Castel, Louis-Bertrand, 50; "discourse of colors," 4, 50, 66; *L'Optique des couleurs,* 50, 52; and natural production of colors, 59; and new philosophy of taste, 59, 60; and Newton, 4, 53, 59–60; ocular harpsichord, 3, 49–50, 61, 68n. 14; and relationship of colors and musical tones, 50–53; and theory of vibrations, 52–53
Chadwick, Whitney: *Myth in Surrealist Painting,* 177
Chambers, Robert: *Vestiges of the Natural History of Creation,* 92–93
Cheselden, William, 55, 65
Chirography, 246
Chthonic myths, 176–77, 181
Cinema, 37; and Aristotelian typology of aesthetics, 37; as basis of modern music, 80–81
Coleridge, Samuel Taylor, 248–50
Collins, Christopher, 16–17; *Poetics of the Mind's Eye,* 251

Color: Newton on, 53; relationship to musical tones, 50–58
Color-tone harmony: Engel on, 64, 66; Mendelssohn on, 63, 66
Condillac, Étienne Bonnot de, 55
Cook, Albert: "The Sign in Klee," 181
Corazzini, Sergio, 157
Crary, Jonathan, 203; *Techniques of the Observer: On Vision and Modernity in the Nineteenth Century,* 216
Crepuscolare movement, 157, 158, 168n. 8
Cryptography: relation to written music, 78

Dante Alighieri: *Commedia,* 255, 257n. 10
Debussy, Claude, 4; *Monsieur Croche,* 77–78; "Music in the Open Air," 80; *Pelléas and Mélisande,* 79–80; tonal ambiguity, 80
de Certeau, Michel: *Heterologies: Discourse of the Other,* 18n. 8
de Chirico, Giorgio: antitraditional aesthetics, 9, 155–56, 166–67; *The Convent on the Mountain,* 161–62; *The Enigma of the Oracle,* 163–64, 170n. 27; lack of narrative responsibility, 161–62; *non-sense* painting, 165; titles of paintings, 165; use of Iserian blanks, 10, 162, 163–65
Degenerate Art (Entartete Kunst) exhibition, 174; "dada wall," 10–11, 174
De Musset, Alfred, 256
Der Dada magazine, 174
Derrida, Jacques: white mythology, 17n. 4
Descartes, René, 112, 113
Detective fiction, 13, 189–90
Diairesis, 39n. 3; Aristotelian, 32–33; Platonic, 30, 39n. 4
Diaphora, 40n. 13
Diderot, Denis: "Lettre sur les aveugles" (Letter on the blind), 58, 66; "Lettre sur les sourds et muets" (Letter on the Deaf and Dumb), 49–50, 52, 64; visit to Castel, 49–50
Diegesis (narrative), 2, 3, 34; defined, 39n. 3; as outer imaging, 16, 244, 247; Platonic, 29, 30; and sign system, 37
Dienst, Richard, 16
Dithyramb, 30
Durfee, Job: *The Panidea,* 93

Edison, Thomas, 84n. 9
Emerson, Ralph Waldo: "The American Scholar," 97; concept of eternal chain,

100; "Divinity School Address," 98; "The Eternal Pan," 97; "The Genuine Man," 97; "The Heart," 98–99; images of amputation, 99; images of divine nature, 94, 96; influence of Goethe taxonomy on, 94–95; influence of Leibniz's theory of monads on, 107n. 5; leaf as model of globe, 95, 100; on loss of son, 106; "Nature," 96–97; "optical relation," 98; pantheism, 90, 97, 101; rhetoric of eyes/use of visual language, 5, 90, 92, 94–101, 107nn. 6, 7; on self-reliant individuals, 95, 100; *Works,* 97

Encyclopédie: on Castel's ocular harpsichord, 61, 66

Engel, Johann Jacob: on singing as discourse, 70n. 26; theory of musical painting, 64, 66; "Über musikalische Malerey" (On musical painting), 64

Enlightenment: and linguistic representation, 112–14; and principle of analytical reasoning, 113; and rationality, 5–6; self-image of, 112

Euler, Leonhard: "Essay on New Music Theory," 4, 76

Eye: metaphors of in *Hyperion* (Hölderlin), 145; movement, 3, 19n. 10, 34, 41n. 19; rhetoric of in American Renaissance transcendentalism, 5, 89–101, 107nn. 6, 7

The Eye (Nabokov), 13, 191, 206–12; dual ontological levels, 208–9; as metaphor for authorship, 207–8; narrator's "constitutive splitting," 211–12; narrator's narcissistic fantasy, 207–8; surveillance in, 207

Faraday, Michael: *History of a Candle,* 74

Fascism: visuality and specularization in, 148n. 1

Feyerabend, Paul, 167n. 2

Fichte, Johann Gottlieb: prereflective unity of consciousness, 120–21

Foucault, Léon; and carbon arc lamp, 74

Foucault, Michel, 1, 2, 6; *Discipline and Punish,* 220, 221; *The Eye of Power,* 224n. 5; on paradigm shift from classical to modern episteme, 113–14, 128n. 6

Fourier, Jean-Baptiste-Joseph: spectral analysis, 4, 76

Frank, Manfred, 129n. 13

Frankfurt school, 2

Frech, Birgit, 217

Freud, Sigmund: on narcissism, 199

Friedrich, Caspar David, 8, 20n. 18

Gadamer, Hans-Georg: hermeneutical circle notion, 167n. 2

Gandelman, Claude, 19n. 10

Ganzfeld, 248–50

Garrett, Jeffrey, 13–14

Geertz, Clifford, 167n. 2

Genette, Gérard, 39n. 3, 43n. 27

German Opera House, 74

German pantheism, 108n. 12

German romanticism, 92, 104, 231–32

Gessinger, Joachim, 3–4

Ghosts, 16; changing representations of, 243, 246; outer imaging of in oral culture, 243–45; in typographic imagination, 252–56; typology of, 243–46

Goethe, Johann Wolfgang von: "Classical Walpurgis Night," 257; *Colour Theory,* 14; effect on American transcendentalism, 93–94; *Farbenlehre,* 53, 216, 219; *Metamorphoses of Plants,* 103; morphology of leaves, 93, 94; pantheism, 5, 90; refutation of Newton's color theory, 74; romantic taxonomy, 91

Goodman, Nelson: *Languages of Art,* 2

Gottfried von Strassburg, 78–79

Gozzano, Guido, 157

Greek drama, 73

Greek myth: chthonic, 176–77, 181

Greek rhetoric, 2–3

Grenzgänger, 14

"Guckkastentheater," 81

Güntert, Georges, 158

Hallucination: relationship to reading, 250–52

Hardack, Richard, 5, 20n. 14

Hardenberg, Friedrich Leopold von. *See* Novalis

Hartley, David: *Observations on Man,* 52–53

Haverkamp, Anselm, 17n. 4

Hegel, Georg Wilhelm Friedrich: inverted world ("verkehrte Welt") concept, 217

Heidegger, Martin: "Die Zeit des Weltbildes" (The Age of the World Picture), 233; influence of Hölderin, 133

Hemsterhuis, François, 67n. 8; "organe morale," 125–26

Herder, Johann Gottfried, 53, 60; on origin of language, 64, 65; "Vom Angenehmen und Schönen," 66
Historiography, 18n. 8
Hitler, Adolph, 174
Hölderlin, Friedrich, 7–8; "Brot und Wein," 257; *Empedokles,* 8, 137, 143; hypervisuality, 132–33; paratactical style, 132; reception of, 8–9, 132–33; use of metaphor and metonymy, 8. *See also Hyperion*
Homer: procession of ghosts in *Odyssey,* 252–53
Horace, 29
Hunt, John: *Pantheism and Christianity,* 92
Hyperion (Hölderlin), 133, 136–48; aggression in, 141–42; alienation in, 135, 143; color leveling in, 137, 138; dynamic of love in, 144; metaphors of eye and viewing, 145; mirroring in, 138, 140; narcissism in, 8, 135, 138–40; psychoanalytic reading of, 136, 140; sadomasochism in, 143–44; touch motifs, 134–35, 140–41, 147; visual isolation in, 142

Image: defined, 230; discursive and figural aspects of, 35–36; text relations, 2, 3, 29, 36–37, 229–30, 235; Walter Benjamin on, 231
Imagination, productive (phantasia), 16, 245–47, 250–52, 257n. 2
Imagination, reproductive (anamnesis), 16, 245, 247
Imaging, inner: anamnesis (reproductive imagination), 16, 245, 247; conditions conducive to, 247–48; phantasia (productive imagination), 16, 245–47, 250–52, 257n. 2; and the supernatural, 252–56; typographic (literate), 246, 250–56
Imaging, outer: and the supernatural, 243–45. *See also* Diegesis; Mimesis
Intellectual intuition ("intellektuelle Anschauung"), 119–21, 129nn. 13, 15; Novalis' concept of, 123
Intertextuality, 9
Interval concept, 76
Iser, Wolfgang, 162; reader-response theory, 9
Iserian blanks: in de Chirico's paintings, 162, 163–65; in Palazzeschi's verse, 162
Italian Opera House, 74, 75

Jacob, Karen, 12–13
Jakobson, Roman, 19n. 10, 42n. 21
James, Henry: as modernist, 205–6; multiple narrative centers in *Wings of the Dove,* 205; painting in *Wings of the Dove,* 212n. 6; repudiation of first-person narration, 204–5. *See also The Sacred Fount*
Jameson, Fredric: *Signatures of the Visible,* 12, 187
Jay, Martin, 12, 188; "antiocular discourse," 11; scopic regimes, 1, 17n. 2, 182n. 6
Jean Paul, 19n. 11, 20n. 16

Kant, Immanuel, 119–20, 127n. 5, 129n. 13; *Critique of Pure Reason,* 113; taxonomic notion of representation, 112–13
Keats, John, 257
Kemp, Martin: *The Science of Art,* 20n. 18
Kepler, Johannes: theory of retinal image, 216
Kirby, John T., 2–3, 19n. 10
Kircher, Athanasius, 50, 60, 67n. 11
Kittler, Friedrich A., 4–5, 20n. 19
Klee, Paul, 10–11; *Bacchanal with Red Wine,* 175, 181; chthonic myth in late works, 176, 179–82; *Creative Credo (Schöpferische Konfession),* 179; and dada movement, 175; in *Degenerate Art* exhibition, 174–75, 176; *Fragments of a Region Long Since Past,* 175; hybridization of mimetic/nonmimetic, 11; *Landscape on the Way to Hades,* 175, 180, 181; late works (1937–40), 10–11, 175–76, 179–82; *Legend of the Nile,* 181; *Lemon Harvest,* 175, 181; *Peach Harvest,* 175, 180, 181; relationship of theory to art, 179–80; *Swamp Legend,* 174, 175, 179, 180; Swiss exile, 175; titles of late works, 181
Kohut, Heinz; mirror transference, 8, 133, 135–36
Konersmann, Ralf, 237
Kramer, Kathryn E., 10–11
Kraus, Karl, 221
Kristeva, Julia, 20n. 19
Krüger, Johann Gottlob: construction of ocular harpsichord, 60–62
Kudszus, Winfried, 150n. 16
Kuzniar, Alice, 20n. 19

Lacan, Jacques, 189–90
Language, 218n. 9; decentralization of, 156; as ideological medium, 156–57; of modern

literature, 113–14; Novalis' philosophy of, 116–17; Romantic concept of, 7, 232; skeptical view of, 57; and supernatural images, 252–56; theory of, 64–66; Walter Benjamin on, 233–34

Leaves, morphology of, 91

Leibniz, Gottfried Wilhelm, 67n. 11, 112; theory of monads, 5, 107n. 5

Light: Newton on, 53; in theory of vibrations, 53

Locke, John: and camera obscura, 216; *Essay Concerning Human Understanding,* 54, 216; rejection of color-tone harmony, 55; skeptical view of language, 57

Locke-Molyneux hypothesis, 55

Logisikon, 31

London Savoy Theater, 73

Luther, Martin, 254

Lyotard, Jean-François, 155, 167; concept of figure-matrix, 10, 179; on Klee's relationship of theory to art, 179–80

Maeterlinck, Maurice: *Pelléas and Mélisande,* 79–80

Malebranche, Nicolas, 53; *La Recherche de Latin America vérité,* 54, 68n. 13

Manning, J. M.: "Pantheism in the Form of Self-Worship," 101; "The Strengths and Weaknesses of Pantheism," 91–92

Marin, Louis, 168n. 4

Masters, Edgar Lee: *Spoon River Anthology,* 257n. 9

Melville, Herman, 5; *The Confidence Man,* 101; depiction of amputees, 90; and Emersonian theories of identity, 101–6; and Goethe's pantheism, 103–6, 108n. 12; *Mardi,* 101–2, 103–4, 106; *Moby Dick,* 102; *Omoo,* 105; and pantheism, 90, 91, 102–3, 105; *Pierre,* 104–6, 108n. 12; *Redburn,* 103; and seeing and reproduction, 105–6

Mendelssohn, Moses: "Briefe über die Empfindungen" (Letters on sensations), 63; reaction to Castel's ocular harpsichord, 63–64, 66, 69n. 22

Menges, Karl, 5–6

Merrell, Floyd, 19n. 10

Metz, Christian, 17n. 2

Meyerbeer, Giacomo: *Le Prophète,* 74

Miller, D. A., 189

Mimesis (imitation), 2, 3, 16, 34, 244, 247; and abstract art, 37; and aleatory art, 38–39; Aristotelian, 32–33, 40n. 10; defined, 39n. 3; as mode of signification, 41n. 16; Platonic, 30–31, 39n. 5, 40nn. 9, 10; relation to diegesis, 29, 30–31, 32

Mirror transference, 8, 133, 135–36

Mitchell, W. J. T.: "pictorial turn," 21n. 21, 213n. 8; *Picture Theory: Essays on Verbal and Visual Representation,* 2

Modernity: emphasis on visual perception, 132; Heidegger on, 233; and language, 113–14; and techniques of detective fiction, 190–91

Music: emancipation of, 77–83; frequency spectrum, 76; intervals, 4, 76; occidental, 76; relationship of tones to color, 50–58; relationship to cryptography, 78

Musical painting, theory of, 64, 66

Nabokov, Vladimir. *See The Eye*

Narcissism, 150n. 16, 199; in Hölderlin's *Hyperion,* 8, 135, 138–40; in James' *The Sacred Fount,* 199–200; in Nabokov's *The Eye,* 207–8

Nazis: use of walls, 221–22

Newton, Issac: circle of colors, 55–57; musical scale, 56–57; *Opticks,* 53; theory of nature of light, 67n. 10; theory of vision, 52, 53–54

Nietzsche, Friedrich: *The Birth of Tragedy,* 177; on Wagner, 81, 84n. 6

Norton, Andrews: *A Discourse on the Latest Form of Infidelity,* 108n. 12

Noton, D., 19n. 10, 34, 41n. 20

Novalis (Hardenberg, Friedrich Leopold von); *Allgemeine Brouillon,* 128n. 11; alternative visual paradigm ("moral astronomy"), 6–7, 111, 114–15, 117, 123–27; concept of Being ("seyn"), 121–22, 126, 128n. 11; concept of feeling ("Gefühl"), 121–23; concept of intellectual intuition, 123, 126; concept of knowledge, 240; critique of rationalistic literacy, 115–16; dialectic between feeling and thought, 122–23; "Die Christenheit oder Europa," 5, 111–12; "Encyclopaedistik," 115; on essence of poetry, 117; *Fichte-Studies,* 119; *Heinrich von Ofterdingen,* 20nn. 16, 19, 115–16, 117–19, 128n. 11; on Hemsterhuis' "organe morale," 126; Klingsohr tale, 6, 115–16; "Monolog," 6, 116; "ordo-inversus" doctrine, 6, 122–23, 126, 128n. 11; on overcoming of temporality, 126; and paradigm shift from classical to modern, 5, 114, 117; philosophy of language, 116–17; poetic theory of telescope, 124; rejection of Fichte's prereflective unity of consciousness, 120–21; rejection of Goethe's modernity, 128n. 11; on representation, 230; "Universalpoesie" concept, 124, 126; "Wenn nicht mehr Zahlen und Figuren/Sind Schlüssel aller Kreaturen," 116

Occidental music, 76
Ocular harpsichord ("clavecin oculaire," "Farbenclavicymbel"), 3, 49–50, 61
Odyssey: procession of ghosts in, 252–53
Opera: as film theater, 81; impact of electric lighting, 4, 73–76
Orlev, Uri: teichoscopic imagery in Haii Berehov Hatziporim (The Island on Bird Street), 14, 215, 219–20, 222–24

Palazzeschi, Aldo: antitraditional aesthetics, 9, 155–56, 166–67; "Ara Mara Amara," 160; "Chi sono?," 157, 166; "Diaphragm of Evanescences," 159; early verse, 158–60; I cavalli bianchi, 158, 162; "Il passo de le Nazarene," 160–61, 162, 169n. 16; "Il pastello del sonno," 159; "I prati di Gesù," 159; Iserian blanks in verse, 162–63; Lanterna, 161; "La vasca delle anguille," 162; "La voce dell'oro," 162; "Le fanciulle bianche," 160; L'incendiario, 157–58, 166, 168n. 7; non-sense verse, 159, 165; "Oro doro odoro dodoro," 160, 162, 163; philosophy of controdolore, 169n. 16; poetics of the saltimbanco, 157, 168n. 13; poetic techniques, 9–10, 157–61; "The Pastel of Boredom," 158; "The Pastel of Sleep," 158, 160
Panopticon, 13–14, 220–21; panopticism, 221; panoptic metaphor in Haii Berehov Hatziporim (Orlev), 222–24
Pantheism, 91, 101; American, 89–90, 106n. 3; and Emerson, 90, 97, 101; German, 108n. 12; and Goethe, 5, 90; and Melville, 90, 91, 102–3, 102–6; seeing in, 105

Paul of Taurus, 254
Peirce, Charles S., 2; definition of sign, 170n. 30
Phantasia (productive imagination), 16, 245–47, 257n. 2; chirography, 246; dreams, 245; hallucination, 246; literate imaging, 246, 250–52; reverie, 245, 251
Phonograph: as basis of modern music, 80–81
Picasso, Pablo, 176
Plato: analogy between poet and painter, 41n. 15; diairesis, 30, 32; Laws, 31–32; and mimesis (imitation), 30–31, 39n. 5, 40nn. 9, 10; narrative theory, 29, 30–31; Phaedrus, 254; Republic, 30–31
Poe, Edgar Allen: "Ligeia," 107n. 7
Porter, Carolyn, 100; Seeing and Being, 108n. 10
Poststructuralism, 232–33
Pound, Ezra: "The Return," 256
Praxis, 35
Psychoanalysis, 18n. 8
Pythagoras, 76

Read, Herbert, 177
Reading: as hallucination, 250–52
Realism: and Cartesian spectator, 188; detective fiction, 189–90; division into form and content, 187–88; narrator in, 12–13
Repraesentatio, 112–13, 127n. 5
Reverie, 245
Ricoeur, Paul, 12, 42n. 21, 188
Rilke, Rainer Maria, 245, 248
Robertson, Etienne Gaspard, 73
Romanticism: concept of language, 7, 232; and Fichte's prereflective unity of consciousness, 120–21; German, 92, 104, 231–32; hypervisuality, 7; intellectual intuition ("intellektuelle Anschauung"), 119–21; model of representation, 6; "new mythology," 239; rejection of Enlightenment model of representation, 114–15
Rorty, Richard, 188; mirror of nature, 12
Rosenberg, Alfred: Myth of the Twentieth Century, 178
Rousseau, G. S., 18n. 9
Rousseau, Jean-Jacques: "Essay on the Origin of Language," 60
Russ, Colin, 217, 218

Saccades, 3, 19n. 10, 34, 41n. 19
The Sacred Fount (James), 13, 191; Cartesian *vs.* Marxist version of camera obscura, 203; collapse of narrator's theory, 202–3; crystal cage metaphor, 193; erosion of distinction between subjective and objective, 192; function of painting *The Man with the Mask,* 196–98; indeterminacy of language, 203–4, 213n. 9; metaphors of light, 194–95; as modernist work, 206; narrator as visual object, 195–96; narrator's aestheticizing practices, 198; narrator's eroticism, 199; narrator's language of economic exchange, 200–201, 213n. 7; narrator's narcissism, 199–200; Orpheus myth in, 201–2, 206; problemization of transparency, 193–94, 202; screening in, 195
Saint-Exupéry, Antoine-Marie-Roger de, 248
Saint-Martin, Fernande, 18n. 9
Salome, 81–83
Sarte, Jean Paul: *No Exit,* 258n. 11
Saussure, Ferdinand de, 19n. 10, 128n. 7
Savoca, Giuseppe, 169n. 16
Scanpath, 3, 34, 41n. 20
Schaf, Philip, 108n. 12
Schneider, Peter: treatment of visuality in *Der Mauersspringer* (The Wall Jumper), 14, 215, 217–19
Schopenhauer, Arthur: reception of Goethe's physiological optics, 216–17
Schwitters, Kurt, 174
Seltzer, Mark, 188
Semiotics, 4, 170n. 29
Seurat, Georges: *Un dimanche après-midi à l'île de la Grande Jatte,* 34–37, 42nn. 22, 24, 25
Seyhan, Azade, 14–15
Shaw, George Bernard: *Man and Superman,* 258n. 11
Shepard, Roger: Shepard tones, 19n. 12
Sign: Peirce's definition of, 170n. 30
Signification: and allegory, 231; binary organization of, 6; as ideological medium, 156–57, 168n. 5; ternary concept of, 6; ternary *vs.* binary concept of, 114; and translation, 231
Silence, 20n. 16
Simonides, 29
Sound: in theory of vibrations, 53
Sprengel, Peter, 19n. 11

Stafford, Barbara, 11, 16; *Body Criticism,* 21n. 21
Stark, L., 19n. 10, 34, 41n. 20
Stoekl, Allan, 178
Sunthesis pragmatôn (muthos), 34, 35
Supernatural images. *See* Ghosts
Surrealists: use of Greek myths, 177
Swan United Electric Light Company, 73

Tamburri, Anthony Julian, 9–10
Teichoscopia (wall-viewing), 14, 224n. 1
Teichoscopic imagery: in *Der Mauerspringer* (The Wall Jumper), 215, 217–19; in *Haii Berehov Hatziporim* (The Island on Bird Street), 215, 222–24
Telemann, Georg Philipp, 61, 69n. 20
Theoria, 112
Theory: aesthetic, 2–3, 29–39; of Classical Greek art, 38; of language, 64–65, 66; of musical painting, 64, 66; of narrative, 29, 30–31; of nature of light and sound, 52; of perception and knowledge, 52, 54; of retinal image, 216; of vibrations, 52–53; of vision, 52, 53–54
Thomistic theorem, 6, 112
Thoreau, Henry David: *Walden,* 94, 107n. 4
Transcendentalism. *See* American Renaissance transcendentalism
Translation, 15, 231, 232
Typographic imaging, 246, 250–56

Uerlings, Herbert, 130n. 19

Van Cromphout, Gustaaf: "Melville as Novelist," 108n. 12
van Reijen, Willem, 234
Vibrations, theory of, 52–53
Virgil's *Aeneid:* procession of not-yet-reborn, 253
Visuality: Cartesian model of, 12; and diegesis, 34; in fascism, 148n. 1; history of, 1; hypervisual, 7, 132–33; intellectual history of, 216–17; languages of, 1, 5, 6, 8; Marxist (Jameson) model of, 12; and modernity, 132; multivisuality, 9; role of saccades in, 34; and self-representation, 5; as sign of alienation and social deterioration, 133–34. *See also* Image
Visual/textual relations, 2, 3, 29, 36–37, 229–30, 235

269

Voltaire, François Marie Arouet de, 50; commentaries on Castel, 58–59; *Elémens de Latin America philosophie de Newton,* 58; on visual and auditory perception, 68n. 12

Wagner, Richard: *Götterdämmerung,* 76, 83; installation of gaslight in Bayreuth opera house, 4, 73; mimesis in art, 4; projection of light and music into action, 75, 76, 78–79; *Rheingold,* 74, 75, 76; *Tristan und Isolde,* 78–79
Walker, Joyce, 128n. 11
Walls: effect on vision, 216; literary treatments of, 217, 219; "Mauer im Kopf" ("wall-in-the-head") in *Der Mauerspringer* (The

Wall Jumper), 219; socio/psychological uses of, 14, 220–21, 222–23, 224n. 1
Weilnböck, Harald, 7–9
Wellek, Albert, 56, 67n. 9
Werckmeister, Otto, 11; and "crypto-mythic" figuration, 176, 182; *Paul Klee in Exile,* 176
West, Nathaniel, 106n. 3
Wittgenstein, Ludwig: *Blue Book,* 20n. 16

Yeats, W. B., 257, 258n. 15; "The Magi," 255–56

Zervos, Christian, 176
Zizek, Slavoj, 189, 190, 195, 212n. 3

Books in the Kritik series

Walter Benjamin: An Intellectual Biography, by Bernd Witte, trans. by James Rolleston, 1991

The Violent Eye: Ernst Junger's Visions and Revisions on the European Right, by Marcus Paul Bullock, 1991

Fatherland: Novalis, Freud, and the Discipline of Romance, by Kenneth S. Calhoon, 1992

Metaphors of Knowledge: Language and Thought in Mauthner's Critique, by Elizabeth Bredeck, 1992

Laocoon's Body and the Aesthetics of Pain: Winckelmann, Lessing, Herder, Moritz, Goethe, by Simon Richter, 1992

The Critical Turn: Studies in Kant, Herder, Wittgenstein, and Contemporary Theory, by Michael Morton, 1993

Reading After Foucault: Institutions, Disciplines, and Technologies of Self in Germany, 1750–1830, edited by Robert S. Leventhal, 1994

Bettina Brentano-von Arnim: Gender and Politics, edited by Elke P. Frederiksen and Katherine R. Goodman, 1995

Absent Mothers and Orphaned Fathers: Narcissism and Abjection in Lessing's Aesthetic and Dramatic Production, by Susan E. Gustafson, 1995

Identity or History? Marcus Herz and the End of the Enlightenment, by Martin L. Davies, 1995

Languages of Visuality: Crossings between Science, Art, Politics, and Literature, edited by Beate Allert, 1996